YO-BYW-150

AIDS Practice Manual: A Legal and Educational Guide

Second Edition

Principal Editors:

Paul Albert

Leonard Graff

Benjamin Schatz

A joint publication of

National Gay Rights Advocates

and the

**National Lawyers Guild
AIDS Network**

ACKNOWLEDGEMENTS

In the course of completing this manual, we depended on the wisdom and assistance of a great many people. In addition to the authors, without whose contribution the Manual would not have been possible, we wish particularly to thank:

Beverly Abplanalp-Gaede, Prisoners Legal Services, Ithaca, New York; Roberta Achtenberg, Executive Director, Lesbian Rights Project, San Francisco, California; the Anti-Sexism Committee of the San Francisco Chapter of the National Lawyers Guild and Clark Boardman, Co. publishers (for permission to reprint "Insurance and AIDS-Related Issues" by Mark Scherzer); Nigel Fazal; Alison Hardy; Lois Heaney and the National Jury Project, Oakland, California; the Miami Herald (for permission to reprint "AIDS virus inmates in 'leper' cell"); Norman Nickens, AIDS Discrimination Officer, San Francisco Human Rights Commission, San Francisco, California; Alice Philipson, Attorney at Law, Berkeley, California; Abby Rubenfeld, Legal Director, Lambda Legal Defense and Education Fund, Inc., New York, New York; the San Francisco Chapter of the National Lawyers Guild; Harvey Schweitzer, Law Offices of James A. Shrybman, Takoma Park, Maryland; Susan K. Steeg, Texas Department of Health, Austin, Texas; Adryann Strauss; David W. Webber, Attorney at Law, Philadelphia, Pennsylvania; Bridget Wilson, Military Law Task Force of the National Lawyers Guild, San Diego, California.

Editorial Committee: Paul Albert, Nanci Clarence, Bruce Fodiman, Leonard Graff, Benjamin Schatz

SUMMARY TABLE OF CONTENTS

TABLE OF CONTENTS

VI. Criminal Law and Procedure
Paul Albert, Cynthia Stewart and Mark Vermeulen

VII. AIDS in Prisons and Jails
Anita P. Arriola

VIII. Insurance

XII. Further issues:

Manual Appendices

FOREWORD

This Practice Manual is a joint project of the AIDS Network of the National Lawyers Guild and National Gay Rights Advocates. It is a second edition of a work published in 1986 which was coproduced with the Anti-Sexism Committee of the San Francisco Bay Area Chapter of the National Lawyers Guild.

This edition - like the first - was written to assist you in providing legal services to persons with AIDS or ARC and to others experiencing AIDS-related legal problems. The Manual contains information regarding the disease and its physical and emotional effects, the particular legal problems faced by persons with AIDS or ARC, and the threats to civil liberties of persons suffering from the disease, as well as persons perceived to be at risk of contracting the disease - including gay men and lesbians, prostitutes, and intravenous drug users.

The Manual is greatly expanded from the first edition. The sections on employment discrimination and the military have been updated; the medical section is fully annotated to provide ready access to medical citations; new chapters have been added on criminal law and prisons, insurance, housing, nursing homes and child custody. In addition, overview sections on taxation, non-citizens, and suicide are included. The Appendix contains an overview article on HIV antibody testing, a survey of discrimination laws, and a resource list of organizations.

In spite of this expansion, the Manual is still designed as an introduction only. Our basic aim has been merely to acquaint you with the legal issues. Although state law is discussed, the Manual is addressed to a national audience. You should be sure to research the applicable law in your jurisdiction.

We hope the Manual is helpful and would appreciate your suggestions and comments. We also urge you to become more actively involved in our organizations:

- The AIDS Network of the National Lawyers Guild was established to assist members of the legal community to become involved in AIDS-related issues. The Guild is an organization of over 10,000 members in 135 chapters nationwide. It has a fifty year history of defense of civil rights and advocacy for progressive social change.

The purpose of the AIDS Network is to encourage lawyers and legal workers to represent people with AIDS and related conditions, to take part in advocacy and public education about the law and AIDS, and to assist local AIDS organizations. In addition to the Manual, the Network publishes a bimonthly newsletter, The Exchange, which focuses on one topic each issue (such as quarantine, jails, health insurance, race, HIV antibody testing, intravenous drug users, women, and criminal law.) It includes a resource list and updates on recent legal developments. A one year subscription is $10 and can be obtained by use of the form at the end of the Manual.

- National Gay Rights Advocates is a nationally renowned public interest law firm promoting equality for gay men and women. Founded in 1978 as a nonprofit, membership supported organization, NGRA focuses on impact litigation coordinated by a professional staff and supported by pro bono assistance from law firms and individual attorneys throughout the country.

From offices in Los Angeles and San Francisco, NGRA's legal activities have extended to all 50 states, 7 of the 12 U.S. Courts of Appeal and the U.S. Supreme Court. Our historic victories in the areas of AIDS, employment discrimination, freedom of speech and domestic partnerships have substantially bettered the quality of life for millions of Americans.

Established in 1985 as a special division of National Gay Rights Advocates, THE AIDS CIVIL RIGHTS PROJECT has initiated precedent-setting litigation in such areas as employment discrimination, family law, insurance services, and forced HIV antibody testing. In conjunction with litigation, the Project provides a full spectrum of educational materials including consumer education and information, litigation manuals and survey research.

National Gay Rights Advocates is a tax exempt (501)(c)(3) organization under the Internal Revenue Service regulations. All contributions are tax deductible to the full extent of the law.

For further information about our organizations, please return the form at the end of the Manual or write us at the addresses below:

AIDS Network
National Lawyers Guild
211 Gough Street, Third Floor
San Francisco, CA 94102
415 861-8884

National Gay Rights Advocates
540 Castro Street
San Francisco, CA 94114
415 863-3624

INTRODUCTION

NLG AIDS NETWORK: FIGHTING THE BACKLASH

Paul Albert

[Note: This article was originally printed in the Summer 1985 edition of Guild Notes, the newspaper of the National Lawyers Guild. It was reprinted in its present form in the First Edition of the Practice Manual. Statistical information current as of the date of publication of the Second Edition is contained in the Appendix to this Introduction.]

———————

A health crisis with broad implications is spreading across the United States. As of February 1986, Acquired Immune Deficiency Syndrome (AIDS) has struck 17,000 persons since 1979, and the number of new cases is doubling each year. It is estimated that the total will exceed 70,000 within two years, and the epidemic could continue into the next century. The timetable for developing a vaccine is uncertain, and it is unlikely that a cure will be found that is of use to the thousands of persons who currently have the disease. People with AIDS have a life expectancy of less than three years from the time of diagnosis.

In addition, an estimated 150,000 people nationwide are ill with AIDS-related conditions (ARC). These persons are infected with the AIDS virus and have infections other than those listed in government guidelines for an AIDS diagnosis. People with ARC, some of whom are relatively healthy and some of whom are dying, face

———————

Paul Albert is Director of the National Lawyers Guild AIDS Network.

many of the same social and legal problems as people with AIDS.

The Guild and its members have an extremely important role to play in this crisis, which raises legal, political and personal issues. A Guild AIDS Network has been established by the Anti-Sexism Task Force to coordinate the NLG response and the involvement of members. For the reasons discussed here, it is important that all members consider joining the Network.

NOT A 'GAY DISEASE'

Many of the issues surrounding this crisis stem from the fact that 73 percent of AIDS cases involve gay and bisexual men. As a result, AIDS has been labeled a "gay disease." Evidence indicates, however, that the largest number of cases have occurred in Zaire, where the syndrome strikes men and women in equal numbers. And the affected population in the United States is increasingly diverse. Twenty-five percent of all people with AIDS are IV drug users. (The 17% figure frequently reported accounts only for heterosexual IV drug users).

AIDS is caused by a virus transmitted through contact with the blood or semen of an infected person. So it has hit intravenous drug users, persons receiving blood transfusions and children born to women with AIDS. Although at first principally confined to a handful of metropolitan areas, a growing number of cases are being reported in all fifty states.

The spread of AIDS and ARC has been accompanied by media hysteria and a backlash against gays. Heterosexuals and children with AIDS are frequently portrayed in the press as innocent victims, while gays are inferentially seen as culprits. Ignorance about the means by which AIDS is transmitted has caused fear of superficial contact with gays.

The New Right has exploited these fears, linking the disease to the Equal Rights Amendment, abortion rights and other civil liberties issues. The rise in homophobia has resulted in assaults on the civil rights won by gays in recent years; an increase in "fag bashing" and other forms of attacks; prejudice against people with AIDS and ARC and an inadequate level of funding for research, treatment and education.

EXTREME MEASURES PROPOSED

Extreme infringements of rights — including quarantine and mass firings of gays — have been seriously discussed within the Reagan Administration, according to former Public Health Service Director Edward Brandt. Such measures also were advocated during a recent election in Houston, and British magistrates have been granted the power to order AIDS patients quarantined. The closing of gay meeting places has already begun in a few U.S. cities, and employment and housing restrictions have been proposed. An additional threat is that employers and insurance carriers may require members of the at-risk population groups to submit to pre-screening through an antibody test.

The problems facing people with AIDS and ARC were illustrated at the Guild's national convention this past March by Glenn McGahee, associate director of the AIDS Atlanta Foundation. In his presentation, Glenn described being denied access to the hospital bedside of his former lover, who was dying of AIDS. He also recounted being locked out of his apartment by the lover's family, and losing all of his possessions as a result. When Glenn later contracted AIDS, he was fired from his job and evicted from his home. Glenn said his sister lost her job as well, after he began speaking publicly on behalf of people with AIDS.

LEGAL HELP NEEDED

As Glenn McGahee's experience shows, people with AIDS need legal assistance to fight housing and employment discrimination. They also frequently need help on medical, insurance and Social Security matters. (For instance, AIDS patients have been denied medical treatment by frightened hospital workers, and insurance companies are increasingly seeking ways to avoid payment of claims for AIDS treatment.) In addition, people with the disease need special counseling with respect to powers of attorney and wills — in order to ensure that the persons

of their choice can visit them in hospitals and supervise their treatment and last rites. People with AIDS in the military and prisons have other special problems.

Many of the problems associated with AIDS are particularly urgent in parts of the country that have a relatively small number of cases. The civil rights of the gay community may be particularly vulnerable to attack in such areas, since there are not likely to be groups to which a recently diagnosed person can turn for practical assistance and reliable information. It can be impossible for a person with AIDS or ARC to locate sympathetic legal assistance under such circumstances.

In these regions — and throughout the nation — the legal skills of NLG members are badly needed to help defend the civil rights of the gay community and to counsel people with AIDS and ARC. It is important that members educate themselves about the nature of AIDS, in order to be able to deal with widespread misinformation about the disease.

The purpose of the Guild AIDS Network is to assist lawyers and legal workers who want to help. Participants in the network will receive information about the disease itself, as well as materials on representing people with AIDS and AIDS-related conditions. A panel of persons with experience in AIDS-related issues will be available for consultation. The Network list will be made available to national, regional and local AIDS organizations. Both fee-generating and pro-bono cases may be referred from it.

PSYCHOLOGICAL AND SOCIAL CONCERNS OF CLIENTS WITH AIDS AND RELATED CONDITIONS

Susan Hawkins

Most legal counselors are experienced in dealing with clients who are troubled by legal, financial and personal problems. Many may not have worked with clients who

Susan Hawkins is Supervising Patients' Rights attorney at Mental Health Advocacy Project in San Jose, California, an agency specializing in mental health law and the rights of the mentally disabled. She is also a volunteer with the Shanti Project in San Francisco.

are suffering from a life-threatening illness. As a legal counselor, you will be primarily concerned with the legal problems of your client. However, to understand your client and his needs, familiarity with the physical, emotional and social aspects of AIDS will be helpful.

Frequently persons learning of an AIDS diagnosis - or a positive HIV antibody status - experience shock and disbelief. Later, intense anger, fear, confusion, depression and a general sense of loss are common. A recently diagnosed person typically must confront feelings of failure, lowered self-esteem, isolation from friends, loss of independence, and fear of dying. Health, social life and expectations for the future are altered. Some people with AIDS (PWAs) must also adjust to the loss of their jobs, their independence, their homes; to reduced personal finances; to lengthy hospital stays, and to tiring treatment programs. Single parents frequently face difficult questions about the upbringing of their children. Seropositive women are faced with the possibility of not being able to bear children. Most jails and prisons segregate anti-body positive prisoners under terrible conditions. Children and teenagers may be expelled from school or socially ostracized.

Many persons react initially to an AIDS diagnosis by denying that they have a life-threatening illness. Your client may be determined to recover, and a hopeful attitude can have a beneficial effect on the course of the illness. However, denial of the seriousness of the illness may make it difficult for the client to discuss wills, burial arrangements, and plans for incapacity and death. A legal counselor has to be sensitive both to the client's attitude about the illness and to the fact that it is frequently important that documents be executed without delay because the mental and physical health of a person with AIDS can deteriorate rapidly. These two considerations require a delicate balance.

People with AIDS and related conditions face special issues because of the erroneous public image that it is a "gay disease". Although heterosexual men and women have developed AIDS, the majority of people with AIDS in the United States are gay and bisexual men. When a man is diagnosed, he is typically presumed to be gay. PWAs - and persons known to be seropositive - may be subjected to homophobic attacks whether they are gay or straight.

An AIDS diagnosis may force a gay man to reveal his sexual orientation to family members and others who may not have known about it. Parents may be shocked,

embarrassed, hurt and angry to discover suddenly that their son is gay. Particular problems are faced by Black and Hispanic gay men and bisexuals because of the high level of homophobia in these communities. These problems can be so severe that persons suffering symptoms of AIDS will put off seeking medical treatment for fear of confronting them.

The combination of the strong negative emotions accompanying the news that a loved one is both gay and dying may cause family members to react negatively to the PWA, his lover and friends. Many gay men have developed an extended family comprised of a number of close relationships with other men and women. It is not uncommon for family members to deny the validity of these relationships and try to exclude the lover or friends from hospital visitation or from decision-making about medical treatment. Family members may also attack a will leaving property to a lover or friend.

These factors are important considerations in the preparation and execution of powers of attorney for health care and wills. To help a PWA make plans, the attorney should determine who are the significant people in the client's life. The attorney should be aware of the potential for friction between the extended family and the biological family. The legal tools for dealing with any such friction are discussed in Section III, Preparing for Illness, Incapacity and Death Due to AIDS.

The situation of heterosexual intravenous drug users is typically very different. Although IV drug users with AIDS come from all socioeconomic backgrounds, the majority are Black or Hispanic, poor, and alienated from most of society. They frequently face severe difficulties with employment, family and friends; finances related to support of their habit; physiological dependence on the drug; and mental illness.

A principal issue facing the legal counselor of an IV drug user may be to help the client gain access to health care and treatment. IV drug users with AIDS have a shorter life expectancy at time of diagnosis than other PWAs, in part because of the poor quality of medical care available to the Black and Hispanic community in our society. The primary source of medical attention for IV drug users prior to diagnosis is often the public hospital emergency room, and many IV drug users may be unaware of other treatment sites or the availability of financial assistance.

IV drug users face discrimination in a wide variety of housing, support service and medical treatment programs established for PWAs. A client wishing to overcome drug dependence may find a three month waiting period to enter a rehabilitation program. The legal counselor may be of assistance in helping a client gain access to some of these programs.

Many women with AIDS face additional problems related to the presence of dependent children. The need to make provisions for the long-term care of their children - many of whom may be seropositive or have AIDS - can be a primary concern for a mother with AIDS. It has proven very difficult to place such children in foster homes when the mother is no longer able to care for them. This situation adds to the already enormous burden a woman faces in dealing with her illness, addiction, poverty, and racial and sexual discrimination.

This discussion illustrates that a legal counselor of persons with AIDS must be sensitive to issues not only related to life and death but also to class, race, sexism, homophobia and social justice. These issues are explored in greater detail in the following resources:

1. Living with AIDS: A Self-Care Manual
   AIDS Project/Los Angeles
   937 North Cole Avenue, Suite 3
   Los Angeles, CA 90038

2. The Exchange is the bimonthly newsletter of the National Lawyers Guild AIDS Network. It focuses on legal and political issues, including quarantine, prisons and jails, health insurance, race, drug use, women, and criminal law . It is available for $10 for six issues from the AIDS Network.

3. The Family's Guide to AIDS (pamphlet)
   San Francisco AIDS Foundation
   333 Valencia Street, Fourth floor
   San Francisco, CA 94103

4. Coping with AIDS and Coping with ARC (booklets)
   Available through the San Francisco AIDS Foundation. For a complete catalogue of AIDS-related publications distributed by the Foundation, get a copy of the Foundation's "AIDS Educator Catalogue".

Appendix

One of the difficulties in dealing with AIDS issues stems from the fact that reports on the scope of the epidemic are unreliable. There are no official figures with respect to ARC, for example, and government reports on AIDS underestimate the number of cases. The World Health Organization reported in December 1987 that government sources worldwide had reported a total of 71,000 cases. However, the WHO in fact estimated the true number of cases to be closer to 150,000. It projected an additional 150,000 cases in 1988, bringing a world-wide total of 300,000 cases by the end of the year.

Statistics for the United States, which has by far the largest number of cases, are compiled by the Centers for Disease Control. These statistics have been criticized on a number of grounds, including underreporting and classification of transmission categories. Set forth on the following pages are portions of the CDC report for February 9, 1988, including the primary disease of persons with AIDS, age and race/ethnicity breakdowns, transmission categories, and the metropolitan areas with the largest number of cases per capita.

APPENDIX

AIDS WEEKLY SURVEILLANCE REPORT(1) - UNITED STATES
AIDS PROGRAM
CENTER FOR INFECTIOUS DISEASES
CENTERS FOR DISEASE CONTROL
FEBRUARY 8, 1988

1. PRIMARY DISEASE REPORTED(2)

	CASES	PERCENT OF TOTAL	DEATHS	PERCENT DEAD
Pneumocystis carinii Pneumonia	33212	62.6	18788	56.6
Other Opportunistic Diseases	14087	26.5	8187	58.1
Kaposi's Sarcoma	5770	10.9	2695	46.7
TOTAL	53069	100.0	29670	55.9

2. AGE

AGE	CASES	PERCENT OF TOTAL
Under 5	696	1.3
05 - 13	124	0.2
13 - 19	221	0.4
20 - 29	10993	20.7
30 - 39	24599	46.4
40 - 49	11036	20.8
Over 49	5400	10.2
Unknown	0	0.0
Total	53069	100.0

3. RACE/ETHNICITY

RACE/ETHNICITY	CASES	PERCENT OF TOTAL
White, not Hispanic	31930	60.2
Black, not Hispanic	13410	25.3
Hispanic	7242	13.6
Other	361	0.7
Unknown	126	0.2
TOTAL	53069	100.0

4. TRANSMISSION CATEGORIES(3)

	MALES		FEMALES		TOTAL	
	CASES	PERCENT OF MALES	CASES	PERCENT OF FEMALES	CASES	PERCENT OF TOTAL
Homosexual/Bisexual Men	33851	69.3	0	0.0	33851	63.8
Intravenous (IV) Drug User	7093	14.5	1951	46.1	9044	17.0
Homosexual (IV) Drug User	3901	8.0	0	0.0	3901	7.4
Hemophilia/Coag Disorder	509	1.0	20	0.5	529	1.0
Heterosexual Cases(4)	961	2.0	1131	26.7	2092	3.9
Transfusion	810	1.7	425	10.0	1235	2.3
Undetermined(5)	1263	2.6	334	7.9	1597	3.0
PEDIATRIC:(6)						
Hemophiliac	44	0.1	3	0.1	47	0.1
Parent at Risk(7)	318	0.7	308	7.3	626	1.2
Transfusion	67	0.1	48	1.1	115	0.2
Undetermined(5)	16	0.0	16	0.4	32	0.1
Total	48833	100.0	4236	100.0	53069	100.0

(1) These data are provisional.

(2) Disease categories are ordered hierarchically. Cases with more than one disease are tabulated only in the disease category listed first. Kaposi's sarcoma has been reported in 273 cases since January 1 and in 9469 cases cumulatively.

(3) Cases with more than one risk factor other than the combinations listed in the tables or footnotes are tabulated only in the category listed first.

(4) Includes 1200 persons (267 men, 933 women) who have had heterosexual contact with a person with AIDS or at risk for AIDS and 892 persons (694 men, 198 women) without other identified risks who were born in countries in which heterosexual transmission is believed to play a major role although precise means of transmission have not yet been fully defined.

(5) Includes patients on whom risk information is incomplete (due to death, refusal to be interviewed or loss to follow-up), patients still under investigation, men reported only to have had heterosexual contact with prostitute, and interviewed patients for whom no specific risk was identified.

(6) Includes all patients under 13 years of age at time of diagnosis.

(7) Epidemiologic data suggest transmission from an infected mother to her fetus or infant during the perinatal period.

6. AIDS Cases Per Million Population (from the 1980 Census),
   by Standard Metropolitan Statistical Area (SMSA) of Residence,
   Reported from JUNE 1, 1981 to FEBRUARY 8, 1988 - United States

SMSA of Residence	Cases	Percentage of Total	Cases per Million Population
San Francisco, CA	4815	9.1	1481.3
New York, NY	12338	23.2	1352.8
Jersey City, NJ	648	1.2	1163.4
Miami, FL	1389	2.6	854.4
Newark, NJ	1496	2.8	760.9
Elsewhere (irrespective of SMSA)	32383	61.0	151.6
Total - United States	53069	100.0	230.6

MEDICAL ASPECTS OF AIDS-RELATED LITIGATION

James M. Campbell[1*]

Proof and Practical Considerations[2]

AIDS-related[3] cases often need expert medical testimony on HIV transmission. The lawyer must become an "expert" to make the best use of medical experts and to cross-examine effectively.[4] AIDS hysteria -- far more contagious than AIDS -- exists among some lawyers, judges, court officers and jurors. AIDS hysteria is explicitly or implicitly intertwined with the many AIDS legal issues, including discrimination in employment (including military and other federal employment), housing, child custody, bail or parole, insurance, public benefits or accommodations; invasion of privacy and violation of confidentiality; tort claims alleging breach of first-party or supposed third-party duties to warn sexual or drug-use partners or to practice safer sex; lack of due process in imposing quarantine or other involuntary measures (and in prisons, lack of even the minimal due-process protections owed prisoners); enhancing criminal charges, e.g., charging spitting as aggravated assault or biting as attempted murder despite the evidence that AIDS has not been transmitted by spitting or biting; tort claims alleging negligent hiring and seeking a segregated workforce; and will contests alleging lack of testamentary capacity or undue influence.[5]

Extensive AIDS education has calmed much anxiety about workplace contagion among health-care workers and could calm anxieties in other settings. AIDS education may enable people to act on facts rather than fears and it should always be considered as part of any settlement or relief requested. Publicity may be a useful deterrent to further discrimination, but sensitivity to the client and the public is essential.[6]

---

* The endnotes are intended to be useful for trial preparation but need not impede a first reading. Note 2 lists resources to obtain now so they will be at hand when needed.

Expert witnesses should review the medical literature before testifying; having your experts comment on this chapter may help you prepare. Helpful studies should normally be introduced as part of the foundation of the experts' opinions. Federal officials seem reluctant to testify but state and local health officials may be cooperative.[7] If expert testimony conflicts, supporting studies can determine which expert will be believed.[8] Affidavits and even briefs can use medical literature to good effect.[9] References on trial practice and discrimination may be useful.[10]

Cases must be expedited. People with AIDS can deteriorate unpredictably and rapidly, both physically and mentally. Opponents know that every hour of delay tends to work in their favor. Judges who do not want people with AIDS in their courtrooms may favor delay. Diminishing health diminishes the motivation and ability to litigate. As time passes some people with AIDS may develop a dementia which effectively precludes relief.

Consider seeking a temporary restraining order immediately and always get the soonest possible hearing date. If appropriate, request that motions be taken under advisement until after hearing so that hearings will not be delayed. Also consider a prompt deposition to perpetuate testimony, perhaps videotaped. Some remedies do not survive the person even if the evidence does, so speed always remains of the essence from a legal as well as human perspective. A medical evaluation, including an evaluation of the client's ability to work, if relevant, should be conducted as soon as possible after the incident complained of. In cases of employment discrimination, a successful claim for unemployment benefits will support arguments that the person was able to work. Disability benefits may be higher, but a successful disability claim will foil arguments that the person was able to work.

Wills of decedents with AIDS may be challenged for lack

of testamentary capacity due to medication or to central nervous system deterioration. Instruments should be drawn with care, the medication schedule should be documented and the instruments executed when medication effects are reduced, and lucidity should be amply witnessed. A videotape of the signing ceremony may be useful.

Educate yourself now to be prepared if a person with AIDS needs immediate help. When health care is being denied, for example, when the ambulance refuses to take a person with AIDS to the hospital, immediate informed advocacy is essential. Even speedy litigation can be fatally slow. Services such as a visiting "buddy" or "red tape brigade" may be more important to the client than brilliant legal argument, and a prepared lawyer will stay aware of the services available in the community.

Medical Basics [11]

HIV (human immunodeficiency virus) is a recently-identified virus which can (perhaps in conjunction with co-factors) damage the human immune system and result in a spectrum of conditions ranging from no visible symptoms, through the various symptoms of so-called "ARC" (AIDS-related complex), to the grave infections and cancers of AIDS.[12] Figure 1 (following the footnotes) indicates some of the complexity of diagnosing AIDS.

Most of the estimated two million people in the United States with HIV infection have no symptoms at all; full-blown AIDS, the end stage of an extended disease process, is the visible tip of the iceberg.[13] People with HIV can be infected for years without knowing it and can unwittingly transmit HIV to others. These apparently healthy people may be the most common transmitters of HIV. As of September 1987, 42,354 cases meeting the then-current surveillance definition of AIDS and 24,412 deaths had been reported to the CDC (Centers for Disease Control).[14]

HIV is spread by virus from one person entering the body of another. The three basic modes of transmission are (1) "horizontally" by injection of infected blood, (2) "horizontally" by unprotected sex with an infected person, and (3) "vertically" from infected mother to fetus or newborn.[15]

Obvious potential routes to spread HIV include receiving blood transfusions (donating blood is completely safe), and sharing needles and syringes during intravenous drug use. Northeastern urban drug users have especially high rates of infection.[16] Since mid-1985, blood donated in the United States has been screened for HIV antibodies and the risk of HIV infection from post-1985 blood transfusions is extremely low.[17] Preventing HIV transmission among intravenous drug users is far more difficult.[18] Some drug users may get prescriptions and sterile needles and syringes, but thousands cannot get sterile needles and syringes, and cannot get into overcrowded and underfunded drug rehabilitation programs. The impoverished, disproportionately Black and Hispanic, may find good health care inaccessible, and they and their children may die more quickly than other people with AIDS.[19]

Unprotected sex is the leading mode of transmission.[20] HIV may be present in semen and cervical secretions, and may enter the body through the mucous membranes in the vagina, rectum, and possibly mouth and throat.[21] Women may spread HIV to partners during intercourse, perhaps through cervical secretions.[22] Proper use of latex condoms (with water-soluble lubricant) from start to finish during intercourse with men is protective because HIV does not penetrate unbroken condoms, but improper or intermittent use, breakage and the other problems which make condoms less than 100% effective in preventing pregnancy may be problems in preventing HIV transmission, as well.[23] Sharing blood or semen during sex is a more important risk factor than simply the number or gender of sexual partners.[24] Men who have had sex with other men make up about three-fourths of the reported cases of AIDS; the proportion of reported cases among sexually active heterosexuals has increased only minimally.[25] Many community groups conduct "safer sex" education for people of both sexes and all sexual orientations to help reduce transmission among all groups.

Perinatal transmission (before, during or shortly after birth) is an increasing problem. Women now constitute 7% of the adults with AIDS in the United States; 50% of the children diagnosed with AIDS in 1987 are female.[26] Women can transmit HIV to others, including their unborn children, and might be more likely to progress from HIV infection without symptoms to full-blown AIDS during pregnancy.[27] Available data suggest that the rate of transmission from infected mother to infant is 30-50%, a rate high enough that women's reproductive rights are likely to be challenged on this basis as well as others.[28] Many women with HIV are intravenous drug users or sexual partners of users, but every woman should be educated about HIV.[29]

HIV is relatively difficult to catch. HIV is not contagious in the popular sense of being airborne and easy to spread, like a cold.[30] Not one case has been reported of HIV transmission by air; tears; sweat; donating blood; shaking hands; hugging; coughing; sneezing; using swimming pools; touching doorknobs, toilet seats, furniture or telephones; massage; masturbation; sharing towels, bed linens, drinking glasses or food utensils; eating in restaurants; being bitten by mosquitoes or other animals; or any other form of everyday contact.[31] Since HIV can be present in extremely low concentrations in saliva, the possibility of transmission by saliva has been minutely scrutinized, but evidence against transmission by saliva is strong. Family members often share saliva by kissing, sharing the same cup for brushing teeth, etc. Even in this secretion-rich environment, family members of people with AIDS' do not acquire HIV except through the usual routes: unprotected intercourse, sharing blood (including failing to wear gloves when handling blood and diarrhea) and mother to neonate.[32] A handful (far fewer than 1%) of health-care workers who failed to follow infection-control recommendations and had unprotected contact with infected blood have become infected, but adherence to CDC recommendations should prevent non-sexual workplace transmission.[33] Sex workers' advocates contend that true professionals often follow safer sex precautions, although published research is so loose with the label "prostitute" that it may suggest otherwise.[34]

HIV is a fragile virus outside the body. HIV is killed by heating and by ordinary disinfectants such as rubbing alcohol, hydrogen peroxide, a 1 to 10 dilution of household bleach in water, and probably by ordinary soaps.[35]

The hepatitis B virus -- bloodborne like HIV -- is a tougher challenge for infection control. The concentration of hepatitis B virus in infected blood is about one million times greater than the concentration of HIV; hepatitis B virus, unlike HIV, is not killed by drying and remains alive in ordinary room conditions for a week or more; health care workers have infected their patients with hepatitis B and a few patients have died, but no non-sexual worker-to-patient transmission of HIV has been found; hepatitis B is transmitted in up to 30% of sticks with contaminated needles, in contrast to transmission to a small fraction of 1% after HIV needlesticks; and more than 200 million people in the world carry hepatitis B virus, whereas between 5 and 10 million people carry HIV.[36]

HIV transmission in a workplace is far less likely than hepatitis B transmission. Following routine infection-control recommendations universally (in **every** case, regardless of whether infection is suspected) should prevent transmission of hepatitis B, HIV and other agents in health-care settings; use of gloves, masks and other barriers in workplace settings where even hepatitis B transmission does not occur is unwarranted (and if barriers are not used in **every** case, ineffective and discriminatory).[37] It is vital to use science rather than discrimination to address infection-control issues.[38]

In some people HIV can remain relatively inactive for several years and possibly for a full lifetime. An estimate that 25-50% of the people who already have HIV (but who currently have no symptoms) will develop AIDS within five to ten years is uncertain but not unreasonable.[39] What triggers viral activity is unclear, but individual differences in genetics or immune response, differences in virulence among different viral strains, repeated exposures, and living habits or other environmental factors have been suggested.[40] People with HIV may be able to transmit it for life.[41]

If HIV multiplies, it destroys its host cell and infects new host cells. Impairment of host cells results in weakening of the immune system which normally fights off infection. As the immune system weakens, familiar infections may become unusually difficult to treat, common organisms which normally cause no problems have an opportunity to cause grave infections, and certain cancers may develop.[42] The presence of specific AIDS-defining neurological impairment, opportunistic infections or cancers, not mere HIV infection, is diagnostic for AIDS.[43]

Some people with AIDS have successfully fought off Pneumocystis carinii pneumonia or other opportunistic infections time and again, but no person diagnosed with full-blown AIDS has reliably been reported to have recovered from the underlying HIV infection.[44] Most people with AIDS die within two years of diagnosis, but some people have lived with AIDS for four years or more.[45] There has been some progress in treating the opportunistic infections and cancers of AIDS and in delaying or preventing the onset of symptoms.[46] Prospects for a vaccine which would prevent infection, or even for one which would prevent people with HIV from spreading it, are uncertain.[47]

Testing

"[W]e are a testing culture"[48] and the testing of blood for evidence of HIV infection has become so politicized that no discussion of the topic can avoid controversy.[49] The August 1987 issue of The Exchange, the newsletter of the National Lawyers Guild AIDS Network, discusses testing policies and is reprinted as an appendix to this manual.[50]

The Public Health Service counseling and testing recommendations state:

> A person is identified as infected with HIV when a sequence of tests, starting with repeated enzyme immunoassays (EIA [commonly called ELISA]) and including a Western blot or similar, more specific assay, are repeatedly reactive. Persons infected with HIV usually develop antibody against the virus within 6-12 weeks after infection.[51]

Blood screening does not test for AIDS.[52] The 1987 revision of the definition of AIDS indicates that a positive test for HIV antibodies[53] is never sufficient for a diagnosis of AIDS and that in rare circumstances a diagnosis of AIDS may be made even if blood screening for HIV antibodies is negative.[54]

Even when screening tests are performed under ideal laboratory conditions false positive and false negative results occur. Positive antibody tests in infants under 15-months-old may simply reflect the continued presence of the mother's antibodies.[55] Antibodies take 6-12 weeks (sometimes longer) to become detectable so samples drawn in this "window" period can yield false negatives.[56] The value of any test in indicating infection depends on the sensitivity and specificity of the technique and on the prevalence of infection in the population tested. If prevalence is low enough, even highly sensitive and specific techniques performed under ideal conditions will yield more false positive than true positive results.[57]

Testing for HIV is often useful in diagnosing and treating individual patients. In conjunction with counseling and confidentiality (or anonymity), testing with informed consent (informed of risk of stigma and other psychosocial effects) may be useful in preventing and controlling HIV transmission in communities.[58] But involuntary testing for forensic purposes is difficult to justify, particularly when the societal impact of violating confidentiality is considered.[59] How would a test result be substantial probative evidence for any genuinely disputed material fact? Is any less intrusive way to gather evidence available? What will be done to the party, inside and outside the courtroom, if the result is positive? What effect will forced testing followed by disclosure and discrimination have on public health efforts to encourage voluntary testing and counseling? Test results are generally highly prejudicial and inflammatory but rarely probative, and lawyers for people affected by AIDS should almost never agree to have clients tested for any forensic purpose.

The Public Health Service has recently emphasized that discrimination (not protection of confidentiality and civil liberty) harms the public health:

> The ability of health departments, hospitals, and other health-care providers and institutions to assure confidentiality of patient information and the public's confidence in that ability are crucial to efforts to increase the number of persons being counseled and tested for HIV infection. Moreover, to assure broad participation in the counseling and testing programs, it is of equal or greater importance that the public perceive that persons found to be positive will not be subject to inappropriate discrimination.
>
> Every reasonable effort should be made to improve confidentiality of test results. The confidentiality of related records can be improved by a careful review of actual record-keeping practices and by assessing the degree to which these records can be protected under applicable state laws. State laws should be examined and strengthened when found necessary. Because of the wide scope of "need to know" situations, and because of established authorization procedures for releasing records, it is recognized that there is no perfect solution to confidentiality problems in all situations. Whether disclosures of HIV-testing information are deliberate, inadvertent, or simply unavoidable, public health policy needs to carefully consider ways to reduce the harmful impact of such disclosures.
>
> Public health prevention policy to reduce the transmission of HIV infection can be furthered by an expanded program of counseling and testing for HIV antibody, but the extent to which these programs are successful depends on the level of participation. Persons are more likely to participate in counseling and testing programs if they believe that they will not experience negative conse-

quences in areas such as employment, school admission, housing, and medical services should they test positive. There is no known medical reason to avoid an infected person in these and ordinary social situations since the cumulative evidence is strong that HIV infection is not spread through casual contact. It is essential to the success of counseling and testing programs that persons who are tested for HIV are not subjected to inappropriate discrimination.[60]

Public Health Education

No effective vaccine or cure for HIV infection -- no "majic bullet" -- appears likely to be available and generally accepted for several years.[61] Prevention of new infection is the strategy which makes sense.[62] The General Accounting Office has reported the medical consensus as follows:

> [E]ducation and prevention activities are the most powerful tools available to reduce the potential impact of the AIDS epidemic. ... officials in areas hit hardest by AIDS and the experts we interviewed concurred that more education must be directed at population groups with low rates of infection, particularly heterosexuals, so they may remain uninfected. They believe it is more cost-effective to fund educational programs in areas currently experiencing low infection rates than to wait and be faced with the costs involved in treating, testing, and counseling after infection rates increase. Keeping rates of infection low in these areas also creates the greatest potential for containing the epidemic and reducing the projected number of cases for the 1990's.[63]

Risk-reduction education to encourage behavioral changes -- practice safer sex (always use condoms) and never share needles or syringes -- is recommended for everyone as the most effective way to help control the epidemic.[64]

Notes

1. A.B. Dartmouth 1973; J.D. Oregon 1982; former chair, Willamette AIDS Resource Council, Eugene, Oregon; currently staff attorney, New York City Commission on Human Rights, 52 Duane Street, New York, New York 10007, telephone (212) 566 0732.

Thanks to Paul Albert, Esq., Joyce Andrews, R.N., Terry Biern, Michael Callen, J. Robert Fackelman, M.D., Wayne Greaves, M.D., Margaret Hartnett, Mitchell Karp, Esq., Azideh Khalili, Art Leonard, Esq., Bertram Lubin, M.D., Robert McAlister, Ph.D., Keith O'Connor, June E. Osborn, M.D., Anne Quinn, R.N., Christie Reed, M.P.H., Jack Rosenberg, D.D.S., Benjamin Schatz, Esq., Dan Sendzik, William E. Shay, M.D., Susan K. Steeg, Esq., Rand Stoneburner, M.D., M.P.H., Katy Taylor and Carol L. Ziegler, Esq., for review and comments on various drafts. Their help does not imply that they or any institutions with which they may be affiliated agree with everything in this chapter, and this is not an official document of any agency or institution.

The acronyms AIDS (acquired immunodeficiency syndrome), ARC (AIDS-related complex), CDC (Centers for Disease Control), HIV (human immunodeficiency virus), HTLV-III (human T-lymphotropic virus, type three), LAV (lymphadenopathy-associated virus) and MMWR (Morbidity and Mortality Weekly Report) are imported into citations for brevity.

Although there is a settled medical consensus regarding basic modes and probabilities of transmission, medical knowledge about AIDS is increasing rapidly. By the time anything on AIDS is published, particularly on treatments, it is probably slightly outdated.

The world's largest computerized medical database (over five million references, with some 25,000 additions each month) is MEDLINE, maintained by the National Library of Medicine, and accessible at major medical libraries or via modem through services including:

(1) PaperChase (Beth Israel Hospital, 330 Brookline Avenue, Boston, Massachusetts 02215; a program emphasizing ease of use, particularly important for those not skilled in MEDLINE's requirement of precise search terms; accessible through WestLaw, CompuServe or directly, (800) 722-2075 or (617) 735- 2253); and

(2) Colleague (BRS/Saunders, 555 East Lancaster Avenue, St. Davids, Pennsylvania 19087; an AIDS database in addition to MEDLINE has been added; accessible at (800) 468-0908 or (215) 254-0233).

A series of letters at 106 Annals of Internal Medicine 168 (1987) discusses various computer search methods. The Index Medicus, available at major medical libraries, makes many but not all additions to MEDLINE available in a monthly printed cumulation. See Cahan's letter under Chlorosis Lives! -- and Slips Through MeSH, 258 J.A.M.A. 1174 (1987).

New references and offprints are welcome; they will help keep revisions of this chapter useful. Please send them to the address above.

Most papers from the III International Conference on AIDS, held in June 1987 in Washington, D.C., are not yet published or peer-reviewed, and the poster presentations are variable in reliability. But as of June 1987 (the original closing date for this chapter) they were the most current available. They will be cited merely to the page and abstract number in the abstracts volume distributed to conference participants, e.g., Conference Abstracts at 210 (F.5.6). The conference is reviewed in Barnes, AIDS: Statistics but Few Answers, Probing the AIDS Virus and Its Relatives and Cytokines Alter AIDS Virus Production, 236 Science 1423, 1523, 1627 (1987); Hoxie, Current Concepts in the Virology of Infection with HIV and Koenig & Rosenberg, Immunology of Infection with HIV, 107 Annals Internal Med. 406, 409 (1987). The abstracts volume is reprinted as a supplement to the 22 June 1987 issue of AIDS Record, which also reviews the conference (Bio-Data Publishers, 1518 K Street, N.W., Washington, D.C. 20005, (202) 783-0110).

This chapter discusses HIV in the United States, which has about two-thirds of the cases reported in the world. Statistics from the World Health Organization and the CDC, 1 AIDS 195 (1987)(40,845 of the 58,880 cases officially reported to WHO by 2 September 1987). For a broader view see World Health Organization, Special Programme on AIDS, Strategies and Structure: Projected Needs, UN Doc. No. WHO/SPA/GEN/87.1 (March 1987); id., Progress Report No. 1, UN Doc. No. WHO/SPA/GEN/87.2 (1987); id., Report of the Consultation on International Travel and HIV Infection, UN Doc. No. WHO/SPA/GLO/87.1 (1987); Panos Institute, AIDS and the Third World (rev. ed. 1987)(North American office: 1045 King Street, Alexandria, Virginia 22314, telephone (703) 960-2791); Quinn, Mann, Curran & Piot, AIDS in Africa: An Epidemiologic Paradigm, 234 Science 955 (1986); Konotey-Ahulu, AIDS in Africa: Misinformation and Disinformation, [1987] 2 Lancet 206 (see also 192); Conference Abstracts, supra, at 5-6 (M.8.1-6), 17-21 (MP.44, 48, 51, 56, 58, 60, 64, 68, 69), 23 (MP.80 & 82), 25-26 (MP.91 & 96), 45 (MP.214), 57 (T.7.6), 71 (TP.52), 77 (TP.90), 78 (TP.94-96), 85 (TP.145), 88 (TP.153), 93 (TP.187), 106 (W.2.4), 115 (WP.32), 120 (WP.59), 123 (WP.77-79), 124 (WP.84), 133 (WP.136), 157 (TH.5.4 & 5), 173 (THP.61), 176-178 (THP.75, 78, 84, 85, 88).

2. AIDS resources to have on hand include:

a. C. Koop, United States Surgeon General, Report on Acquired Immune Deficiency Syndrome (n.d. [October 1986])(free from AIDS, P.O. Box 14252, Washington, D.C. 20044). Introductory, authoritative and useful. Any "expert" who diverges significantly from Koop's report on the basic outlines of transmission is unreliable. The Public Health Service AIDS hotline is (800) 342-2437.

b. Centers for Disease Control of the Public Health Service of the U.S. Department of Health and Human Services, Morbidity and Mortality Weekly Report. Technical, but easier than most medical journals and indispensable for AIDS litigation. Subscriptions are $46 annually from Massachusetts Medical Society, C.S.P.O. Box 9120, Waltham, Massachusetts 02254-9120. CDC recommendations on preventing transmission are highly authoritative.

Single copies of the recommendations and guidelines on AIDS are free from Technical Information Activity, CDC, 1600 Clifton Road, Atlanta, Georgia 30333, (404) 639-3311. ext. 2891; the current "Orange Book" (November 1986) is being revised to include the most recent recommendations, see notes 32-33, which are also available from CDC. MMWR reports on AIDS are periodically collected and indexed; the current (May 1986) collection is $8.75 prepaid from the National Technical Information Service, 5285 Port Royal Road, Springfield, Virginia 22161, (703) 487 4650.

c. N. Krieger & R. Appleman, The Politics of AIDS (1987)($4.80 prepaid from Frontline Pamphlets, P.O. Box 2809, Oakland, California 94609). An explicitly left-wing but readable and factually reliable 64-page booklet.

The best book on AIDS science written for a wide range of readers is Institute of Medicine/National Academy of Sciences, Mobilizing Against AIDS: The Unfinished Story of a Virus (1986)(Harvard University Press, paperbound $7.95).

The most authoritative study is Committee on a National Strategy for AIDS, Institute of Medicine/National Academy of Sciences, Confronting AIDS: Directions for Public Health, Health Care, and Research (1986)[Confronting AIDS] (paperbound $24.95 prepaid from National Academy Press, 2101 Constitution Avenue, N.W., Washington, D.C. 20418). As one reviewer says, "it is comprehensive, well-referenced, superbly edited, and well-organized ... a thoughtful blueprint for mobilizing and coordinating the efforts necessary to cope with the epidemic. ... Although it does not appear likely that the present administration will follow this sound advice, we might expect more from its successor." Polk, Book Review, 317 New Eng. J. Med. 389 (1987). The membership of the Presidential Commission on the HIV Epidemic, announced 23 July 1987 and distinguished by the absence of recognized AIDS experts, has strengthened fears that Reagan's "advisory commission is designed more as an ideological screen for Reagan policies than as a blue-ribbon panel above political reproach." Inglehart, Financing the Struggle Against AIDS, 317 New Eng. J. Med. 180, 184 (1987)(Inglehart is here reporting rather than endorsing the fears); Bad Advice on AIDS and Reagan AIDS Panel Disappoints Health-Care Professionals, 328 Nature 366, 372 (1987). The commission is established by Executive Order 12601 of 24 June 1987. 52 Fed. Reg. 24,129 (29 June 1987).

There are also anthologies convenient for lawyers and medical experts, including:

a. American Civil Liberties Union, AIDS: Basic Documents (April 1987; periodically updated)($3 from ACLU, 132 West 43rd Street, New York, New York 10036, telephone (212) 944-9800)(reproduces various CDC recommendations for preventing transmission, six medical studies, and four judicial opinions).

b. AIDS: Papers from Science, 1982-1985 (R. Kulstad ed. 1986)(paperbound $21.45 from American Association for the Advancement of Science Sales Department, 1333 H Street, N.W., Washington, D.C. 20005).

c. AIDS: From the Beginning (H. Cole & G. Lundberg edd. 1986)(articles from the Journal of the American Medical Association 1982-1986; paperbound $24.95 prepaid from JAMA Circulation and Fulfillment Division, 535 North Dearborn Street, Chicago, Illinois 60610).

d. AIDS: Epidemiological and Clinical Studies (1987)(reprints from the New England Journal of Medicine 1981 to February 1987; paperbound $28.50 prepaid from NEJM, Box 9130, Waltham, Massachusetts 02254-9130).

e. AIDS and the Law: A Guide for the Public (H. Dalton & S. Burris, edd.) (1987)(Yale AIDS Law Project; paperbound $8.95; Yale University Press).

A valuable work of perspective, now available paperbound, is Allan M. Brandt's No Magic Bullet: A Social History of Venereal Disease in the United States Since 1880 (Oxford University Press, rev. ed. 1987). Brandt abbreviates his book in AIDS: From Social History to Social Policy, 14 Law, Medicine & Health Care 231 (1986) and in the Yale anthology: A Historical Perspective, in AIDS and the Law 37.

3. AIDS - acquired immunodeficiency syndrome - is a disease resulting from a virus, human immunodeficiency virus (HIV), which can suppress the immune system and result in devastating, often fatal, opportunistic infections and cancers. The official surveillance definition for reporting cases to the federal authorities is more detailed; the 1987 revision runs to 15 pages. Revision of the CDC Surveillance Case Definition for AIDS, 36 MMWR, Supp. No. 1 (1987). Figure 1 of this definition is reproduced preceding these notes.

For earlier definitions, see Update: AIDS, 32 MMWR 688 (1984); Revision of the Case Definition of AIDS for National Reporting -- United States, 34 MMWR 373 (1985); Selik, Jaffe, Solomon & Curran, CDC's Definition of AIDS, 315 New Eng. J. Med. 761 (1986)(letter); Classification System for HIV Infection in Children under 13 Years of Age, 36 MMWR 225 (1987). See also Colebunders, Mann, Francis, Bila, Izaley, Kakonde, Kabasele, Ifoto, Nzilambi, Quinn, Van der Groen, Curran, Vercauteren & Piot, Evaluation of a Clinical Case-Definition of AIDS in Africa, [1987] 1 Lancet 492, responding letter, [1987] 2 Lancet 569; Colebunders, Greenberg, Nguyen-Dinh, Francis, Kabote, Izaley, Davachi, Quinn & Piot, Evaluation of a Clinical Case Definition of AIDS in African Children, 1 AIDS 155 (1987).

4. The usual considerations apply: get an expert with technical expertise, some prior courtroom experience (showing ability to withstand vigorous cross-examination), and good teaching and communication skills; avoid professionals who support themselves by testifying rather than doing; review all relevant prior statements and other materials which may be used in cross-examination; prepare thoroughly, preferably with videotaped mock examinations rather than documents; and clarify and control costs. See generally E. Cleary, McCormick on Evidence ~~ 13-17 (3d ed. 1984); R. Keeton, Trial Tactics and Methods ~ 9.8 (2d ed. 1973); 4 M. Belli, Modern Trials ch. 62 (2d ed. 1982 & Supp. 1984); Scientific and Expert Evidence (E. Imwinkelreid ed. 1981); Locating Medical Experts, 2 Am. Jur. Trials 357 (1964 & Supp. 1986).

General discussions of scientific evidence include Symposium on Science and the Rules of Evidence, 99 F.R.D. 187 (1983); Symposium on Science and the Rules of Legal Procedure, 101 F.R.D. 599 (1984); Rules for Admissibility of Scientific Evidence, 115 F.R.D. 81 (1987).

Experts were used well in District 27 School Board v. Board of Education, 130 Misc. 2d 398, 502 N.Y.S.2d 325 (Sup. Ct. Queens County 1986). See Schwarz & Schaffer, AIDS in the Classroom, 14 Hofstra L. Rev. 163 (1985); Nelkin & Hilgartner, Disputed Dimensions of Risk: A Public School Controversy over AIDS, 64 Milbank Q., Supp. 1, at 118 (1986).

5. See generally, in addition to this manual, Matthews & Neslund, The Initial Impact of AIDS on Public Health Law in the

United States -- 1986, 257 J.A.M.A. 344 (1987); Yale anthology, AIDS and the Law, supra note 2.

6. On images of AIDS, see Brandt, supra note 2 (all three Brandt references); Fuentes, Karp & Brack, AIDS Discrimination and Its Implications for People of Color and Other Minorities, 8 August 1987 (presentation at AIDS and Minority Populations in the United States conference; available from AIDS Unit, New York City Commission on Human Rights, 52 Duane Street, New York, New York 10007); What to Do about AIDS: Physicians and Mental Health Professionals Discuss the Issues (L. McKusick ed. 1986); Mills, Attitudes and Trends: Public Perception of AIDS, Focus, December 1986 (from AIDS Health Project, University of California at San Francisco, Box 0884, San Francisco, California 94143-0884); Cooke, Learning to Care: Health Care Workers Respond to AIDS, Focus, June 1987; Gordin, Willoughby, Levine, Gure & Neill, Knowledge of AIDS Among Hospital Workers: Behavioral Correlates and Consequences, 1 AIDS 183 (1987); and Dolgin, AIDS: Social Meanings and Legal Ramifications, 14 Hofstra L. Rev. 193 (1985).

According to an April 1987 Media General-Associated Press poll, reported in the New York Times, 12 May 1987, at C3, AIDS rivals cancer as the most feared disease in the nation and 60% of respondents favor mandatory "AIDS tests". Cf. Schuman & Scott, Problems in the Use of Survey Questions to Measure Public Opinion, 236 Science 957 (1987)(typical opinion surveys are unreliable for showing absolute preferences or rankings). Acute fear regarding AIDS is unsurprising: risks which are perceived as unknown or unobservable to those exposed, new, delayed in effect, risky to future generations, uncontrollable and fatal are perceived as far more threatening than familiar risks such as smoking, regardless of the actual frequency and severity of consequences. Slovic, Perception of Risk, 236 Science 280 (1987); see generally Wilson & Crouch, Risk Assessment and Comparisons: An Introduction, 236 Science 267 (1987).

Books recommended for patients, partners, family and friends include L. Martelli, When Someone You Know Has AIDS: A Practical Guide (1987); PWA Coalition, Surviving and Thriving with AIDS: Hints for the Newly Diagnosed (1987; rev. ed. forthcoming)(rev. ed. $10.40 from National AIDS Network, 1012 Fourteenth Street, N.W., Suite 601, Washington, D.C. 20005); and Living with AIDS: A Self Care Manual (J. Lang, J. Spiegel & S. Strigle edd. 1985)(AIDS Project/Los Angeles, 937 North Cole Avenue, Suite 3, Los Angeles, California 90038).

Concrete educational suggestions are found in Task Force on AIDS of the American College Health Association, AIDS on the College Campus 22-33 (1986)(available for $7.50 prepaid from ACHA, 15879 Crabbs Branch Way, Rockville, Maryland 20855) and Conference Abstracts, supra note 1, at 155 (TH.3.4).

7. Litigators report that federal experts will not voluntarily appear and will resist subpoena; researchers want to spend their time in laboratories rather than courtrooms. Reluctance to testify is not necessarily an endorsement of the massive program of forced testing and exclusion used by the military and some other federal agencies.

8. Medical knowledge about AIDS is constantly being updated, but there is a settled expert consensus regarding basic modes and probabilities of transmission, and regarding appropriate and effective infection-control measures. Sources are cited in note 2 above. There will always be differences of detail and emphasis among experts, but any "expert" who diverges significantly from the basic consensus is suspect.

A relatively accessible introduction to epidemiology, helpful for understanding and examining experts, is Fraser, Epidemiology as a Liberal Art, 316 New Eng. J. Med. 309 (1987).

9. Sample briefs include:

(1) Brief Amici Curiae of Doctors for AIDS Research and Education 9-40, School Board of Nassau County v. Arline, 107 S. Ct. 1123 (1987)(No. 85 1277)(available from ACLU Foundation of Southern California, 633 South Shatto Place, Los Angeles, California 90005);

(2) Brief Amici Curiae National Gay Rights Advocates and ACLU Foundation of Southern California 3-16, Barlow v. Superior Court, 190 Cal. App. 3d 1652, 236 Cal. Rptr. 134 (4th Dist. 1987)(No. D005427)(available from National Gay Rights Advocates, 540 Castro Street, San Francisco, California 94114), review denied & opinion depublished by Cal. Supreme Ct., 26 May 1987 (opinion deleted from bound volumes and citation forbidden); and

(3) Opening Brief of Complainant Estate of Chadbourne 6-22, 30-43, Dep't of Fair Employment & Housing v. Raytheon, Daily Labor Rep. (BNA) E-1 (Cal. Fair Emp. & Housing Comm'n 13 Feb. 1987)(No. FEP83-84, L1-0310p, L33998)(also available from NGRA at address above).

10. Mechanics of proof are discussed in Employment Discrimination Action under Federal Civil Rights Acts, 21 Am. Jur. Trials 1 (1974 & Supp. 1986); Housing Discrimination Litigation, 28 Am. Jur. Trials 1 (1981 & Supp. 1986). Social security disability and workers' compensation manuals may be instructive on ability to work in employment cases. One available text (West Publishing Company) is D. Morton, Medical Proof of Social Security Disability (1987); workers' compensation manuals are often specific to a particular state's workers' compensation scheme.

For general consciousness-raising on disability, not on AIDS specifically, see R. Murphy, The Body Silent (1987).

In addition to discrimination based on fear, misinformation and prejudice, people with HIV face all the difficulties other people in the United States face in getting affordable quality medical care. Major players in the battle over who pays are the insurance industry, the hospital industry, the pharmaceutical industry, state and local governments and the federal government. See Inglehart, Financing the Struggle Against AIDS, 317 New Eng. J. Med. 180 (1987); Arno, The Economic Impact of AIDS, 258 J.A.M.A. 1376 (1987). Minorities and others less likely to have adequate private financial resources may be less likely to be able to obtain decent care. See, e.g., Torres, Lefkowitz, Kales & Brickner, Homelessness Among Hospitalized Patients with AIDS in New York City, 258 J.A.M.A. 779 (1987).

11. An article often cited is Francis & Chin, The Prevention of AIDS in the United States, 257 J.A.M.A. 1357 (1987)[Preventing AIDS].

A series in the British Medical Journal under the general title ABC of AIDS includes the following articles: Adler, Development of the Epidemic, 294 Brit. Med. J. 1083 (1987); Adler, Range and Natural History of Infection, 294 Brit. Med. J. 1145 (1987); Mindel, Management of Early HIV Infection, 294 Brit. Med. J. 1214 (1987); Smith & Spittle, Tumours, 294 Brit. Med. J. 1272 (1987); Carne, Neurological Manifestations, 294 Brit. Med. J. 1399 (1987); Weller, Gastrointestinal and Hepatic Manifestations, 294 Brit. Med. J. 1474 (1987); Beverley & Sattentau, Immunology of AIDS, 294 Brit. Med. J. 1536 (1987); Mortimer, The Virus and the Tests, 294 Brit. Med. J. 1602 (1987); Jeffries, Control of Infection Policies, 295 Brit. Med. J. 33 (1987); Elliott, Nursing Care, 295 Brit. Med. J. 104 (1987); Weller, Treatment of Infections and Antiviral Agents, 295 Brit. Med. J. 200 (1987); Grimshaw, Being HIV Antibody Positive, 295 Brit. Med. J. 256 (1987); Madeley, Having AIDS, 295 Brit. Med. J. 320 (1987); Johnson & Adler, Strategies for Prevention, 295 Brit. Med. J. 373 (1987).

Recent medical texts have entries on AIDS, although these texts are substantially less detailed and up-to-date than journal articles. See, e.g., Maxcy-Rosenau Public Health and Preventive Medicine 459-465 (J. Last 12th ed. 1986); Cecil Textbook of Medicine 1861-63 (J. Wyngaarden & L. Smith 17th ed. 1985); Principles and Practice of Infectious Diseases 1670-73 (G. Mandell, R. Douglas & E. Bennett 2d ed. 1985). There are also medical texts devoted solely to AIDS, including AIDS: Modern Concepts and Therapeutic Challenges (S. Broder ed. 1987).

12. A standard medical reference is Harrison's Principles of Internal Medicine (E. Braunwald, K. Isselbacher, R. Petersdorf, J. Wilson, J. Martin & A. Fauci 11th ed. 1987)(AIDS at 1392-96).

HIV - human immunodeficiency virus - is a retrovirus identified in 1984 as the cause of AIDS; specific co-factors are being sought but have not yet been confirmed. Confronting AIDS, supra note 2, at 39; Robert-Guroff & Gallo, A Virological Perspective on AIDS, in AIDS: From the Beginning, supra note 2, at xxvii; Essex, The Etiology of AIDS: Introduction and Overview, in AIDS: Papers from Science, 1982-1985, supra note 2, at 3; Gluckman, Klatzmann & Montagnier, LAV Infection and AIDS, 4 Annual Rev. Immunology 97 (1986); Gallo, The AIDS Virus, Scientific American, January 1987, at 46; Schuepbach, Veronese & Gallo, Human Retroviruses, in Clinical Virology Manual 451, 453-54 (S. Specter & G. Lancz edd. 1986); Gabuzda & Hirsch, Neurologic Manifestations of Infection with HIV: Clinical Features and Pathogenesis, 107 Annals Internal Med. 383, 387-88 (1987)(lentivirus taxonomy); citations in note 40, infra.

A small minority of researchers continues to doubt that HIV, even with co-factors, causes AIDS. Duesberg, Retroviruses as Carcinogens and Pathogens: Expectations and Reality, 47 Cancer Research 1199 (1987); Volsky, Sakai, Stevenson & Dewhurst, Retroviral Etiology of AIDS, 2 AIDS Research, Supp. 1, at 35 (1986). Even if some bloodborne agent other than HIV were the true cause of AIDS (African swine fever virus, on which see Feorino, Schable, Schochetman, Jaffe, Curran, Witte & Hess, AIDS and African Swine Fever Virus, [1986] 2 Lancet 815 and syphilis are the obsession of one gay newspaper), following the routine infection-control guidelines cited in note 32, infra, should prevent transmission. And even if the infectious agent were a CIA germ-warfare experiment gone public (another suggestion in the press, see Shively, AIDS and Genes, Gay Community News, 4-10 Oct. 1987, at 3), routine infection control should suffice.

Earlier acronyms for HIV include HTLV-III (human T-cell lymphotropic virus type three, U.S. National Cancer Institute) and LAV (lymphadenopathy-associated virus, Pasteur Institute, Paris). Confronting AIDS, supra note 2, at 39, 353, 356, 357; Brown, Human Immunodeficiency Virus, 232 Science 1486 (1986)(letter); World Health Organization Working Group on Characterization of HIV-Related Retroviruses, Criteria for Characterization and Proposal for a Nomenclature System, 1 AIDS 189 (1987). With the settlement of the NCI/Pasteur patent dispute, use of "HIV" should become universal. See Gallo & Montagnier, The Chronology of AIDS Research, 326 Nature 435 (1987).

Various viral types, all sharing the same basic modes of transmission, are being identified; the names "HIV-1" and "HIV-2" have begun to appear. See Clavel, HIV-2, the West African AIDS Virus, 1 AIDS 135 (1987); Guyader, Emerman, Sonigo, Clavel, Montagnier & Alizon, Genome Organization and Transactivation of HIV-2, 326 Nature 662 (1987); Clavel, Mansinho, Chamaret, Guetard, Favier, Nina, Santos-Ferreira, Champalimaud & Montagnier, HIV-2 Infection Associated with AIDS in West Africa, 316 New Eng. J. Med. 1180 (1987);

Newmark, Variations of AIDS Virus Relatives, 326 Nature 548 (1987); Kornfeld, Riedel, Viglianti, Hirsch & Mullins, Cloning of HTLV-4 and Its Relation to Simian and Human Immunodeficiency Viruses, 326 Nature 610 (1987)(letter); Kanki, M'Boup, Ricard, Barin, Denis, Boye, Sangare, Travers, Albaum, Marlink, Romet-Lemonne & Essex, HTLV-4 and HIV in West Africa, 236 Science 827 (1987). Related monkey viruses are described in Kanki, West African Human Retroviruses Related to STLV-III, 1 AIDS 141 (1987); Franchini, Gurgo, Guo, Gallo, Collalti, Fargnoli, Hall, Wong-Staal & Reitz, Sequence of Simian Immunodeficiency Virus and Its Relationship to HIV, 328 Nature 539 (1987); Chakrabarti, Guyader, Alizon, Daniel, Desrosiers, Tiollais & Sonigo, Sequence of Simian Immunodeficiency Virus from Macaque and Its Relationship to Other Human and Simian Retroviruses, 328 Nature 543 (1987); Arya, Beaver, Jagodzinski, Ensoli, Kanki, Albert, Fenyo, Biberfeld, Zagury, Laure, Essex, Norrby, Wong-Staal & Gallo, New Human and Simian HIV-related Retroviruses Possess Functional Transactivator (tat) Gene, 328 Nature 548 (1987).

Recent reviews of what is now known about the mechanisms of the disease include Ho, Pomerantz & Kaplan, Pathogenesis of Infection with HIV, 317 New Eng. J. Med. 278 (1987) and Seligmann, Pinching, Rosen, Fahey, Khaitov, Klatzmann, Koenig, Luo, Ngu, Riethmueller & Spira, Immunology of HIV Infection and AIDS, 107 Annals Internal Med. 234 (1987).

13. Estimates of the number of people with HIV for each person with AIDS [PWA] range from 30:1 to 300:1. Moss, What Proportion of HTLV-III Antibody Positives Will Proceed to AIDS?, [1985] 2 Lancet 223 (letter)(30:1); Sivak & Wormser, How Common Is HTLV-III Infection in the United States?, 313 New Eng. J. Med. 1352 (1985)(letter)(300:1).

The low end of Curran's estimate of roughly 50-100 to 1 in 1985 has been multiplied by the number of reported cases and rounded to the nearest hundred thousand to produce the estimate in the text. If in 1987 there are roughly 100 people with HIV for each person with AIDS as defined by the 1985 criteria, the figure is roughly four million people with HIV in the United States. Curran, Morgan, Hardy, Jaffe, Darrow & Dowdle, The Epidemiology of AIDS: Current Status and Future Prospects, 229 Science 1352 (1985).

These estimates and projections are controversial. See Confronting AIDS, supra note 2, at 69; May & Anderson, Transmission Dynamics of HIV Infection, 326 Nature 137 (1987), responding letter, 328 Nature 767 (1987); Rees, The Sombre View of AIDS, 326 Nature 343 (1987), responding letters 326 Nature 734, 328 Nature 582, 673 (1987); Anderson, Medley, Blythe & Johnson, Is It Possible to Predict the Minimum Size of the AIDS Epidemic in the United Kingdom?, [1987] 2 Lancet 1073, and responding letters, [1987] 2 Lancet 98 & 99; Luzi, Aiuti, Rezza & Greco, Italian HIV Infection Updated, 328 Nature 385 (1987); Medley, Anderson, Cox & Billard, Incubation Period of AIDS in Patients Infected via Blood Transfusion, 328 Nature 719 (1987).

The U.S. Public Health Service has recently published an estimate that 1.0 to 1.5 million people in the United States have HIV; this estimate is lower than many others. Public Health Service Guidelines for Counseling and Antibody Testing to Prevent HIV Infections and AIDS, 36 MMWR 509 (1987). The higher estimate in the text, two million, is in agreement with Kessler, Blaauw, Spear, Paul, Falk & Landay, Diagnosis of HIV Infection in Seronegative Homosexuals Presenting with an Acute Viral Syndrome, 258 J.A.M.A. 1196, 1199 (1987).

PWA - person with AIDS - is the term accepted by people with AIDS. Many PWAs find "AIDS victim" or "AIDS sufferer" demeaning and offensive because it suggests helplessness and passivity. See PWA Stands For..., PWA Coalition Newsline, Nov. 1986, at 20 (subscription $20 annually from PWA Coalition, 263A West 19th Street, No. 125, New York, New York 10011).

14. CDC, AIDS Weekly Surveillance Report -- United States, 28 September 1987. With the expanded definition of AIDS, effective September 1987, the number of reported cases may jump sharply. Revision of the CDC Surveillance Case Definition for AIDS, 36 MMWR, Supp. No. 1 (1987).

The CDC surveillance report is the authoritative source of numbers of cases, shown by "risk group", gender, race/ethnic group and geography. (Talking of risk groups rather than risky behavior encourages the mistaken impression that status rather than action spreads HIV. "Homosexual or bisexual" is an inaccurate way of referring to men who have had sex with men. The phrase impairs educational outreach because many adolescent and other males may experiment sexually with men, yet not consider themselves homo- or bisexual or at risk for AIDS. This is acknowledged in blood donor deferral guidelines. See Update: Revised PHS Definition of Persons Who Should Refrain from Donating Blood and Plasma, 34 MMWR 547 (1985).) Similar variation appears in New York City Department of Health AIDS Surveillance Unit, AIDS Surveillance Update, 26 August 1987, although the clear and accurate description "sex with men" appears more often than does the comparatively misleading "gay/bisexual."

The CDC in 1986 described a four-stage classification for HIV infection in adults; the terms "group I, II, III or IV HIV infection" may replace "AIDS" and the ill-defined term "ARC" (AIDS-related complex) in precise discourse. Classification System for HTLV-III/LAV Infections, 35 MMWR 334 (1986). (See Green, The Transmission of AIDS [sic], in AIDS and the Law, supra note 2, at 30, the term "ARC" has never been defined or accepted by the CDC, and since people die as a result of HIV infection without always developing the specific conditions which define AIDS, it is misleading to say that "ARC by itself is not fatal.") The newly expanded definition of AIDS may result in an altered staging classification. See Revision of the CDC Surveillance Case Definition for AIDS, 36 MMWR, Supp. No. 1 (1987).

Group I is people with the transient vaguely flu-like symptoms of initial infection with HIV; Group II is people with laboratory evidence of HIV infection but no visible symptoms, the largest group by far; Group III is people with persistent generalized lymphadenopathy (swollen lymph nodes), a symptom which some consider sufficient for a diagnosis of ARC. (There is evidence that laboratory findings may permit finer staging in Groups II and III even though clinical findings may be unrevealing. See Zolla-Pazner, Des Jarlais, Friedman, Spira, Marmor, Holzman, Mildvan, Yancovitz, Mathur-Wagh, Garber, El-Sadr, Cohen, Smith, Kalyanaraman, Kaplan & Fishbein, Nonrandom Development of Immunologic Abnormalities after Infection with HIV: Implications for Immunologic Classification of the Disease, 84 Proc. Nat'l Acad. Sciences U.S.A. 5404 (1987); McDougal, Kennedy, Nicholson, Spira, Jaffe, Kaplan, Fishbein, O'Malley, Aloisio, Black, Hubbard & Reimer, Antibody Response to HIV in Homosexual Men: Relation of Antibody Specificity, Titer, and Isotype to Clinical Status, Severity of Immunodeficiency, and Disease Progression, 80 J. Clinical Investigation 316 (1987); Lange, de Wolf, Krone, Danner, Coutinho & Goudsmit, Decline of Antibody Reactivity to Outer Viral Core Protein p17 Is an Earlier Serological Marker of Disease Progression in HIV Infection than Anti-p24 Decline, 1 AIDS 155 (1987).)

Group IV, "other disease," is the most complex, with five subgroups, one of which is subdivided into two categories.

Subgroup A, constitutional disease, includes people with persistent fever or diarrhea or involuntary weight loss of more than 10%, but with no condition other than HIV infection to explain the findings.

Subgroup B, neurologic disease, includes people with dementia but with no condition other than HIV infection to explain the findings. The newly expanded definition of AIDS categorizes these cases as AIDS. Revision of the CDC Surveillance Case Definition for AIDS, 36 MMWR, Supp. No. 1, at 11S (1987)(appendix II); see also note 43, infra.

Subgroup C, secondary infectious diseases, includes people with infectious diseases indicative of immune deficiency. The two categories are C-1, including people with Pneumocystis carinii pneumonia, chronic cryptosporidiosis, toxoplasmosis, extraintestinal strongyloidiasis, isosporiasis, candidiasis (esophageal, bronchial, or pulmonary), cryptococcosis, histoplasmosis, mycobacterial infection with Mycobacterium avium complex or Mycobacterium kansasii, cytomegalovirus infection, chronic mucocutaneous or disseminated herpes simplex infection or multifocal leukoencephalopathy; and C-2, including people with oral hairy leukoplakia, multidermatomal herpes zoster, recurrent Salmonella bacteremia, nocardiosis, tuberculosis or oral candidiasis (thrush). Category C-1 generally meets the expanded surveillance definition of AIDS but category C-2 often does not unless serologic testing for anti-HIV is positive.

Subgroup D, secondary cancers, includes people with Kaposi's sarcoma, non-Hodgkin's lymphoma or primary lymphoma of the brain. This subgroup meets the surveillance definition of AIDS. Subgroup E, other conditions, is a catch-all for findings which may be attributable to HIV or which indicate immune deficiency but which are not in the other subgroups.

A distinct pediatric classification has been described. Classification System for HIV Infection in Children under 13 Years of Age, 36 MMWR 225 (1987). Table 1, summary of the definition of HIV infection in children, states:

Infants and children under 15 months of age with perinatal infection

1) Virus in blood tissues or

2) HIV antibody and both cellular and humoral immune deficiency and one or more categories in Class P-2 [table 2] or

3) Symptoms meeting CDC case definition for AIDS

Older children with perinatal infection and children with HIV infection acquired through other modes of transmission

1) Virus in blood or tissues or

2) HIV antibody or

3) Symptoms meeting CDC case definition for AIDS

Table 2, summary of the classification of HIV infection in children under 13 years of age, states:

Class P-0. Indeterminate infection [antibody to HIV but under 15 months of age and not classified as definitely infected]

Class P-1. Asymptomatic infection

Subclass A. Normal immune function
Subclass B. Abnormal immune function
Subclass C. Immune function not tested

Class P-2. Symptomatic infection

Subclass A. Nonspecific findings
Subclass B. Progressive neurological disease
Subclass C. Lymphoid interstitial pneumonitis
Subclass D. Secondary infectious diseases
  Category D-1. Specified secondary infectious diseases listed in the CDC surveillance definition for AIDS

Category D-2.Recurrent serious bacterial infections

Category D-3.Other specified secondary infectious diseases

Subclass E.   Secondary cancers
Category E-1.Specified secondary cancers listed in the CDC surveillance definition for AIDS

Category E-2. Other cancers possibly secondary to HIV infection

Subclass F. Other diseases possibly due to HIV   infection

The text accompanying these tables in MMWR explains these bare categories more fully.

15. Confronting AIDS, supra note 2, at 50. The CDC introduced recent recommendations with the following paragraph:

> Human immunodeficiency virus (HIV), the virus that causes acquired immunodeficiency syndrome (AIDS), is transmitted through sexual contact and exposure to infected blood or blood components and perinatally from mother to neonate. HIV has been isolated from blood, semen, vaginal secretions, saliva, tears, breast milk, cerebrospinal fluid, amniotic fluid, and urine and is likely to be isolated from other body fluids, secretions, and excretions. However, epidemiologic evidence has implicated only blood, semen, vaginal secretions, and possibly breast milk in transmission.

Recommendations for Prevention of HIV Transmission in Health-Care Settings, 36 MMWR, Supp. No. 2, at 2S (1987).

16. Des Jarlais & Friedman, HIV Infection Among Intravenous Drug Users: Epidemiology and Risk Reduction, 1 AIDS 67 (1987).

17. HIV Infection in Transfusion Recipients and Their Family Members, 36 MMWR 137 (1987); Confronting AIDS, supra note 2, at 115-117, 309-313; Bove, Transfusion-Associated Hepatitis and AIDS: What Is the Risk?, 317 New Eng. J. Med. 242 (1987); Busch & Samson, Transfusion-Associated AIDS: Past, Present, and Future, Focus, supra note 6, July 1987; Deitch, Counseling the HIV Seropositive Transfusion Recipient, Focus, supra note 6, July 1987; Barnes, Keeping the AIDS Virus Out of Blood Supply, 233 Science 514 (1986); AIDS: The Safety of

Blood and Blood Products (J. Petrucciani, I. Gust, P. Hoppe & H. Krijnen edd. 1987)(based on 1986 World Health Organization meeting); HIV Infection and Pregnancies in Sexual Partners of HIV-Seropositive Hemophiliac Men -- United States, 36 MMWR 593 (1987).

One report has contrasted the resources expended to prevent transmission by transfusion with the resources expended to prevent transmission by the more important routes of needle sharing and unsafe sex. Conference Abstracts, supra note 1, at 139 (WP.175).

18. Stein & Branson, New AIDS Prevention Strategies for the I.V. Drug User, Focus, supra note 6, September 1987; Dotman, Now Is the Time to Prevent AIDS, 77 Am. J. Pub. Health 143 (1987) (editorial); Des Jarlais & Friedman, HIV Infection Among Intravenous Drug Users: Epidemiology and Risk Reduction, 1 AIDS 67 (1987); Marmor, Des Jarlais, Cohen, Friedman, Beatrice, Dubin, El-Sadr, Mildvan, Yancovitz, Mathur & Holzman, Risk Factors for Infection with HIV among Intravenous Drug Abusers in New York City, 1 AIDS 39 (1987); Black, Dolan, DeFord, Rubenstein, Penk, Robinowitz & Skinner, Sharing of Needles Among Users of Intravenous Drugs, 314 New Eng. J. Med. 446 (1986); Committee on Medicine and Law, Association of the Bar of the City of New York, Legalization of Non-prescription Sale of Hypodermic Needles: A Response to the AIDS Crisis, 41 Record A.B.C.N.Y. 809 (1986).

19. See CDC, AIDS Weekly Surveillance Report (as of 28 September 1987, 54% of children with AIDS were non-hispanic Blacks, 24% were Hispanics); AIDS Among Black and Hispanics -- United States, 35 MMWR 655, 695 (1986); AIDS Unit, New York City Commission on Human Rights, AIDS and People of Color: The Discriminatory Impact (rev. ed. August 1987), November 1986 version reprinted in AIDS: The Legal Complexities of a National Crisis 177 (Law Journal Seminars-Press 1987); Mays & Cochran, AIDS and Black Americans: Special Psychosocial Issues, 102 Pub. Health Rep. 224 (1987); Faltz & Madover, AIDS and Substance Abuse: Issues for Health Care Providers, Focus, supra note 6, August 1986; Bakeman, Lumb, Jackson & Smith, AIDS Risk-group Profiles in Whites and Members of Minority Groups, 315 New Eng. J. Med. 191 (1986)(letter); Samuel & Winkelstein, Prevalence of HIV Infection in Ethnic Minority Homosexual/Bisexual Men, 257 J.A.M.A. 1901 (1987)(letter); Schmidt, High AIDS Rate Spurring Efforts for Minorities, N.Y. Times, 2 August 1987, at A1, col. 1; Conference Abstracts, supra note 1, at 77 (TP.88), 171 (THP.46), 178 (THP.87)(no invited papers found).

The CDC sponsored a conference in Atlanta on 8-9 August 1987, AIDS and Minority Populations in the United States.

20. See generally Peterman & Curran, Sexual Transmission of HIV, 256 J.A.M.A. 2222 (1986).

The term "unprotected sex" is used rather than "unsafe sex" because "protected" has a closer intuitive connection with using condoms than does "safe". The term "safer sex" will be used rather than "safe sex" because "safe" may misleadingly connote reduction of risk to absolutely zero; practicing safer sex reduces risk of transmission in any situation, but risk can rarely be reduced to zero.

21. Particularly during infection, white blood cells infected with HIV may be present in semen or cervical secretions (and various other bodily fluids, but ability to detect an infectious agent in or on a surface, tissue or fluid does not necessarily imply that the agent can be transmitted by contact with that surface, tissue or fluid).

On oral sex, see Preventing AIDS, supra note 11, at 1359 (oral mucosa appear relatively inhospitable to HIV transmission, yet infection of one infant, presumably through breast feeding, leaves room for concern); Lyman, Winkelstein, Ascher & Levy, Minimal Risk of Transmission of AIDS-associated Retrovirus by Oral-Genital Contact, 255 J.A.M.A. 1703 (1986)(letter); Mayer & De Gruttola, HIV and Oral Intercourse, 107 Annals Internal Med. 428 (1987)(data insufficient to assess risk).

Developing definitive answers on the risk of oral sex would require identifying a large number of people without HIV; dividing them into groups and deliberately exposing them never, once, twice, thrice, ..., many times to unprotected oral sex with HIV-infected people; monitoring them for decades to ensure they never had any other kind of sex or engaged in any other risk behavior; withholding a vaccine or treatment which might become available; counting how many people became infected and how many became how ill how soon after how many exposures; and analyzing the data for statistically significant correlations. Such an experiment would obviously be unethical and impractical. Definitive experiments to answer many other questions about HIV transmission, prevention and treatment would be similarly unethical and impractical. See generally Osborn, The AIDS Epidemic: Multidisciplinary Trouble, 314 New Eng. J. Med. 779 (1986).

22. See Heterosexual Transmission of HTLV-III/LAV, 34 MMWR 561 (1985); Preventing AIDS, supra note 11, at 1358; Fischl, Dickinson, Scott, Klimas, Fletcher & Parks, Evaluation of Heterosexual Partners, Children, and Household Contacts of Adults with AIDS, 257 J. A.M.A. 640 (1987), and responding letter, 257 J.A.M.A. 2288 (1987); Blaser, Isolation of HIV from Cervical Secretions During Menses, 106 Annals Internal Med. 912 (1987); Archibald, Witt, Craven, Vogt, Hirsch & Essex, Antibodies to HIV in Cervical Secretions from Women at Risk for AIDS, 156 J. Infectious Disease 240 (1987); Conference Abstracts, supra note 1, at 75 (TP.75), 105-106 (W.2.1, 2, 5, 6).

The U.S. data suggest that sexual transmission from a woman to her partner is extremely rare. See Schultz, Milberg, Kristal & Stoneburner, Female-to-Male Transmission of HTLV-III, 255 J.A.M.A. 1703 (1986); Callen, Challenging the Proposition of Female to Male Transmission, PWA Coalition Newsline, supra note 13, May 1987, at 26. However, African data, where the number of women with AIDS appears approximately equal to the number of men with AIDS, suggest that it may be prudent to assume that women can transmit HIV sexually to their partners, although other explanations for the African data are plausible. See Quinn, Mann, Curran & Piot, AIDS in Africa: An Epidemiologic Paradigm, 234 Science 955 (1986). The assumption that women can transmit HIV to sexual partners may encourage heterosexual men to practice safer sex and reduce the transmission of HIV and other sexually transmitted diseases.

Reports of possible female-to-female sexual transmission are extraordinarily rare. In one report, blood contact was involved. Marmor, Weiss, Lynden, Weiss, Saxinger, Spira & Feorino, Possible Female-to-Female Transmission of HIV, 105 Annals Internal Med. 969 (1986)(letter). Blood contact may have been involved in another case. Monzon & Capellan, Female-to-Female Transmission of HIV, [1987] 2 Lancet 40. The third report excludes blood transfusions, "intravenous drug use, male partners with AIDS or I.V. drug use, or Haitian origin," but concludes only "This would suggest that females may harbor the AIDS agent as healthy carriers." Sabatini, Patel & Hirschman, 1 AIDS Research 135, 136 (1984). Artificial insemination could carry risks similar to unsafe heterosexual intercourse. Conference Abstracts, supra note 1, at 22 (MP.75).

23. Goldsmith, Sex in the Age of AIDS Calls for Common Sense and 'Condom Sense', 257 J.A.M.A. 2261 (1987); Preventing AIDS, supra note 11, at 1360; Mann, Quinn, Piot, Bosenge, Nzilambi, Kalala, Francis, Colebunders, Byers, Azila, Kabeya & Curran, Condom Use and HIV Infection among Prostitutes in Zaire, 316 New Eng. J. Med. 345 (1987); Van De Perre, Jacobs & Sprecher-Goldberger, The Latex Condom: An Efficient Barrier Against Sexual Transmission of AIDS-Related Viruses, 1 AIDS 49 (1987); Conference Abstracts, supra note 1, at 138 (WP.171), 140 (WP.181), 178 (THP.92).

24. Moss, Osmond, Baccheti, Barre-Sinoussi & Carlson, Risk Factors for AIDS and HIV Seropositivity in Homosexual Men, 125 Am. J. Epidemiology 1035 (1987); van Griensven, Tielman, Goudsmit, van der Noordaa, de Wolf, de Vroome & Coutinho, Risk Factors and Prevalence of HIV Antibodies in Homosexual Men in the Netherlands, 125 Am. J. Epidemiology 1048 (1987); Kingsley, Detels, Kaslow, Polk, Rinaldo, Chmiel, Detre, Kelsey, Odaka, Ostrow, Van Raden & Visscher, Risk Factors for Seroconversion to HIV among Male Homosexuals, [1987] 1 Lancet 345; Padian, Marquis, Francis, Anderson, Rutherford, O'Malley & Winkelstein, Male-to-Female Transmission of HIV, 258 J.A.M.A. 788 (1987).

Since more men than women carry HIV, unsafe sex with men is statistically more likely to expose partners to HIV than is unsafe sex with women, and increasing the number of partners increases the statistical chance that one or more of them will carry HIV. See Peto, AIDS and Promiscuity, [1986] 2 Lancet 979.

25. This should not induce complacency among heterosexuals. Grant, Wiley & Winkelstein, Infectivity of HIV: Estimates from a Prospective Study of Homosexual Men, 156 J. Infectious Disease 189, 192 (1987); Conference Abstracts, supra note 1, at 57 (T.7.4), 117 (WP.45), 125 (WP.90); CDC, AIDS Weekly Surveillance Report, 29 June 1987; Confronting AIDS, supra note 2, at 71, 86; Preventing AIDS, supra note 11, at 1358.

The phrase "general population" is to be avoided because it is often simply a code for dismissing gays, drug users, and any others who are not considered sufficiently mainstream by the speaker.

26. CDC, AIDS Weekly Surveillance Report, 28 September 1987.

27. This seems intuitively plausible because pregnancy depresses the immune system of the mother; otherwise the mother's immune system would reject the fetus like any other foreign tissue. And the immune system of the fetus does not become fully functional for months after birth. See Pinching & Jeffries, AIDS and HTLV-III Infection: Consequences for Obstetrics and Perinatal Medicine, 92 Brit. J. Obstet. Gynaecology 1211 (1985). But empirical data to support the theory that pregnancy accelerates development of symptoms are not conclusive.

28. Novick & Rubenstein, AIDS -- The Paediatric Perspective, 1 AIDS 3, 6 (1987); CDC, Recommendations for Assisting in the Prevention of Perinatal Transmission of HTLV-III/LAV and AIDS, 34 MMWR 721 (1985); Mok, Giaquinto, Grosch-Woerner, Ades & Peckham, Infants Born to Mothers Seropositive for HIV, [1987] 1 Lancet 1164; Grimes, The CDC and Abortion in HIV-Positive Women, 258 J.A.M.A. 1176 (1987); Confronting AIDS, supra note 2, at 56-57; Conference Abstracts, supra note 1, at 36 (MP.156), 76 (TP.83), 120 (WP.62), 136 (WP.157), 157-158 (TP.7.2, 4-6), 178 (THP.91), 186 (THP.140), 214 (F.9.6).

29. "[I]t is important to educate all women about their risk of sexually acquired AIDS and to encourage risk-reducing sexual behavior." Guinan & Hardy, Epidemiology of AIDS in Women in the United States, 1981 Through 1986, 257 J.A.M.A. 2039 (1987); Wofsy, HIV Infection in Women, 257 J.A.M.A. 2074 (1987) (excellent editorial, noting that condoms are far more realistic than celibacy or lifetime monogamy, and that of the more than 70% of women with AIDS who are Black or Hispanic,

more than 80% were of childbearing age); Shaw & Paleo, Women and AIDS, in What To Do About AIDS, supra note 6, at 142; Worth & Rodriguez, Latina Women and AIDS, SIECUS Report, Jan.-Feb. 1987, at 5; International Working Group on Women and AIDS, An Open Letter to the Planning Committees of the International Conference on AIDS (June 1987) reprinted in PWA Coalition Newsline, supra note 13, July/August 1987 at 49; Conference Abstracts, supra note 1, at 119 (WP.57), 120 (WP.60), 125 (WP.91), 174 (THP.66).

30. "There is no well documented evidence that the virus is spread by saliva. It is not spread by casual or social contact. ... there is no evidence that the virus is spread by mosquitoes, lice, bed bugs, in swimming pools, or by sharing cups, eating and cooking utensils, toilets, and air space with an infected individual. Hence, HIV infection and AIDS are not contagious." Adler, Development of the Epidemic, 294 Brit. Med. J. 1083, 1084 (1987).

31. New HIV infection is preventable. However, the current AIDS epidemic is entrenched among people who were infected before HIV and its modes of transmission were discovered or widely known in communities; therefore, numbers of reported cases will continue to climb as asymptomatic carriers develop AIDS over the years.

The evidence against casual transmission is compelling: HIV has been spreading in the U.S. for at least a decade and that unprotected sex, shared blood, and mother to fetus are the identified routes in virtually every case. If casual contact could spread AIDS, at least a few thousand of the millions of people who have knowingly (health-care workers caring for people with AIDS) or unknowingly (notably family members living with a person with HIV but not diagnosed with AIDS) been exposed to a person with AIDS should themselves have AIDS, but they don't. See Surgeon General's Report, supra note 2, at 21; Confronting AIDS, supra note 2, at 6, 50-57, 98, 189-191, 271; Preventing AIDS, supra note 11 at 1358; Gerberding, Bryant-LeBlanc, Nelson, Moss, Osmond, Chambers, Carlson, Drew, Levy & Sande, Risk of Transmitting HIV, Cytomegalovirus, and Hepatitis B to Health Care Workers Exposed to Patients with AIDS and ARC, 156 J. Infectious Diseases 1 (1987); Evaluation of Heterosexual Partners, Children, and Household Contacts of Adults with AIDS, supra note 22; Sande, The Case against Casual Contagion, 314 New Eng. J. Med. 380 (1986); Update: AIDS - United States, 35 MMWR 757 (1986); Berthier, Chamaret, Fauchet, Fonlupt, Genetet, Gueguen, Pommereuil, Ruffault & Montagnier, Transmissibility of HIV in Haemophilic and Non-haemophilic Children Living in a Private School in France, [1986] 2 Lancet 598; Jason, McDougal, Dixon, Lawrence, Kennedy, Hilgartner, Aledort & Evatt, HTLV-III/LAV Antibody and Immune Status of Household Contacts and Sexual Partners of Persons with Hemophilia, 255 J.A.M.A. 1703 (1986); Conference Abstracts, supra note 1, at 73 (TP.67), 76 (TP.84).

There is strong evidence that HIV is not transmitted by insects, including the lack of cases among children older than infants (who may have perinatal transmission) but younger than adolescents (who may experiment with sex and drugs). AIDS in Western Palm Beach County, Florida, 35 MMWR 609 (1986); Norman, Sex and Needles, Not Insects and Pigs, Spread AIDS in Florida Town, 234 Science 415, 1486 (1986); Booth, AIDS and Insects, 237 Science 355 (1987), responding letter, 238 Science 143 (1987); Jupp & Lyons, Experimental Assessment of Bedbugs (Cimex lectularius and Cimex hemipterus) and Mosquitoes (Aedes aegypti formosus) as Vectors of HIV, 1 AIDS 171 (1987).

32. "[S]aliva has not been implicated in HIV transmission." Recommendations for Prevention of HIV Transmission in Health-Care Settings, 36 MMWR, Supp. No. 2, at 6S (1987)(recommendation 4). Justice Hyman agreed in the Queens school case, District 27 School Board v. Board of Education, 130 Misc. 2d 398, 502 N.Y.S.2d 325 (Sup. Ct. Queens County 1986); so did Judge Stotler in Thomas v. Atascadero Unified School District, 662 F. Supp. 376, 380 (C.D. Cal. 1987).

Dental treatment bloodies saliva and dentists have extensive contact with saliva. Yet of 1231 dental personnel recently surveyed (many of whom treated people with AIDS) only one, a dentist who rarely wore gloves, sustained repeated needlestick injuries, practiced with cuts on his hands and had never knowingly treated a person with AIDS, has seroconverted. Recommendations for Prevention of HIV Transmission in Health-Care Settings, 36 MMWR, Supp. No. 2, at 5S (1987); Conference Abstracts, supra note 1, at 155 (TH.3.5)(note 19 in preceding reference); Affidavits of Robert S. Klein, M.D., and of Jack Rosenberg, D.D.S., at 36, both in Opposition to Motion to Dismiss, Campanella v. Hurwitz, No. GA-00021030487-DN (New York City Commission on Human Rights, filed 3 March 1987).

Antibodies to HIV were detected in saliva shortly after the virus was identified. Groopman, Salahuddin, Sarngadharan, Markham, Gonda, Sliski & Gallo, HTLV-III in Saliva of People with AIDS-Related Complex and Healthy Homosexual Men at Risk for AIDS, 226 Science 447 (1984). Other researchers suggested that HIV was rarely present in saliva. Ho, Byington, Schooley, Flynn, Rota & Hirsch, Infrequency of Isolation of HTLV-III Virus from Saliva in AIDS, 313 New Eng. J. Med. 1606 (1985). More sensitive research techniques suggest that HIV antibody is often present in saliva, at least in minuscule concentrations, but hypothesize that the immunoglobulin A also present in saliva prevents viral transmission. Archibald, Zon, Groopman, McLane & Essex, Antibodies to HTLV-III in Saliva of AIDS Patients and in Persons at Risk for AIDS, 67 Blood 831 (1986). One report urges that screening saliva may be an accurate alternative to screening blood serum. Parry, Perry & Mortimer, Sensitive Assays for Viral Antibodies in Saliva: An Alternative to Tests on Serum, [1987] 2 Lancet 72.

Two reports have suggested saliva as a mode of transmission: Wahn, Kramer, Voit, Bruester, Scrampical & Scheid, Horizontal Transmission of HIV Infection between Two Siblings, [1986] 2 Lancet 694; Salahuddin, Groopman, Markham, Sarngadharan, Redfield, McLane, Essex, Sliski & Gallo, HTLV-III in Symptom-free Seronegative Persons, [1984] 2 Lancet 1418, 1419 (Partner 3). In these cases, family members denied other types of contact but admitted biting and kissing, respectively. As the quote opening this note indicates, these reports are not generally accepted as adequate evidence of salivary transmission. See also Smith, HIV Transmitted by Sexual Intercourse but Not by Kissing, 294 Brit. Med. J. 446 (1987); Drummond, Seronegative 18 Months After Being Bitten by a Patient with AIDS, 256 J.A.M.A. 2342 (1986).

33. Recommendations for Prevention of HIV Transmission in Health-Care Settings, 36 MMWR, Supp. No. 2 (1987). Universal precautions are strongly recommended in health-care settings:

> Since medical history and examination cannot reliably identify all patients infected with HIV or other blood-borne pathogens, blood and body-fluid precautions should be consistently used for all patients. This approach, previously recommended by CDC, and referred to as "universal blood and body-fluid precautions" or "universal precautions," should be used in the care of all patients, especially including those in emergency-care settings in which the risk of blood exposure is increased and the infection status of the patient is usually unknown.

Id. at 5S (notes omitted; emphases in original).

One 1987 report on three health-care workers received sufficient inflammatory publicity to warrant quotation of CDC's summary of the facts:

> Health-Care Worker 1 [attempt to insert catheter directly into artery] had chapped hands, and the duration of the contact with the blood of the patient experiencing a cardiac arrest may have been as long as 20 minutes. Health-Care Worker 2 [several milliliters of blood spattered around room, on her face and into her mouth] sustained contamination of oral mucous membranes. This individual also had acne but did not recall having open lesions. In addition, she had sustained a scratch from a needle used to draw blood from an intravenous drug abuser of unknown HIV-infection status. Health-Care Worker 3 [blood spill covering most of her hands and forearms] had a history of dermatitis involving an ear. Health-Care Workers 1 and 3 were not wearing gloves when direct contact with blood occurred. Health-Care Worker 2 was wearing gloves, but blood contaminated her face and mouth.

In a study at the National Institutes of Health through April 30, 1987, none of the 103 workers with percutaneous exposures and none of the 229 workers with mucous-membrane exposures to blood or body fluids of patients with AIDS was seropositive. At the University of California, none of the 63 workers with open wounds or mucous membranes exposed to blood or body fluids of patients with AIDS was seropositive. Although the precise risk of transmission during exposures of open wounds or mucous membranes to contaminated blood cannot be defined, these studies indicate that it must be very low....

Three ongoing prospective studies provide data on the magnitude of the risk of HIV infection incurred when health-care workers are exposed to blood of infected patients through needle-stick wounds or contamination of an open wound or mucous membrane. In a CDC cooperative surveillance project, a total of 1,097 health-care workers with parenteral or mucous-membrane exposure to the blood of patients with AIDS or other manifestations of HIV infection had been enrolled as of March 31, 1987. ... One (0.3%) seroconverted indicating that the risk of transmission during these exposures is very low. In addition, 70 health-care workers had open wounds exposed to blood, and 58 had mucous membranes exposed to blood. Postexposure serum samples from 82 of these 128 workers have been tested for antibody to HIV; none was seropositive.

Update: HIV Infections in Health-Care Workers Exposed to Blood of Infected Patients, 36 MMWR 285 (1987)(notes omitted).

See also Flynn, Pollet, van Horne, Elvebakk, Harper & Carlson, Absence of HIV Antibody Among Dental Professionals Exposed to Infected Patients, 146 Western J. Med. 437 (1987); Preventing AIDS, supra note 11, at 1358; Henderson, Saah, Zak, Kaslow, Lane, Folks, Blackwelder, Schmitt, LeCamera, Masur & Fauci, Risk of Nosocomial Infection with HTLV-III/LAV in a Large Cohort of Intensively Exposed Health Care Workers, 104 Annals Internal Med. 644 (1986)(risk "extremely low"); McCray & Cooperative Needlestick Surveillance Group, Occupational Risk of AIDS among Health Care Workers, 314 New Eng. J. Med. 1127 (1986); McEvoy, Porter, Mortimer, Simmons & Shanson, Prospective Study of Clinical, Laboratory, and Ancillary Staff with Accidental Exposures to Blood or Body Fluids from Patients Infected with HIV, 294 Brit. Med. J. 1595 (1987); Conference Abstracts, supra note 1, at 200 (THP.223).

The "transmission categories" heading in the CDC weekly surveillance report categorizes 3% of adult cases as "undetermined." CDC note 4 explains: "Includes patients on whom risk information is incomplete (due to death, refusal to be interviewed or loss to follow-up), patients still under investigation,

men reported only to have had heterosexual contact with a prostitute, and interviewed patients for whom no specific risk was identified." CDC, AIDS Weekly Surveillance Report, 27 July 1987.

The various CDC recommendations, in chronological order, are AIDS: Precautions for Clinical and Laboratory Staffs, 31 MMWR 577 (1982); Prevention of AIDS: Report of Inter-Agency Recommendations, 32 MMWR 101 (1983); AIDS: Precautions for Health-Care Workers and Allied Professionals, 32 MMWR 450 (1983); Provisional Public Health Service Inter-Agency Recommendations for Screening Donated Blood and Plasma for Antibody to the Virus Causing AIDS, 34 MMWR 1 (1985); Testing Donors of Organs, Tissues, and Semen for Antibody to HTLV-III/LAV, 34 MMWR 294 (1985); Education and Foster Care of Children Infected with HTLV-III/LAV, 34 MMWR 517 (1985); Recommendations for Preventing Possible Transmission of HTLV-III/LAV from Tears, 34 MMWR 533 (1985)(eye and contact lens examinations); Update: Revised Public Health Service Definition of Persons Who Should Refrain from Donating Blood and Plasma -- United States, 34 MMWR 547 (1985); Recommendations for Preventing Transmission of Infection with HTLV-III/LAV in the Workplace, 34 MMWR 681 (1985); Recommendations for Assisting in the Prevention of Perinatal Transmission of HTLV-III/LAV and AIDS, 34 MMWR 721 (1985); Additional Recommendations to Reduce Sexual and Drug-Abuse Related Transmission of HTLV-III/LAV, 35 MMWR 152 (1986); Recommendations for Preventing Transmission of Infection with HTLV-III/LAV during Invasive Procedures, 35 MMWR 221 (1986); Recommended Infection-Control Practices for Dentistry, 35 MMWR 237 (1986); Recommendations for Providing Dialysis Treatment to Patients Infected with HTLV-III/LAV, 35 MMWR 376 (1986); Diagnosis and Treatment of Mycobacterial Infection and Disease in Persons with HTLV-III/LAV Infection, 35 MMWR 448 (1986); HTLV-III/LAV: Agent Summary Statement, 35 MMWR 540 (1986)(laboratory safety); Immunization of Children Infected with HTLV-III/LAV, 35 MMWR 595 (1986); Public Health Service Guidelines for Counseling and Antibody Testing to Prevent HIV Infection and AIDS, 36 MMWR 509 (1987); Recommendations for Prevention of HIV Transmission in Health-Care Settings, 36 MMWR, Supp. No. 2 (1987).

On the workplace recommendations, the most generally important, see Mason, Statement on the Development of Guidelines for the Prevention of AIDS Transmission in the Workplace, 101 Pub. Health Rep. 6 (1986). Other groups have proposed additional specialized guidelines, e.g., MacArthur & Schneiderman, Infection Control and the Autopsy of Persons with HIV, 15 Am. J. Infection Control 172 (1987).

34. Sex Work: Writings by Women in the Sex Industry (F. Delacoste & P. Alexander edd. 1987). Professional sex workers risk occupational exposure to HIV, but money is not a mode of transmitting HIV, and amateurs are more likely to ignore

precautions. Reported seropositivity rates are not as high as some expected. Antibody to HIV in Female Prostitutes, 36 MMWR 157 (1987)(defines anyone who has ever exchanged "physical-sexual services for money or drugs" since beginning of 1978 as a "prostitute"); AIDS and People of Color: The Discriminatory Impact, supra note 19, at 15-16.

35. Recommendations for Prevention of HIV Transmission in Health-Care Settings, 36 MMWR, Supp. No. 2, at 9S-12S (1987); Resnick, Veren, Salahuddin, Tonreau & Markham, Stability and Inactivation of HTLV-II/LAV under Clinical and Laboratory Environments, 255 J.A.M.A. 1887 (1986)(viral infectivity undetectable and reduced more than ten million times within one minute by 1 to 10 dilution of bleach and by standard 70% rubbing alcohol); Martin, McDougal & Loskoski, Disinfection and Inactivation of HTLV-III/LAV, 152 J. Infectious Disease 400 (1985), responding letter and reply, 153 J. Infectious Disease 694 (1987)(letter on whether heating blood products interferes with subsequent serological testing); Conference Abstracts, supra note 1, at 169 (THP.37). Vodka and wine are also effective (though not EPA-approved) disinfectants, but beer and cola are not. Conference Abstracts, supra note 1, at 42 (MP.191). Drying may kill 90% or more of the virus. Recommendations for Prevention of HIV Transmission in Health-Care Settings, 36 MMWR, Supp. No. 2, at 10S; Conference Abstracts, supra note 1, at 48 (MP.229), 50 (MP.239).

36. Hepatitis B is the target disease when discussing issues of infection control because of its modes of transmission, the virulence and infectivity of the virus, and because of the epidemiology of hepatitis B in the general population and health care workers....

Hepatitis B is an insidious disease. The majority of infections are asymptomatic or, more correctly, subclinical in nature and undiagnosed.... [O]nly about one-fourth of patients actually demonstrate jaundice.

Approximately 80% of all hepatitis B infections are undiagnosed.... Thus, the patient never knew he or she had hepatitis B and could not provide the dentist [or other people coming in contact with the person] with positive history of disease....

Regardless of the medical history, occupational group, or other subcategory of population, all patients should be regarded as potential HBV [hepatitis B virus] carriers. ...

Cottone, Hepatitis B: Transmission and Epidemiology in the Dental Profession, in Proceedings: National Conference on Infection Control in Dentistry 9, 11, 13 (1986)(sponsored by American Dental Association, CDC & National Institute for Dental Research).

In the blood of a patient infected with hepatitis B, it is not unusual to find anywhere from 100 million (10^8) to 1 billion (10^9) viruses per milliliter of blood or serum, an extraordinarily high number of viruses to be contained in approximately 15 to 20 drops of blood. In fact, a drop of whole blood not even visible to the naked eye can contain hundreds of thousands of viruses. To add to this disturbing fact, the hepatitis B virus is stable after drying and will remain viable at ambient [room] conditions for up to 1 week and perhaps much longer.... [N]umbers of microorganisms are directly related to the efficiency of transmission by a particular route, which is what makes hepatitis so dangerous in terms of a blood-contaminated environment.

In comparison, a patient infected with the AIDS virus has only 1 to 100 viruses per milliliter of blood, and this is probably a high estimate of the actual titer [concentration].... Since the numbers of microorganisms in an inoculum [the droplet or whatever containing virus] are directly related to the efficiency of transmission of that organism, the risk of transmitting AIDS virus infection by a single event should be at least six orders of magnitude [one million] times less than that for hepatitis B in a comparable event....

Throughout the health care professions today, there is an altogether too common myth that microorganisms responsible for serious diseases require extraordinary or exotic physical or chemical treatments to eliminate real or simply perceived transmission hazards from contaminated inanimate surfaces.

... [A]ll data indicate that the virus [HIV] is extremely sensitive to heat and also to a wide range of disinfectant chemicals, at levels well within accepted sterilizing, disinfecting, and even some sanitizing regimens. This broad sensitivity to physical or chemical stress, coupled with the very low titers in the blood of infected patients, are two major reasons why the virus is extremely difficult to transmit except under the most favorable conditions.

Bond, Modes of Transmission of Infectious Diseases, in Proceedings: National Conference on Infection Control in Dentistry, Id. at 34-35.

See also Gerberding, Hopewell, Kaminsky & Sande, Transmission of Hepatitis B without Transmission of AIDS by Accidental Needlestick, 312 New Eng. J. Med. 56 (1985); Piazza, Guadagnino, Picciotto, Borgia & Nappa, Contamination by

Hepatitis B Surface Antigen in Dental Surgeries, 295 Brit. Med. J. 473 (1987) (extensive contamination); Recommendations for Preventing Transmission of Infection with HTLV-III/LAV in the Workplace, 34 MMWR 681 (1985); Harrison's Internal Medicine, supra note 12, at 1329 (et pace 1334); Recommended Infection-Control Practices for Dentistry, 35 MMWR 237 (1986); Jonas, Schiff, O'Sullivan, Medina, Reddy, Jeffers, Fayne, Roach & Steele, Failure of CDC Criteria to Identify Hepatitis B Infection in a Large Municipal Obstetrical Population, 107 Annals Internal Med. 335 (1987)(even thorough history of risk factors to identify hidden carriers fails to identify half of the women found to be infected when tested); Council on Dental Material and Devices, Council on Dental Therapeutics, American Dental Association, Guidelines for Infection Control in the Dental Office and the Commercial Dental Laboratory, 97 J. Am. Dental Ass'n. 673 (1978).

The estimate of world HIV infection is from World Health Organization, Special Programme on AIDS, Strategies and Structure: Projected Needs, supra note 1, at annex I-3.

37. Compliance, not the adequacy of the infection-control guidelines, is the problem. See Gerberding & University of California at San Francisco Task Force on AIDS, Recommended Infection-Control Policies for Patients with HIV Infection, 315 New Eng. J. Med. 1562 (1986), and responding letter and reply, 316 New Eng. J. Med. 1479 (1987); Lynch, Jackson, Cummings & Stamm, Rethinking the Role of Isolation Practices in the Prevention of Nosocomial Infections, 107 Annals Internal Med. 243 (1987)(briefly indicates rationale for various recommendations); Conference Abstracts, supra note 1, at 155 (TH.3.6); Outbreak of Hepatitis B Associated with an Oral Surgeon -- New Hampshire, 36 MMWR 132 (1987)("The repeated occurrence of outbreaks associated with dentists or oral surgeons is especially disturbing because there are easily available and widely recommended measures to prevent them. A safe, effective vaccine against hepatitis B became available in 1982, and, since the late 1970's, national dental authorities have urged dental practitioners to wear gloves during all procedures involving hand contact with patients' mouths. In March 1986, a national random telephone survey revealed that 44% of non-federal, practicing dentists and oral surgeons in the United States had been vaccinated against hepatitis B. Only 15% of respondents used gloves routinely for all procedures.")(notes omitted).

The Recommendations for Prevention of HIV Transmission in Health-Care Settings, 36 MMWR, Supp. No. 2 (1987), appear likely to be more strongly enforced than previous guidelines, although as of this writing the Occupational Safety and Health Administration has not implemented its rumored plan to mandate compliance with the guidelines.

38. Mackie-Bailey, Abhorrent, Unethical and Impractical for Nurses to Refuse to Care for AIDS Patients, Nursing Standards,

6 Nov. 1986, at 5.

Accommodating any person with a transmissible disease requires an individualized determination, based on reasonable medical judgments given the state of medical knowledge, which considers, among other factors, (a) the nature of the risk (how the disease is transmitted), (b) the duration of the risk (how long the carrier is infectious), (c) the severity of the risk (the potential harm to third parties) and (d) the probabilities the disease will be transmitted and will cause varying degrees of harm. (After School Board of Nassau County v. Arline, 107 S. Ct. 1123 (1987).)

The consensus among the recognized and experienced experts is that there is no medical basis for blanket discrimination against people with AIDS. Public Health Service Guidelines for Counseling and Antibody Testing to Prevent HIV Infection and AIDS, 36 MMWR 509, 514 (1987)(quoted in testing section); Confronting AIDS, supra note 2, at 19; Gillon, Refusal to Treat AIDS and HIV Positive Patients, 294 Brit. Med. J. 1332 (1987). People who have AIDS may also have active pulmonary tuberculosis or another airborne contagious infection requiring unusual protections. See Lynch, Jackson, Cummings & Stamm, Rethinking the Role of Isolation Practices in the Prevention of Nosocomial Infections, 107 Annals Internal Med. 243, 245 (1987). But need for unusual protections is based upon the medical complications, not upon risk of transmitting HIV or the classical opportunistic infections, which are generally difficult to transmit.

Brandt has placed AIDS in the context of other "deep cultural fears about disease and sexuality," recalling the earlier hysteria about syphilis and gonorrhea, and suggesting that ideology preserves unreasonable fears of people with AIDS despite overwhelming evidence against casual contagion:

> [P]hysicians now [ca. 1910] asserted that syphilis and gonorrhea could be transmitted in any number of ways. Doctors catalogued the various modes of transmission. Pens, pencils, toothbrushes, towels and bedding, and medical procedures were all identified as potential means of communication. ... One indication of how seriously these casual modes of transmission were taken is the fact that the Navy removed doorknobs from its battleships during the First World War, claiming that they had been a source of infection for many of its sailors (a remarkable act of denial). We now know, of course, that syphilis and gonorrhea cannot be contracted in these ways. This poses a difficult historical problem: why did physicians believe that they could be?
>
> Theories of casual transmission reflected deep cultural fears about disease and sexuality in the early twentieth century. In these approaches to venereal disease, concerns about hygiene, contamination, and contagion were expressed, anxieties

that reflected a great deal about the contemporary society and culture. Venereal disease was viewed as a threat to the entire late Victorian social and sexual system, which placed great value on discipline, restraint, and homogeneity. ...

Perhaps the most dramatic public health intervention designed to combat sexually transmitted diseases was the campaign to close red-light districts.... The crackdown on prostitutes constituted the most concerted attack on civil liberties in the name of public health in American history.... Prostitutes were now subject to quarantine, detention, and internment....

Although many of these interventions were challenged in the courts, most were upheld; the police powers of the state were deemed sufficient to override any constitutional concerns. The program of detention and isolation, it should be noted, had no impact on rates of venereal disease, which increased dramatically during the [1914-1918] war. Although this story is not well known, it is not unlike the internment of Japanese-Americans during World War II.

In light of the history of sexually transmitted diseases in the last century, it is almost impossible to watch the AIDS epidemic without experiencing a sense of deja vu. AIDS raises a host of concerns traditional to the debates about venereal infection, from morality to medicine, sexuality and deviancy, prevention and intervention....

Despite considerable evidence that AIDS is not easily communicated, there are widespread fears. The anxiety that AIDS can be casually transmitted is reminiscent of the earlier belief that syphilis could be communicated by shared drinking cups, toilet seats, and doorknobs. What were late Victorian concerns are now cast in a contemporary light. In the fall of 1985 a New York Times/CBS poll found that 47 percent of Americans believed that AIDS could be transmitted via a shared drinking glass, while 28 percent believed that toilet seats could be the source of contamination. Another survey found that 34 percent of those polled believed it unsafe to "associate" with an AIDS victim even when no physical contact was involved.

Brandt, supra note 2, 14 Law, Medicine & Health Care at 232-234 (notes omitted).

39. Confronting AIDS, supra note 2, at 91; Carne, Weller, Loveday & Adler, From Persistent Generalised Lymphadenopathy to AIDS: Who Will Progress?, 294 Brit. Med. J. 868 (1987);

Conference Abstracts, supra note 1, at 1-2 (M.3.1 & 3), 171 (THP.49).

Some recent studies have predicted that more than 25-50% of people with HIV infection will develop AIDS. But extrapolating from data found in a small study to national averages is fraught with hazard and predictions remain controversial. See note 13, supra.

40. This issue can overlap with the search for co-factors and is under intensive study. See Preventing AIDS, supra note 11, at 1359; Haverkos, Factors Associated with the Pathogenesis of AIDS, 156 J. Infectious Diseases 251 (1987)(report on NAIAD workshop); Polk, Fox, Brookmeyer, Kanchanaraksa, Kaslow, Visscher, Rinaldo & Phair, Predictors of AIDS Developing in a Cohort of Seropositive Men, 316 New Eng. J. Med. 61 (1987) and responding letters, 317 New Eng. J. Med. 245; Brookmeyer, Gail & Polk, The Prevalent Cohort Study and AIDS, 126 Am. J. Epidemiology 14 (1987); Holzman, Walsh & Karpatkin, Risk for AIDS Among Thrombocytopenic and Nonthrombocytopenic Homosexual Men Positive for HIV, 106 Annals Internal Med. 383 (1987); Eales, Nye, Parkin, Weber, Forster, Harris & Pinching, Association of Different Allelic Forms of Group Specific Component with Susceptibility to and Clinical Manifestation of HIV Infection, [1987] 1 Lancet 999, and responding letters, 317 New Eng. J. Med. 630 & 631 (1987); Des Jarlais, Friedman, Marmor, Cohen, Mildvan, Yancovitz, Mathur, El-Sadr, Spira, Garber, Beatrice, Abdul-Quader & Sotheran, Development of AIDS, HIV Seroconversion, and Potential Co-factors for T4 Cell Loss in a Cohort of Intravenous Drug Users, 1 AIDS 105 (1987); Zagury, Bernard, Leonard, Cheynier, Feldman, Savin & Gallo, Long-Term Cultures of HTLV-III-infected T Cells: A Model of Cytopathology of T-cell Depletion in AIDS, 231 Science 850 (1986); Taylor, Schwartz & Detels, The Time from Infection with HIV to the Onset of AIDS, 154 J. Infectious Disease 694 (1986); Conference Abstracts, supra note 1, at 2 (M.4.1 & 2), 25 (MP.89), 71 (TP.53), 73 (TP.64 & 65), 81 (TP.111), 83 (TP.124), 123 (WP.76), 124 (WP.83 & 86), 125 (WP.92), 206 (F.1.2-6); citations in note 12, supra.

41. HIV is a retrovirus which inserts its genetic material into the genes of the host whence the viral material cannot be removed by any of the usual chemical or biological methods of treatment, so theory indicates that infection with HIV will persist for the life of the host. See Broder & Gallo, A Pathogenic Retrovirus (HTLV-III) Linked to AIDS, 311 New Eng. J. Med. 161 (1984). Once within the body, HIV can spread from cell to cell without having to produce and release infective virus particles. Strebel, Daugherty, Clouse, Cohen, Folks & Martin, The HIV 'A' (sor) Gene Product Is Essential for Virus Infectivity, 328 Nature 728 (1987); Matthews, Weinhold, Lyerty, Langlois, Wigzell & Bolognesi, Interaction between the HTLV-III$_B$ Envelope Glycoprotein gp 120 and the Surface Antigen CD4, 84 Proc. Nat'l Acad. Sciences U.S.A. 5424 (1987); Dowsett, Roff,

Greenaway, Elphick & Farrer, Syncitia -- A Major Site for the Production of HIV?, 1 AIDS 147 (1987). Empirically, HIV can be cultured from many people who are seropositive (have detectable antibodies indicating exposure to HIV) even though they have no symptoms. See Falk, Paul, Landay & Kessler, HIV Isolation from Plasma of HIV-Infected Persons, 316 New Eng. J. Med. 1547 (1987).

The handful of cases of apparent seroconversion (change in antibody status) from positive back to negative remain under study. Conference Abstracts, supra note 1, at 53 (T.3.2.).

Conclusive data are unavailable, but there are indications that the two times of greatest infectivity may be in the window period immediately after infection (before antibody testing can reveal infection) and later, often years after the initial infection, when the T4 (CD4+ or OKT4 lymphocyte) cell count falls. Id. at 95 (TP.195; the poster abstract does not mention the data on high infectivity before antibodies form and the data are not decisive, but high early infectivity, before the body has mounted a neutralizing immune response, is common in other infections), 106 (W.2.6); Mortimer, The Virus and the Tests, 294 Brit. Med. J. 1602, 1603 (1987).

42. See Confronting AIDS, supra note 2, at 46-50, 281-303; Revision of the CDC Surveillance Case Definition for AIDS, 36 MMWR, Supp. No. 1 (1987). HIV infection also complicates treatment of several conditions not caused by HIV, including tuberculosis and syphilis. Tuberculosis and AIDS -- Connecticut, 36 MMWR 133 (1987); Johns, Tierney & Selsenstein, Alteration in the Natural History of Neurosyphilis by Concurrent Infection with HIV; 316 New Eng. J. Med. 1569 (1987); Berry, Hooten, Collier & Lukehart, Neurologic Relapse after Benzathine Penicillin Therapy for Secondary Syphilis in a Patient with HIV Infection, 316 New Eng. J. Med. 1587 (1987); Tramont, Syphilis in the AIDS Era, 316 New Eng. J. Med. 1600 (1987); Increases in Primary and Secondary Syphilis -- United States, 36 MMWR 393 (1987).

43. Confronting AIDS, supra note 2, at 292-297.

The neurological manifestations of HIV infection are under study. Gabuzda & Hirsch, Neurologic Manifestations of Infection with HIV: Clinical Features and Pathogenesis, 107 Annals Internal Med. 383 (1987); Revision of the CDC Surveillance Case Definition for AIDS, 36 MMWR, Supp. No. 1, at 12S (1987)(definition of HIV encephalopathy; see also note 14, supra); Barnes, Brain Damage by AIDS under Active Study, 235 Science 1574 (1987); Lee, Ho & Gurney, Functional Interaction and Partial Homology Between HIV and Neuroleukin, 237 Science 1047 (1987), and discussion in same issue, 237 Science 971; Pamarola-Sune, Navia, Cordon-Carlo, Cho & Price, HIV Antigen in the Brains of Patients with the AIDS Dementia Complex, 21 Annals Neurology 490 (1987); Koyangi, Miles, Mitsuyasu, Merrill, Vinters & Chen, Dual Infection of the Central Nervous System by AIDS Viruses with Distinct Cellular Tropisms, 236 Science 819 (1987); Goudsmit-Epstein, Paul, van der Helm, Dawson, Asher, Yanagihara, Wolff, Gibbs & Gajdusek, Intra-blood-brain Barrier Synthesis of HIV Antigen and Antibody in Humans and Chimpanzees, 84 Proc. Nat'l Acad. Sciences U.S.A. 3876 (1987); Boussin, Dormont, Merrouche, Fleury, Dubreaux, Bequet, Goasguen & Brunet, Possible Involvement of HIV in Neuropsychiatric Episode in Patient Seronegative for Two (or More) Years, [1987] 2 Lancet 571; Bach & Boothby, Dementia Associated with HIV with a Negative ELISA, 315 New Eng. J. Med. 891 (1986)(letter); Conference Abstracts, supra note 1, at 4 (M.5.3), 34 (MP.145), 55 (T.5.1 & 2), 115 (WP.29), 135 (WP.148 & 149), 153 (TH.1.3), 182 (THP.115), 187 (THP.146), 189 (THP.153 & 155).

Cases of tuberculosis or other diseases which disproportionately affect poor and minority people did not meet the surveillance definition of AIDS until its recent expansion. Revision of the CDC Surveillance Case Definition for AIDS, 36 MMWR, Supp. No. 1 (1987). Even when it was clear that a person with, for example, tuberculosis, would not have died if an underlying HIV infection had not made the usual tuberculosis treatments ineffective, no diagnosis of AIDS could be reported to CDC. Thus the number of official diagnoses of AIDS systematically understated the impact of HIV infection on populations with higher endemic rates of tuberculosis and certain other diseases. See Des Jarlais & Friedman, HIV Infection Among Intravenous Drug Users, 1 AIDS 67, 74 (1987); AIDS and People of Color: The Discriminatory Impact, supra note 19, at 11. On the other hand, there are rumors that some physicians with middle- or upper-class patients selectively fail to make or report AIDS diagnoses to spare their patients the stigma and discrimination often attendant on a diagnosis of AIDS. Published data may not support this hypothesis. Hardy, Starcher, Morgan, Druker, Kristal, Day, Kelly, Ewing & Curran, Review of Death Certificates to Assess Completeness of AIDS Case Reporting, 102 Pub. Health Rep. 386 (1987).

44. Surprising preliminary data suggest that a handful of people with HIV infection but no clinical or laboratory symptoms may have eliminated their HIV infections. See note 41, supra. There are no reliably reported preliminary data suggesting that people who have developed full-blown AIDS have eliminated their HIV infections.

45. The percentages of deaths reported to the CDC as of the 28 September 1987 surveillance report include 91% of people reported in the first half of 1981, 88% from the first half of 1983, 76% from the first half of 1985 and 27% from the first half of 1987. Reporting of deaths is incomplete. Since AIDS is defined in terms of extremely serious manifestations of HIV infection, a high fatality rate is unsurprising, but the supposition that all HIV infections are fatal is far from established. Dassey, AIDS and Testing for AIDS, 255 J.A.M.A. 743 (1986).

46. See Kaplan, Wofsy & Volberding, Treatment of Patients with AIDS and Associated Manifestations, 247 J.A.M.A. 1367 (1987); DeVita, Developmental Therapeutics and AIDS, 106 Annals Internal Med. 568 (1987)(report on NIH conference); American Foundation for AIDS Research, AmFAR Directory of Experimental Treatments for AIDS & ARC (June 1987; bi-monthly supplements scheduled); Confronting AIDS, supra note 2, at 139-175.

The drug recently approved for treatment of some people with AIDS is discussed in Yarchoan & Broder, Development of Retroviral Therapy for AIDS and Related Disorders, 316 New Eng. J. Med. 557 (1987)(life cycle of HIV and use of AZT (azidothymidine, newly christened "retrovir" (brand name) and "zidovudine" (generic name)), and letter and reply, 317 New Eng. J. Med. 629 (1987); Fischl, Richman, Grieco, Gottlieb, Volberding, Laskin, Leedom, Groopman, Mildvan, Schooley, Jackson, Durack & King, The Efficacy of Azidothymidine (AZT) in the Treatment of Patients with AIDS and AIDS-Related Complex, New Eng. J. Med. 185 (1987); Richman, Fischl, Grieco, Gottlieb, Volberding, Laskin, Leedom, Groopman, Mildvan, Hirsch, Jackson, Durack & Nusinoff-Lehrman, The Toxicity of Azidothymidine (AZT) in the Treatment of Patients with AIDS and AIDS-Related Complex, New Eng. J. Med. 192 (1987); Yarchoan, Berg, Brouwers, Fischl, Spitzer, Wichman, Grafman, Thomas, Safai, Brunetti, Perno, Schmidt, Larson, Myers & Broder, Response of HIV-associated Neurological Disease to 3'-Azido-s'-deoxythymidine, [1987] 1 Lancet 132.

On stimulating production of blood cells, see Groopman, Mitsuyasu, DeLeo, Oette & Golde, Effect of Human Granulocyte-Macrophage Colony-Stimulating Factor on Myelopoiesis in AIDS, 317 New Eng. J. Med. 599 (1987); Nathan, Hope for Hematopoietic Hormones, 317 New Eng. J. Med. 626 (1987); Stella, Ganser & Hoelzer, Defective In Vitro Growth of the Hemopoietic Progenitor Cells in AIDS, 80 J. Clinical Investigation 286 (1987); Clark & Kamen, The Human Colony-Stimulating Factors, 236 Science 1229 (1987)(general review of CSFs; on AIDS see 1235-36).

There is an active self-treatment movement among people with AIDS. See Michaud, AIDS Drug Underground Helps Spread the Word on Treatments, Reuter wire, New York, 27 July 1987; AIDS Treatment News (published biweekly by John S. James, P.O. Box 411256, San Francisco, California 94141, (415) 282-0110), $25/quarter ($8 for people with AIDS or ARC).

47. See Merz, HIV Vaccine Approved for Clinical Trials, 258 J. A.M.A. 1433 (1987); Barnes, Solo Actions of AIDS Virus Coat, 237 Science 971 (1987); Barnes, Broad Issues Debated at AIDS Vaccine Workshop, 236 Science 255 (1987); Salk, Prospects for the Control of AIDS by Immunizing Seropositive Individuals, 327 Nature 473 (1987); Confronting AIDS, supra note 2, at 221-229; Hu, Fultz, McClure, Eichberg, Thomas,

Zarling, Singhal, Kosowski, Swenson, Anderson & Todaro, Effect of Immunization with a Vaccinia-HIV env Recombinant of HIV Infection of Chimpanzees, 328 Nature 721 (1987); Adams, Dawson, Gull, Kingsman & Kingsman, The Expression of Hybrid HIV:Ty Virus-like Particles in Yeast, 328 Nature 68 (1987).

48. Meyer & Pauker, Screening for HIV: Can We Afford the False Positive Rate?, 317 New Eng. J. Med. 238, 240 (1987)("We are a testing culture: we test our urine for drugs; we test our sweat for lies. ... If the false positive rate is not virtually zero, screening a population in which the prevalence of HIV is low will unavoidably stigmatize and frighten many healthy people. How will these mistakes change the lives of the unfortunate persons who are incorrectly identified as infected? Will such screening affect the course of the AIDS epidemic? ... The AIDS epidemic frightens us all. But we should not allow our fear to cloud our judgment. Hasty and indiscriminate screening for antibody to HIV is imprudent and potentially dangerous, whether we suggest the tests to young women, require them of engaged couples, or impose them on our veterans.").

49. Krieger and Appleman preface The Politics of AIDS, supra note 2, with the following quotation from H.E. Sigerist's The Philosophy of Hygiene:

It is quite obvious that the means and methods used in prevention of disease are those provided by medicine and science. And yet whether these methods are applied or not does not depend on medicine alone but to a much higher extent on the philosophical and social tendencies of the time ... From whatever angle we approach these problems, over and over we find that hygiene and public health, like medicine at any age, are but an aspect of the general civilization of the time and are largely determined by the cultural conditions of that time.

50. See Confronting AIDS, supra note 2, at 119-130; Cleary, Barry, Mayer, Brandt, Gostin & Fineberg, Compulsory Premarital Screening for HIV: Technical and Public Health Considerations, 258 J.A.M.A. 1757 (1987); Meyer & Pauker, supra note 48; Bayer, Levine & Wolf, HIV Antibody Screening: An Ethical Framework for Evaluating Proposed Programs, 256 J.A.M.A. 1768 (1986); Gostin & Curran, The Limits of Compulsion in Controlling AIDS, Hastings Center Report, December 1986, reprinted in AIDS: The Legal Complexities of a National Crisis 44 (Law Journal Seminars-Press 1987); Gostin & Curran, AIDS Screening, Confidentiality, and the Duty to Warn, 77 Am. J. Pub. Health 361 (1987); Dlugosch, Gold & Dilley, AIDS Antibody Testing: Evaluation and Counseling, Focus, supra note 6, July 1986; Adler & Jeffries, AIDS: A Faltering Step, 295 Brit.

Med. J. 73 (1987); Miller, Jeffries, Green, Harris & Pinching, HTLV-III: Should Testing Ever Be Routine?, 292 Brit. Med. J. 941 (1986); Antibody Testing: A Consensus Statement (February 1987)(joined by 19 AIDS, civil rights and gay/lesbian organizations; available from Gay Men's Health Crisis, Box 274, 132 West 24th Street, New York, New York 10011, Attention: Tim Sweeney); Surgeon General, Report on AIDS, supra note 2, at 30, 33-34; Conference Abstracts, supra note 1, at 4-5 (M.6.1-6).

Minorities, prisoners, prostitutes, immigrants, child-bearing women and other relatively disempowered groups are the targets most often suggested for mass screening. Young Black males are disproportionately excluded from the Job Corps and the military, employers of last resort, by screening. See Burke, Brundage, Herbold, Berner, Gardner, Gunzenhauser, Voskovitch & Redfield, HIV Infections Among Civilian Applicants for United States Military Service, October 1985 to March 1986, 317 New Eng. J. Med. 131 (1987); Trends in HIV Infection Among Civilian Recruits for Military Service -- United States, October 1985-December 1986, 36 MMWR 273 (1987).

51. Recommendations for Prevention of HIV Transmission in Health-Care Settings, 36 MMWR, Supp. No. 2, at 13S (1987). These recommendations may have been biased toward excessive testing and contact tracing by political pressure.
Cf. Gostin, Curran & Clark, The Case Against Compulsory Casefinding in Controlling AIDS -- Testing, Screening and Reporting, 12 Am. J. L. & Med. 7 (1987)(based on study undertaken for CDC).

52. The misnomer "AIDS test" falsely equates having HIV with having AIDS, and heightens panic and discrimination. See Dassey, AIDS and Testing for AIDS, 255 J.A.M.A. 743 (1986)(misleading heading supplied by JAMA letters editor).

Important recent documents include Public Health Service Guidelines for Counseling and Antibody Testing to Prevent HIV Infection and AIDS, 36 MMWR 509 (1987); Revision of the CDC Surveillance Definition for AIDS, 36 MMWR, Supp. No. 1 (1987); Recommendations for Prevention of HIV Transmission in Health-Care Settings, 36 MMWR, Supp. No. 2, at 13S-15S (1987); National Institutes of Health Consensus Development Panel, The Impact of Routine HTLV-III Antibody Testing on Public Health (n.d. [1987]; available from Office of Medical Applications of Research, DHHS/PHS/NIH, Building 1, Room 216, Bethesda, Maryland 20892).

ELISA (or EIA) - enzyme-linked immunosorbent assay - is a general method which can detect various substances depending upon which enzymes are used. Shekarchi & Sever, Enzyme Immunoassay, in Clinical Virology Manual 133-146 (S. Specter & G. Lancz edd. 1986). This method, with enzymes keyed to HIV antibody proteins, is the initial screening test for antibodies to HIV. Confronting AIDS, supra note 2, at 113-114;

Schuepbach, Veronese & Gallo, Human Retroviruses, in Clinical Virology Manual 451, 468-478 (S. Specter & G. Lancz edd. 1986).

The current protocol for accurate HIV testing requires repeating a positive ELISA and then confirming it with either indirect immunofluorescence assay (IFA) or Western blot immunoelectrophoresis. Confronting AIDS, supra note 2, at 304-308; NIH Consensus Statement 5, 7-9; 1987 CDC Surveillance Definition 10S (appendix 1). A single positive ELISA may be unreliable. See NIH Consensus Statement 2, 4 ("the odds are great that any single ELISA-positive reading comes from an uninfected person").

A typical indirect ELISA method proceeds as follows: HIV is grown in a particular line of cancerous blood cells which are not killed by HIV. The cell membranes are then chemically disrupted to release HIV antigens (viral products to which people infected by HIV normally develop antibodies). The antigen is diluted to a standard concentration and attached to small beads or to the lining of small chambers (microtiter wells). Blood serum is then added to the antigen-coated surface and incubated according to instructions. If HIV antibodies are present in the serum they will attach to the antigen-coated surface during incubation. The unattached blood serum is then washed away. Goat anti-human immunoglobulin G (IgG) linked to an enzyme (horseradish peroxidase) is added and the test is reincubated. During reincubation, the anti-human IgG (with enzyme) attaches to any human IgG on the antigen-coated surface. In a perfectly specific test, the only human IgG attached to the antigen-coated surface would be bound to HIV antibody. The unattached anti-human IgG is then washed away. A substrate on which the enzyme acts is added. If enzyme is present it will cause the sample to change color. (Enzyme should be present only if anti-human IgG attached to the antigen-coated surface during reincubation; anti-human IgG should have attached only if HIV antibodies attached to HIV antigens during the first incubation; all the unattached potentially reactive substances should have been removed by the washings.) The amount of color is measured by a spectrophotometer. Any sample with more than the specified cutoff amount of color is positive. For screening blood donations, the cutoff value is deliberately set low to detect as many reactions as possible, although this increases the rate of false positives. See Council on Scientific Affairs, American Medical Association, Status Report on AIDS: HTLV-III Testing, 254 J.A.M.A. 1342 (1985); Carlson, Bryant, Hinrichs, Yamamoto, Levy, Yee, Higgins, Levine, Holland, Gardner & Pedersen, AIDS Serology Testing in Low- and High-Risk Groups, 253 J.A.M.A. 3405 (1985); Schuepbach, Haller, Vogt, Luethy, Joller, Oelz, Popovic, Sarngadharan & Gallo, Antibodies to HTLV-III in Swiss Patients with AIDS and Pre-AIDS and in Groups at Risk for AIDS, 312 New Eng. J. Med. 265 (1985), Hirsch, Wormser, Schooley, Ho, Felsenstein, Hopkins, Joline, Duncanson, Sarngadharan, Saxinger & Gallo, Risk of Nosocomial Infection with HTLV-III, 312 New Eng. J. Med. 1 (1985). These references also describe the IFA and Western blot confirmatory tests.

More direct tests are being developed, e.g., reliably culturing HIV from infected blood; finding HIV antigens -- actual HIV components or products -- by purified HIV DNA or RNA probes, or by ELISA or radioimmunoassay (RIA) or radioimmunoprecipitation assay (RIPA) methods keyed to HIV structural core proteins, rather than to antibodies; or detecting HIV-specific immunoglobulin M. NIH Consensus Statement 6-7; Kwok, Mack, Mullis, Poiesz, Ehrlich, Blair, Friedman-Klein & Sninsky, Identification of HIV Sequences by Using In Vitro Enzymatic Amplification and Oligomer Cleavage Detection, 61 J. Virology 1690 (1987); Parry & Mortimer, Place of IgM Antibody Testing in HIV Serology, [1986] 2 Lancet 979; Wittek, Phelan, Wells, Vujcic, Epstein, Lane & Quinlan, Detection of HIV Core Protein in Plasma by Enzyme Immunoassay, 107 Annals Internal Med. 286 (1987); Conference Abstracts, supra note 1, at 207 (F.2.2-6). A rapid, simple and economical test is urgently needed, especially for underdeveloping countries. Id. at 108 (W.4.6.), 115 (WP.30), 166 (THP.18); but see Konotey-Ahulu, Clinical Epidemiology, Not Seroepidemiology, Is the Answer to Africa's AIDS Problem, 294 Brit. Med. J. 1593 (1987). Claims to have such a test have begun to appear. E.g., Carlson, Mertens, Yee, Gardner, Watson-Williams, Ghrayeb, Jennings & Biggar, Rapid, Easy, and Economical Screening Test for Antibodies to HIV, [1987] 2 Lancet 361.

53. HIV antibodies are markers of exposure to HIV. (The immune system generally forms antibodies to foreign substances, such as infectious agents. Not all antibodies are effective in fighting infection, particularly when other components of the immune system are damaged.) The current screening test detects antibodies formed in reaction to HIV rather than detecting HIV directly. See citations in preceding note.

HIV disrupts cells which are required for proper functioning of the immune system so HIV antibodies may be ineffective. Some people, however, may form at least partially protective antibodies. See Seligmann, Pinching, Rosen, Fahey, Khaitov, Klatzmann, Hoenig, Luo, Ngu, Riethmueller & Spira, Immunology of HIV Infection and AIDS, 107 Annals Internal Med. 234 (1987); Chatterjee, Rinaldo & Gupta, Immunogenicity of HIV Reverse Transcriptase: Detection of High Levels of Antibodies to HIV Reverse Transcriptase in Sera of Homosexual Men, 7 J. Clinical Immunology 218 (1987); Wahren, Morfeldt-Mansson, Biberfeld, Moberg, Sonnerborg, Ljungman, Werner, Kurth, Gallo & Bolognesi, Characteristics of the Specific Cell-Mediated Immune Response in HIV Infection, 61 J. Virology 2017 (1987); McDougal, Kennedy, Nicholson, Spira, Jaffe, Kaplan, Fishbein, O'Malley, Aloisio, Black, Hubbard & Reimer, Antibody Response to HIV in Homosexual Men, 8 J. Clinical Investigation 316 (1987); Weber, Clapham, Weiss, Parker, Roberts, Duncan, Weller, Carne, Tedder, Pinching & Cheingsong-Popov, HIV Infection in Two Cohorts of Homosexual Men: Neutralising Sera and Association of Anti-gag Antibody with Prognosis, [1987] 1 Lancet 119; Prince, Pascual, Kosolapov, Kurokawa, Baker & Rubenstein, Prevalence, Clinical Significance, and Strain Specificity of Neutralizing Anti-

body to HIV, 156 J. Infectious Disease 268 (1987); Ho, Pomerantz & Kaplan, supra note 12; Conference Abstracts, supra note 1, at 8 (M.10.4&5), 53 (T.3.3), 76 (TP.81), 107 (W.3.5), 183 (THP.117), 207 (F.2.1).

There are also reports of lymphocytes which kill HIV-infected cells. Walker, Chakrabarti, Moss, Paradis, Flynn, Durno, Blumberg, Kaplan, Hirsch & Schooley, HIV-specific Cytotoxic T Lymphocytes in Seropositive Individuals, 328 Nature 345 (1987); Plata, Autran, Martins, Wain-Hobson, Raphael, Mayaud, Denis, Guillon & Debre, AIDS Virus-specific Cytotoxic T Lymphocytes in Lung Disorders, 328 Nature 348 (1987).

The immune response of the chimpanzee, the only animal other than the human which has been successfully infected with HIV-1, appears far more effective than the human immune response. Nara, Robey, Gonda, Carter & Fischinger, Absence of Cytotoxic Antibody to HIV-infected Cells in Humans and Its Induction in Animals after Infection or Immunization with Purified Envelope Glycoprotein gp 120, 84 Proc. Nat'l Acad. Sciences U.S.A. 3797 (1987); Letvin, Daniel, Sehgal, Yetz, Solomon, Kannagi, Schmidt, Silvan, Montagnier & Desrosiers, Infection of Baboons with HIV-2, 156 J. Infectious Disease 406 (1987).

54. Revision of the CDC Surveillance Case Definition for AIDS, 36 MMWR, Supp. No. 1 (1987); Kessler, Blaauw, Spear, Paul, Falk & Landay, Diagnosis of HIV Infection in Seronegative Homosexuals Presenting with an Acute Viral Syndrome, 258 J.A.M.A. 1196 (1987); Vernon, Hoagland & Perlman, AIDS Wrongly Diagnosed, 258 J.A.M.A. 2063 (1987).

55. Classification System for HIV Infection in Children under 13 Years of Age, 36 MMWR 225 (1987); Preventing AIDS, supra note 11, at 1359; Harnish, Hammerberg, Walker & Rosenthal, Early Detection of HIV Infection in a Newborn, 316 New Eng. J. Med. 272 (1987); Johnson, Nair & Alexander, Early Diagnosis of HIV Infection in the Neonate, 316 New Eng. J. Med. 273 (1987); Borkowsky, Krasinski, Paul, Moore, Bebenroth & Chanwani, HIV Infections in Infants Negative for anti-HIV by Enzyme-linked Immunoassay, [1987] 1 Lancet 1168; Pyun, Ochs, Dufford & Wedgewood, Perinatal Infection with HIV: Specific Antibody Responses by the Neonate, 317 New Eng. J. Med. 611 (1987); Pahwa, Good & Pahwa, Prematurity, Hypogammaglobulinemia, and Neuropathy with HIV Infection, 84 Proc. Nat'l Acad. Sciences U.S.A. 3826 (1987).

56. Transfusion-associated HTLV-III/LAV Infection from a Seronegative Donor -- Colorado, 35 MMWR 389 (1986); HIV Infection Transmitted from an Organ Donor Screened for HIV Antibody -- North Carolina, 36 MMWR 306 (1987); Phair, HIV Antigenemia, 258 J.A.M.A. 1218 (1987); Marlink, Allan, McLane, Essex, Anderson & Groopman, Low Sensitivity of

ELISA Testing in Early HIV Infection, 315 New Eng. J. Med. 1549 (1986) (letter); Mayer, Stoddard, McCusker, Ayotte, Ferriani & Groopman, HTLV-III in High-risk, Antibody-negative Homosexual Men, 104 Annals Internal Med. 194 (1986); Conference Abstracts, supra note 1, at 186 (THP.139).

A recent report indicates that seroconversion can take a year or more. Ranki, Valle, Krohn, Antonen, Allain, Leuther, Franchini & Krohn, Long Latency Period Precedes Overt Seroconversion in Sexually Transmitted HIV Infection, [1987] 2 Lancet 589.

57. A rather skeptical view of diagnostic testing generally is Begg, Biases in the Assessment of Diagnostic Tests, 6 Statistics in Med. 411 (1987). For a general explanation of Bayes' theorem describing the mathematical relationship of sensitivity, specificity and prevalence in determining the predictive value of a test, see Harrison's Internal Medicine, supra note 12, at 7-9; Clinical Diagnosis and Management by Laboratory Methods 526-531 (J. Henry ed. 1979). Application to HIV screening is discussed in Kanter, AIDS and Testing for AIDS, 255 J.A.M.A. 743 (1986).

HIV screening should meet higher standards of accuracy than other medical tests because false positives may be stigmatized as much as true positives. Meyer & Pauker, Screening for HIV: Can We Afford the False Positive Rate?, 317 New Eng. J. Med. 238 (1987). Drs. Meyer and Pauker calculate that in a low-incidence population such as female blood donors (0.01% reported rate of HIV infection), if a testing program has only 0.5% false positives "then 50 women without HIV infection will be stigmatized for every truly infected person identified." Id. at 240.

A study in New Mexico, a state with a low incidence of AIDS (less than 4% of New York City's) and HIV seropositivity (2.4% of men and 0% of women attending sexually transmitted disease clinics) judged 55% of positive ELISA results to be falsely positive. Fleming, Cochi, Steece & Hull, AIDS in Low-Incidence Areas: How Safe Is Unsafe Sex?, 258 J.A.M.A. 785 (1987).

On testing the tests, see Confronting AIDS, supra note 2, at 203-04, 306-07; Ward, Grindon, Feorino, Schatle, Parvin & Allen, Laboratory and Epidemiologic Evaluation of an Enzyme Immunoassay for Antibodies to HTLV-III, 256 J.A.M.A. 357 (1986); Gaines, von Sydow, Soennerborg, Albert, Czajkowski, Pehrson, Chiodi, Moberg, Fenyoe, Asjoe & Forsgren, Antibody Response in Primary HIV Infection, [1987] 2 Lancet 1249; Burke, Brandt, Redfield, Lee, Thorn, Beltz & Hung, Diagnosis of HIV Infection by Immunoassay Using a Molecularly Cloned and Expressed Virus Envelope Polypeptide, 106 Annals Internal Med. 671 (1987); Conference Abstracts, supra note 1, at 77 (TP.92).

"[F]alse positive results and lack of uniformity in the results of various methods" have been noted in screening frozen blood serum in southern Africa to test suggestions that HIV originated in Africa. Sher, Antunes, Reid & Falcke, Seroepidemiology of HIV in Africa from 1970 to 1974, 317 New Eng. J. Med. 450 (1987).

For views favorable to testing (and largely ignoring the psychosocial impact), see American Council of Life Insurance v. District of Columbia, 645 F. Supp. 84 (D.D.C. 1986); Davis, Wisconsin State Epidemiologist, Serologic Tests for the Presence of Antibody to HTLV-III: Information Pursuant to the Purposes of Wisconsin Statute s. 631.90 Regarding Their Use in Underwriting Individual Life, Accident and Health Insurance Policies (July 28, 1986) (available from Jeffery P. Davis, M.D., Wisconsin Health Division, P.O. Box 309, Madison, Wisconsin 53701-0309).

58. Recommendations for Prevention of HIV Transmission in Health-Care Settings, 36 MMWR, Supp. No. 2, at 14S (1987). Traditional public health measures may be inappropriate. See Gostin, Curran & Clark, The Case Against Compulsory Casefinding in Controlling AIDS -- Testing, Screening and Reporting, 12 Am. J. Law & Med. 7 (1987). Informed consent and counseling for adolescents may be particularly difficult in light of parental and medical paternalism. See Evans, HIV and the Law, [1987] 2 Lancet 574.

59. Hunter, AIDS Prevention and Civil Liberties: The False Security of Mandatory Testing (1987)(ACLU position paper; available from ACLU, 132 West 43rd Street, New York, New York 10036); see Rasmussen v. South Florida Blood Service, 500 So. 2d 533 (Fla. 1987).

60. Recommendations for Prevention of HIV Transmission in Health-Care Settings, 36 MMWR, Supp. No. 2, at 514 (1987).

61. Osborn, The AIDS Epidemic: Multidisciplinary Trouble, 314 New Eng. J. Med. 779 (1986). Dean Osborn's piece is succinct, sophisticated, realistic and recommended.

62. See generally Confronting AIDS, supra note 2 (the committee's educational recommendations are summarized at 9-13); Board of Trustees, American Medical Association, Prevention and Control of AIDS: An Interim Report, 258 J.A.M.A. 10977 (1987).

63. United States General Accounting Office, AIDS Prevention: Views on the Administration's Budget Proposals, Briefing No. GAO/HRD-87-126BR, at 2, 4 (1987). This report contains sharp criticism of the federal response to the AIDS crisis.

64. Osborn, <u>AIDS, Social Sciences, and Health Education: A Personal Perspective</u>, 13 Health Ed. Q. 287 (1986); <u>Confronting AIDS</u>, <u>supra</u> note 2, at 96-112, 230-238; <u>see</u> <u>Self-Reported Changes in Sexual Behaviors Among Homosexual and Bisexual Men from the San Francisco City Clinic Cohort</u>, 36 MMWR 187 (1987); <u>AIDS Education in the United Kingdom</u>, Focus, <u>supra</u> note 6, June 1987; Coates, Morin & McKusick, <u>Behavioral Consequences of AIDS Antibody Testing Among Gay Men</u>, 258 J.A.M.A. 1889 (1987). Efforts to implement and evaluate various educational programs are underway. Wertz, Sorenson, Liebling, Kessler & Heeren, <u>Knowledge and Attitudes of Health Care Providers Before and After Education Programs</u>, 102 Pub. Health Rep. 248 (1987); <u>Conference Abstracts</u>, <u>supra</u> note 1, at 56 (T.6.1-6), 60 (T.10.1-6), 91 (TP.171, 173-176), 92-94 (TP. 181-186, 189-191, 194), 139-142 (WP.177-180, 182-189, 191-195), 156-157 (TH.5.1-3, 5-6), 192-196 (THP.173, 176, 177-187, 190-194, 196, 198), 213 (F.8.1-6).

Some authorities ignore safer sex and recommend measures based simply on antibody status; as the Public Health Service, the Surgeon General and others have concluded, such measures encourage segregation of and discrimination against people with actual or perceived HIV, and will be less effective in combatting the epidemic than risk-reduction counseling in conjunction with voluntary, confidential testing and education which is independent of testing. A recent example of the constricted thinking which ignores the psychosocial context of preventing HIV transmission is Horsburgh, Douglas & LaForce, <u>Preventive Strategies in Sexually Transmitted Diseases for the Primary Care Physician</u>, 258 J.A.M.A. 815 (1987).

<u>Preventing AIDS</u>, <u>supra</u> note 11, at 1360 (Table 2)(editorial comment supplied) suggests the following relatively genteel guidelines:

The AIDS Prevention Message to the Community:

To Stop Needle-Borne Transmission: Don't share unsterile needles or syringes

To Stop Sexual Transmission: If you have vaginal or rectal intercourse, use the following guidelines to decrease your chance of infection:

Absolutely Safe: Mutually monogamous relationship between uninfected partners;

Extremely Safe: Noninsertive sexual relations (no vaginal or rectal intercourse);

Very Safe: Vaginal or rectal intercourse using a condom (and spermicide containing non-oxynol-9);

Risky: Anything else [this should be "Any other vaginal or rectal intercourse"].

To Stop Perinatal Transmission: If you could have been exposed to HIV, get tested for antibodies; if you are positive, don't become pregnant

Many authorities stick with the simple "condoms always" or, in two prepositions, "on me, not in me," rather than complicating the safer sex message. Dr. Francis himself summarizes the safer sex message as "If you are going to have sex, use a condom." <u>Conference Abstracts</u>, <u>supra</u> note 1, at 87 (TP.152). And some consider "don't become pregnant" utterly unhelpful advice, particularly for women whose economic or cultural situation gives them little opportunity to insist that their men wear condoms, practice safer sex or take responsibility for preventing transmission.

FIGURE I. Flow diagram for revised CDC case definition of AIDS, September 1, 1987

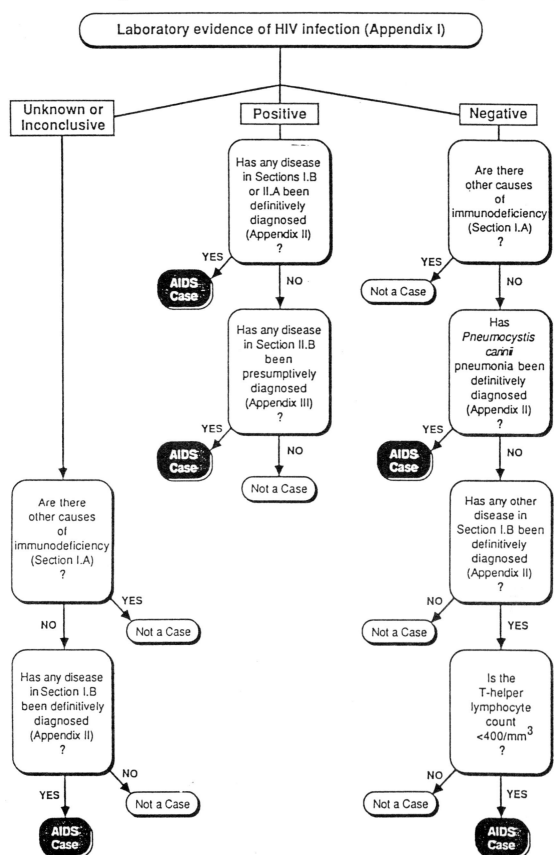

PREPARING FOR ILLNESS, INCAPACITY AND DEATH DUE TO AIDS

Susan Hawkins

A. GETTING ONE'S AFFAIRS IN ORDER

Persons diagnosed with AIDS or ARC frequently seek legal assistance in getting their affairs in order. This section discusses primarily the legal issues involved in planning for the individual's personal care as well as asset management and disposition. There are, however, other steps the client can take. Making a contingency plan for serious illness or death will give the client some peace of mind and ensure minimal difficulties for his or her significant others in the event of incapacity or death.

The attorney should advise a person with AIDS to consider the following questions:

1. Can your personal papers be easily located by you or a trusted friend? These include insurance policies; employee benefit handbooks; bank, savings and loan and credit union records; real estate documents; credit card records; will; safe deposit box.

2. In case of emergency or death, do you have certain out-of-town friends or relatives you want notified? Who?

3. Do you want to add another person's name to your bank accounts or safe deposit box?

Susan Hawkins is Supervising Patients' Rights Attorney at Mental Health Advocacy Project in San Jose, California, an agency specializing in mental health law and the rights of the mentally disabled. She is also a volunteer with the Shanti Project in San Francisco.

This Chapter includes material adapted from several sources, in particular from Sexual Orientation and the Law (Clark Boardman 1985), produced by the Anti-Sexism Committee of the San Francisco Chapter of the National Lawyers Guild.

4. Do you want to change the beneficiary on any of your insurance policies?

5. Do you want another person to have a set of keys to your car or home?

6. Do you have a will? Have you listed all your special possessions in your will?

7. If you have a collection of personal correspondence, a journal or private papers, who do you want to have these?

Answering these questions may be difficult for a person faced with a life-threatening disease, depending on the individual's level of denial or acceptance. The attorney can remind the client that organizing one's personal affairs relates to living well. Planning will make it easier for friends and family to help in emergencies and ease their burdens should they become the client's survivors.

B. HEALTH, FINANCIAL AND ESTATE PLANNING.

The attorney should describe to the client the legal instruments available to implement plans for individual care, asset management and distribution. These include powers of attorney, conservatorships and directives to physicians, wills and trusts. See Appendix for sample forms. The legal issues involved in planning for illness, incapacity and death of a person with AIDS are similar to those involved in such planning for any individual. However, some special considerations do apply.

Because a person with AIDS may live for some time after becoming incapacitated, the various legal instruments related to making medical and financial decisions are crucially important. These include powers of attorney, conservatorships and directives to physicians. These instruments enable PWAs who generally feel out of control of the effects of the disease on their body, to exert some control over how the doctors and hospital treat them. For example, the person can decide in advance whether he or she wants to receive extraordinary life-prolonging treatments.

Clients with AIDS or ARC may require assistance in making financial plans for the duration of their illness. AIDS, like cancer and other catastrophic illnesses, requires long and expensive treatment. The attorney and client should explore the availability of insurance, personal assets and public benefits to pay for medical care and personal support. Insurance may not cover medical care. Some people with AIDS do not have insurance, some lose insurance benefits when they become unable to work and some insurers are delaying or denying payment on AIDS claims. The attorney should always ask if the client has group insurance through an employer and whether this can be converted to an individual policy after termination of employment. This is crucial because a PWA will not otherwise be able to get individual health insurance. Generally, conversion must occur with 30 days of employment termination. (See Chapter 8 for a discussion of insurance issues.)

An important aspect of financial planning for PWAs is to establish eligibility for public benefits programs that will pay medical, food and personal support costs. The client should apply for these programs as soon as possible because there may be a delay of weeks or months before payment. For benefit programs and eligibility requirements, see below "Obtaining Public Benefits". Wealthier PWAs can be caught in a painful cash-flow situation if they have non-liquid assets that nonetheless render them ineligible for need-based public benefits. An applicant for need-based public benefits must deplete his or her personal resources before becoming eligible. PWAs who have substantial assets should be advised to arrange these instruments so that cash is readily accessible. Real estate, for example, should be sold.

Time is an important factor in handling any legal matter for a person with AIDS. Since 73% become incapacitated or die within two years of a diagnosis of AIDS, wills and other documents should be executed as quickly as possible. Even though a client may appear healthy, acting promptly is extremely important. Some individuals have died within a week of diagnosis.

Other special considerations arise if the client is gay, as are the majority of AIDS patients to date. The legal issues involved in planning for the illness, incapacity and death of gay men and lesbians are similar to those applying to any unmarried individual. The following material presents a general overview of these legal issues, raising specific concerns of persons with AIDS and gay men and lesbians where relevant.

Execution of written documents is important for everyone, but especially for gay men and lesbians, who often create close ties with people who are not related by blood or marriage. Since marriage between persons of the same sex is not recognized in any state, even a lifelong partner of a gay decedent or incapacitated person will have none of the rights and preferences that the law affords to legally recognized spouses. Only by executing documents in advance of incapacity or death can a gay man or lesbian have control of their personal care, if incapacitated, and of their estate. Generally speaking, to discourage successful contests, it is important to create a comprehensive written plan that is absolutely clear regarding the client's intent.

C. OBTAINING PUBLIC BENEFITS

When assisting the client with AIDS or ARC in making financial plans, the attorney should explore the availability of public benefits. People with AIDS or ARC are often too sick to work. Loss of income, frequently combined with loss of insurance benefits tied to the job, raises immediate concerns about paying medical and living expenses. Obtaining public benefits should be discussed with every PWA regardless of personal resources because some programs are not need-based. Further, the high costs of AIDS care can rapidly deplete one's savings.

Federal, state and local public benefit programs can provide assistance. These programs are administered by different agencies, each with its own eligibility rules. Further, benefits received under one program may adversely affect eligibility under another program. E.g., SSI recipients are not eligible for food stamps; SSI benefits will be reduced by the amount of state disability benefits. Because the regulations are complex and change frequently, this section is intended only as an introduction. Additional information can be obtained from the administering agency or from a social worker, especially one employed by a government or private AIDS organization. It is advisable to specify that the applicant for benefits has AIDS because some programs have special expedited processing for PWAs.

1. Federal Programs

a. Social Security Disability Insurance (Title II)
(Also known as "Social Security" or "SSI")

This program is administered by the Social Security Administration. To be eligible for Social Security Disability Insurance, the applicant must be disabled and must have paid into the Social Security System through his or her employer (FICA deductions on the wage stub).

For purposes of Social Security Disability Insurance and Supplemental Security Income (SSI - see below), "disability" is defined as any medical condition (physical or mental) which prevents or is expected to prevent a person from working for a minimum of 12 months. Persons who have been diagnosed with AIDS according to the Center for Disease Control (CDC) criteria are automatically presumed to be disabled. 20 CFR Sec. 416.934 (k).

Persons with ARC are not automatically presumed to be disabled, but are evaluated on a case by case basis by the Social Security Administration. Here an attorney or other advocate can be extremely helpful since many people with ARC have been denied benefits. Physicians' statements and other documentary evidence have been successfully used to show that the applicant is disabled under the regulations. See Appendix 8 for a decision by an SSA Administrative Law Judge finding that a person with ARC had the substantial medical equivalent of AIDS and was therefore entitled to disability benefits. It is extremely important for people with ARC to supply adequate documentation of disability when applying for benefits because even a successful appeal of an initial denial can take months of delay. The amount of Social Security Disability benefits varies, depending on earnings and amount paid into the Social Security System. Benefits are payable no earlier than five months after the onset of disability. To apply for benefits, the applicant should go to the local Social Security offices and, if possible, bring the following documents:

(1) A signed letter from the physician stating diagnosis and date of diagnosis.

(2) Social Security Number and card, and any other Social Security Numbers through which benefits were ever received (i.e., parents, spouse).

(3) Certified copy of birth certificate.

(4) W-2 forms for the previous two years or names and addresses of employers during the last two years.

(5) If previously or currently married, name of spouse, dates of marriage, social security number.

(6) A list of all doctors, hospitals and clinics visited and dates and types of treatment received. A list of all medications being taken. A list of restrictions on activity imposed by physician. A list of all physical and emotional aspects of condition that prevent the applicant from working.

b. Social Security Income (SSI)

SSI, like Social Security Disability, is administered by the Social Security Administration. To qualify for SSI, the applicant must be disabled and have financial need. The disability requirement for SSI is the same as for Social Security Disability (see previous discussion). To meet the financial need criteria, the applicant must have no more than $1,600 in assets (excluding a home occupied by the applicant) and no more than $524 in monthly income (1985 figures).

To apply for SSI, the applicant should go to the local Social Security Office and bring, if possible, the following documents.

(1) Documents listed in (1), (2), (3) and (6) in previous section a. regarding Social Security.

(2) Proof of any current or expected income, including claim number under which benefits are received (i.e., V.A. number, welfare number, etc.).

(3) Bank statements for the last two months.

(4) Car registration, life insurance policies, stocks, etc., if any.

(5) Proof of rent payment. Proof of household expenses (utilities, food).

c. Medicaid

Medicaid is a Federally mandated program to pay medical

bills for people who cannot pay for them from their own resources. In some states, the program has other names, (e.g., in California, Medicaid is called MediCal.) Medicaid is funded by Federal, state and local governments. Because it is administered by state and county governments, application procedures and eligibility rules vary. Medicaid is a huge, complicated system. Attorneys and clients can seek assistance from a local legal aid office which will be familiar with Medicaid. In general, the medical and financial criteria for eligibility to Medicaid are similar to the requirements for SSI (see above). People who have an AIDS diagnosis are presumed to be disabled for purposes of Medicaid. Persons who have established eligibility for SSI are automatically eligible for Medicaid. If a person has income above the maximum limit, he or she may nevertheless qualify for benefits if medical bills are very high.

d. Medicare

Medicare pays medical bills for persons who are not entitled to Supplemental Security Income (SSI) because they have assets above the maximum limit but who are eligible for Social Security Disability Insurance (Title II). However, there is a two year waiting period. Legislation has been introduced in Congress to eliminate the two year waiting period for PWAs and to include payment for experimental treatments, which are usually excluded. The attorney and client should contact the administering agency for current regulations.

e. Food Stamps

Food Stamps is a Federally funded program administered by local county governments to assist low-income people. To be eligible, the applicant must demonstrate little or no income and assets. (The specific eligibility requirements vary from state to state). To apply, the applicant should take proof of income and expenses to the county social services office.

f. Veterans Benefits

PWAs who are veterans may be entitled to the following Benefits: medical care, dental treatment, disability compensation, group life insurance, unemployment compensation, burial and others. Contact the local office of the Veterans Administration for a booklet entitled, "Federal Benefits for Veterans and Dependents" (January 1984).

2. State and Local Programs

a. State Disability Insurance

Each state has its own disability insurance program. These programs usually cover persons who have paid into the system through their employer and whose disability (any illness or injury, either physical or mental) prevents them from doing their customary work. State disability programs are often administered by the state labor or employment department. Attorneys and clients should contact the applicable state government office for more information.

b. General Assistance/Welfare

General Assistance and Welfare are county and city funded programs to provide financial assistance to persons with limited or no income and assets. Contact the county department of social services for more information.

c. Unemployment Benefits

It may be possible for the lover or family member of a PWA who quits his or her job in order to care for the PWA to obtain state unemployment benefits. An Administrative Law Judge for the California State Employment Development Department recently awarded benefits to a gay man who quit his job to care for his lover. A letter from the physician stated that in order for the PWA to die at home, the lover needed to be there because he was the primary care provider. The Administrative Law Judge found that non-blood and non-legal relationships may be established which are as meaningful or more meaningful than relationships created by blood or marriage. This decision does not have precedential value, but the reasoning should apply in similar cases elsewhere. (Case number SF-24774; Decision of the Office of Appeals of the California Unemployment Insurance Appeals Board; Robert P. Mason, Administrative Law Judge. For more information, contact the Lesbian Rights Project, 1370 Mission Street, San Francisco, CA 94110).

d. Other Benefit Programs

The attorney and client should consider other city, county and private programs to assist the disabled and/or financially needy. In many cities, the local gay and lesbian community has organized to provide financial assistance, food banks, legal advice and other services for PWAs. Major cities may have city AIDS agencies to provide information and services.

D. CONSERVATORSHIPS

Conservatorship is a statutory mechanism in which someone is appointed by the court to assist another who has become incapacitated during his or her lifetime and needs assistance in management of his or her assets and/or personal care. A conservator is appointed by the court, on the petition of a relative, friend or anyone with a good faith belief that he is acting in the best interests of the proposed conservatee. Some states appoint a "guardian' for an incapacitated adult. Since the terminology, scope and limitations of conservatorships and guardianships vary from state to state, the attorney should become familiar with the statutes in the relevant jurisdiction.

There are generally two forms of conservatorship (or guardianship) that can be established separately or concurrently. A conservator for the estate is legally responsible for managing the conservatee's assets and financial affairs. A conservator for the person is legally responsible for ensuring that health, food, clothing and shelter needs of the conservatee are met.

A person with AIDS may need both kinds of conservatorships during his or her illness. Because court approval is required for most actions taken by the conservator, a conservatorship can be costly. The attorney should consider alternatives, such as an intervivos trust or power of attorney. However, even if such alternatives are used, the client should also execute a written and witnessed nomination of conservator. This will prevent appointment of a blood relative, as is specified by most state statutes, instead of the lover or friend in the event a conservatorship becomes necessary.

E. POWER OF ATTORNEY

A power of attorney is a written authorization to an agent to perform specified acts on behalf of the principal. It is a powerful tool for management of another's assets during physical absence or physical incapacity. Traditionally, however, powers do not survive the principal's mental incapacity or death. Some jurisdictions have provided for durable powers of attorney where the agent's authority continues beyond the principal's incapacity. A durable power may become effective upon execution or upon the incapacity of the principal. By executing a durable power of attorney, persons with AIDS can ensure that the persons they select, rather than court appointed conservators, will be managing their affairs. See Appendix 1 for a sample form of durable power of attorney.

It is not clear whether an ordinary durable power of attorney can be used to delegate authority regarding acts personal in nature (e.g., consenting to medical treatment) after the principal is incapacitated. Inclusion of such powers is advisable, provided there is a severability clause, since it may aid the attorney in fact in caring for the incapacitated principal.

Some states, including California, have enacted a Durable Power of Attorney for Health Care. See, e.g., Cal. Civ. Code Sec. 2430 et seq. and Appendix 2. This statute enables the signer to assure that only the person they designate will make decisions about their medical treatment and have priority in visitation. It may also specifically direct the attorney in fact to refuse any life sustaining or prolonging treatment. The principal may also designate a Durable Power of Attorney for Deposition of Remains. Such provision may be incorporated within a Durable Power of Attorney for Health Care in some jurisdictions.

In states with no durable power of attorney for health care, it is advisable for the client who wants someone other than a biological family member to make medical decisions to execute a separate document authorizing the designated agent to make such decisions. Such written authorization may be persuasive in dealing with a physician, especially where the client's intent is clear and unequivocal.

See Appendix 3 for a chart showing each state's statutes regarding powers of attorney.

F. DIRECTIVES TO PHYSICIANS (LIVING WILLS)

Some jurisdictions have enacted statutes which allow a person to authorize, in advance, removal of artificial life-support systems where brain death has occurred or where the condition is irreversible and terminal. See, e.g., Cal. Prob. Code Section 7185-95. The writing invoking such powers must conform precisely in language and in procedure to rigid requirements imposed by the statutes. The writing is directed to the patient's physician and must be executed by the patient personally. Additional written evidence of the patient's intent may be useful where the lover or friend is requesting that the physician cease life-support and the patient's family is opposed. In addition to giving the physician a copy of the directive, persons with AIDS or ARC may be advised to write a letter to their doctor expressing their wishes in advance of a serious decline in health.

In states that have no provision for living wills, such as New York, a client may want to execute one anyway in hopes that his or her wishes will be followed.

See Appendix 5 for a sample living will.

G. WILLS.

A will is essential if the client wants to leave any portion of his or her estate to anyone other than a biological family member. Each state has its own statutory scheme which prescribes who shall inherit the assets of someone who dies without a will. In all states, the intestate heirs are limited to the legal spouse and blood relatives of the decedent and, in some states, to the relatives of a predeceased legal spouse.

Even when a plan has been designed to dispose of assets in ways other than by will, such as by trust or joint tenancy, a will should be executed as well. This will avoid intestate succession if the plan is lost or invalidated. The will also serves as further evidence of intent and covers any assets that may have been inadvertently omitted or subsequently acquired. It is essential that the plan for disposition contained in the will be absolutely consistent with the total estate plan. For example, if the client establishes a living trust, it can be incorporated by reference into the will.

Homosexuality is generally irrelevant to the validity of a will in the absence of other grounds for contest. While gathering information regarding a gay male client's assets, (see Appendix 6, sample will questionnaire), the attorney should discuss with the client the possibility of a will contest. The purpose of the discussion is to identify possible contestants and to reduce the client's fear of a successful contest. Questions the attorney might ask include:

Does the family know the testator is gay?

Does the family know the testator intends to benefit his or her lover or friend through his or her will or benefit an AIDS organization or a gay and lesbian rights group?

Is there anything the testator can do to minimize the shock that his or her biological family members might feel when they discover that a large portion of the estate will go to an "unrelated" person or to a gay and lesbian organization?

1. Execution

All procedural formalities regarding execution of wills should be strictly followed. Witnesses should be able, if necessary, to provide strong testimony based on personal knowledge that the testator had testamentary capacity when the will was executed. It is best if witnesses are persons with whom the testator is acquainted. Sometimes the attorney may need to take a will to a person with AIDS in the hospital to be executed. The attorney should arrange in advance for witnesses since many hospitals prohibit nurses and other staff from witnessing such documents. The client may be able to arrange for friends (only those who are not beneficiaries) to be witnesses.

2. Special Concerns For People With AIDS: Testamentary Capacity and Undue Influence

When a client is terminally ill or in a weakened mental or physical state at the time of execution, the will may be particularly vulnerable to contest based on alleged incapacity or undue influence. In situations where the client's lover is the intended beneficiary, the attorney should make sure the lover is not present when the will is discussed or executed. Although the lover may be a ready messenger service between a bedridden client and the attorney, it might create the appearance of undue influence if the lover is involved in any way in the preparation of the will.

The attorney should also create documentation of the client's capacity. If the client is in the hospital, the attending physician should be asked to make a determination of the client's capacity and to note it in the medical record. If the client is taking any medication that affects his of her mental abilities, the attorney should ask that he be taken off these drugs the day prior to the execution of the will and request that this fact also be noted on the medical chart. All evidence of the client's capacity should be preserved, including medical records, statements by medical personnel, and names of other persons who could serve as competent witnesses as to the client's capacity.

The attorney should ascertain if any potential contestant to the will could qualify as a pretermitted heir. If so, that person should be named and specifically omitted in the will. If there is a spouse, children (natural or adopted) or grandchildren to whom no bequests are intended, a statement of specific omission must be made in the will.

3. Selecting An Executor

The client should be advised to select an executor based on reliability and competency to carry out administration of the estate. The client may choose a lover, a friend or an institution which he believes would properly handle the administration of the estate. At least two successors or alternates should be named and it may be desirable to give one or more of the nominees power to nominate a co-executor, alternate or successor.

4. Providing For Minor Children

If the client has a minor child, the will should contain provisions for management of assets being left to the minor. These may include testamentary trust provisions or a gift under the state's provision for gifts to minors or may provide for a guardianship of the estate of the child. The will should nominate a fiduciary which may be any adult, including the client's lover, and at least one successor. Generally, this person will be appointed by the court even if someone else is appointed as guardian of the person of the child. The client should also nominate a guardian of the person of the minor child to oversee the child's personal care. Where the client is the custodial parent and wants to nominate as guardian someone other than the surviving natural parent, the nomination should clearly state the name of the nominee and the reasons for the nomination. The test regarding appointment of a guardian is whether the welfare of the child will be benefitted by the appointment.

5. Funeral Plans and Burial Instructions

The attorney should ask the client what plans he or she has regarding funeral and burial. It is especially important for gay and lesbian clients to execute documents that clearly express what they want done with their body. This can prevent painful controversies between the biological family and a lifelong partner over where the decedent should be buried. There have been numerous cases reported recently where the family has prevented the lover from seeing his or her partner after death and then has taken the body far away for burial or cremation. Such events can be very disruptive to the grieving process.

Funeral and burial instructions can be included in the will, in which case they will be carried out immediately in most jurisdictions regardless of challenges to the will's validity. Will clauses should contain the testator's wishes regarding funeral and burial arrangements, prepaid funeral plans and disposition of anatomical parts, if desired. Because the will may not be found immediately upon death, the client should be advised to tell his or her lover, family and friends what he wants done with his or her body. It is also useful to have written instructions separate from the will in an accessible location.

Some persons with AIDS or ARC may be resistant to making specific funeral and burial plans due to denial of the life-threatening nature of the disease, or a determined attitude to survive until a cure is found, or some other factor. Such a client may be more comfortable with a provision that designates a specific person - lover, friend or family member - to make funeral and burial decisions when the time comes.

6. Will Contests

Grounds for contest include mental incapacity, undue influence, fraud, duress and lack of procedural formality in execution of the will. As discussed earlier, the will of a person with AIDS may be subjected to contest on the grounds of mental incapacity or undue influence because the decedent was already ill at the time of execution. In general, the wills of gay men and lesbians are often contested by families who are disgruntled by bequests left to "unrelated' persons.

Lifestyle or sexual orientation alone is not grounds for contest in any jurisdiction. Even in states where same gender sexual activity is illegal, the existence of such a relationship between the testator and the beneficiary is only one factor to be considered in determining if undue influence was brought to bear on the testator. The weight, effect and use of proof of the relationship varies from state to state.

H. TRUSTS

A trust is a contractual arrangement in which a fiduciary agrees with the trustor to manage and ultimately distribute the trustor's assets to intended beneficiaries according to specific directions contained in the trust document. A testamentary trust, contained in a will, has no effect until death. An intervivos trust, created during the life of the trustor, can be used to avoid the cost and delays of probate.

An intervivos trust may be useful for a persons with AIDS or ARC who are presently capable of managing their affairs but anticipate becoming incapacitated in the future. A provision in the trust instrument for a successor trustee (the lover or a trusted friend) to manage the trustor's assets in the event of incapacity will avoid the need for a conservatorship of the estate. In the event of incapacity, the successor trustee is immediately able to manage the assets without needing to get a court order. The trust may also contain directions to the trustee to look after certain personal matters of the trustor thereby avoiding need for a conservatorship of the person.

I. APPENDIX

Please note: this appendix contains sample forms which are intended as examples only. The reader should check statutes in the relevant jurisdiction for specific requirements.

1. General Durable Power of Attorney (sample form).

2. Durable Power of Attorney for Health Care (two sample forms).

3. Chart of state statutes regarding Durable Powers of Attorney.

4. Model Nomination of Conservator.

5. Directive to Physician (Living Will) (sample form).

6. Basic questions for a person needing a simple will.

7. Last Will and Testament (sample form).

8. A written decision from a Social Security administrative hearing finding that a person with an AIDS-related condition is disabled for purposes of SSI and SSDI eligibility.

APPENDIX 1

DURABLE POWER OF ATTORNEY

I, _____, resident of _____ County, State of ____, do hereby appoint _____, who resides at _____ as my attorney in fact, for me and in my name, place and stead, and for my use and benefit to act as follows:

1. To ask, demand, sue for, recover, collect and receive all such sums of money, debts, dues, accounts, legacies, bequests, interest, dividends, annuities, and demands whatsoever as are now or shall hereafter become due, owing, payable, or belonging to me and have, use, and take all lawful ways and means in my name or otherwise for the recovery thereof, by attachments, arrests, distress, or otherwise, and to compromise and agree for the same and acquittances or other sufficient discharges for the same.

2. For me and in my name, to make, seal, and deliver, to bargain, contract, agree for, purchase, receive, and take lands, all deeds and other assurances, in the law therefor, and to lease, let, demise, bargain, sell, remise, release, convey, mortgage, and hypothecate lands, tenements, and properties upon such terms and conditions and under such covenants as he/she shall think fit.

3. To bargain and agree for, buy, sell, mortgage, hypothecate, and in any and every way and manner deal in and with goods, wares, and merchandise, choses in action, and other property in possession or in action, and to make, do, and transact all and every kind of business of whatsoever nature and kinds.

4. For me and in my name, and as my act and deed, to sign, seal, execute, deliver, and acknowledge such deeds, leases, mortgages, hypothecations, bills of lading, bills, bonds, notes, receipts, evidence of debt, releases and satisfactions of mortgage, judgments and other debts, and such other instruments in writing of whatsoever kind and nature as may be necessary or proper in the premises.

5. For me and in my name, to employ, retain, hire, and discharge, when necessary, an attorney at law, for counsel, advice, representation, and litigation, when necessary for discharge of powers and authority granted to my attorney in fact by this document.

6. In addition to the foregoing, this document is specifically to be construed and interpreted as a general power of attorney in favor of ___ and the enumeration of specific items, acts, rights, or powers herein does not in any way limit or restrict, and is not to be construed or interpreted as limiting or restricting, the general powers herein granted to said _____ as my attorney in fact, giving and granting unto my said attorney in fact full power and authority to do and perform every act necessary, requisite, or proper to be done in and about the premises as fully as I might or could if personally present, with full power of substitution and revocation, hereby ratifying and confirming all that my said attorney shall lawfully do or cause to be done by virtue hereof.

7. This document shall at all times be governed by and construed in accordance with the laws of the State of _____. If any part, provision, or term of this document is found to be invalid by a court of competent jurisdiction, such finding shall not impair the operation or affect the remaining parts, terms or provisions of this document, and the latter are to continue to be given full force and effect.

8. My heirs, successors, representatives, and assigns shall be bound by all acts taken by my attorney in fact pursuant to the provisions of this document.

9. I authorize that all acts of my attorney in fact be given full force and effect, without inquiry by any third party concerning the nature and extent of the authority given to my said attorney in fact. 10. I understand that this document provides my attorney in fact with serious and broad powers concerning my person and my assets, and that such powers are expressly to continue if I become incapacitated at any time. I further understand that I can revoke and cancel this document at any time.

11. I specifically acknowledge that this is a Durable Power of Attorney executed pursuant to Civil Code Sections ____ and that this document shall not be affected by my subsequent incapacity.

12. The rights, powers and authority of my attorney in fact to execute any and all of the rights and powers herein granted shall commence and shall be in full force and effect as of the date this document is executed by me, and shall remain in full force and

effect thereafter, unless and until revoked and cancelled by me, expressed in a duly written document.

This document is signed voluntarily and of my own free will. I have read and understood the contents of this document, and have been advised of its legal effects by an attorney at law chosen by me to advise me regarding this document.

     IN WITNESS WHEREOF, this Durable Power of Attorney is executed on ___, 19 _, at _____.

_____

[NOTE: Under California law either of the two following attestation clauses may be used. Check the statute in your state for the required form of attestation and attorney certification.]

WITNESSES

(1)

I declare under penalty of perjury under the laws of _____ that the principal is personally known to me, that the principal signed or acknowledged this durable power of attorney in my presence, that the principal appears to be of sound mind and under no duress, fraud, or undue influence, that I am not the person appointed as attorney in fact by this document, and that I am not a health care provider, an employee of a health care provider, the operator of a community care facility, nor an employee of an operation of a community care facility.

I further declare that I am not related to the principal by blood, marriage, or adoption, and to the best of my knowledge I am not entitled to any part of the estate of the principal upon the death of the principal under a will now existing or by operation of law.

WITNESSED AND EXECUTED, at_____, this _____ day of _, 19_ .

WITNESSES   ADDRESSES

_____   _____

_____   _____

_____   _____

or (2)

STATE OF _____)

COUNTY OF _____) ss

On this ___ day of ___, 19_, before me, the undersigned, a Notary Public in and for the state of ____, personally appeared _____, known to me (or proven to me on the basis of satisfactory evidence to be) the person whose name is subscribed to the within instru-

ment, and acknowledged to me that he/she executed the same.

I declare under penalty of perjury that the person whose name is subscribed to this instrument appears to be of sound mind and under no duress, fraud or undue influence.

     WITNESS my hand and official seal.

_____

ATTORNEY'S CERTIFICATE

I, _____, being duly admitted to practice law in the State of _____, hereby certify that I have advised my client, _____, concerning his/her rights in connection with this Durable Power of Attorney and the law applicable thereto, including, but not limited to, the matters listed in subdivision ____ of Section __ of the Civil Code, and the consequences of signing or not signing this Durable Power of Attorney, and my client, after being so advised, has executed this Durable Power of Attorney.

Dated: ___, 19_.

_____
Attorney At Law

APPENDIX 2

HEALTH CARE POWER OF ATTORNEY

WARNING TO PERSON EXECUTING THIS DOCUMENT

This is an important legal document. It creates a durable power of attorney for health care. Before executing this document you should know these important facts:

1. This document gives the person you designate as your attorney in fact the power to make health care decisions for you, subject to the limitations or statement of desires that you include in this document. The power to make health care decisions for you may include consent, refusal of consent or withdrawal of consent to any care, treatment service or procedure to maintain, diagnose, or treat a physical or mental condition. You may state in this document any types of treatment or placements that you do not desire.

2. The person you designate in this document has a duty to act consistently with your desires as stated in this document, or otherwise made known, or, if your desires are unknown, to act in your best interests.

3. Except as you otherwise specify in this document, the power of the person you designate to make health care decisions for you may include the power to consent to your doctor not giving you treatment or stopping treatment which would keep you alive.

4. Unless you specify a shorter period in this document, this power will exist for seven years from the date you execute this document, and if you are unable to make health care decisions for

yourself at the time when this seven year period ends, this power will continue to exist until the time when you become able to make health care decisions for yourself.

5. Notwithstanding this document, you have the right to make medical and other health care decisions for yourself so long as you can give informed consent with respect to the particular decision. In addition, no treatment can be given to you over your objection, and health care necessary to keep you alive may not be stopped if you object.

6. You have the right to revoke the appointment of the person designated in this document by notifying that person of the revocation orally or in writing.

7. You have the right to revoke the authority granted to the person designated in this document to make health care decisions for you by notifying the treating physician, hospital or health care provider orally or in writing.

8. The person designated in this document to make health care decisions for you has the right to examine your medical records and to consent to their disclosure, unless you limit this right in this document.

9. If there is anything in this document you do not understand, you should ask a lawyer to explain it to you. This power of attorney will be not valid for making health care decision unless it is either signed by two qualified witnesses who are personally known to you and who are present when you sign, or acknowledged before a notary public in California.

DURABLE POWER OF ATTORNEY FOR HEALTH CARE

(Short Form)

KNOW ALL MEN BY THESE PRESENTS:

I, _____, of _____Street, _____, do hereby make constitute, and appoint _____ of _____ Street, _____, my true and lawful attorney in fact, for me and in my name, place and stead, and for my use and benefit, to do any and all of the following:

1. To make health care decisions for me, including, but not limited to, the granting, refusing, or withdrawing of consent to any care, treatment, service or procedure; to maintain, diagnose, or treat any physical or mental condition; to have access to my medical records; and _____ shall have priority under visiting regulations of any health care institution.

2. To receive into his/her possession any and all items of personal property and effects which may be recovered from, on, or about my person by any hospital, police agency or any other person at the time of my illness, disability or death.

3. To authorize the release of my body from any hospital or any other authority having possession of my body at the time of my death and to make all decisions necessary for the removal and transportation of my body from the place of my death.

I FURTHER GIVE to my said attorney in fact full power and authority to do and perform all and every act and thing which may be necessary, or convenient, in connection with any of the foregoing, as fully as I might or could do if personally present, to all intents ratifying and confirming all that my said attorney in fact shall lawfully do or cause to be done by authority hereof.

This power of attorney shall not be affected by subsequent incapacity of the principal.

IN WITNESS WHEREOF, I have signed and acknowledged this Durable Power of Attorney this ____ day of ___, 19_.

_____

[See Note concerning witness attestation forms and attorney certificate set forth in appendix 1.]

DURABLE POWER OF ATTORNEY FOR HEALTH CARE

(Long Form)

I, _____, of ____, State of ____, do hereby nominate, constitute and appoint _____ of the City and County of _____, State of , as my true and lawful attorney in fact, to act for me and in my name, place and stead, with regard to any and all medical and health care decisions to be made concerning my medical condition, treatment and care, including, but not limited to, the following powers:

A. Priority in Visitation . To be given first priority in visitation should. I be a patient in any hospital, health care facility, or institution including, but not limited to, any intensive care or coronary care units of any medical facility, and should I be unable to express a preference on account of my illness or disability.

B. Employment of Health Care Personnel. To employ such physicians, dentists, nurses, therapists, and other professionals or non-professionals, as my attorney in fact may deem necessary or appropriate for my physical or mental well-being; and to pay from my funds reasonable compensation for all services performed by such persons.

C. Gain Access to Medical and Other Personal Information To request, review, and receive any information, verbal or written, regarding my personal affairs or my physical or mental health, including medical and hospital records, and to execute any releases or other documents that may be required in order to obtain this information.

D. Consent or Refuse Consent to Medical Care. To give or withhold consent to medical care, surgery or any other medical procedures or tests; to arrange for my hospitalization, convalescent care or home care; and to revoke, withdraw, modify or change consent to such medical care, surgery, or any other medical procedures or tests, hospitalization, convalescent care or home care which I or my attorney in fact may have previously allowed or consented to. I ask my attorney in fact to be guided in making such decisions by what I have told my attorney in fact about my personal preferences regarding such care. Based on those same preferences, my attorney in fact may also summon paramedics or other emergency medical personnel and seek emergency treatment for me, or choose not to do so, as my attorney in fact deems appropriate given my wishes and my medical status at the time of the decision. My attorney in fact is authorized, when dealing with hospitals and physicians, to sign documents entitled or purporting to be a "Refusal to Permit Treatment" and "Leaving Hospital Against Medical Advice" as well as any necessary waivers of or releases from liability required by the hospitals or physicians to implement my wishes regarding medical treatment or non-treatment.

E. Refuse Life-Prolonging Treatment or Procedures. To request that aggressive medical therapy not be instituted or be discontinued, including (but not limited to) cardiopulmonary resuscitation, the implantation of cardiac pacemaker, renal dialysis, parenteral feeding, the use of respirators or ventilators, nasogastric tube use, endotracheal tube use, and organ transplants. My attorney in fact should try to discuss the specifics of any such decision with me if I am able to communicate in any manner. If I am unconscious, comatose, senile or otherwise unreachable by such communication, my attorney in fact should make the decision guided by any preferences which I may have previously expressed and the information given by the physicians treating me as to my medical diagnosis and prognosis. My attorney in fact may specifically request and concur with the writing of a "no-code" (do not resuscitate) order by the attending or treating physician.

F. Provide Relief From Pain. To consent to and arrange for the administration of pain-relieving drugs of any type, or other surgical or medical procedures calculated to relieve any pain even though their use may lead to permanent physical damage, addiction, or even hasten the moment of (but not intentionally cause) my death. My attorney in fact may also consent to and arrange for unconventional pain-relief therapies such as biofeedback, guided imagery, relaxation therapy, acupuncture, skin stimulation or cutaneous stimulation, and other therapies which I or my attorney in fact believe may be helpful to me.

G. Protect My Right of Privacy. To exercise my right of privacy to make decisions regarding my medical treatment and my right to be left alone even though the exercise of my right may hasten death or be against conventional medical advice. My attorney in fact may take appropriate legal action, if necessary in the judgment of my attorney in fact, to enforce my right in this regard.

H. Execute Documents and Contracts To sign, execute, deliver, acknowledge, and make declarations in any document(s) that may be necessary or proper in order to exercise any of the powers described in this document, to enter into contracts and to pay reasonable compensation or costs in the exercise to any such powers.

This Durable Power of Attorney shall take effect upon my incapacity. Said incapacity shall be defined as my failure, due to deteriorating physical or mental health, to be able to make informed decisions regarding the course of my medical treatment, or my failure, due to deteriorating physical or mental health, to be able to sign any documents or perform any act necessary to decisions regarding the course of my medical treatment.

IN WITNESS WHEREOF, I have hereunto signed my name this day of ___, 19 _.

_____

[See Note concerning witness attestation forms and attorney certificate set forth in appendix 1.]

APPENDIX 3

DURABLE POWERS OF ATTORNEY

STATE	CODE SECTION	BASIC TEXT
Alabama	26-1-2	Similar to Uniform Probate Act (UPA) (attached following chart).
Alaska	13.26.325 13.26.330	Similar to UPA
Arizona	14-5501 14-5502	Similar to UPA
Arkansas	58-701 to 58-740	Power of attorney for care of person, property or both.
California	Civil Code 2400-2407	Uniform Durable Power of Attorney with health care addition.
Colorado	15-14-501 15-14-502	Similar to UPA
Connecticut	45-69	Similar to UPA
Delaware	title 12, sec. 4901 et seq.	Uniform Durable Power of Attorney Act
District of Columbia	citation not available	
Florida	709.08	Only designated relatives ma be nominated attorney in fact.
Georgia	10-6-36	Any power of attorney is durable unless the instrument expressly provides otherwise.
Hawaii	560:5-501 560:5-502	Similar to UPA
Idaho	15-5-5O1 15-5-502	Similar to UPA
Illinois	110 1/2, 11A-6	
Indiana	30-2-11-1 to 30-2-11-7	Similar to UPA
Iowa	633.705 633.706	Similar to UPA

Kansas	58-610 to 58-617	Uniform Durable Power of Attorney Act
Kentucky	386-093	Similar to UPA
Louisiana	C.C. Art. 3072	
Maine	tit. 18-Al 5-5O1	Similar to UPA
Maryland	Est. & Trusts 13-601 13-602	Similar to UPA
Massachusetts	ch. 201B 1 to 7	Uniform Durable Power of Attorney Act
Michigan	No Law	
Minnesota	524.5-501 524.5-502	Similar to UPA
Mississippi	87-3-13	Similar to UPA
Missouri	486.550 to 486.595	Uniform Durable Power of Attorney Act
Montana	72-5-501 72-5-502	Similar to UPA
Nebraska	30-2664 30-2672	Similar to UPA
Nevada	111.460, 111.470	Similar to UPA
New Hampshire	506:6	Similar to UPA
New Jersey	46:2B-8 46:2B-9	Similar to UPA
New Mexico	45-5-501 45-5-502	Similar to UPA
New York	Gen. Obl. 5-1601	Similar to UPA
North Carolina	32A-8,9	Similar to UPA
North Dakota	30.1-30-01 30.1-30-02	Similar to UPA
Ohio	title 13, vol.II 1337.09 1337.091	Similar to UPA
Oklahoma	tit. 58 1051, 1056	Power of attorney for care of person, property or both
Oregon	126-407	Similar to UPA
Pennsylvania	tit. 20 5601, 5602	Similar to UPA

Rhode Island	34-22-6.1	Similar to UPA
South Carolina	32-13-10	Similar to UPA
South Dakota	59-7-2.1	Similar to UPA
Tennessee	34-6-101 to 34-6-107	Uniform Durable Power of Attorney Act
Texas	Prob. Code tit. 17A 36A	Similar to UPA
Utah	75-5-5O1 75-5-502	Similar to UPA
Vermont	tit. 14 3051, 3052	Similar to UPA
Virginia	11-9.1 11-9.2	Similar to UPA
Washington	11.94.010 11.94.020	Similar to UPA
West Virginia	39-4-1 to 39-4-7	Similar to UPA
Wisconsin	243.07	Uniform Durable Power of Attorney Act
Wyoming	34-9-101 to 34-9-116	1. Power of attorney for care of person, property or both 2. Power of attorney must be approved by a court

UNIFORM PROBATE ACT

POWERS OF ATTORNEY

[When Power of Attorney Not Affected by Disability.]

Whenever a principal designates another his/her attorney in fact or agent by power of attorney in writing and the writing contains the words "This power of attorney shall not be affected by disability of the principal," or "This power of attorney shall become effective upon the disability of the principal," or similar words showing the intent of the principal that the authority conferred shall be exercisable notwithstanding his/her disability, the authority of the attorney in fact or agent is exercisable by him as provided in the power on behalf of the principal notwithstanding later disability or incapacity of the principal at law or later uncertainty as to whether the principal is dead or alive. All acts done by the attorney in fact or agent pursuant to the power during any period of disability or incompetence or uncertainty as to whether the principal is dead or alive have the same effect and inure to the benefit of and bind the principal or his/her heirs, devisees and personal representative as if the principal were alive, competent and not disabled. If a conservator thereafter is appointed for the principal, the attorney in fact or agent, during the continuance of the appointment, shall account to the conservator rather than the principal. The conservator has the same power the principal would have had if he/she were not disabled or incompetent to revoke, suspend, or terminate all or any part of the power of attorney or agency.

[Other Powers of Attorney Not Revoked Until Notice of Death or Disability]

(a) The death, disability, or incompetence of any principal who has executed a power of attorney in writing other than a power as described above does not revoke or terminate the agency as to the attorney in fact, agent or other person who, without actual knowledge of the death, disability, or incompetence of the principal, acts in good faith, under the power of attorney or agency. Any action so taken, unless otherwise invalid or unenforceable, binds the principal and his/her heirs, devisees, and personal representatives.

(b) An affidavit, executed by the attorney in fact or agent stating that he/she did not have, at the time of doing an act pursuant to the power of attorney, actual knowledge of the revocation or termination of the power of attorney by death, disability or incompetence, is, in the absence of fraud, conclusive proof of the nonrevocation or nontermination of the power at that time. If the exercise of the power requires execution and delivery of any instrument which is recordable, the affidavit when authenticated for record is likewise recordable.

(c) This section shall not be construed to alter or affect any provision for revocation or termination contained in the power of attorney.

APPENDIX 4

MODEL NOMINATION OF CONSERVATOR

NOMINATION

I, _____, a resident of _____County, (State), being of sound and disposing mind and memory, and not acting under duress, menace, fraud, or undue influence of any person whomsoever, do make, publish, and declare this instrument nominating a Conservator and do expressly revoke all other and former instruments nominating Conservators executed by me.

1. PURPOSE: My purpose in executing this instrument is to nominate a Conservator of my person and estate who will act in the event that I am unable properly to provide for my personal needs for physical health, food, clothing or shelter, or am substantially unable to manage my own financial resources or business affairs, or in the event that for any reason a Conservator could be appointed by the appropriate court and there should be good cause for appointment of a Conservator.

2. NOMINATION: I nominate (1st Nominee) to act as the Conservator of my person and estate, with power to nominate a successor. If _ shall for any reason be unable or unwilling to act in that capacity, I nominate (2nd Nominee) to serve as the Conservator of my person and estate with power to nominate a successor.

3. BOND: No nominee named in this instrument or designated under the power given herein to act at any time as the Conservator of my person and estate shall be required at any time to give bond in order to act in that capacity.

4. POWERS: It is my intention that the Court grant to my Conservator such powers as are needed for appropriate management of my estate. Further, it is my intention that if my Conservator or nominee so requests the Court grant the following powers if not otherwise inherently vested in law in my Conservator: To make all medical decisions, and do all that is necessary to maintain my health, both physical and psychological, including, but not limited to consenting or refusing to consent to treatment, and authorizing any and all medical and psychiatric care and expenses. These powers are to include the authority to specify or remove life support systems, and shall supersede any power vested by law in any other person.

If the Court for any reason refuses to grant these powers or to approve my waiver of any requirement for bond, such refusal shall not invalidate this Nomination of Conservator, and the remaining provisions shall be carried into effect.

Executed this _____, at _____, _____.

_____

On the date last above written, (Client) declared to us that the above instrument, consisting of _____ pages, including the page signed by us as witnesses, is (His/Her) Nomination of Conservator and requested us to act as witnesses to it. Each of us at (His/Her) request now signs as a witness in (His/Her) presence and in the presence of each other, and declares that (He/She) appears to be of sound mind and under no duress, fraud, or undue influence. Each of us observed the signing by (Client) and the signing by each other. Each of us knows that each signature appearing herein is a true signature of the person whose name was signed.

We declare under penalty of perjury that the foregoing is true and correct.

Executed this _____, at _____, _____.

_____   Address _____

_____   Address _____

_____   Address _____

DIRECTIVE TO PHYSICIANS

Directive made this ____ day of ___, 19_.

I, _____, being of sound mind, willfully, and voluntarily make known my desire that my life shall not be artificially prolonged under the circumstances set forth below, and do hereby declare:

1. If at any time I should have an incurable injury, disease, or illness certified to be a terminal condition by two physicians, and where the application of life-sustaining procedures would serve only to artificially prolong the moment of my death and where my death is imminent whether or not life-sustaining procedures are utilized, I direct that such procedures be withheld or withdrawn, and that I be permitted to die naturally.

2. In the absence of my ability to give directions regarding the use of such life sustaining procedures, it is my intention that this directive shall be honored by my family and physician(s) as the final expression of my legal right to refuse medical or surgical treatment and accept the consequences from such refusal.

3. If I have been diagnosed as pregnant and that diagnosis is known to my physician, this directive shall have no force or effect during the course of my pregnancy.

4. I have been diagnosed and notified at least fourteen days ago as having a terminal condition by _____, M.D., whose address is ____, and whose telephone number is ____. I understand that if I have not filled in the physician's name and address it shall be presumed that I did not have a terminal condition when I made out this directive.

5. This directive shall have no force of effect five years from the date filled in above.

6. I understand the full import of this directive and I am emotionally and mentally competent to make this directive.

_____

City of ____ County of

State of

The declarant has been personally known to me and I believe him to be of sound mind.

Witnessed by:

_____   Address: _____

_____   Address:_____

BASIC QUESTIONS FOR A PERSON NEEDING A SIMPLE WILL

1. Testator's name and address.

2. Disposition of body.

3. Beneficiary(s)
   a) Alternate beneficiary if first beneficiary dies before testator or in common accident with testator.

4. Executor - name and address
   a) Alternate

NOTES REGARDING SAMPLE WILL

1. The enclosed form is for simple estates. For large estates, tax planning, testamentary trusts, and complicated bequests seek professional advice.

2. Witnesses must not be heirs at law or beneficiaries under the will. They must all strictly abide by statement in first paragraph of attestation.

3. Check your state's laws to determine the number of witnesses required or if notarization is required.

LAST WILL AND TESTAMENT

I, _____ , domiciled and residing at ____ Street, _____, _____, _____do hereby declare, make and publish this to be my Last Will and Testament and hereby revoke any and all wills and codicils at any time heretofore made by me.

I direct that my body be cremated and that the expenses be paid out of my estate in such amount as my Executor may deem proper and without regard to any limitation in the applicable law as to the amount of such expenses and without necessity of prior court approval. And, I further direct that my Executor shall have full and complete authority to make any and all arrangements regarding the disposition of my remains thereafter.

I direct that all estate, inheritance, succession and other taxes and duties occasioned by my death, whether incurred with respect to property passing by this Will or otherwise, shall be paid by my Executor out of the principal of my residuary estate with no right of reimbursement from any recipient of any such property.

I hereby confirm my intention that the beneficial interest in all property, real or personal, tangible or intangible (including joint checking or savings accounts), which is registered or held, at the time of my death, jointly in the names of myself and any other person, shall pass by right of survivorship or operation of law and outside of the terms of this Will to such other person, if that person is alive. To the extent that my intention may be defeated by any rule of law, I give, devise and bequeath all such jointly held property to such other person or persons who shall survive me.

I give, bequeath, and devise my entire estate, both real and personal and mixed, tangible and intangible to _____, ___ Street, , ___ provided he/she survives me by 90 days. If he/she shall fail to survive me by 90 days, then I give my entire estate to _____, Street, ____ , ____ .

{NOTE: If property is to be divided among several beneficiaries, use the following two paragraphs instead of the preceding paragraph:

I give and bequeath to _____ the following property: (describe property).][This paragraph may be repeated as often as desired.]

All the rest, residue and remainder of my property and estate, of whatsoever character, whensoever acquired and wheresoever situated, and to which I or my estate may be in any manner entitled at the time of my death, including any property or estate as to which I may have any power of disposition or appointment, shall be disposed of as follows ____ . }

I nominate and appoint_____ as Executor of this my Last Will and Testament. Should my Executor be unable or unwilling to serve, or fail to qualify within a reasonable time after receiving notice of the nomination, I nominate and appoint _____, Street, ____, ____ as my Executor's successor, and I direct that neither my Executor nor the successor be required to give bond or undertaking in any jurisdiction.

If my designated fiduciary shall be unable to qualify as Executor under this my Last Will and Testament in any jurisdiction in which it becomes necessary to administer my estate, I hereby authorize and direct my Executor to appoint a qualified individual or corporation to serve as my Executor. Any person or corporation, so appointed, shall have all the powers herein conferred upon my Executor, and I direct that no bond be required of any fiduciary so appointed.

My Executor shall not be liable for any loss, including insufficient rate of return or appreciation of principal, destruction or other injury of or to the assets in my Executor's possession, unless such loss is occasioned by willful fraud, default or misconduct.

My Executor shall have full discretionary power, without order or approval of any court, to take any action desirable for the administration of my estate, including the power to sell at public or private sale, any real or personal property belonging to my estate at whatever prices and upon whatever terms deemed advisable, to retain, invest or reinvest in any property without responsibility for diversification and without being restricted by any rule of law or court limiting investments, to hold any securities in the name of a nominee, to compromise any claims to the same extent I could, if living, and to distribute in kind or in money, or partly in each, even if shares be composed differently.

If any beneficiary named in this Will, or any heir or other person whether or not named in this Will, shall contest the validity of this will or any provision thereof, such person and the person's issue shall forfeit all interest in my estate hereunder.

I hereby declare that I have thought of and considered each and every person who (a) would inherit from me had I died intestate, or (b) who is not mentioned in this Will, and I hereby declare that I do not desire to devise or bequeath to such person or persons any sum whatsoever and I hereby disinherit such person or persons.

IN WITNESS WHEREOF, I have set my hand to this my Last Will and Testament this ____ ·day of ___ , 19_.

TESTATOR:

The foregoing instrument was signed, published and declared by the testator as and for his/her Last Will and Testament in the presence of us, and we, at his/her request, and in his/her presence, and the presence of each other, have hereunto subscribed our names as witnesses the day, date and year above written.

Each of us is an adult and a competent witness and resides at the address set forth after his/her or her name below written.

We are all acquainted with _____ . At this time he/she is an adult, and to the best of our knowledge he/she is of sound mind and is not acting under duress, menace, fraud, misrepresentation or undue influence.

We declare under penalty of perjury that the foregoing is true and correct.

NAME   ADDRESS

_____   _____
Signature   Address
_____   _____
Printed

_____   _____
Signature   Address

_____   _____
Printed

DEPARTMENT OF
HEALTH AND HUMAN SERVICES
Social Security Administration
OFFICE OF HEARINGS AND APPEALS

DECISION

IN THE CASE OF: CLAIM FOR:

                                         Period of Disability,
                                         Disability Insurance Benefits, and
                                         Supplemental Security Income

(Claimant)

                                         (Social Security Number)

This case is before the Administrative Law Judge on a request for hearing.
The Administrative Law Judge has carefully considered all the documents
identified in the record as exhibits, the testimony at the hearing and
arguments presented.

ISSUES

The general issues are whether the claimant is entitled to a period of
disability and disability insurance benefits under section 216(i) and 223,
respectively, of the Social Security Act, as amended; and whether the claimant
is disabled under section 1614(a)(3)(A) of the Act. The Social Security Act
defines "disability" as the inability to engage in any substantial gainful
activity due to physical or mental impairment(s) which can be expected to
either result in death or last for a continuous period of not less than 12
months.

The specific issues are whether the claimant was under a "disability" and, if
so, when such disability commenced and the duration thereof; and whether the
disability insured status requirements of the Act are met for the purpose of
entitlement to a period of disability and disability insurance benefits.

APPLICABLE REGULATIONS AND EVALUATION OF THE EVIDENCE

Pursuant to the Act, the Secretary has established Regulations No. 4 and No.
16. The Regulations provide steps for evaluating disability (20 CFR
404.1520(a) and 416.920(a)). In addition, a claimant's impairment must meet
the 12 month duration requirement before being found disabling. A set order
is followed to determine whether an individual is disabled. If it is
determined that a claimant is or is not disabled at any point in the review,
further review is not necessary.

Social Security Administration Regulations No. 4 and No. 16 require the
Administrative Law Judge to consider the following in sequence:

1. An individual who is working and engaging in substantial gainful
   activity will not be found to be "disabled" regardless of medical
   findings (20 CFR 404.1520(b) and 416.920(b));

2. If an individual is not working and is suffering from a severe
   impairment which meets the duration requirement and which "meets or
   equals a listed impairment in Appendix 1" of Subpart P of
   Regulations No. 4, a finding of "disabled" will be made without
   consideration of vocational factors (20 CFR 404.1520(d) and
   416.920(d));

3. If an individual is capable of performing work he or she has done in
   the past, a finding of "not disabled," must be made (20 CFR
   404.1520(e) and 416.920(e));

4. If an individual's impairment is so severe as to preclude the
   performance of past work, other factors including age, education,
   past work experience and residual functional capacity must be
   considered to determine if other work can be performed (20 CFR
   404.1520(f) and 416.920(f)).

The rules set out in Appendix 2 of Subpart P of Regulations No. 4 are
considered in determining whether a claimant with exertional impairments is or
is not disabled. The regulations also provide that if an individual suffers
from a nonexertional impairment as well as an exertional impairment, both are
considered in determining residual functional capacity (20 CFR 404.1545 and
416.945). If a finding of disabled cannot be made based on strength
limitations alone, the rules established in Appendix 2 are used as a framework
in evaluating "disability." In cases where the individual has solely a
nonexertional impairment, a determination as to whether disability exists
shall be based on the principles in the appropriate sections of the
regulations, giving consideration to the rules for specific case situations in
Appendix 2.
In applying the sequential steps outlined above, the Administrative Law Judge
concludes that a decision on whether the claimant is disabled cannot be made
based on work activity. After considering the medical facts alone, the
Administrative Law Judge further concludes that the claimant has a severe
impairment which is medically equivalent to an impairment listed in Appendix
1, Subpart P, Regulations No. 4. Consequently, it must be found that the
claimant became disabled within the meaning of the Social Security Act on
August, 14,1983. Prior to that date, he retained the residual functional
capacity to perform his past relevant work.

EVALUATION OF THE EVIDENCE

The claimant was given a hearing in May 1984. Thereafter, the undersigned
determined that the claimant was a member of the class identified in Dixon v.
Heckler, 83 Civ. 7001 (MEL), S.D.N.Y., July 25, 1984 and entitled to a new
hearing. Since the claimant is a member of the class covered by the Dixon v.
Heckler case, his case is required to be evaluated under the evaluation

-3-

criteria set forth in that case. Accordingly, all references to 20 CFR 404.1520 (c), 404.15621, 416.920(c) and 416.921 herein are hereby deleted. Since the claimant is not working and the evidence provides a basis for a finding that he has an impairment which equals an impairment listed in Appendix 1, his case is now being decided on the basis of Appendix 1.

The claimant alleges that he became unable to work in June 1983 as a result of a psychiatric condition and possible Acquired Immune Deficiency Syndrome. The evidence shows that the claimant voluntarily sought hospitalization on August 18. 1983. At that time, the claimant stated that he had become depressed four days earlier and had taken an overdose of pills. The claimant was found to be very depressed, with low psychomotor activity and very poor self esteem. He was treated, but showed only a slight improvement as of September 6th when he was discharged (Exhibit 17). A significant factor of the claimant's depression was the diagnosis of possible Acquired Immune Deficiency Syndrome (Exhibits 15, 17).

Dr. Richard Wagman, a medical advisor, appeared at the hearing and testified. He thoroughly reviewed the medical reports and noted the diagnosis of possible A.I.D.S.. The doctor also referred to the claimant's history of a variety of infections, the abnormalities of his immune system, his weight loss and his fatigue. Based upon an October 1984 finding of pneumocystic pneumonia (Exhibit 31), Dr. Wagman concluded that the claimant clearly had A.I.D.S. as of that time. While the claimant's impairment did not meet the level of severity of any impairment listed in Appendix 1 to the Regulations, the medical advisor testified that, as there was no therapy available, the claimant's condition was equivalent in severity to that set out in section 13.02(B) of the Listing of Impairments. Dr. Wagman also testified that, although the claimant did not have evidence of true A.I.D.S. prior to the October 1934 report from Dr. Siroty (Exhibit 31), there were significant abnormalities going back as far as August of 1983. The medical advisor testified that, as the result of the combination of the claimant's fatigue, weight loss, weakness, chronic depression, abnormalities in chemical analysis and history of substance abuse, the claimant had been unable to engage in substantial gainful activity on a sustained basis since the time he was hospitalized for an overdose of Valium.

The objective medical evidence shows that the claimant was hospitalized on August 18, 1983 following an attempted suicide by an overdose of Valium tablets because of severe depression (Exhibit 17). Since that time, the claimant has sought medical treatment for a variety of maladies, physical as well as psychological. Dr. Zeiguer noted on September 16, 1983 that the claimant's concentration and memory were impaired and that his judgment, insight and impulse control were poor (Exhibit 18). The records from the A.I.D.S. Clinic of the Beth Israel Medical Center establish a variety of infections and abnormalities related to the poor functioning of the claimant's immune system (Exhibits 22, 24). Dr. Robert LaPlaca, the treating psychiatrist, concluded that the claimant was unable to work as the result of a dysthymic disorder (Exhibit 23). Dr. William Siroty advised that the claimant's weight loss, fatigue and shortness of breath precluded him from working (Exhibit 31). The medical evidence is consistent with the opinions of the treating physicians as well as with that of the medical advisor. I find that the claimant is "disabled" as that term is defined in the Social Security Act, as amended.

Although the claimant alleged an onset of disability of June 14, 1983 (Exhibit 1), the earliest medical report is from August, 1983. The claimant related

Form HA-514-C8 (10-83)   REPRESENTATIVE

that, about four days prior to his admission on August 18th, he was depressed and attempted suicide (Exhibit 17). There are no reports of any earlier treatment. The claimant listed work activities as a cook in private residences in the summer of 1983 in his work history report (Exhibit 26). At the hearing, the medical advisor testified that the record established an inability to perform substantial gainful activity from the time of the hospitalization onward. Based upon the evidence before me, I find that the claimant is precluded from engaging in substantial gainful activity by a combination of exertional and non-exertional restrictions which equal the level of severity of that set out in section 13.02(B) of the Listing of Impairments. I find that, beginning 4 days before entering the hospital, on August 14, 1983, this claimant has been disabled as that term is defined in the Social Security Act, as amended. Prior to August 14, 1983, however, the claimant apparently continued to work (Exhibit 26), and there is no evidence to suggest that he was precluded from performing his regular job as a cook.

FINDINGS

After careful consideration of the entire record, the Administrative Law Judge makes the following findings:

1. The claimant met the disability insured status requirements of the Act on June 14, 1983, the date the claimant stated he became unable to work, and continues to meet them.

2. The claimant has not engaged in substantial gainful activity since July 1983.

3. The medical evidence establishes that the claimant has a severe pneumonic infection, as well as other abnormalities characteristic of Acquired Immune Deficiency Syndrome.

4. Prior to August 14, 1983, the claimant had the residual functional capacity to perform his usual work (20 CFR 404.1545, 404.1567, 416.945 and 416.967).

5. The claimant indicated that he worked at private residences in July 1983. There is no objective evidence of any impairment prior to 4 days before the claimant's hospitalization in August 1983.

6. The claimant's impairments did not prevent him from performing his past relevant work as a cook prior to August 14, 1983.

7. Since August 14, 1983, but not prior thereto, the severity of the claimant's impairments have equalled the requirements of section 13.02, Appendix 1, Subpart P, Regulations No. 4 (20 CFR 404.1526 and 416.926).

8. The claimant has been under a "disability," as defined in the Social Security Act, since August 14, 1983, but not prior thereto (20 CFR 404.1520(d), (e) and (f), and 416.920(d), (e) and (f)).

DECISION

It is the decision of the Administrative Law Judge that, based on the application filed on August 30, 1983, the claimant is entitled to a period of disability commencing on August 14, 1983 and to disability insurance benefits under sections 216(i) and 223, respectively, of the Social Security Act.

REPRESENTATIVE

5

It is the further decision of the Administrative Law Judge that, based on the application filed on August 30, 1983, the claimant has been disabled since August 14, 1933 under 1614(a)(3)(A) of the Social Security Act, and that the claimant's disability has continued at least through the date of this decision.

The component of the Social Security Administration responsible for authorizing supplemental security income payments will advise the claimant regarding the nondisability requirements for these payments, and if eligible, the amount and the month(s) for which payment will be made.

Peter B. Devine
Administrative Law Judge

December 26, 1984
Date

REPRESENTATIVE

LIST OF EXHIBITS

_____   _____   _____   _____
                (Claimant)

_____
(Wage Earner) (Leave blank in Title XVI Cases or if name is
same as above)

EXHIBIT NO	DESCRIPTION	NO OF PAGES
1	Application for Disability Insurance Benefits dated August 30, 1983	4
2	Disability Determination and Transmittal dtd 11/9/83	9
3	Social Security Notice of Disapproved Claim dated November 21, 1983	3
4	Request for Reconsideration dated November 28, 1983	1
5	Disability Determination and Transmittal dtd 1/9/84	3
6	Social Security Notice of Reconsideration dtd 1/13/84	2
7	Application for Supplemental Security Income 8/30/83 dated August 30, 1983	10
8	Disability Determination and Transmittal dtd 11/9/83	1
9	Supplemental Security Income Notice of Disapproved Claim - Disability dated November 21, 1983	3
10	Disability Determination and Transmittal dtd 1/9/84	1
11	Supplemental Security Income Notice of Reconsideration - Disability dated January 10, 1984	3
12	Request for Hearing dated January 19, 1984	1
13	Earnings record dated August 31, 1983	2
14	Disability Report dated August 30, 1983	8
15	Reconsideration Disability Report undated	6
16	Claimant's statement when request for hearing is filed and the issue is disability dated 1/19/84	1
17	Medical report from Kingsboro Psychiatric Center dated June 9, 1953 to August 18, 1983	14
18	Medical report from L. Zeiger, M.D. dtd 9/16/83	3
19	Medical report from Beth Israel Medical Center dated December 23, 1983	14
20	Medical report from R. LaPlaca, M.D. dtd 1/1/84	

Form HA-540-US (4-82)
Prior editions may be used

ATTACH TO REPRESENTATIVE'S COPY OF THE DECISION

LIST OF EXHIBITS

(Wage Earner) (Leave blank in Title XVI Cases or if name is
same as above)

EXHIBIT NO	DESCRIPTION	NO OF PAGES
21	Letter to Medical Advisor with attached professional qualifications dated April 20, 1984	5
22	Medical Records from Beth Israel MED. Ctr. from 2/3/84 thru 4/24/84	11
23.	Medical Report from R.W.LaPlaca, M.D.dtd 5/1/84	1
24.	Medical Report from U.Mathur, M.D. dtd 5/1/84	1
25.	Claimant's Medications dtd 5/14/84	2
26.	List of Claimant's Employment	12
27	Letter from Atty. Morrison, dtd. 7-19-84	4
28	Letter from Atty. Morrison, dtd. 9-5-84	12
29	PQ of Dr. Richard Wagman	2
30	Claimant's Medication, dated 10-22-84	2
31	Medical Report from William C. Siroty, dtd. 10-31-84	1

EMPLOYMENT DISCRIMINATION AND AIDS: A PRACTICAL GUIDE FOR PLAINTIFFS' LAWYERS

Benjamin Schatz

THE PROBLEM

The problems associated with acquired immune deficiency syndrome and employment discrimination are numerous and varied. Some employers openly admit that they have fired or refused to hire an employee because he or she has AIDS or AIDS-related complex (ARC.) Others may be more subtle, devising more legitimate-sounding pretexts for dismissal, or deferring to the fears of co-workers. Still others may make working conditions intolerable by placing the employee with AIDS or ARC in isolation, or by encouraging the spread of rumors among co-workers, thereby adding to the employee's stress and inducing his or her "voluntary resignation."

Furthermore, a large number of employment discrimination complaints involve people who do not actually have AIDS or ARC. Most of the employment complaints reaching National Gay Rights Advocates involve people who are discriminated against because they are perceived to have a high risk of developing AIDS. Some employers, especially those in businesses such as restaurants which involve employee-client contact, have gone so far as to fire all Haitians, gay (or unmarried) men and others commonly associated with AIDS. Other employers who are more informed about the medical facts may nonetheless bow to public prejudice. Such employers may be willing to hire men whom they know are gay -- but only if these employees are willing and able to "pass" as heterosexual.

The HIV antibody test[1] is another tool for discriminating against healthy individuals in high incidence groups. Some employers have fired employees who confided in co-workers, company physicians or managers after taking the test on their own initiative. Others-have gone even farther, requiring all of their employees and job applicants to take

Benjamin Schatz is the Director of the AIDS Civil Rights Project of National Gay Rights Advocates in San Francisco.

the test. Those who test positive or refuse to submit to testing are denied employment. Other employers may require only certain applicants to take the test. Thus, men who are known or thought to be gay, members of other high incidence groups, and friends and relatives or people with AIDS may be required to test negative in order to keep their jobs. Members of high incidence groups who show any signs of illness -- even those with common colds -- are particularly vulnerable to such discrimination.

It is important to note that employee dismissal is not the only employment discrimination problem associated with AIDS. People associated with AIDS may be moved to isolated environments, denied work assignments, or be discriminated against in other conditions of employment. Others may effectively be fired by being forced to take a medical leave even though they are perfectly capable of working. For those who are fired, the loss of a job is only the beginning of their problems. Many employers have attempted to deprive their former employees of their insurance, pension and medical benefits as well. People with AIDS are especially vulnerable in this regard: many employers have gambled -- often correctly -- that a person with AIDS will quickly die or be too ill or demoralized to defend his or her legal rights.

POTENTIAL SOLUTIONS

In considering how to tackle a case involving AIDS-related employment discrimination, it is important to understand that your client is probably experiencing an enormous amount of pain. Not only has the client been humiliated by discrimination, he or she may also be confronting critical issues of life and death as well. Add to this the social stigmatization of homosexuality and I.V. drug usage, and the additional stigma attached to AIDS, and it is hardly surprising that many clients are reluctant to pursue their claims vigorously. The vast majority hope instead to settle their cases quietly and go on with their lives.

It is perhaps less obvious that most employers who discriminate on the basis of AIDS share this desire to keep things quiet. The great majority of employers have yet to formulate well thought-out policies regarding AIDS and ARC. As a result, most employers who discriminate against people associated with AIDS are, bluster and bravado notwithstanding, quite uncertain about the legality and the medical validity of their actions. They are typically extremely concerned about public reaction to the news that one of their employees may have AIDS or ARC, and usually believe that firing (or not hiring) the employee is the best way to keep things quiet.

Not surprisingly, the threat of litigation and press coverage is extremely threatening to these employers. Such publicity, after all, will do precisely what they fear the most: associate them in the public's mind with AIDS. Consequently, your perceived willingness to publicize your client's case may become your most important bargaining chip in negotiations with employers. Most employers realize that AIDS is a "hot issue" and can attract a tremendous amount of media attention. Even if your client does not actually desire publicity, there's no reason for you to volunteer this fact to the employer.

Whether or not you opt for publicity, you will be able to confront the employer with a very strong legal argument. A few cities such as Austin, Texas, Los Angeles, San Francisco, Sacramento, Oakland, Berkeley, Hayward, Riverside and West Hollywood have enacted legislation specifically designed to prohibit AIDS-related discrimination. In addition, executive orders by the governor of Minnesota and the mayor of Philadelphia prohibit AIDS-based discrimination against public employees. Moreover, virtually every state has adopted a law forbidding discrimination on the basis of physical disability. In most states, AIDS should fit squarely within the meaning of disability as defined by statute or case law.

AIDS AND STATE DISABILITY LAW

As the NGRA survey, AIDS and Handicap Discrimination (see Manual Appendix at end of volume) shows, most agencies charged with enforcing state handicap laws have either categorized AIDS as a physical handicap or declared that they are investigating AIDS discrimination complaints under state disability statutes. In the first case decision of its type, the Florida Commission on Human Relations ruled in Shuttleworth v. Broward County Office of Budget and Management Policies, FCHR No. 85-0624, Dec. 11, 1985 that an employee fired because he had AIDS was a victim of unlawful handicap discrimination. This decision can be found in the BNA Daily Labor Report, 12-17-85, No. 242. Similarly, in People v. 49 W. 12 Tenants Corp. (Docket No. 43604/83, NY Sup. Ct., NY Co.), a New York state trial judge ruled in a housing case that AIDS is a disability for purposes of the state's Human Rights Law. Although this decision is not officially published, it was reported in the New York Law Journal, October 17, 1983, page 2. A New York Court also ruled that a ban on school attendance by children with AIDS would violate federal disability law as well as the Equal Protection Clause of the U.S. Constitution. (See District 27 Community School Board et al. v. Board of Education of the City of New York et al., 502 N.Y.S. 2d 325, sup. 1986.) Other important decisions declaring AIDS to be a protected physical handicap include Chadbourne v. Raytheon (employment -- California; reprinted in BNA's Daily Labor Report, E-1, Feb. 13, 1987), and Cronan v. New England Telephone Company (employment -- Massachusetts) (denial of motion to dismiss)(opinion reprinted in BNA Daily Labor Reporter D-1, Sept. 19, 1986.)

The statutory language and judicial interpretation of differing state disability statutes vary considerably. Thus, remedies and procedural requirements (such as the availability of a private cause of action) differ from state to state. A few state laws protect only state employees; others protect those employees who are actually handicapped, but have no provisions for non-handicapped individuals who are discriminated against because they are perceived to be disabled. It thus becomes crucial for you to examine the wording of the laws of your particular state.

One important caution, however: the wording itself can be misleading. For example, several statutes which on their face protect only the disabled have been interpreted by the courts or state agencies to prohibit discrimination on the basis of perceived disability as well. Furthermore, while a few statutes explicitly exclude "infectious" or "communicable" diseases from coverage, such exceptions were clearly drafted to protect co-workers from being infected in the workplace, and thus should not apply to AIDS. As we shall discuss below, AIDS can not be contracted from routine, non-sexual contact with an infected individual.

THE FEDERAL REHABILITATION ACT

In addition to being protected by state statutes, many workers are safeguarded by federal antidiscrimination legislation as well. The Federal Rehabilitation Act of 1973 (29 U.S.C. 701 et seq.) prohibits discrimination against handicapped individuals by federal agencies (501)[2] federal contractors or subcontractors doing more than $2,500 in business with the federal government (503),[3] and recipients of federal funds (504).[4] An individual is handicapped, according to the Act, if he or she "has a physical or mental impairment which substantially limits one or more of such person's major life activities." (29 U.S.C. 706[7][B]). The Act also explicitly protects those who have a "record of...impairment" or are "regarded as having such an impairment." Thus, healthy gay men (and members of other high incidence groups) should be protected against discrimination which is based on an employer's fears that they might develop AIDS. The irony here is that while federal, and most state and local laws, do not prohibit an employer from firing a man simply because he is gay, such discrimination may now be attacked if it can be linked to the issue of AIDS. (See, for example, Poff v. Caro [New Jersey Superior Court], holding that under state handicap law the fear of AIDS cannot be used to justify the denial of housing to healthy gay men. [Case reported in BNA's AIDS Policy and Law, April 8, 1987 at 3.])

That AIDS is a protected physical handicap under the Act seems almost certain in light of the U.S. Supreme Court decision in School Board of Nassau County v. Arline, 107 S. Ct. 1123 (1987). Although the case involved a teacher with tuberculosis, the real debate centered around the validity of the Department of Justice's memorandum on AIDS, issued in June of 1986 and re-fashioned by the D.O.J. to apply to tuberculosis as well. By a 7 - 2 vote, the court rejected the D.O.J.'s argument that the Act permits discrimination based upon (unreasonable) fears of contagion. Instead, the Court stated that:.

> "Allowing discrimination based on the contagious effects of a physical impairment would be inconsistent with the basic purpose of Section 504, which is to ensure that handicapped individuals are not denied jobs or other benefits because of the prejudiced attitudes or the ignorance of others. By amending the definition of 'handicapped individual' to include not only those who are actually physically impaired, but also those who are regarded as impaired and who, as a result are substantially limited in a major life activity, Congress acknowledged that society's accumulated myths and fears about disability and disease are as handicapping as are the physical limitations that flow from actual impairment."

It should be noted that the Court declared in a footnote (in its only reference to AIDS) that it was not deciding whether HIV seropositivity constitutes a handicap under the Act,

because the issue was not directly raised in the case. (Ms. Arline had an actual, and not a perceived, impairment.) Nonetheless, the language of the opinion is extremely broad, and most analysts agree that both HIV seropositivity and AIDS are clearly covered. Moreover, there have already been at least two federal court rulings holding that AIDS is a protected handicap under Section 504. Chalk v. U.S. District Court, 87-6418, __ F.2d __ (9th Cir., 1987), Thomas v. Atascadero Unified School District, 662 F. Supp. 376 (C.D. Cal. 1987). In Chalk, the ninth circuit ordered a teacher to be reinstated after he was suspended because he had AIDS. In Thomas, the court refused to allow a school district to bar from school a child with AIDS who had bitten another child.

The differing sections of the Federal Rehabilitation Act each contain their own peculiar procedural requirements. For example, while a private cause of action is authorized under 501, complaints under 503 must be filed with the U.S. Department of Labor's Office of Federal Contract Compliance Programs. Complaints under 504 should be brought before the civil rights division of the regional office of the Department which is providing federal funding; thus, a complaint against a hospital would be filed with the U.S. Department of Health and Human Services, and a complaint involving education would be brought before the U.S. Department of Education.

Substantive provisions may differ as well. For example, sections 501 and 503 both require reasonable accommodation of and affirmative action for handicapped workers. Section 504, however, does not mandate affirmative action, and requires plaintiffs alleging discrimination to prove that they can perform all necessary tasks in spite of their handicap. (Please note: some of these issues are presently being litigated in the courts, and interpretations of the varying sections are therefore subject to change.)

DISABILITY LAW: BURDENS OF PROOF
AND DEFENSES

The burden of proof needed to prevail in a discrimination suit varies from statute to statute. Nonetheless, the requirements of federal and most state laws are fairly similar. Generally, a plaintiff alleging discrimination on the basis of disability must present a prima facie case that he or she:

1) has or is perceived to have an ailment which qualifies as a handicap.

2) is qualified to perform the essential functions of the job in question if afforded reasonable ac-

commodations (including flexible hours or, in some cases, the opportunity to work at home), and

3) was discriminated against in whole or in part because of his or her handicap (or perceived handicap.)

The defense must then prove either that the handicap was not a factor in the decision or that the exclusion of people with the particular disability is justified by business necessity (41 C.F.R. 60-741.6 [c][2][1983.]) Consequently, the employer can allege one of three things:

1) that the employee/applicant cannot perform the essential functions of the job, or that accommodation would cause the employer undue hardship. (You may have a problem here if your client's illness causes chronic absenteeism.)

2) that the absence of handicap is a bona fide occupational qualification of the job (this defense is rarely successful), or

3) that the employee/applicant cannot perform his or her duties without endangering his or her own safety or that of others.

The issue of transmissibility is obviously of key importance here. In this regard, the holding in NYS Association for Retarded Children v. Carey 466 F. Supp. 479 should be very helpful. In Carey, a federal district court ruled that segregating retarded children with Hepatitis B violated their rights under Section 504 of the Federal Rehabilitation Act. (Hepatitis B is known to be transmitted far more easily than AIDS. See Public Health Service Guidelines in Appendix at end of chapter.) Even more directly on point are the rulings in Chadbourne, supra ("Chadbourne's co-workers were at no risk of contracting AIDS by working alongside him") and Thomas, supra ("The overwhelming weight of medical evidence is that the AIDS virus is not transmitted by human bites, even bites that break the skin...Any theoretical risk of transmission of the AIDS virus by Ryan in connection with his attendance in regular kindergarten class is so remote that it cannot form the basis for any exclusionary action by the school district.") In addition, the Public Health Service of the U.S. Department of Health and Human Services has issued detailed workplace guidelines which state that employees with AIDS present no danger to customers or co-workers. The evidence cited in these guidelines is sufficient to refute any argument that AIDS can be casually transmitted.

Clever employers may also attempt to argue that employees with AIDS endanger themselves by remaining on the job and exposing themselves to other people's illnesses. Given the fact that AIDS is usually fatal, however, an employer will have a difficult time demonstrating that it is the job which endangers an employee who has AIDS. The argument must also fail when applied to employees who test HIV antibody positive, since the majority of these individuals are no more susceptible to illness than are others.

Employees with ARC, however, may in fact have a heightened susceptibility to illness. Any argument that people with ARC will be harmed by continued employment, however, is easily refuted upon examination of the alternatives. Most people with ARC, after all, are expected to live for many years, during which time they cannot possibly live in total isolation. Indeed, such isolation (not to mention unemployment and poverty) is certain to cause tremendous stress, which many physicians believe to be a co-factor in the development of AIDS.

A few other general points should be made about disability laws. First, they can be used to attack not only employee dismissals and discriminatory working conditions, but also to challenge the routine testing of employees or applicants for evidence of HIV antibodies. Under the Federal Rehabilitation Act, for example, employers are forbidden to give pre-employment physicals until after an offer of employment has been extended. Moreover, given the fact that the HIV antibody test has only limited diagnostic use, an employer will have a difficult time showing that it is being used for a purpose other than discrimination.

Secondly, there may, in a given situation, be several handicap laws which apply. In addition to the laws which we have already discussed, municipal and county disability laws have also been enacted. Furthermore, according to Professor Arthur Leonard of New York Law School, governors in several states have issued executive orders prohibiting discrimination against the physically disabled by state contractors.

Finally, there are two employer defenses which, although commonly raised, are easily rebutted. First, an employer's fear of increased costs (because of higher insurance premiums, extra medical costs, etc.) is not a defense to discrimination against the handicapped. Several courts which have analyzed this issue have reasoned that allowing such a defense would undercut the very purpose of disability statutes. (See, for example, Chrysler Outboard Corp. v. Department of Industry, Labor and human Relations [1976], CCH Employment Practices Guide, 13 Employment Practices Decisions, par. 11,526 [Wisconsin.] See also Sterling Transit Co. v. FEPC [1981], 121 Cal. App. 3d. 791 [California.])

Customer or co-worker prejudice is also not a valid defense. If co-workers are fearful, an employer is obligated to educate them or to restructure the work environment in a manner which does not infringe upon the rights of the AIDS-associated employee. Should the co-workers refuse to work at all, an employer may legally discipline them. (While non-unionized employees have a right under the Taft-Hartley Act [21 U.S.C. 141 et al.] to cease working without retaliation if they believe themselves to be in danger, recent decisions by the National Labor Relations Board have indicated that work stoppages of this type are valid only when employee fears are reasonable and in good faith.)

OTHER CAUSES OF ACTION

In addition to pursuing your client's claims under disability law, keep in mind the fact that you may have several other possible causes of action. Your client may, for example, have a valid claim for breach of contract The provisions of his or her collective bargaining agreement may also have been violated. Furthermore, in some states the tort of wrongful discharge may apply.

You may, in addition, wish to pursue some more imaginative claims; the more facially valid arguments you are able to present, the greater your likelihood becomes of successfully settling your case. AIDS-related litigation is a very recent phenomenon, and the applicable legal theories are far from fully developed. Think creatively: the far-fetched thought which you are tempted to dismiss may in fact be successful.

In the spirit of creative thinking, the following approaches are offered for your consideration:

1) Sexual orientation discrimination: check to see if state or local law (or your client's contract or collective bargaining agreement) prohibits anti-gay discrimination.

2) Gender or marital status discrimination if your client's employer is firing or testing the blood of only males, or only single males, the employer is violating state and federal statutory prohibitions against discrimination on the basis of gender and/or marital status. Constitutionally-based equal protection arguments may also be raised if state action is involved.

3) Title VII adverse impact -- gender or race: any employment policy which systematically excludes people with AIDS, ARC or positive HIV antibody test results will have a highly disproportionate impact upon males. Furthermore, since 40% of people with AIDS are Black and Hispanic (double the percentage of these groups in the national population), any systematic AIDS-based exclusion is likely to have a disproportionate impact upon racial minorities as well.

If such disparate impact can be sufficiently demonstrated, the burden will shift to the employer to demonstrate business necessity. Griggs v. Duke Power Co., 401 U.S. 424, 91 S. Ct. 849 (1971.) This burden can be a difficult one: the courts have struck down such employer practices as favoring applicants with honorable military discharges or refusing to hire employees with arrest records as unjustified in the face of their disproportionate impact upon members of racial minority groups. Dozier v. Chupka, 395 F. Supp. 836, Gregory v. Litton Systems, 316 F. Supp. 401.) It should be noted, however, that the Griggs approach has been increasingly restricted during recent years.

A claim under Title VII should be filed with the U.S. Equal Employment Opportunity Commission or with a comparable state agency, usually within 180 days of the discriminatory act. After investigating the case, the E.E.O.C. will either file suit or issue a "right to sue" letter. Procedures differ somewhat for federal employees.

4) ERISA The federal Employee Retirement Income Security Act (29 U.S.C. 1140) forbids employer discrimination against employees in order to deprive them of benefits to which they are entitled under an ERISA-qualified benefit plan. Those employers engaging in interstate commerce who have company-funded benefit programs are covered by ERISA. Thus, ERISA should prohibit a broad spectrum of employers from firing an employee if the dismissal is motivated in part by a desire to avoid the costs associated with future AIDS-related medical benefits.

5) Constitutional Law: when state action is implicated in an employment discrimination case, your client may have a claim for violation of his or her rights to equal protection or due process. Freedom of speech and freedom of association may also be denied if your client is singled out because he or she has talked about AIDS or associated with people with AIDS or high-risk individuals. Finally, mandatory drug testing by employers may be an illegal fourth amendment search and violate employees' constitutional right to privacy.

6) Privacy torts (common law): if, in the process of firing a person with an AIDS-related condition, an employer discloses the employee's medical status to co-workers, the dismissed employee may have a claim for public disclosure of private facts (Keep in mind, however, that courts will generally deny relief unless the disclosure was to a significant number of people.) If the employer misinforms co-workers that your client has AIDS while in fact he or she has, for example, merely tested HIV antibody positive, a suit for slander may be appropriate. In addition, a claim of intrusion may be worth exploring if your client has been forced to take an HIV antibody test. Finally, if an employee's dismissal is based upon information gained from a company physician, the employer may be liable for damages under statutory or common law guarantees of the confidentiality of employee medical records. The employee may also have a claim for breach of confidentiality against the physician.

7) Employment termination and insurance benefits: most states have enacted legislation which requires that employees be allowed to "convert" their group insurance to individual insurance upon leaving a job. If employers actively discourage or forbid employees to convert, they are probably violating the law. Unfortunately, the conversion period is usually very short -- typically only 30 days. Moreover, premiums are usually astronomical, and coverage very restricted. A far better option is available under the Congressional Omnibus Budget Reconciliation Act of 1985 (COBRA). Under COBRA, terminated employees are entitled to continue the same coverage provided by their employers for a period of 18 months. The costs of continuation may be charged to the employee -- but the charge may not exceed 102% of the cost paid by the employer for active employees. COBRA applies not only to insurance plans, but also to health maintenance organizations (HMO's) and self-funded employee benefit plans. But note: employers with fewer than 20 workers, religious employers, and the federal government are exempt.

Given the increasing amount of discrimination in the area of insurance, you should advise unemployed clients during their first consultation to obtain new health insurance if possible, or to continue or convert their group policies. Since the former choice will be impossible for those already diagnosed with AIDS or ARC, it is imperative that they be advised to continue or convert their policies immediately. Without such coverage, they will probably be wiped out financially. (Please note: many insurance policy manuals describe their conversion procedures in fine print, in language which is incomprehensible to non-lawyers. You may, therefore, wish to ask your client to bring in his or her policy so that you can review it yourself.)

A FINAL NOTE

The information included in this article is not exhaustive. It is my hope, however, that it will serve as a launching point for further research by practicing attorneys. Should you desire further information, feel free to contact National Gay Rights Advocates or any of the other resource organizations listed in the appendix. See also "Employment Discrimination Against Persons With AIDS," by Professor Arthur Leonard of New York Law School, 10 U. of Dayton Law Review 681 (Spring, 1985), and Leonard, "AIDS and Employment Law Revisited", 14 Hofstra L. Rev. 11 (Fall, 1985) for excellent discussions of AIDS and employment law.

FOOTNOTES

[1] The HIV antibody test -- when accurate -- measure presence in the blood of antibodies to the Human Immunodeficiency Virus, a probable causative agent of AIDS. Medical evidence currently indicates that the majority of people who develop these antibodies will not develop AIDS. Indeed, some do not even have the live HIV virus in their blood. (Please note that HIV has also been called HTLV-III and LAV.)

The test was originally licensed by the U.S. Food and Drug Administration solely for the purpose of protecting the nation's blood supply. For this reason, F.D.A. labeling language declares that: "It is inappropriate to use this test as a screen for AIDS in the general population." (Note: this language may have been changed by the time you read this to permit some diagnostic uses of the test.)

[2] 29 U.S.C. 791.

[3] 29 U.S.C. 793.

[4] 29 U.S.C. 794.

Appendix

Centers for Disease Control, Summary: Recommendations for Preventing Transmission of Infection with Human T-Lymphotropic Virus Type III/Lymphadenopathy-Associated Virus in the Workplace, 34 MMWR 681 (1985).

CENTERS FOR DISEASE CONTROL

MMWR

MORBIDITY AND MORTALITY WEEKLY REPORT

November 15, 1985 / Vol. 34 / No. 45

681 Summary: Recommendations for Preventing Transmission of Infection with HTLV-III/LAV in the Workplace
682 Recommendations for Preventing Transmission of Infection with HTLV-III/LAV in the Workplace

Current Trends

Summary:
Recommendations for Preventing Transmission of Infection with Human T-Lymphotropic Virus Type III/ Lymphadenopathy-Associated Virus in the Workplace

The information and recommendations contained in this document have been developed with particular emphasis on health-care workers and others in related occupations in which exposure might occur to blood from persons infected with HTLV-III/LAV, the "AIDS virus." Because of public concern about the purported risk of transmission of HTLV-III/LAV by persons providing personal services and those preparing and serving food and beverages, this document also addresses personal-service and food-service workers. Finally, it addresses "other workers"—persons in settings, such as offices, schools, factories, and construction sites, where there is no known risk of AIDS virus transmission.

Because AIDS is a bloodborne, sexually transmitted disease that is not spread by casual contact, this document does *not* recommend routine HTLV-III/LAV antibody screening for the groups addressed. Because AIDS is not transmitted through preparation or serving of food and beverages, these recommendations state that food-service workers known to be infected with AIDS should not be restricted from work unless they have another infection or illness for which such restriction would be warranted.

This document contains detailed recommendations for precautions appropriate to prevent transmission of all bloodborne infectious diseases to people exposed—in the course of their duties—to blood from persons who may be infected with HTLV-III/LAV. They emphasize that health-care workers should take all possible precautions to prevent needlestick injury. The recommendations are based on the well-documented modes of HTLV-III/LAV transmission and incorporate a "worst case" scenario, the hepatitis B model of transmission. Because the hepatitis B virus is also bloodborne and is both hardier and more infectious than HTLV-III/LAV, recommendations that would prevent transmission of hepatitis B will also prevent transmission of AIDS.

Formulation of specific recommendations for health-care workers who perform invasive procedures is in progress.

Recommendations for Preventing Transmission of Infection with Human T-Lymphotropic Virus Type III/ Lymphadenopathy-Associated Virus in the Workplace

Persons at increased risk of acquiring infection with human T-lymphotropic virus type III/lymphadenopathy-associated virus (HTLV-III/LAV), the virus that causes acquired immuno-deficiency syndrome (AIDS), include homosexual and bisexual men, intravenous (IV) drug abusers, persons transfused with contaminated blood or blood products, heterosexual contacts of persons with HTLV-III/LAV infection, and children born to infected mothers. HTLV-III/LAV is transmitted through sexual contact, parenteral exposure to infected blood or blood components, and perinatal transmission from mother to neonate. HTLV-III/LAV has been isolated from blood, semen, saliva, tears, breast milk, and urine and is likely to be isolated from some other body fluids, secretions, and excretions, but epidemiologic evidence has implicated only blood and semen in transmission. Studies of nonsexual household contacts of AIDS patients indicate that casual contact with saliva and tears does not result in transmission of infection. Spread of infection to household contacts of infected persons has not been detected when the household contacts have not been sex partners or have not been infants of infected mothers. The kind of nonsexual person-to-person contact that generally occurs among workers and clients or consumers in the workplace does not pose a risk for transmission of HTLV-III/LAV.

As in the development of any such recommendations, the paramount consideration is the protection of the public's health. The following recommendations have been developed for all workers, particularly workers in occupations in which exposure might occur to blood from individuals infected with HTLV-III/LAV. These recommendations reinforce and supplement the specific recommendations that were published earlier for clinical and laboratory staffs (1) and for dental-care personnel and persons performing necropsies and morticians' services (2). Because of public concern about the purported risk of transmission of HTLV-III/LAV by persons providing personal services and by food and beverages, these recommendations contain information and recommendations for personal-service and food-service workers. Finally, these recommendations address workplaces in general where there is no known risk of transmission of HTLV-III/LAV (e.g., offices, schools, factories, construction sites). Formulation of specific recommendations for health-care workers (HCWs) who perform invasive procedures (e.g., surgeons, dentists) is in progress. Separate recommendations are also being developed to prevent HTLV-III/LAV transmission in prisons, other correctional facilities, and institutions housing individuals who may exhibit uncontrollable behavior (e.g., custodial institutions) and in the perinatal setting. In addition, separate recommendations have already been developed for children in schools and day-care centers (3).

HTLV-III/LAV-infected individuals include those with AIDS (4); those diagnosed by their physician(s) as having other illnesses due to infection with HTLV-III/LAV; and those who have virologic or serologic evidence of infection with HTLV-III/LAV but who are not ill.

These recommendations are based on the well-documented modes of HTLV-III/LAV transmission identified in epidemiologic studies and on comparison with the hepatitis B experience. Other recommendations are based on the hepatitis B model of transmission.

COMPARISON WITH THE HEPATITIS B VIRUS EXPERIENCE

The epidemiology of HTLV-III/LAV infection is similar to that of hepatitis B virus (HBV) infection, and much that has been learned over the last 15 years related to the risk of acquiring hepatitis B in the workplace can be applied to understanding the risk of HTLV-III/LAV transmission in the health-care and other occupational settings. Both viruses are transmitted through

HTLV-III/LAV — Continued

sexual contact, parenteral exposure to contaminated blood or blood products, and perinatal transmission from infected mothers to their offspring. Thus, some of the same major groups at high risk for HBV infection (e.g., homosexual men, IV drug abusers, persons with hemophilia, infants born to infected mothers) are also the groups at highest risk for HTLV-III/LAV infection. Neither HBV nor HTLV-III/LAV has been shown to be transmitted by casual contact in the workplace, contaminated food or water, or airborne or fecal-oral routes (5).

HBV infection is an occupational risk for HCWs, but this risk is related to degree of contact with blood or contaminated needles. HCWs who do not have contact with blood or needles contaminated with blood are not at risk for acquiring HBV infection in the workplace (6-8).

In the health-care setting, HBV transmission has not been documented between hospitalized patients, except in hemodialysis units, where blood contamination of the environment has been extensive or where HBV-positive blood from one patient has been transferred to another patient through contamination of instruments. Evidence of HBV transmission from HCWs to patients has been rare and limited to situations in which the HCWs exhibited high concentrations of virus in their blood (at least 100,000,000 infectious virus particles per ml of serum), and the HCWs sustained a puncture wound while performing traumatic procedures on patients or had exudative or weeping lesions that allowed virus to contaminate instruments or open wounds of patients (9-11).

Current evidence indicates that, despite epidemiologic similarities of HBV and HTLV-III/LAV infection, the risk for HBV transmission in health-care settings far exceeds that for HTLV-III/LAV transmission. The risk of acquiring HBV infection following a needlestick from an HBV carrier ranges from 6% to 30% (12,13), far in excess of the risk of HTLV-III/LAV infection following a needlestick involving a source patient infected with HTLV-III/LAV, which is less than 1%. In addition, all HCWs who have been shown to transmit HBV infection in health-care settings have belonged to the subset of chronic HBV carriers who, when tested, have exhibited evidence of exceptionally high concentrations of virus (at least 100,000,000 infectious virus particles per ml) in their blood. Chronic carriers who have substantially lower concentrations of virus in their blood have not been implicated in transmission in the health-care setting (9-11,14). The HBV model thus represents a "worst case" condition in regard to transmission in health-care and other related settings. Therefore, recommendations for the control of HBV infection should, if followed, also effectively prevent spread of HTLV-III/LAV. Whether additional measures are indicated for those HCWs who perform invasive procedures will be addressed in the recommendations currently being developed.

Routine screening of all patients or HCWs for evidence of HBV infection has never been recommended. Control of HBV transmission in the health-care setting has emphasized the implementation of recommendations for the appropriate handling of blood, other body fluids, and items soiled with blood or other body fluids.

TRANSMISSION FROM PATIENTS TO HEALTH-CARE WORKERS

HCWs include, but are not limited to, nurses, physicians, dentists and other dental workers, optometrists, podiatrists, chiropractors, laboratory and blood bank technologists and technicians, phlebotomists, dialysis personnel, paramedics, emergency medical technicians, medical examiners, morticians, housekeepers, laundry workers, and others whose work involves contact with patients, their blood or other body fluids, or corpses.

Recommendations for HCWs emphasize precautions appropriate for preventing transmission of bloodborne infectious diseases, including HTLV-III/LAV and HBV infections. Thus, these precautions should be enforced routinely, as should other standard infection-control precautions, regardless of whether HCWs or patients are known to be infected with HTLV-III/LAV or HBV. In addition to being informed of these precautions, all HCWs, including students and housestaff, should be educated regarding the epidemiology, modes of transmission, and prevention of HTLV-III/LAV infection.

Risk of HCWs acquiring HTLV-III/LAV in the workplace. Using the HBV model, the highest risk for transmission of HTLV-III/LAV in the workplace would involve parenteral exposure to a needle or other sharp instrument contaminated with blood of an infected patient. The risk to HCWs of acquiring HTLV-III/LAV infection in the workplace has been evaluated in several studies. In five separate studies, a total of 1,498 HCWs have been tested for antibody to HTLV-III/LAV. In these studies, 666 (44.5%) of the HCWs had direct parenteral (needlestick or cut) or mucous membrane exposure to patients with AIDS or HTLV-III/LAV infection. Most of these exposures were to blood rather than to other body fluids. None of the HCWs whose initial serologic tests were negative developed subsequent evidence of HTLV-III/LAV infection following their exposures. Twenty-six HCWs in these five studies were seropositive when first tested; all but three of these persons belonged to groups recognized to be at increased risk for AIDS (*15*). Since one was tested anonymously, epidemiologic information was available on only two of these three seropositive HCWs. Although these two HCWs were reported as probable occupationally related HTLV-III/LAV infection (*15,16*), neither had a preexposure nor an early postexposure serum sample available to help determine the onset of infection. One case reported from England describes a nurse who seroconverted following an accidental parenteral exposure to a needle contaminated with blood from an AIDS patient (*17*).

In spite of the extremely low risk of transmission of HTLV-III/LAV infection, even when needlestick injuries occur, more emphasis must be given to precautions targeted to prevent needlestick injuries in HCWs caring for any patient, since such injuries continue to occur even during the care of patients who are known to be infected with HTLV-III/LAV.

Precautions to prevent acquisition of HTLV-III/LAV infection by HCWs in the workplace. These precautions represent prudent practices that apply to preventing transmission of HTLV-III/LAV and other bloodborne infections and should be used routinely (*18*).

1. Sharp items (needles, scalpel blades, and other sharp instruments) should be considered as potentially infective and be handled with extraordinary care to prevent accidental injuries.

2. Disposable syringes and needles, scalpel blades, and other sharp items should be placed into puncture-resistant containers located as close as practical to the area in which they were used. To prevent needlestick injuries, needles should not be recapped, purposefully bent, broken, removed from disposable syringes, or otherwise manipulated by hand.

3. When the possibility of exposure to blood or other body fluids exists, routinely recommended precautions should be followed. The anticipated exposure may require gloves alone, as in handling items soiled with blood or equipment contaminated with blood or other body fluids, or may also require gowns, masks, and eye-coverings when performing procedures involving more extensive contact with blood or potentially infective body fluids, as in some dental or endoscopic procedures or postmortem examinations. Hands should be washed thoroughly and immediately if they accidentally become contaminated with blood.

4. To minimize the need for emergency mouth-to-mouth resuscitation, mouth pieces, resuscitation bags, or other ventilation devices should be strategically located and available for use in areas where the need for resuscitation is predictable.

5. Pregnant HCWs are not known to be at greater risk of contracting HTLV-III/LAV infections than HCWs who are not pregnant; however, if a HCW develops HTLV-III/LAV infection during pregnancy, the infant is at increased risk of infection resulting from

HTLV-III/LAV — Continued

perinatal transmission. Because of this risk, pregnant HCWs should be especially familiar with precautions for the preventing HTLV-III/LAV transmission (*19*).

Precautions for HCWs during home care of persons infected with HTLV-III/LAV. Persons infected with HTLV-III/LAV can be safely cared for in home environments. Studies of family members of patients infected with HTLV-III/LAV have found no evidence of HTLV-III/LAV transmission to adults who were not sexual contacts of the infected patients or to children who were not at risk for perinatal transmission (*3*). HCWs providing home care face the same risk of transmission of infection as HCWs in hospitals and other health-care settings, especially if there are needlesticks or other parenteral or mucous membrane exposures to blood or other body fluids.

When providing health-care service in the home to persons infected with HTLV-III/LAV, measures similar to those used in hospitals are appropriate. As in the hospital, needles should not be recapped, purposefully bent, broken, removed from disposable syringes, or otherwise manipulated by hand. Needles and other sharp items should be placed into puncture-resistant containers and disposed of in accordance with local regulations for solid waste. Blood and other body fluids can be flushed down the toilet. Other items for disposal that are contaminated with blood or other body fluids that cannot be flushed down the toilet should be wrapped securely in a plastic bag that is impervious and sturdy (not easily penetrated). It should be placed in a second bag before being discarded in a manner consistent with local regulations for solid waste disposal. Spills of blood or other body fluids should be cleaned with soap and water or a household detergent. As in the hospital, individuals cleaning up such spills should wear disposable gloves. A disinfectant solution or a freshly prepared solution of sodium hypochlorite (household bleach, see below) should be used to wipe the area after cleaning.

Precautions for providers of prehospital emergency health care. Providers of prehospital emergency health care include the following: paramedics, emergency medical technicians, law enforcement personnel, firefighters, lifeguards, and others whose job might require them to provide first-response medical care. The risk of transmission of infection, including HTLV-III/LAV infection, from infected persons to providers of prehospital emergency health care should be no higher than that for HCWs providing emergency care in the hospital if appropriate precautions are taken to prevent exposure to blood or other body fluids.

Providers of prehospital emergency health care should follow the precautions outlined above for other HCWs. No transmission of HBV infection during mouth-to-mouth resuscitation has been documented. However, because of the theoretical risk of salivary transmission of HTLV-III/LAV during mouth-to-mouth resuscitation, special attention should be given to the use of disposable airway equipment or resuscitation bags and the wearing of gloves when in contact with blood or other body fluids. Resuscitation equipment and devices known or suspected to be contaminated with blood or other body fluids should be used once and disposed of or be thoroughly cleaned and disinfected after each use.

Management of parenteral and mucous membrane exposures of HCWs. If a HCW has a parenteral (e.g., needlestick or cut) or mucous membrane (e.g., splash to the eye or mouth) exposure to blood or other body fluids, the source patient should be assessed clinically and epidemiologically to determine the likelihood of HTLV-III/LAV infection. If the assessment suggests that infection may exist, the patient should be informed of the incident and requested to consent to serologic testing for evidence of HTLV-III/LAV infection. If the source patient has AIDS or other evidence of HTLV-III/LAV infection, declines testing, or has a positive test, the HCW should be evaluated clinically and serologically for evidence of HTLV-III/LAV infection as soon as possible after the exposure, and, if seronegative, retested after 6 weeks and on a periodic basis thereafter (e.g., 3, 6, and 12 months following exposure) to determine if

HTLV-III/LAV — Continued

transmission has occurred. During this follow-up period, especially the first 6-12 weeks, when most infected persons are expected to seroconvert, exposed HCWs should receive counseling about the risk of infection and follow U.S. Public Health Service (PHS) recommendations for preventing transmission of AIDS (*20,21*). If the source patient is seronegative and has no other evidence of HTLV-III/LAV infection, no further follow-up of the HCW is necessary. If the source patient cannot be identified, decisions regarding appropriate follow-up should be individualized based on the type of exposure and the likelihood that the source patient was infected.

Serologic testing of patients. Routine serologic testing of all patients for antibody to HTLV-III/LAV is not recommended to prevent transmission of HTLV-III/LAV infection in the workplace. Results of such testing are unlikely to further reduce the risk of transmission, which, even with documented needlesticks, is already extremely low. Furthermore, the risk of needlestick and other parenteral exposures could be reduced by emphasizing and more consistently implementing routinely recommended infection-control precautions (e.g., not recapping needles). Moreover, results of routine serologic testing would not be available for

(Continued on 691)

HTLV-III/LAV — Continued

emergency cases and patients with short lengths of stay, and additional tests to determine whether a positive test was a true or false positive would be required in populations with a low prevalence of infection. However, this recommendation is based only on considerations of occupational risks and should not be construed as a recommendation against other uses of the serologic test, such as for diagnosis or to facilitate medical management of patients. Since the experience with infected patients varies substantially among hospitals (75% of all AIDS cases have been reported by only 280 of the more than 6,000 acute-care hospitals in the United States), some hospitals in certain geographic areas may deem it appropriate to initiate serologic testing of patients.

TRANSMISSION FROM HEALTH-CARE WORKERS TO PATIENTS

Risk of transmission of HTLV-III/LAV infection from HCWs to patients. Although there is no evidence that HCWs infected with HTLV-III/LAV have transmitted infection to patients, a risk of transmission of HTLV-III/LAV infection from HCWs to patients would exist in situations where there is both (1) a high degree of trauma to the patient that would provide a portal of entry for the virus (e.g., during invasive procedures) and (2) access of blood or serous fluid from the infected HCW to the open tissue of a patient, as could occur if the HCW sustains a needlestick or scalpel injury during an invasive procedure. HCWs known to be infected with HTLV-III/LAV who do not perform invasive procedures need not be restricted from work unless they have evidence of other infection or illness for which any HCW should be restricted. Whether additional restrictions are indicated for HCWs who perform invasive procedures is currently being considered.

Precautions to prevent transmission of HTLV-III/LAV infection from HCWs to patients. These precautions apply to all HCWs, regardless of whether they perform invasive procedures: (1) All HCWs should wear gloves for direct contact with mucous membranes or nonintact skin of all patients and (2) HCWs who have exudative lesions or weeping dermatitis should refrain from all direct patient care and from handling patient-care equipment until the condition resolves.

Management of parenteral and mucous membrane exposures of patients. If a patient has a parenteral or mucous membrane exposure to blood or other body fluids of a HCW, the patient should be informed of the incident and the same procedure outlined above for exposures of HCWs to patients should be followed for both the source HCW and the potentially exposed patient. Management of this type of exposure will be addressed in more detail in the recommendations for HCWs who perform invasive procedures.

Serologic testing of HCWs. Routine serologic testing of HCWs who do not perform invasive procedures (including providers of home and prehospital emergency care) is not recommended to prevent transmission of HTLV-III/LAV infection. The risk of transmission is extremely low and can be further minimized when routinely recommended infection-control precautions are followed. However, serologic testing should be available to HCWs who may wish to know their HTLV-III/LAV infection status. Whether indications exist for serologic testing of HCWs who perform invasive procedures is currently being considered.

Risk of occupational acquisition of other infectious diseases by HCWs infected with HTLV-III/LAV. HCWs who are known to be infected with HTLV-III/LAV and who have defective immune systems are at increased risk of acquiring or experiencing serious complications of other infectious diseases. Of particular concern is the risk of severe infection following exposure to patients with infectious diseases that are easily transmitted if appropriate precautions are not taken (e.g., tuberculosis). HCWs infected with HTLV-III/LAV should be counseled about the potential risk associated with taking care of patients with transmissible infections and should continue to follow existing recommendations for infection control to minimize

HTLV-III/LAV — Continued

their risk of exposure to other infectious agents (*18,19*). The HCWs' personal physician(s), in conjunction with their institutions' personnel health services or medical directors, should determine on an individual basis whether the infected HCWs can adequately and safely perform patient-care duties and suggest changes in work assignments, if indicated. In making this determination, recommendations of the Immunization Practices Advisory Committee and institutional policies concerning requirements for vaccinating HCWs with live-virus vaccines should also be considered.

STERILIZATION, DISINFECTION, HOUSEKEEPING, AND WASTE DISPOSAL TO PREVENT TRANSMISSION OF HTLV-III/LAV

Sterilization and disinfection procedures currently recommended for use (*22,23*) in health-care and dental facilities are adequate to sterilize or disinfect instruments, devices, or other items contaminated with the blood or other body fluids from individuals infected with HTLV-III/LAV. Instruments or other nondisposable items that enter normally sterile tissue or the vascular system or through which blood flows should be sterilized before reuse. Surgical instruments used on all patients should be decontaminated after use rather than just rinsed with water. Decontamination can be accomplished by machine or by hand cleaning by trained personnel wearing appropriate protective attire (*24*) and using appropriate chemical germicides. Instruments or other nondisposable items that touch intact mucous membranes should receive high-level disinfection.

Several liquid chemical germicides commonly used in laboratories and health-care facilities have been shown to kill HTLV-III/LAV at concentrations much lower than are used in practice (*25*). When decontaminating instruments or medical devices, chemical germicides that are registered with and approved by the U.S. Environmental Protection Agency (EPA) as "sterilants" can be used either for sterilization or for high-level disinfection depending on contact time; germicides that are approved for use as "hospital disinfectants" and are mycobactericidal when used at appropriate dilutions can also be used for high-level disinfection of devices and instruments. Germicides that are mycobactericidal are preferred because mycobacteria represent one of the most resistant groups of microorganisms; therefore, germicides that are effective against mycobacteria are also effective against other bacterial and viral pathogens. When chemical germicides are used, instruments or devices to be sterilized or disinfected should be thoroughly cleaned before exposure to the germicide, and the manufacturer's instructions for use of the germicide should be followed.

Laundry and dishwashing cycles commonly used in hospitals are adequate to decontaminate linens, dishes, glassware, and utensils. When cleaning environmental surfaces, housekeeping procedures commonly used in hospitals are adequate; surfaces exposed to blood and body fluids should be cleaned with a detergent followed by decontamination using an EPA-approved hospital disinfectant that is mycobactericidal. Individuals cleaning up such spills should wear disposable gloves. Information on specific label claims of commercial germicides can be obtained by writing to the Disinfectants Branch, Office of Pesticides, Environmental Protection Agency, 401 M Street, S.W., Washington, D.C., 20460.

In addition to hospital disinfectants, a freshly prepared solution of sodium hypochlorite (household bleach) is an inexpensive and very effective germicide (*25*). Concentrations ranging from 5,000 ppm (a 1:10 dilution of household bleach) to 500 ppm (a 1:100 dilution) sodium hypochlorite are effective, depending on the amount of organic material (e.g., blood, mucus, etc.) present on the surface to be cleaned and disinfected.

Sharp items should be considered as potentially infective and should be handled and disposed of with extraordinary care to prevent accidental injuries. Other potentially infective waste should be contained and transported in clearly identified impervious plastic bags. If the

HTLV–III/LAV – Continued

outside of the bag is contaminated with blood or other body fluids, a second outer bag should be used. Recommended practices for disposal of infective waste (*23*) are adequate for disposal of waste contaminated by HTLV-III/LAV. Blood and other body fluids may be carefully poured down a drain connected to a sanitary sewer.

CONSIDERATIONS RELEVANT TO OTHER WORKERS

Personal-service workers (PSWs). PSWs are defined as individuals whose occupations involve close personal contact with clients (e.g., hairdressers, barbers, estheticians, cosmetologists, manicurists, pedicurists, massage therapists). PSWs whose services (tattooing, ear piercing, acupuncture, etc.) require needles or other instruments that penetrate the skin should follow precautions indicated for HCWs. Although there is no evidence of transmission of HTLV-III/LAV from clients to PSWs, from PSWs to clients, or between clients of PSWs, a risk of transmission would exist from PSWs to clients and vice versa in situations where there is both (1) trauma to one of the individuals that would provide a portal of entry for the virus and (2) access of blood or serous fluid from one infected person to the open tissue of the other, as could occur if either sustained a cut. A risk of transmission from client to client exists when instruments contaminated with blood are not sterilized or disinfected between clients. However, HBV transmission has been documented only rarely in acupuncture, ear piercing, and tattoo establishments and never in other personal-service settings, indicating that any risk for HTLV-III/LAV transmission in personal-service settings must be extremely low.

All PSWs should be educated about transmission of bloodborne infections, including HTLV-III/LAV and HBV. Such education should emphasize principles of good hygiene, antisepsis, and disinfection. This education can be accomplished by national or state professional organizations, with assistance from state and local health departments, using lectures at meetings or self-instructional materials. Licensure requirements should include evidence of such education. Instruments that are intended to penetrate the skin (e.g., tattooing and acupuncture needles, ear piercing devices) should be used once and disposed of or be thoroughly cleaned and sterilized after each use using procedures recommended for use in health-care institutions. Instruments not intended to penetrate the skin but which may become contaminated with blood (e.g., razors), should be used for only one client and be disposed of or thoroughly cleaned and disinfected after use using procedures recommended for use in health-care institutions. Any PSW with exudative lesions or weeping dermatitis, regardless of HTLV-III/LAV infection status, should refrain from direct contact with clients until the condition resolves. PSWs known to be infected with HTLV-III/LAV need not be restricted from work unless they have evidence of other infections or illnesses for which any PSW should also be restricted.

Routine serologic testing of PSWs for antibody to HTLV-III/LAV is not recommended to prevent transmission from PSWs to clients.

Food-service workers (FSWs). FSWs are defined as individuals whose occupations involve the preparation or serving of food or beverages (e.g., cooks, caterers, servers, waiters, bartenders, airline attendants). All epidemiologic and laboratory evidence indicates that bloodborne and sexually transmitted infections are not transmitted during the preparation or serving of food or beverages, and no instances of HBV or HTLV-III/LAV transmission have been documented in this setting.

All FSWs should follow recommended standards and practices of good personal hygiene and food sanitation (*26*). All FSWs should exercise care to avoid injury to hands when preparing food. Should such an injury occur, both aesthetic and sanitary considerations would dictate that food contaminated with blood be discarded. FSWs known to be infected with HTLV-III/LAV need not be restricted from work unless they have evidence of other infection or illness for which any FSW should also be restricted.

HTLV-III/LAV — Continued

Routine serologic testing of FSWs for antibody to HTLV-III/LAV is not recommended to prevent disease transmission from FSWs to consumers.

Other workers sharing the same work environment. No known risk of transmission to co-workers, clients, or consumers exists from HTLV-III/LAV-infected workers in other settings (e.g., offices, schools, factories, construction sites). This infection is spread by sexual contact with infected persons, injection of contaminated blood or blood products, and by perinatal transmission. Workers known to be infected with HTLV-III/LAV should not be restricted from work solely based on this finding. Moreover, they should not be restricted from using telephones, office equipment, toilets, showers, eating facilities, and water fountains. Equipment contaminated with blood or other body fluids of any worker, regardless of HTLV-III/LAV infection status, should be cleaned with soap and water or a detergent. A disinfectant solution or a fresh solution of sodium hypochlorite (household bleach, see above) should be used to wipe the area after cleaning.

OTHER ISSUES IN THE WORKPLACE

The information and recommendations contained in this document do not address all the potential issues that may have to be considered when making specific employment decisions for persons with HTLV-III/LAV infection. The diagnosis of HTLV-III/LAV infection may evoke unwarranted fear and suspicion in some co-workers. Other issues that may be considered include the need for confidentiality, applicable federal, state, or local laws governing occupational safety and health, civil rights of employees, workers' compensation laws, provisions of collective bargaining agreements, confidentiality of medical records, informed consent, employee and patient privacy rights, and employee right-to-know statutes.

DEVELOPMENT OF THESE RECOMMENDATIONS

The information and recommendations contained in these recommendations were developed and compiled by CDC and other PHS agencies in consultation with individuals representing various organizations. The following organizations were represented: Association of State and Territorial Health Officials, Conference of State and Territorial Epidemiologists, Association of State and Territorial Public Health Laboratory Directors, National Association of County Health Officials, American Hospital Association, United States Conference of Local Health Officers, Association for Practitioners in Infection Control, Society of Hospital Epidemiologists of America, American Dental Association, American Medical Association, American Nurses' Association, American Association of Medical Colleges; American Association of Dental Schools, National Institutes of Health, Food and Drug Administration, Food Research Institute, National Restaurant Association, National Hairdressers and Cosmetologists Association, National Gay Task Force, National Funeral Directors and Morticians Association, American Association of Physicians for Human Rights, and National Association of Emergency Medical Technicians. The consultants also included a labor union representative, an attorney, a corporate medical director, and a pathologist. However, these recommendations may not reflect the views of individual consultants or the organizations they represented.

References
1. CDC. Acquired immune deficiency syndrome (AIDS): precautions for clinical and laboratory staffs. MMWR 1982;31:577-80.
2. CDC. Acquired immunodeficiency syndrome (AIDS): precautions for health-care workers and allied professionals. MMWR 1983;32:450-1.
3. CDC. Education and foster care of children infected with human T-lymphotropic virus type III/lymphadenopathy-associated virus. MMWR 1985;34:517-21.
4. CDC. Revision of the case definition of acquired immunodeficiency syndrome for national reporting—United States. MMWR 1985;34:373-5.

HTLV-III/LAV — Continued

5. CDC. ACIP recommendations for protection against viral hepatitis. MMWR 1985;34:313-24, 329-335.

6. Hadler SC, Doto IL, Maynard JE, et al. Occupational risk of hepatitis B infection in hospital workers Infect Control 1985;6:24-31.

7. Dienstag JL, Ryan DM. Occupational exposure to hepatitis B virus in hospital personnel: infection or immunization? Am J Epidemiol 1982;115:26-39.

8. Pattison CP, Maynard JE, Berquist KR, et al. Epidemiology of hepatitis B in hospital personnel. Am J Epidemiol 1975;101:59-64.

9. Kane MA, Lettau LA. Transmission of HBV from dental personnel to patients. JADA 1985;110: 634-6.

10. Hadler SC, Sorley DL, Acree KH, et al. An outbreak of hepatitis B in a dental practice. Ann Intern Med 1981;95:133-8.

11. Carl M, Blakey DL, Francis DP, Maynard JE. Interruption of hepatitis B transmission by modification of a gynaecologist's surgical technique. Lancet 1982;i:731-3.

12. Seeff LB, Wright EC, Zimmerman HJ, et al. Type B hepatitis after needlestick exposure: prevention with hepatitis B immune globulin. Ann Intern Med 1978;88:285-93.

13. Grady GF, Lee VA, Prince AM, et al. Hepatitis B immune globulin for accidental exposures among medical personnel: Final report of a multicenter controlled trial. J Infect Dis 1978;138:625-38.

14. Shikata T, Karasawa T, Abe K, et al. Hepatitis B e antigen and infectivity of hepatitis B virus. J Infect Dis 1977;136:571-6.

15. CDC. Update: evaluation of human T-lymphotropic virus type III/lymphadenopathy-associated virus infection in health-care personnel — United States. MMWR 1985;34:575-8.

16. Weiss SH, Saxinger WC, Rechtman D, et al. HTLV-III infection among health care workers: association with needle-stick injuries. JAMA 1985;254:2089-93.

17. Anonymous. Needlestick transmission of HTLV-III from a patient infected in Africa. Lancet 1984;ii:1376-7.

18. Garner JS, Simmons BP. Guideline for isolation precautions in hospitals. Infect Control 1983;4: 245-325.

19. Williams WW. Guideline for infection control in hospital personnel. Infect Control 1983;4:326-49.

20. CDC. Prevention of acquired immune deficiency syndrome (AIDS): report of inter-agency recommendations. MMWR 1983;32:101-3.

21. CDC. Provisional Public Health Service inter-agency recommendations for screening donated blood and plasma for antibody to the virus causing acquired immunodeficiency syndrome. MMWR 1985;34:1-5.

22. Favero MS. Sterilization, disinfection, and antisepsis in the hospital. In: Manual of Clinical Microbiology. 4th ed. Washington, D.C.: American Society for Microbiology, 1985;129-37.

23. Garner JS, Favero MS. Guideline for handwashing and hospital environmental control, 1985. Atlanta Georgia: Centers for Disease Control, 1985. Publication no. 99-1117.

24. Kneedler JA, Dodge GH. Perioperative patient care. Boston: Blackwell Scientific Publications, 1983: 210-1.

25. Martin LS, McDougal JS, Loskoski SL. Disinfection and inactivation of the human T-lymphotropic virus type III/lymphadenopathy-associated virus. J Infect Dis 1985;152:400-3.

26. Food Service Sanitation Manual 1976. DHEW publication no. (FDA) 78-2081. First printing June 1978.

FAIR HOUSING LAW AND PRACTICE

Holly D. Ladd

Just as AIDS has no sexual or racial preference, it also is without economic preference. As more of our clients with ARC/AIDS, and those perceived to be at risk for contagion, experience rejection in their own communities and by society in general, their access to a home will be increasingly jeopardized. This will be true whether our clients rent expensive apartments or are residents of public housing. Housing should not be viewed as only an economic issue, but as a major civil rights issue as well.

Fair housing laws have promised homeseekers the right to live where they choose, but shootouts in Cleveland and marches in Forsyth County, Georgia serve as painful reminders of how little progress we have made since the enactment of the Fair Housing provision of the 1968 Civil Rights Act (Title VIII). Litigation to enforce fair housing laws has been fairly infrequent. More active advocacy by civil rights lawyers is needed to make the promise more of a reality.

The advocacy and enforcement of fair housing laws for our clients, however, may mean the difference between their ability to stay in their homes while they are well enough to do so and their forced eviction. Filing complaints with local enforcement agencies may halt an eviction or get utilities turned back on when landlords harass people with AIDS or people perceived to be at risk. While there are limits on the amount of damage awards, in most statutes or ordinances there are important reasons to pursue fair housing actions, if only to commit local political officials to support the rights of people with AIDS and send a message to the local real estate community.

Holly D. Ladd is General Council of the Boston Fair Housing Commission and the Chair of the Board of the Fenway Community Health Center in Boston (a gay and lesbian health center that serves many people with ARC/ AIDS and related medical problems).

I. CIVIL RIGHTS LEGISLATION

A. GENERAL APPLICABILITY OF CIVIL RIGHTS LAWS

State and local civil rights laws which cover housing are modeled on Title VIII of the Civil Rights Act of 1968. (See list of state and local laws accompanying this article.) Title VIII does not currently include the physically or mentally disabled as a protected class (but see the discussion of section 504 below). Most states and municipalities, however, do include protections for the disabled in their legislation.

The U.S. Congress has attempted to pass amendments to the fair housing law which would add handicapped to the list of protected groups. Such legislation is currently pending in both the House and the Senate, and adding this protection should be a vital concern. While most of the debate so far has been focused on the enforcement provisions, we should anticipate that more conservative members of Congress will challenge the handicap provision in response to the Supreme Court's decision in School Board of Nassau County v. Arline, 106 S.Ct. 1633 (1987), holding that discrimination based on fears of the contagious effects of a physical impairment was prohibited by section 504 of the Federal Rehabilitation Act of 1973.

As a result of the Supreme Court decision in Arline, protections contained in fair housing laws for disabled or handicapped persons should be read to include people with AIDS/ARC and those perceived to have the disease. In addition, some local ordinances and the State of Wisconsin include protections from discrimination based upon sexual orientation. Finally, some local ordinances are being amended to explicitly prevent discrimination on the basis of AIDS.

This review will address fair housing law as it relates to handicap and disability, presuming that most AIDS-related discrimination cases will be filed on that basis. However, there may be some instances where it is as, or more, appropriate to file under sexual orientation provisions or those concerning special AIDS related protections. In general, most of the procedural issues will be the same. Since this is an overview, the practitioner must consider this as only a guide and must consult applicable local law.

The seriousness of these cases cannot be overestimated. They range from harassment to actual threats on the lives of our clients. This past summer, a young gay man was ordered to move out of the room he rented in a rooming house in a Boston neighborhood. He was told by his landlady that other tenants had complained they were afraid of contracting AIDS from him if he were allowed to continue living in the building. He filed a complaint with the Boston Fair Housing Commission against the landlady and against one of the other tenants for interfering with his right to remain in the building. The case was successfully resolved; the young man got a cash settlement and the landlady made an additional contribution to a local AIDS organization. However, because of the ill will that had developed, the young man decided to move out of the rooming house.

The New York City Human Rights Commission has received numerous complaints from people with AIDS whose landlords have turned off their heat and tap water knowing they were ill in an attempt to harass them out of their units. These cases generally fall under the "discrimination in the terms and conditions" provisions of most fair housing laws and may also be enjoined as attempts at constructive evictions. In one particularly egregious case, a person with AIDS was actually threatened at knife-point by his landlord, who then told police not to believe the tenant because he was nothing but a "faggot with AIDS."

While the primary focus of activity in the area of AIDS discrimination has been in employment and insurance benefits, civil rights agencies in San Francisco, New York and Boston have seen an increase in the number of AIDS related housing discrimination cases in 1986-1987. In 1985, the New York City Human Rights Commission received 96 complaints of discrimination in the areas of housing and public accommodations. In 1986, the Commission received 314 complaints. In the period from 1985 through 1986, the San Francisco Commission received 20 housing discrimination complaints. Many of the calls agencies receive from people with ARC/AIDS involve the inability to continue to pay for housing, though the level of direct discrimination is on the increase.

People are denied housing opportunities or evicted as a direct result of the AIDS crisis. In New York City, cases growing from neighborhood panic, such as the case discussed above, were more common two or three years ago. Areas such as Boston, which have fewer reported cases of AIDS than New York and San Francisco, are only now catching up in the kind and level of discrimination experienced. One focus of case activity in New York has concerned the rights of surviving life partners to retain apartments and the more generalized discrimination against two men renting together. Like the case in Boston, persons denied housing may not even have AIDS, but because they are gay they are perceived as a potential threat by others.

B. PRIVATE HOUSING

In general, the rental of privately owned apartments and the sale of private dwellings are covered by federal, state and local fair housing laws (of which only state and local laws currently cover the handicapped). Exemptions from coverage are usually related to the presence of an owner-occupant and the number of units in an owner-occupied building. These are not the only exemptions, however, so the practitioner should check applicable local law. The most common exemptions are for rooms rented in an owner-occupied single family home or for an owner-occupied building with fewer than two to four units. Local ordinances usually have fewer exemptions than state law. Many statutes exempt housing that is owned by non-profit, religious or fraternal organizations.

C. PUBLIC HOUSING

In addition to Title VIII and/or state fair housing laws, any housing which receives federal financial assistance is also covered by another federal civil right statute, section 504 of the Rehabilitation Act of 1973. This law deals with discrimination on the basis of handicap and provides, in part, that:

> [n]o otherwise qualified handicapped individual in the United States ... shall, solely by reason of his handicap, be excluded from participation in, be denied the benefit of, or be subjected to discrimination under any program or activity

receiving Federal financial assistance. 29 U.S.C. sec. 794 (1973)(emphasis added).

While mandated by Executive Order 11914 in 1974 to develop regulations for the implementation of section 504 in the area of housing, the U.S. Department of Housing and Urban Development has yet to do so. The Department proposed regulations in 1978 modeled on those adopted by the Department of Health, Education and Welfare, but they were dropped in response to a flood of comments. See 43 Fed. Reg. 16,6652 (proposed April 19, 1978). In 1983, HUD tried again to issue "interim rules" establishing procedures and policies for the implementation of section 504, but revoked the publication in order to allow 'additional comment.' 48 Fed. Reg. 27,528(proposed June 15, 1983). Because there are no rules for implementation, HUD continues to utilize the definitions adopted by Health and Human Services. Both the draft regulations and the draft interim rules provide some clue to HUD's thinking on the issue of handicap access to federally funded housing, but neither are controlling.

HUD regional offices will accept and investigate complaints of discrimination in housing under section 504 in addition to Title VIII. This may be important for our clients who qualify for housing subsidies or public housing placement, including local public housing, federally subsidized housing certificates or voucher programs (under section 8 of the Housing and Community Redevelopment Act of 1974), and HUD assisted housing that may be privately owned but built with federal money or HUD loan or mortgage guarantees. Complaints should be filed with the HUD office, although experience shows that these cases should be filed in court as well.

D. DEFINITIONS

As you will note in reviewing the attached list of state and local laws, there are several different ways to include the disabled in the scope of protections provided by the various laws. The most common statement of the protection is "physical handicap." However, the laws include: physical disability, mental or physical disability, disability, handicap, and physical or mental impairment. The Washington, D.C. ordinance, for example, states physical handicap as the protected basis, but it defines it to include "bodily or mental disablement." The inclusion of mental disability may become an important issue, depending upon how dementia related to HIV infection is defined. Few statutes provide definitions, and not all regulations provide further

definition. Phone numbers of the agencies have been provided in order to help you obtain copies of the regulations.

The Supreme Court has resolved the question of the inclusion of a contagious disease in the definition of handicap under section 504. However, Georgia and Kentucky specifically exclude contagious diseases from coverage under their statues. Ga. Code Ann. sec. 34-6a-3(b); Ky. Rev. Stat. Ann. sec. 207.140(a)(c).

New York City's Administrative Code sec. B1-2.0(16)(a) (Human Rights Ordinance) does not explicitly include those who are "regarded as having ... impairment" as do certain federal programs. See 29 U.S.C. sec. 706(8)(B) (USCA Supp. 1987). This inclusion is important to protect people who are not diagnosed with AIDS, but who are discriminated against because they are perceived as being at risk for the disease. The New York City Human Rights Commission will, however, interpret the City's handicap protection to include those perceived as being handicapped. Many other jurisdictions may also extend the coverage beyond those who are actually diagnosed to those who are perceived as handicapped, following the language of section 504. See, for example, Dairy Equipment Co. v. Dept. of Industry, Labor & Human Resources, 95 Wis.2d 319, 290 N.W.2d 330 (1980), which held that an employee with one kidney who suffered no functional limitation was protected under state law despite lack of explicit reference to "perceived" handicap. The language of the court in the this case is helpful in this regard:

> It would be both ironic and insidious if the legislative intent in providing the protection of the [Wisconsin] Fair Employment Act were afforded to persons who actually have a handicap that ... limits their capacity to work, but the same protection is denied to those whom employers perceive as being handicapped. 290 N.W.2d at 335.

The practitioner may have to encourage the local agency to give its law the broad construction normally accorded civil rights legislation.

E. REASONABLE ACCOMMODATION

Under section 504, it is incumbent upon the defendant to prove that he or she is unable to make reasonable accommodation for the disabled individual. (Mantolete v. Bolger, 767 F.2d 1416, 1423 (5th Cir. 1985); Doe v. NYU, 666 F.2d

761, 776 (2d Cir. 1981); New York State Association for Retarded Children v.Carey, 512 F.2d 644, 649 (2d Cir. 1979)). Several states have included language specifically stating that a landlord need not make any physical modifications in or on the property to accommodate a disabled tenant.

F. ZONING

As AIDS continues to strike greater numbers of people, the need for alternative housing options will also increase. Organizations which decide to operate homes to accommodate people with AIDS may face opposition from the neighborhood residents who fear contagion or who are motivated out of a desire to discriminate against gay people or people with AIDS. In Jackson, Mississippi, for example, residents vowed to fight approval by the Mayor of a proposal for the operation of a boarding house in a city neighborhood for persons with AIDS. BNA, AIDS Policy & Law, Dec. 31, 1986.

Opposition to residences for the physically or mentally disabled has led to a good deal of litigation on equal protection grounds. See, e.g., City of Cleburne, Texas v. Cleburne Living Center, 473 U.S. ___, 105 S.Ct. 3249 (1985)(home for mentally retarded); Sullivan v. City of Pittsburgh, 617 F.Supp. 1488 (D.Pa 1985)(neighborhood fears and opposition cannot be the basis for local zoning decisions affecting group residences for home and treatment programs for recovering alcoholics). Zoning ordinances which attempt to exclude handicapped persons must be shown to meet legitimate governmental concerns although, with regard to the mentally retarded, the Supreme Court in Cleburne would not apply a "heightened scrutiny" standard. The Court stated that since the retarded "have a reduced capacity to cope with and function in the everyday world" they would not be accorded special consideration under the equal protection clause. The Court then employed the rational basis test in overturning the zoning ordinance.

Civil rights statutes are also useful in dealing with zoning issues. For example, relying upon 42 U.S.C. sec. 1985(3) and the New York Human Rights Act, the Second Circuit upheld the claim of residents of a home for the mentally retarded that a neighborhood group's purchase of a home that they sought to buy, in order to block the plaintiffs' purchase, was illegally motivated. People by Abrams v. 11 Cornwell Co., 695 F.2d 287 (3d Cir. 1984).

G. SOURCE OF INCOME

A few state and local fair housing laws also provide protection on the basis of source of income or receipt of public benefits. (E.g., Mass. Gen. Law ch. 151B; Boston Fair Housing Ordinance; and the Cambridge Human Rights Ordinance). This is an important addition to the traditional bases of protection because landlords often will refuse to rent to a tenant because of race, for example, but say that they do not want to accept the tenant because that person receives a housing subsidy. AIDS clients who receive SSI or some other form of support may find a landlord unwilling to rent to them, or eager to evict them because they are no longer employed. The defense of an unacceptable source of income is often a pretext for prohibited, discriminatory exclusion.

H. FILING COMPLAINTS

Another area where state and local laws may differ is in the type of case that an agency is prepared to handle. This may be related to the size and resources of the agency. Normally, AIDS related housing discrimination cases will be filed by the individual, so it is important to determine the appropriate forum in order to maximize your client's opportunity to recover damages.

Most agencies will accept complaints from individuals or those filed on behalf of individuals and will investigate and resolve the cases from the position of a fact finder. Following Title VIII, most fair housing laws require the agencies to attempt to conciliate cases after a finding of probable cause and will either order or suggest an award of damages to the complainant upon a finding or after a hearing. A few jurisdictions will only consider cases upon an allegation of a pattern or practice of discrimination (systemic cases). This generally requires repeated instances of discrimination or the consistent application of a policy that has a discriminatory effect. The agency then may choose to file the case itself and proceed as the complainant.

As with employment discrimination, most jurisdictions have a 180-day statute of limitations for filing with the agency. However, some jurisdictions have a 120-day statute of limitations for filing.

I. PROOF AND INTENT

Fair housing, as compared to equal employment, is a rather underdeveloped area of civil rights law. Few cases exist which address the area of handicapped discrimination in housing under most state statutes or federal law. Where cases do exist, they usually involve questions of zoning and site selection. It is common, therefore, in fair housing cases to look to equal employment cases for both definition and precedent. Some states, however, differ in the definitions of handicap between the employment and public accommodations sections of the statute and the housing sections. For example, Mass. Gen. Laws ch. 1518 provides protection for handicap in employment and public accommodations, but limits the protections in housing to the blind and hearing impaired.

Important differences do exist between housing and employment discrimination and other civil rights laws which work to the advantage of the housing plaintiff. As with employment law, a prima facie case presented by the plaintiff includes the availability of the housing, the qualification of the plaintiff, the membership of the plaintiff in a protected class, the denial of housing and the subsequent continued availability or occupancy of the housing to or by a person who is not a member of the protected class.

The plaintiff need not establish intent in the same manner as an equal protection claim, however, but can rely upon the effect or impact of a policy or practice. Betsey v. Turtle Creek Associates, 736 F.2d 983 (4th Cir. 1984). The plaintiff in a fair housing case does not need to prove that discriminatory intent was the only or even the prevailing consideration. Smith v. Sol D. Adler Realty Co., 436 F.2d 344 (7th Cir. 1970). Plaintiffs need only show that their membership in a protected class was a factor in the denial of housing. Kaplan v. 442 Willington Co-op Bldg. Corp., 567 F.Supp. 53, 57 (N.D. Ill. 1983; plaintiffs must show that race played "some part, be it ever so small," in defendant's refusal to deal).

J. REMEDIES AND ENFORCEMENT

The issue of remedies in fair housing cases is unresolved. Most state statutes and some local ordinances give the agencies the power to enter cease and desist orders. In housing cases, it is important to seek temporary restraining orders or preliminary injunctions to prevent evictions or to keep units in dispute from being rented or sold to third parties. This is a step complainants may have to take themselves in addition to filing with the agency.

The practice of consolidating the preliminary injunction hearing with the trial on the merits is common in federal fair housing cases. Upon a finding of probable cause, the agency will attempt to conciliate the case. Conciliation agreements often include provisions for damages in addition to agreements to rent or sell the disputed unit to the complainant, or not evict the complainant. Most statutes limit the amount an agency can award in damages at hearing. For example, the Massachusetts Commission Against Discrimination is limited to $2,000 per violation.

The area that is unresolved is the amount of damages one can receive in a court action or from a local agency which has no power to enforce in its ordinance. Until recently, court awards for damages in fair housing cases have been relatively low, usually only slightly more than the agency was able to award. Currently, relying on theories of constitutional torts, emotional distress, and dignitory torts, plaintiffs have been recovering damages in the $100,000 to $300,000 range. Court awards in this area are expected to continue to grow.

Practitioners sometimes avoid local agencies because the agency may not have the ability to enforce their orders in court. While that is true of the Boston Fair Housing Commission, for example, cases conciliated by it have compared favorably with the amount of settlements obtained by the state agency. Because there is no statutory limit on damages, which tends to keep settlement offers low, that agency was able to conciliate one case with settlements of over $5,000 for each of three complainants. Local agencies which have reputations for quality investigations and which can complete work quickly are usually able to obtain relief from landlords. In addition, there may be important political reasons for our clients' obtaining an opinion from, if not the support of, the municipality. And, as apparent from the list of state and local fair housing laws, in some jurisdictions there may be no alternative to the local agency. With the exception of Wisconsin, only local agencies offer protection from discrimination based upon sexual preference. Finally, where an agency either has added AIDS as a protected basis or has announced its intention to include AIDS as a protected basis under its definition of handicap, it would be the forum of choice. It is good practice in fair housing cases to file under as many bases and with as many agencies as applicable for your client.

II. RESOURCES

In addition to the telephone link to the many gay and/or AIDS civil rights organizations nationally and to the agencies listed below, you may want to check out the following publications:

Housing Discrimination Law, Robert Schwemm, Bureau of National Affairs, Inc., 1983;

Housing Discrimination Law Supplement, Robert Schwemm, Bureau of National Affairs, Inc., 1986;

Fair Housing, Discrimination in Real Estate, Community Development and Revitalization, James A. Kushner, Shepard's/McGraw-Hill, Colorado Springs, 1983 (with annual supplement);

Fair Housing - Fair Lending, Prentice-Hall, Inc., Englewood Cliffs, N.J., (reporter series);

Directory of State and Local Fair Housing Agencies, U.S. Commission on Civil Rights, Clearinghouse Publication 86, March 1985;

AIDS Policy & Law, Buraff Publications, Inc., Bureau of National Affairs, Inc. Washington, D.C. (bi-weekly publication).

This author relied as well on a memorandum of law provided by the New York City Human Rights Commission, drafted by the office of the Corporation Counsel for New York City examining the applicability of the U.S. Justice Department's Memorandum on AIDS-Related Discrimination, dated July 25, 1986.

Appendices

Appendix A: The following is a compilation of local and state fair housing laws and/or human rights agencies that have been recognized as substantially equivalent to HUD in the types of protections and procedures that they offer to enforce fair housing laws. In every case, they exceed the protections provided by HUD under Title VIII, for the protection of housing rights of persons with AIDS or who are discriminated against because of AIDS related factors. There are a few agencies listed that have not yet been granted the equivalency status, but have been included because they prohibit discrimination on the basis of sexual orientation.

This list may not be complete and agencies that have not been included may want to write to the author so that they may be included in future updates.

Appendix B: A comparison of state and local enabling legislation and Title VIII prepared by legal counsel to HUD.

AGENCY	PROTECTION PROVIDED
Alaska Anchorage Equal Rights Comm'n (907) 264-4342 Ordinance, ch. 5.10-5.30	Provides protection for those discriminated against on the basis of physical handicap.
California	See California Civil code sec. 54.1 et seq. -- Blind and Other Physical Handicapped -- Rights Concerning Housing Accommodations. Provides protection against discrimination in housing based upon physical handicap. Also, five counties and the Cities of Los Angeles, Hollywood and West Hollywood have adopted ordinances specifically preventing discrimination based upon AIDS. These counties include: Sonoma, San Mateo, Riverside, San Luis Obispo.
San Francisco Human Rights	Provides protection from discrimination based upon physical handicap and sexual orientation, and AIDS (prohibits discrimination against persons with AIDS, a related medical condition, or those perceived as having AIDS).
Colorado Civil Rights Comm'n (303) 866-4170 Colo. Rev. Stat. sec. 24-34-301 Conn. Gen. Stat. Ann. sec. 46a-51 et seq.	Provides protection based upon handicap.
Connecticut State Comm'n on Human Rights & Opportunities (203) 566-5423 Conn. Gen. Stat. Ann. sec. 46a-51 et seq. sec. 47a-2a	Provides protection on the basis of physical disability which as defined "includes but [is] not limited to chronic physical handicap, infirmity, or impairment whether congenital or as a result of bodily injury or organic process, change from illness, epilepsy, deafness or hearing impairment."
New Haven Equal Opportunity Comm'n (203) 787-8163 Ordinance, ch. 12 1/2	Provides protection on the basis of physical or mental disability.
Delaware Division of Human Relations Comm'n (302) 571-3485 Del. Code Ann., Title 6, ch. 46	Provides protections based upon handicap which it defines as physical or mental impairment.
District of Columbia Office of Human Rights (202) 727-3100 D.C. Code, Title 1, sec. 2501 et seq.	Provides protection on the basis of sexual orientation and physical handicap, defined as "bodily or mental disablement as a result of injury, illness, or congenital condition for which reasonable accommodation can be made."
Florida Clearwater Office of Community Relations (813) 462-6884 Code of Ord., ch. 78	Provides protection on the basis of handicap.

Dade County Fair Housing and Employment Appeals Board (305) 547-7840 Dade County Code, ch. 11A	Provides protection on the basis of physical handicap.
Excambia-Pensacola Human Relations Comm'n (904) 434-2431 City Code, ch. 80, art. II	Provides protection on the basis of physical disability.
St. Petersburg Human Relations Dep't (813) 893-7345 Ord. No. 466-F, ch. 12 1/2	Provides protection on the basis of handicap.
Hawaii Regulated Industries Complaints Office (808) 548-7640 Rev. Stat. sec. 515-1 et seq.	Provides protection on the basis of physical handicap.
Illinois Dep't of Human Rights (312) 793-6221 Ann. Stat., ch. 68, sec. 1-101, et seq.	Provides protection on the basis of physical or mental disability.
Bloomington Human Relations Comm'n (309) 828-7361 City Ordinance, ch. 22.2	Provides protection on the basis of physical or mental handicap (unrelated to ability).
Evanston Human Relations Commission (312) 323-2100 ch. 5, sec. 5-5-1 et seq.	Provides protection on the basis of sexual orientation.
Springfield Fair Housing Board (217) 789-2270 City Code, sec. 31.55-31.60 and sec. 2.45.70-2.435.72	Provides protection on the basis of physical or mental handicap.
Urbana Human Relations Comm'n (217) 384-2460 City Code sec. 2.68a as amended by Ordinance No. 7879-92	Provides protection on the basis of physical or mental handicap.
Indiana Civil Rights Comm'n (317) 232-2600 Ind. Code sec. 22-9-1 et seq.	Provides protection on the basis of handicap (a mental or physical disability).
Columbus Human Rights Comm'n (812) 376-2532 Ord. No. 2663 (1978)	Provides protection on the basis of mental or physical disability. (To be classified as disabled under Columbus law, a person must be certified as such by the Indiana Rehabilitation Services Board).
East Chicago Human Rights Comm'n (219) 392-8236 Ord. No. 3286	Provides protection on the basis of handicap (a physical or mental disability).

Fort Wayne Metropolitan
Human Relations Comm'n
(219) 427-1146
Gen Ord. No. G 21-78

Provides protection on the basis of handicap (a physical or mental disability).

Gary Human Relations Comm'n
(219) 883-4151 or (219) 882-0100
Civil Rights Ord., Title VII

Provides protection on the basis of physical or mental disability.

South Bend Human Rights Comm'n
(219) 284-9355
Municipal Code, ch. 2, art. IX, sec. 2-126-2-136

Provides protection on the basis of physical or mental handicap.

Iowa Civil Rights Comm'n
(515) 281-4121
Iowa Code, sec. 601A.1 et seq.

Provides protection on the basis of disability (a mental or physical condition that constitutes a substantial handicap).

Iowa City Human Rights Comm'n
(319) 356-5022
Code of Ord., ch. 18

Provides protection on the basis of sexual orientation.

Kansas Kansas City Human Relations Dep't
(913) 573-5460
Code of Ord., ch.11

Provides protection on the basis of physical handicap.

Salina Human Relations Comm'n and Dep't
(913) 823-2792
Ord. ch. 13

Provides protection on the basis of physical handicap.

Wichita Citizen Rights and Services Board
(316) 268-4488
City Code, sec. 2.12.900-2.12.955

Provides protection on the basis of physical handicap.

Kentucky
Lexington-Fayette Urban County
Human Rights Comm'n
(606) 252-4931
Code of Ord., ch. 2, art. II, sec. 2-45

Provides protection on the basis of physical handicap.

Maine Human Rights Comm'n
Me. Rev. Stat. Ann. Tit. 5
(207) 289-2326, sec. 4551 et seq.
and Tit. 14, sec. 6027

Provides protection on the basis of physical or mental handicap.

Maryland Comm'n on Human Relations
(301) 659-1744 or (301) 659-1715
Md. Code Ann., art. 49B, sec. 1-30

Provides protection on the basis of physical or mental disability.

Howard County Human Rights Comm'n
and Office of Human Rights
(301) 992-2162 or (301) 992-2163
County Code, sec. 12.200 et seq.

Provides protection on the basis of physical or mental handicap and sexual orientation

Montgomery County Human Relations Comm'n (301) 468-4260 County Code, ch. 27, art. I	Provides protection on the basis of handicap (physical, mental or emotional impairment) and sexual orientation.
Prince George's County Human Relations Comm'n (301) 952-3070 County Code, Div. 12, sec. 2-185 et seq.	Provides protection on the basis of physical or mental disability.
Massachusetts Boston Fair Housing Comm'n (617) 725-4408 City Code, Ord., Title 10, ch.5	Provides protection on the basis of handicap and sexual preference.
Cambridge Human Rights Comm'n (617) 498-9000 Cambridge Human Ordinance	Provides protection on the basis of handicap.
Somerville Fair Housing (617) 625-6600 Somerville Fair Housing Ord.	Provides protection on the basis of handicap.
Michigan Dep't of Civil Rights (313) 256-2643 Mich. Comp. Laws Ann., sec. 37.2101 et seq.	Provides protection on the basis of physical or mental disability.
Minnesota Dep't of Human Rights (612) 296-5676 or (612) 296-5663 Minn. Stat. Ann., sec. 363.01 et seq.	Provides protection on the basis of physical or mental disability.
Minneapolis Dep't of Civil Rights (612) 348-7736 Code of Ord., Title 7, ch. 139 and ch. 141	Provides protection on the basis of disability or affectional preference.
Saint Paul Dep't of Human Rights (612) 298-4288 Ord. No. 13706, as amended, Leg. Code sec. 183.01 et seq.	Provides protection on the basis of physical or mental disability.
Missouri Comm'n on Human Rights (314) 751-3325 Mo. Ann. Stat., sec. 213.100 et seq.	Provides protection on the basis of physical or mental disability.
Kansas City Dep't of Human Relations (816) 274-1432 Code of Gen. Ord., art. IX, sec. 26.201 et seq.	Provides protection on the basis of physical or mental disability.
Montana Human Rights Comm'n (406) 444-2884 Mont. Code Ann., sec. 49-1-101 et seq.	Provides protection on the basis of physical or mental disability.
Nebraska Lincoln Comm'n on Human Rights (402) 471-7624 Mun. Code, title 11	Provides protection on the basis of physical or mental disability.

Omaha Human Relations Dep't (402) 444-5050 Omaha Code, art. III, sec. 13-81 et seq.	Provides protection on the basis of physical or mental disability.
New Hampshire Comm'n for Human Rights (603) 271-2767 N.H. Rev. Stat. Ann., sec. 354.A:1 et seq.	Provides protection on the basis of physical or mental disability.
New Jersey Dep't of Law and Public Safety Division on Civil Rights (201) 648-2700 N.J. Stat. Ann., sec. 10:5-1 et seq.	Provides protection on the basis of physical or mental disability.
New Mexico Human Rights Comm'n (505) 827-6420 N.M. Stat. Ann., sec. 4-33-1 et seq.	Provides protection on the basis of physical or mental disability.
New York State Division of Human Rights (202) 488-5750 N.Y. Exec. Law, sec. 290 et seq.	Provides protection on the basis of physical or mental disability.
City of New York Comm'n on Human Rights (212) 233-3984 Admin. Code, ch. I, titles B and C	Provides protection on the basis of physical disability and sexual orientation.
Ohio Civil Rights Comm'n (614) 446-2785 Ohio Rev. Code Ann., sec. 4112.01 et seq.	Provides protection on the basis of disability.
Montgomery County Fair Housing Center (513) 228-8991 Ord. sec. 32.01 et seq.	Provides protection on the basis of physical disability.
Oregon Bureau of Labor and Industries (503) 229-5900 Or. Rev. Stat., sec. 659.010 et seq.	Provides protection on the basis of physical or mental disability.
Pennsylvania Human Relations Comm'n (717) 787-4410 Pa. Stat. Ann.. sec. 951 et seq.	Provides protection on the basis of handicap or disability.
Harrisburg Human Relations Comm'n (717) 255-3087 Ord. part 7, art. 725	Provides protection on the basis of handicap or disability.
Philadelphia Comm'n on Human Relations (215) 686-4670 Code, ch. 9-1100	Provides protection on the basis of physical disability.
Pittsburgh Comm'n on Human Relations (412) 255-2600 Code ch. 651-659	Provides protection on the basis of handicap or disability.

York City Human Relations Comm'n (717) 846-2926 Code, arts. 183 and 185	Provides protection on the basis of handicap or disability.
Rhode Island Comm'n for Human Rights (401) 277-2661 R.I. Gen. Laws, sec, 34-37-1 et seq.	Provides protection on the basis of physical disability.
South Dakota Sioux Falls Human Relations Comm'n (605) 339-7039 Code, ch. 13	Provides protection on the basis of physical, mental or social disability.
Texas Austin Human Relations Comm'n	Prohibits use of AIDS-related factors in real estate or housing transactions.
Virginia Real Estate Board, Attn: Fair Housing Section 1-800-552-3016	Provides protection on the basis of handicap.
Washington State Human Rights Comm'n (509) 456-4473 Wash. Rev. Code, sec. 49.60.010 et seq.	Provides protection on the basis of physical or mental disability. Has adopted guidelines for AIDS cases.
King County Affirmative Action Office (206) 344-7652 Ord. 5280	Provides protection on the basis of physical or mental handicap.
Seattle Human Rights Dep't (206) 625-4381 Ord. 104839, Code, ch. 14.08	Provides protection on the basis of sexual orientation.
Tacoma Human Relations Dep't (206) 591-5151 Code, ch. 1.29	Provides protection on the basis of physical or mental handicap.
West Virginia Human Rights Comm'n (304) 348-2616 W. Va. Code, sec. 5-11-1 et seq.	Provides protection on the basis of physical or mental handicap.
Charleston Human Rights Comm'n (304) 348-6880 Code sec. 15-1 et seq.	Provides protection on the basis of physical or mental disability.
Wisconsin Dep't of Industry, Labor and Human Relations (608) 266-6860 Wis. Stat. Ann., sec. 101.22(1) et seq.	Provides protection on the basis of physical or mental disability or sexual orientation.
Beloit Equal Opportunities Comm'n (608) 364-6700 City Code, ch. 20	Provides protection on the basis of handicap.

Appendix B

Commonalities and Differences of Substantially Equivalent Jurisdiction's Enabling Legislation and Title VIII

State or Locality	Substantive Rights Protected (by covered category)				Procedures Followed by Administrative Agency		Remedies Available to Administrative Agency					Judicial Review of Agency Action (w/o De Novo Review)	
	Race, Color, Religion, Nat'l Origin	Sex	Handicap	Familial Status (Children)	Investigation (including subpoena power)	Administrative Hearings	Conciliation	Compensation for Damages	Civil Penalty (Maximum Amount)	Injunctive or Affirmative Relief	Preliminary Relief	Comp.	Resp.
TITLE VIII	X	X			X		X						
Alaska	X	X			X	X	X	X		X	X	X	X
California	X	X	X		X	X	X	X	$1000 punitive	X	X	X	X
Colorado	X	X	X		X	X	X			X	X	X	X
Connecticut	X	X	X	X	X	X	X	X		X	X	X	X
Delaware	X	X	X*		X	X	X						
Florida	X	X			X	X	X						
Hawaii	X	X	X		X	X	X			X	X	X	X
Illinois	X	X	X	X	X	X	X	X		X	X	X	X
Indiana	X	X	X		X	X	X	X		X		X	X
Iowa	X	X	X		X	X	X	X		X	X	X	X
Kansas	X	X	X		X	X	X			X			
Kentucky	X	X	X		X	X	X	X		X	X	X	X
Maine	X	X	X	X	X	X	X				X		

State or Locality	Substantive Rights Protected (by covered category)				Procedures Followed by Administrative Agency		Remedies Available to Administrative Agency					Judicial Review of Agency Action (w/o De Novo Review)	
	Race, Color, Religion, Nat'l Origin	Sex	Handicap	Familial Status (Children)	Investigation (including subpoena power)	Administrative Hearings	Conciliation	Compensation for Damages	Civil Penalty (Maximum Amount)	Injunctive or Affirmative Relief	Preliminary Relief	Comp.	Resp.
Maryland	X	X	X		X	X	X			X	X	X	
Massachusetts	X	X	X -blind and deaf		X	X	X	X	$2000	X	X		
Michigan	X	X	X		X	X	X	X		X	X		
Minnesota	X	X	X	X	X	X	X	X		X	X	X	X
Montana	X	X	X		X	X	X	X		X	X		
Nebraska	X	X	X		X	X	X				X		
Nevada	X	X			X	X	X			X			
New Hampshire	X	X	X		X	X	X			X		X	X
New Jersey	X	X	X		X	X	X	X	$5000	X	X	X	X
New Mexico	X	X	X		X	X	X	X		X	X	X	X
New York	X	X	X	X	X	X	X	X	Limited to profit realized because of discrimination; in finance cases limit is $10,000	X	X	X	X

State or Locality	Substantive Rights Protected (by covered category)				Procedures Followed by Administrative Agency		Remedies Available to Administrative Agency					Judicial Review of Agency Action (w/o De Novo Review)	
	Race, Color, Religion, Nat'l Origin	Sex	Handicap	Familial Status (Children)	Investigation (including subpoena power)	Administrative Hearings	Conciliation	Compensation for Damages	Civil Penalty (Maximum Amount)	Injunctive or Affirmative Relief	Preliminary Relief	Comp.	Resto.
North Carolina	X	X	X		X		X						
Oklahoma	X	X	X		X	X	X	X		X	X	X	X
Oregon	X	X	X		X	X	X			X		X	X
Pennsylvania	X	X	X		X	X	X			X	X	X	
Rhode Island	X	X	X	X	X	X	X			X	X	X	X
South Dakota	X	X			X	X	X			X		X	X
Tennessee	X	X	X		X	X	X	X		X	X	X	X
Virginia	X	X	X	X	X	X	X						
Washington	X	X	X		X	X	X	X	$1000	X	X	X	X
West Virginia	X	X	X		X	X	X			X	X		
Wisconsin	X	X	X		X	X	X				X	X	

State or Locality	Substantive Rights Protected (by covered category)				Procedures Followed by Administrative Agency		Remedies Available to Administrative Agency					Judicial Review of Agency Action (w/o De Novo Review)	
	Race, Color, Religion, Nat'l Origin	Sex	Handicap	Familial Status (Children)	Investigation (including subpoena power)	Administrative Hearings	Conciliation	Compensation for Damages	Civil Penalty (Maximum Amount)	Injunctive or Affirmative Relief	Preliminary Relief	Comp.	Resp.
ALASKA													
Anchorage	X	X	X		X	X	X			X	X	X	X
ARIZONA													
Phoenix	X	X			X		X				X		
CONNECTICUT													
New Haven	X	X	X		X	X	X	X		X	X	X	X
DISTRICT OF COLUMBIA													
Washington	X	X	X	X	X	X	X	X		X	X	X	X
FLORIDA													
Clearwater	X	X	X		X	X	X			X		X	X
Dade County (Metropolitan)	X	X	X		X	X	X	X	$500	X	X	X	X
Escambia County	X	X	X		X	X	X						
Hillsborough County	X	X			X	X	X		$500	X			
Jacksonville	X	X			X	X	X						

State or Locality	Substantive Rights Protected (by covered category)				Procedures Followed by Administrative Agency		Remedies Available to Administrative Agency					Judicial Review of Agency Action (w/o De Novo Review)	
	Race, Color, Religion, Nat'l Origin	Sex	Handicap	Familial Status (Children)	Investigation (including subpoena power)	Administrative Hearings	Conciliation	Compensation for Damages	Civil Penalty (Maximum Amount)	Injunctive or Affirmative Relief	Preliminary Relief	Comp.	Resp.
Orlando	X	X			X	X	X	X		X			
Pensacola	X	X	X		X	X	X	X					
Pinellas County	X	X	X		X	X	X	X	Unlimited Punitive Damages				
St. Petersburg	X	X	X		X	X	X	X		X			
Tallahassee	X	X			X	X	X		$500				
Tampa	X	X			X	X	X	X	$500	X		X	X
ILLINOIS													
Bloomington	X	X	X		X	X	X	X	$1000		X		
Evanston	X	X		X	X	X	X	X	$ 500	X	X	X	X
Park Forest	X	X	X		X	X	X		$ 500	X	X		
Springfield	X	X	X		X	X	X				X		
Urbana	X	X	X	X	X	X	X	X	$ 500	X			
INDIANA													
Columbus	X	X	X		X	X	X	X		X			
East Chicago	X	X	X		X	X	X	X	$ 300	X		X	X

State or Locality	Substantive Rights Protected (by covered category)				Procedures Followed by Administrative Agency		Remedies Available to Administrative Agency					Judicial Review of Agency Action (w/o De Novo Review)	
	Race, Color, Religion, Nat'l Origin	Sex	Handicap	Familial Status (Children)	Investigation (including subpoena power)	Administrative Hearings	Conciliation	Compensation for Damages	Civil Penalty (Maximum Amount)	Injunctive or Affirmative Relief	Preliminary Relief	Comp.	Resp.
INDIANA (Cont.)													
Ft. Wayne	X	X	X		X	X	X	X		X			
Gary	X	X			X	X	X	X		X			
South Bend	X	X	X		X	X	X	X		X	X	X	X
IOWA													
Dubuque	X	X	X		X	X	X	X		X	X		X
Iowa City	X	X	X		X	X	X	X		X		X	X
KANSAS													
Kansas City	X	X	X		X	X	X						
Lawrence	X	X	X		X	X	X	X		X			
Olathe	X	X	X		X	X	X		$ 500	X	X		
Salina	X	X	X		X	X	X	X		X			
KENTUCKY													
Jefferson County	X	X	X		X	X	X		$ 100	X	X	X	X
Lexington-Payette	X	X			X	X	X	X		X	X	X	X

State or Locality	Substantive Rights Protected (by covered category)				Procedures Followed by Administrative Agency		Remedies Available to Administrative Agency					Judicial Review of Agency Action (w/o De Novo Review)	
	Race, Color, Religion, Nat'l Origin	Sex	Handicap	Familial Status (Children)	Investigation (including subpoena power)	Administrative Hearings	Conciliation	Compensation for Damages	Civil Penalty (Maximum Amount)	Injunctive or Affirmative Relief	Preliminary Relief	Comp.	Resp.
MARYLAND													
Howard County	X	X	X		X	X	X	X	$1000	X	X	X	X
Montgomery County	X	X	X	X	X	X	X	X		X	X	X	X
Prince George's County	X	X	X		X	X	X	X		X			
MASSACHUSETTS													
Boston	X	X	X	X	X	X	X						
MINNESOTA													
Minneapolis	X	X	X		X	X	X	X		X		X	X
St. Paul	X	X	X	X	X	X	X	X		X			
MISSOURI													
Kansas City	X	X	X		X	X	X	X		X	X	X	X
St. Louis	X	X			X	X	X	X		X		X	X
NEBRASKA													
Lincoln	X	X	X		X	X	X	X		X			
Omaha	X	X	X		X	X	X	X		X	X	X	X

State or Locality	Substantive Rights Protected (by covered category)				Procedures Followed by Administrative Agency		Remedies Available to Administrative Agency					Judicial Review of Agency Action (w/o De Novo Review)	
	Race, Color, Religion, Nat'l Origin	Sex	Handicap	Familial Status (Children)	Investigation (including subpoena power)	Administrative Hearings	Conciliation	Compensation for Damages	Civil Penalty (Maximum Amount)	Injunctive or Affirmative Relief	Preliminary Relief	Comp.	Resp.
NEW YORK													
New York	X	X	X		X	X	X	X		X	X	X	X
N. CAROLINA													
Charlotte	X	X			X	X	X				X		
Mecklenberg County	X	X			X	X	X						
New Hanover County	X	X			X	X	X			X		X	X
Raleigh	X	X			X	X	X	X		X			
Winston-Salem	X	X			X	X	X				X		
OHIO													
Dayton	X	X	X		X	X	X	X		X	X	X	X
PENNSYLVANIA													
Allentown	X	X	X		X	X	X		$ 300	X	X	X	X
Harrisburg	X	X			X	X	X		$ 300	X	X	X	X
Philadelphia	X	X			X	X	X	X		X	X	X	X
Pittsburgh	X	X			X	X	X	X		X	X		
Reading	X	X			X	X	X		$ 300	X	X		
York	X	X	X		X	X	X		$ 300	X	X		

State or Locality	Substantive Rights Protected (by covered category)				Procedures Followed by Administrative Agency		Remedies Available to Administrative Agency					Judicial Review of Agency Action (w/o De Novo Review)	
	Race, Color, Religion, Nat'l Origin	Sex	Handicap	Familial Status (Children)	Investigation (including subpoena power)	Administrative Hearings	Conciliation	Compensation for Damages	Civil Penalty (Maximum Amount)	Injunctive or Affirmative Relief	Preliminary Relief	Comp.	Resp.
S. DAKOTA													
Sioux Falls	X	X	X		X	X	X	X		X		X	X
TENNESSEE													
Knoxville	X	X			X	X	X			X		X	X
TEXAS													
Fort Worth	X	X			X	X	X		$ 200				
VIRGINIA													
Arlington County	X	X			X	X	X			X	X		
WASHINGTON													
King County	X	X	X	X	X	X	X	X	$ 500	X			
Seattle	X	X		X	X	X	X	X	$ 500	X			
Tacoma	X	X	X		X	X	X	X		X	X	X	X
W. VIRGINIA													
Beckley	X	X			X	X	X			X			
Charleston	X	X			X	X	X			X	X		X
Huntington	X	X			X	X	X			X			X
WISCONSIN													
Beloit	X	X			X	X	X		$ 200		X	X	

CRIMINAL LAW AND PROCEDURE

Paul Albert, Cynthia Stewart and Mark Vermeulen

AIDS issues have permeated all aspects of the criminal justice system, from arrest through court proceedings through release from custody. Although these issues have arisen previously in different settings, they require serious reconsideration in light of the magnitude of the AIDS epidemic and its propensity for provoking irrational fear and prejudice. When combined with the current push for "law and order" and "victim's rights," the potential for infringement on criminal defendants' rights is indeed grave.

This chapter is intended to point up a number of junctures in the criminal justice system where AIDS related issues may arise and to provide the practitioner with a few starting points and possible avenues for analysis. The issues addressed relating to conditions of confinement are covered in greater depth in the chapter on prisons and jails.

Overview.

Most criminal charges against seropositive persons[1] do not involve AIDS as an element of the offense. Persons infected with HIV are arrested for the same spectrum of crimes as persons who are not seropositive. In most such cases, the medical status of the defendant with AIDS or ARC may be relevant, if at all, only in sentencing. Although the criminal charge against a seropositive defendant may not directly involve AIDS, the issue of AIDS can affect all aspects of the proceedings. An air of hys-

Paul Albert is the Director of the National Lawyers Guild AIDS Network. Cynthia Stewart is a criminal lawyer practicing with the firm of Moore & Stewart in Jackson, Mississippi. Mark Vermeulen is a criminal lawyer in San Francisco with the Law Offices of Judd Iversen. Paul Albert and Mark Vermeulen are members of the Editorial Board of The Exchange, the newsletter of the National Lawyers Guild AIDS Network. The authors wish to thank for their assistance Ron Albers, a member of the office of the San Francisco Public Defender, and Stuart Hanlon, an attorney with the San Francisco firm of Tamburello, Hanlon & Bresciani, as well as Lois Heaney and the National Jury Project, Oakland, California.

teria often surrounds the cases of seropositive defendants, which severely prejudices their rights.

Conditions of pretrial confinement may affect the disposition of the case. A 1986 study of the National Institute of Justice revealed that 27 percent of local jails and 16 percent of state and federal prisons segregate asymptomatic seropositive prisoners.[2] The conditions of isolation not only restrict access of prisoners to jail programs but also interfere with their ability to aid their attorney and take part in the proceedings pending against them.

A study published by the Association of the Bar of New York revealed that segregated inmates frequently had difficulty seeing their lawyers. The report found that defense counsel "rarely if ever visit defendants who are incarcerated in the AIDS unit" of the jail system. In addition, defendants in this unit were not always produced in court for proceedings in their cases because of claimed logistical problems in transporting them or because court personnel refused to have contact with them.[3] This can result in substantial delays in their cases.

The stigma associated with AIDS may well follow the defendant into the courtroom. The Bar Association Report revealed that court-appointed counsel have refused to represent people with AIDS and one judge even required a defendant to wear a mask during the proceedings. This hysteria has been legitimized by January 1988 guidelines issued by New York State's Chief Administrative Judge which recommend that court officers guard defendants who may have AIDS from 10 feet away and, at the judge's discretion, wear surgical gloves and masks.[4]

In some cases, seropositivity may also relate to an element of the charged crime. In a growing number of cases, prosecutors have aggravated the charges against persons suspected of being seropositive who commit assaults or acts of prostitution. A number of persons have been charged with assault with a deadly weapon or attempted murder after having bitten or spat on other persons. Defendants alleged to be seropositive have also been charged with attempted murder and reckless endangerment for having consensual sexual relations[5] or for selling blood to a blood bank. In 1986, new laws were enacted in five states making it a crime to knowingly transmit the AIDS virus in some circumstances,[6] and calls for greater use of the criminal law in controlling AIDS are increasing.

Much public attention has been focused on AIDS and prostitutes, who are seen by many as a bridge for infecting the heterosexual community.[7] Prostitutes have been denied bail and quarantined. A Florida prostitute with AIDS was confined to her home and ordered to wear an electronic monitor that signaled the police if she strayed more than 200 feet from her telephone.[8] Prostitutes suspected of being seropositive have also faced aggravated charges and received stiffer sentences even in the absence of allegations that they engaged in unsafe sexual practices.

Prosecutors, judges and public health officials have been anxious to establish whether a prostitute is seropositive. Courts have offered reduced sentences or conditioned bail on a defendant submitting to an HIV antibody test. An ordinance passed unanimously by the Newark, New Jersey, City Council would require convicted prostitutes and their customers to take the HIV antibody test. The Georgia Department of Human Resources has enacted a regulation requiring the testing of all convicted prostitutes (including persons convicted in other states). A bill introduced in California would make HIV testing mandatory upon conviction of prostitution. The defendant would be told of the result and, if seropositive, subsequent prostitution charges would have to be charged at the felony level.

This overview has obviously raised a huge number of legal issues relating to both criminal law and procedure. Discussed below are issues related to bail, the right to a fair trial, elements of AIDS-related criminal charges, evidentiary and search issues, plea bargaining and sentencing, and diminished capacity as a defense.

A. Bail.

Bail issues are especially likely to arise in cases involving prostitutes suspected of being seropositive whom prosecutors allege will engage in unsafe sex practices if released. In such cases, denial of bail altogether or the setting of extremely high bail has been used as a means of control. In Mississippi, for example, a prostitute represented by one of the authors was denied bail because he was thought to pose a danger to the community based

upon his positive antibody status. He was held in custody for sixty days before a grand jury refused to indict him.

The purpose of denying bail in such situations is preventive detention rather than insuring that the defendant will appear at subsequent proceedings. The United States Supreme Court has recently ruled that under certain circumstances denial of bail for reasons relating to preventive detention does not violate the constitution. In U.S. v. Salerno, 107 S. Ct. 2095 (1987), the Court upheld a provision of the 1984 Bail Reform Act which permits detention of an arrestee pending trial if the government demonstrates by clear and convincing evidence that no release conditions "will reasonably assure ... the safety of any other person and the community." The defendant is entitled to an evidentiary hearing on this issue and enumerated procedural rights. 18 U.S.C.A. 3142(f)(1987 Supp.).

It may therefore be necessary to look to state law to challenge the denial of bail for reasons related to preventive detention. The law in this area is controversial and differs dramatically from state to state. See Pretrial Preventive Detention, 75 A.L.R.3d 956 (1977). In jurisdictions which permit preventive detention, it has been suggested that defense counsel may forestall invocation of the doctrine by proposing conditions of the client's release, such as a prohibition against going to certain designated areas. Counsel can be creative in proposing alternative bail conditions to fit the individual defendant's circumstances and charges.

In addition to denial of bail, counsel may face the imposition of inappropriate conditions associated with bail. For example, a New York State appellate court recently overturned a bail requirement imposed by a trial court that a defendant show seronegativity as a condition of pretrial release.[9]

B. The Right to a Fair Trial.

Numerous issues may arise relating to a defendant's right to a fair trial. A few are discussed below.

1. Effective assistance of counsel requires that a defendant be present at all pretrial proceedings in which substantial rights are involved. U.S. v. Washington, 705 F.2d 489 (D.C. Cir. 1983). Refusal of jail personnel to produce a defendant may violate this right. In addition, the right to counsel may be violated if a defendant does not have an adequate opportunity to confer with counsel

due to the nature of the jail facilities or if counsel fails to visit a prisoner because of the isolated location of confinement. See 21A Am. Jur. 2d Crim. Law sec. 985.

2. Defendants have a right to a trial "in an atmosphere of judicial calm." State v. Marchand, 156 A.2d 245 (N.J. 1959). The wearing of masks by court room personnel or other extraordinary measures lends an air of hysteria to the proceedings which is obviously prejudicial to the defendant. Analogies to cases prohibiting the shackling of a defendant before a jury or requiring his or her appearance in prison garb are clear.[10]

3. Delays before trial can impair a defendant's ability to present a defense. If, during a delay, a defendant with AIDS or ARC becomes increasingly ill, develops memory problems, or if symptoms of dementia occur, it may become impossible to try the defendant.[11] San Francisco Public Defender Ron Albers reports that all minor cases he has handled involving physically disabled defendants with AIDS who are not in custody have been delayed and ultimately have never come to trial. The physical or mental decline of a defendant can also be used to buttress a motion to dismiss in the interest of justice.

4. The procedures for the issuance of quarantine orders may violate state and federal constitutions. In most states, such orders can be issued by local health officers without affording the subjected person such due process rights as the right to confront and cross-examine witnesses or the right to counsel. The health officer charged with responsibilities related to quarantining is generally given broad discretion. In California, for example, a person may be quarantined "when such action is necessary for the protection of the public health," and refusal to obey a quarantine order is a misdemeanor. Cal. Health & Safety Code secs. 3123, 3354 (West 1988 Supp.).

Courts have traditionally upheld such statutes, evaluating them under a minimum scrutiny standard which presumes validity unless they bear no reasonable relationship to the achievement of a public health purpose. With the development of due process rights over the past decades, however, courts are more likely to require procedural safeguards in any proceeding which involves a deprivation of liberty.[12] As a result, new regulations have been proposed in some states which would couple broad discretion on the part of health officials to quarantine persons suspected of being seropositive with the right to counsel and other due process trappings.[13] Such regulations and laws, as well as the quarantine orders themselves, should be strictly scrutinized to ensure that they represent the least restrictive alternative necessary to

meet their stated public health purpose.[14] Relevant in this regard would be such matters as the counseling and educational measures undertaken by public health authorities, efforts to involve community organizations, and the availability of measures short of isolation.

5. A basic component of the right to a fair trial is the right to an impartial jury. Actual bias of a juror violates this right,[15] and, in theory at least, a defendant in a criminal case has the right to "probe for the hidden prejudices of the jurors." Lurding v. U.S., 179 F.2d 410, 421 (6th Cir. 1950). The defense must be given a full and fair opportunity to expose bias or prejudice on the part of potential jurors (Morford v. United States, 339 U.S. 258 (1950)), and there must be sufficient information elicited on voir dire to permit a defendant to intelligently exercise not only challenges for cause, but also peremptory challenges. Swain v. Alabama, 380 U.S. 202 (1965).

The voir dire is important both as a means of educating the jurors and as a method of obtaining a more favorable jury. Education of a prospective juror occurs both in the context of the questions themselves and through listening to the answers given by other panel members.

Issues related to AIDS are highly inflammatory. On the one hand, jurors may feel sympathy for a defendant with AIDS under certain circumstances. On the other, polls have shown that irrational fear of persons with AIDS is widespread. A survey distributed by the Centers for Disease Control in January 1988 found that 26 percent of respondents thought they would probably get AIDS from giving blood and 36 percent believed they could get AIDS by eating at a restaurant where the cook had the disease.[16] As a result of a combination of such misinformation and bias, a significant proportion of the public favor oppressive measures against seropositive persons. A survey conducted by the Los Angeles Times in July 1987 revealed that 29 percent favored the tattooing of seropositive persons, for example.[17] In jury trials in which a defendant has AIDS or is seropositive, these studies indicate the importance of extended voir dire into possible prejudice and irrational fear.[18]

State and federal courts permit questioning of jurors in various ways. In some jurisdictions, defense counsel is very limited in the questions that can be asked, while in others the defense is given broad latitude to explore the attitudes of jurors. Attorneys are well advised to seek improved voir dire conditions in a case in which AIDS will be an issue. Even in jurisdictions where there may be extensive attorney-conducted voir dire, it may prove valuable to discuss with the court the areas of bias which you believe should form the bases of challenges for cause. In addition, traditional large group voir dire may be inappropriate in an AIDS case. As the areas of inquiry during the voir dire are sensitive and personal, the large group setting will inhibit many prospective jurors and thus limit the kind and amount of information elicited by the questioning. Attorneys should therefore consider a motion for small group (in which four to six people are in the jury box and other prospective jurors are excluded from the courtroom) or individual sequestered voir dire.

The way in which the motion is brought is a strategic decision. A well conceived request presents the court with social science evidence and legal precedent. Attorneys should consider the prevailing voir dire conditions as well as the judge's own practice and preference for resolving such matters. Judges are likely to be more receptive to such motions when the proposal includes an efficient method of impaneling jurors, one which is designed to minimize inconvenience to the court and prospective jurors.[19]

While the voir dire conditions will influence the kind and amount of information elicited from prospective jurors, so too will the phrasing of the questions. Reliance upon closed-ended questions alone, those which call for a "yes" or "no," agree-or-disagree response, curtails an attorney's ability to eliminate bias and prejudice. Closed-ended questions generally communicate to jurors the "correct" response, one which leads to inclusion rather than exclusion from the jury panel. For example, a closed-ended question which generally accomplishes little toward revealing bias is:

> Is there anything about the (race)(background) (sexual preference) of the defendant which would prevent you from being fair and impartial?

The correct answer is obviously "no," and few jurors want to say they are prejudiced, unfair or partial, especially to a judge. Only open-ended questions which require jurors to formulate their thoughts into their own words will actually separate those who are without unfair prejudice from those who may just be unaware of their prejudices. Sample voir dire questions dealing with homosexuality and AIDS issues are set forth in an appendix to this article.

C. Plea bargaining and sentencing.

The fact that a defendant is seropositive or has AIDS or ARC may be relevant in the plea bargaining or sentenc-

ing stage of criminal proceedings. A number of cases have been dismissed "in the interests of justice" because of the defendant's AIDS-related medical condition.[20] Medical factors can be used in fashioning numerous other dispositions short of dismissal. Conditioning probation on participation in programs provided by local AIDS agencies is just one example.

The shortened life span of persons with AIDS and ARC is a relevant factor in sentencing. A study of New York prisoners found that the average length of time from the onset of AIDS-related symptoms to confirmation of a diagnosis of AIDS was three to four months, and the average length of time from diagnosis to death ranged from five to six months.[21] For this reason, the pretrial confinement alone of a prisoner with AIDS or ARC may represent a substantial proportion of the defendant's life expectancy, and even a short jail sentence may constitute confinement for life.

In addition, sentencing a person with AIDS or ARC to jail or prison may deprive that person of adequate medical care. This fact has both equitable and constitutional dimensions. In systems which segregate seropositive prisoners, a defendant may be unable to obtain basic services available to the general population. In addition, the sentencing of a defendant with AIDS or ARC to confinement in a prison system which has shown a "deliberate indifference to the serious medical needs" of prisoners would violate the constitutional proscription against cruel and unusual punishment.[22] Evidence of the standard of treatment afforded prisoners with AIDS in a prison system may be a relevant in the sentencing stage of the proceedings.

D. Proving elements of AIDS-related crimes.

The ability of a person to transmit the HIV has been an issue in a series of cases involving allegations of assaults or unsafe conduct. Charges of assault with a deadly weapon or attempted murder have been filed against persons who have spat upon or bitten others. These cases have usually arisen during an arrest, when the defendant is alleged to have admitted to being seropositive after biting or spitting upon the arresting officer. Charges of aggravated assault and attempted murder have also been brought against persons alleged to be seropositive who have sold their blood or had sexual relations with others to whom they did not reveal their condition.

Although the laws relating to such charges vary from state to state, in general the elements of an assault require that the defendant have both the ability and the intent to inflict harm. This requires that the prosecution prove that the defendant (1) was seropositive, (2) knew of this condition, (3) knew that the act committed could result in transmission of the virus, and (4) intended that the virus be transmitted.[23] In addition, the prosecutor must prove that (5) the virus can be transmitted by the act.

These elements may provide various avenues for the defense. Charges of assault with a deadly weapon stemming from biting or spitting have been dismissed because of evidence that there are no documented cases of AIDS being transmitted in this manner.[24] For this reason, in charges stemming from consensual sexual relations, counsel may wish to introduce evidence that it is extremely unlikely that the AIDS virus will be passed through oral-genital sex[25] or sexual intercourse with a condom.

This line of reasoning applies also to prostitution cases. Many prostitutes are engaging in safe sexual practices, and it cannot be assumed that a seropositive defendant engaging in an act of prostitution was endangering his or her client. Studies have shown the relatively routine insistence by prostitutes that their patrons use condoms during coitus and that coitus is not even an issue in many (if not most) transactions.[26] In addition to safe sex precautions, the court can be educated that in spite of 300 million acts of prostitution annually in the United States, there has to date not been a single case of AIDS definitively traced to a female prostitute in this country.[27]

Another difficulty faced by the prosecution is proving that the defendant is seropositive. Evidence of seropositivity may be suppressed if the test was performed in a confidential program.[28] Evidence may also be inadmissable if the blood sample was obtained without a search warrant. Although courts permit the taking of blood samples during an arrest for purposes of proving blood alcohol levels, the justification for such warrantless searches stems from the need to avoid destruction of evidence by the passage of time.[29] For evidence of seropositivity, no such rush applies.[30] Similarly, the lack of ability to pinpoint the time of infection because of the varying incubation period for development of HIV antibodies can complicate proof of seropositivity and the defendant's knowledge of seropositivity.

E. Mental Capacity

It is not uncommon that persons with AIDS suffer some form of physiological and/or psychological impairment

as a result of the disease. AIDS dementia may be relevant in the disposition of a case or as a defense.

The law related to diminished capacity, mental capacity or lessened culpability varies greatly from state to state. In general, this issue arises when a defendant is competent to stand trial but may not be capable of having the state of mind necessary to commit the crime charged. In some cases, a defendant may be found guilty of a lesser charge due to diminished capacity. See People v. Martanez, 90 A.D.2d 476, 455 N.Y.S.2d 268 (1982) (charge reduced from first to third degree because of the defendant's mental, emotional and psychological history).

Conclusion.

This discussion has touched only the surface of the numerous criminal law and procedure issues raised by AIDS. Unfortunately, because the use of criminal and quarantine-related sanctions to deal with AIDS is politically safe and convenient, it can be expected that many new AIDS-related criminal laws will be enacted. There has to date been very little written about this aspect of the AIDS crisis, and it is our hope that criminal defense organizations will respond with seminars and advanced workshops on AIDS-related medical and legal issues.

Notes

1. Another aspect of AIDS-related criminal law involves recently enacted statutes imposing criminal penalties on persons who violate the rights of people with AIDS. These types of statutes are the subject of much recent legislative activity, some of which strengthen and some of which eliminate confidentiality protections. Examples include statutes making it a crime to violate the confidentiality of medical records concerning HIV status or for an employer to require an HIV test as a condition of employment. See, e.g., Cal. Health & Safety Code sec. 199.21 (West Supp. 1987); Fla. Stat. sec. 384.29 (Supp. 1987); Ky. Rev. Stat. Ann. secs. 214.420, 214.990 (Baldwin 1986 at 655); Wis. Stat. Ann. secs. 103.15, 103.20 (West Supp. 1987).

Persons seeking to obtain prosecutions under such laws have had great difficulty. Alice Philipson, a Berkeley, California, attorney, has requested county and state prosecutors to bring charges against doctors who revealed the antibody status of their patients to insurance carriers. All such requests have been turned down, and she is seeking redress under provisions in the statutes for monetary damages.

2. Hammett, AIDS in Correctional Facilities: Issues and Options xxii (1987)(sponsored by the National Institute of Justice and the American Correctional Association).

3. There have been instances in which defendants with AIDS have been left all day in a van parked outside the courthouse (regardless of weather and lack of basic amenities) because court officers have refused to deal with them. Joint Subcomm. on AIDS in the Criminal Justice System of the Comm. on Corrections and the Comm. on Criminal Justice Operations and Budget, AIDS and the Criminal Justice System: A Preliminary Report and Recommendations, 42 Record of the Ass'n of the Bar of the City of New York 901, 908 n.27, 909 n.30 (1987) (available by contacting the Association at 42 W. 44th St., New York, NY 10035). A report published by the National Institute of Justice recommends extensive AIDS education of police and other law enforcement personnel. See Hammett, AIDS and the Law Enforcement Officer: Concerns and Policy Responses (1987).

4. See New York Times, Jan. 23, 1988. These aspects of the guidelines were criticized by New York City Health Commissioner Stephen C. Joseph as having "no basis in scientific fact." Id.

5. It can be predicted that laws passed earlier in this century to deal with syphilis and other venereal diseases which make it unlawful to knowingly infect another with a dangerous disease will be used by some prosecutors for cases such as these. See, e.g., Cal. Health & Safety Code sec. 3353.

6. See, e.g., Fl. Stats. Ann. sec. 384.24 (West 1987 Supp); Idaho Code sec. 39-601 (1987 Supp). The criminal laws have also been passed in Louisiana, Nevada, and Alabama. See New York Times, October 14, 1987.

7. Historically, there is precedent for singling out prostitutes in an effort to contain sexually transmitted diseases. During the First World War, for example, prostitutes were blamed for the spread of venereal disease and subjected to forced examination and quarantine. See generally Decker, Prostitution: Regulation and Control (1979); Brandt, No Magic Bullet: A Social History of Venereal Disease in the United States since 1880 (1987).

8. Mills, Wofsy & Mills, The Acquired Immune Deficiency Syndrome and Public Health Law, 314 New Eng. J. Med. 931, 934 (1986).

9. People v. McGreevy, 514 N.Y.S.2d 622 (Sup. Ct. 1987).

10. See Annot., 26 A.L.R. Fed. 535(1976); Annot., 90 A.L.R.3d 17 (1979); 3 A.B.A. Standards for Criminal Justice, Trial by Jury, 15-3.1 (1986 Supp.). The decision in the case of Coy v. Iowa, No. 86-6757, argued Jan. 13, 1988 before the United States Supreme Court, may well be relevant. 42 Crim. L. Rep. (BNA) 4121 (1988). In this case, a state supreme court found that a defendant's right to a fair trial was not violated even though, in front of the jury, a screen was placed in front of him so that a child witness did not have to see him. See 397 N.W.2d 730 (Ia. 1986).

11. See, e.g., U.S. v. Dreyer, 533 F.2d 112 (3d Cir. 1976)(defendant's mental suffering, culminating in a suicide attempt, during inordinate delay required dismissal where prosecution could not justify the delay); State v. Jenkins, 565 P.2d 758 (Or. App. 1977)(dimming of memory by defendant during extensive delay as basis for dismissal).

12. See Green v. Edwards, 263 S.E.2d 661, 663 (W. Va. 1980) (proceedings for the quarantine of tuberculosis patients must

include (1) an adequate written notice detailing the grounds and underlying facts on which commitment is sought; (2) the right to counsel and, if indigent, the right to appointed counsel; (3) the right to present, to cross-examine, and to confront witnesses; (4) proof by clear, cogent and convincing evidence; and (5) the right to a verbatim transcript of the proceedings for purposes of appeal.) See also Parmet, AIDS and Quarantine: The Revival of an Archaic Doctrine, 14 Hofstra L. Rev. 53 (1985); Annot., 97 A.L.R.3d 780 (1980).

13. For example, the press has reported that under a policy proposed by the Florida Department of Health and Rehabilitative Services, any person who believed someone was knowingly spreading HIV could notify the Health Department. The agency would attempt to have the person tested. People who refused to be tested could be presumed to be positive and health officials would seek to gather evidence that the accused had been sharing needles for drug use or engaging in promiscuous sexual activity. The accused would have the right to an attorney, to cross-examine witnesses and submit to testing to disprove the allegation. If the accused did not respond to education and counseling, the agency could obtain a court order to intervene, ranging from daily monitoring by a probation officer to commitment to a locked ward. Commitment would be reviewed every three months. Those making malicious reports to health authorities would face unspecified sanctions. The proposal advocated setting aside $1.1 million for committing up to 22 adults to confinement. New York Times, Jan. 27, 1987.

14. See Note, The Constitutional Rights of AIDS Carriers, 99 Harv. L. Rev. 1274 (1986); Special Report: The Acquired Immunodeficiency Syndrome 314 New Eng. J. of Med. 931 (1986). A quarantine order which interferes with the family life of a person is subject to special scrutiny for violation of the right to privacy (under federal and some state laws). See, e.g., City of Akron v. Akron Center for Reproductive Rights, 103 S. Ct. 2481 (1986).

15. U.S. v. Dellinger, 472 F.2d 340, 367 (9th Cir. 1972) (the Chicago 8 case).

16. New York Times, Jan. 30, 1988.

17. San Francisco Chronicle, July 31, 1987.

18. The courts have acknowledged the special need for "searching voir dire examination" where the case involves "matters concerning which either the local community or population at large is commonly known to harbor strong feelings that may stop short of presumptive bias in law, yet significantly skew deliberations in fact." United States v. Robinson, 475 F.2d 376 (D.C. Cir. 1973).

19. See National Jury Project, Jurywork: Systematic Techniques (Clark Boardman 1987) for a more complete discussion of motions to improve voir dire conditions and for sample questions.

20. See 1987 Lesbian and Gay Law Notes at 11. This publication is available from the Bar Association for Human Rights of Greater New York, P.O. Box 1899, Grand Central Station, New York, NY 10163.

21. New York State Commission of Correction, Acquired Immune Deficiency Syndrome: A Demographic Profile of New York State Inmate Mortalities, 1981-85 23, 31 (March 1986) cited in Record,

note 3 above, at 906 n.22.

22. Estelle v. Gamble, 429 U.S. 978 (1976).

23. Variations on the law include requiring only apparent ability (instead of actual ability) and requiring the prosecution to show only that the defendant engaged in gross negligence or reckless and wanton conduct (instead of acting with the intent to inflict harm). See Annot., 6 Am. Jur. 2d, Assault and Battery, sec. 32.

24. New York Times, June 10, 1987. In a school case, a federal district court in California found explicitly that "[t]he overwhelming weight of medical evidence is that the AIDS virus is not transmitted by human bites, even bites that break the skin." Thomas v. Atascadero Unified School District, No. 86-6609, Amended Findings of Fact at 5 (C.D. Cal. Feb. 19, 1987) reprinted in ACLU, AIDS: Basic Documents (April 1987)(available from ACLU, 132 West 43rd St., New York, NY 10036).

Nonetheless, at least one conviction has been obtained in an aggravated assault charge involving biting. In that case, however, the jury foreman indicated that the defendant's seropositivity was not a factor in the verdict as the jurors relied on the defendant's statement that he wanted to kill the guards he assaulted and the attendant viciousness of the biting. Gay Community News, July 19, 1987.

25. See Winkelstein, Lyman, Padian, Grant, Samuel, Wiley, Anderson, Lang, Riggs & Levy, Sexual Practices and Risk of Infection by the Human Immunodeficiency Virus: The San Francisco Men's Health Study, 257 JAMA 321 (Jan 16, 1987) reprinted in ACLU, AIDS: Basic Documents (April 1987).

26. See Decker, Prostitution as a Public Health Issue in AIDS and the Law: A Guide for the Public (Dalton, Burris & Yale AIDS Law Project ed. 1987) at 84.

27. Id.

28. For example, evidence proffered in a court martial was suppressed by a trial court because the armed forces' antibody test program is confidential. However, at the time of publication, the ruling has been overturned by a court of review, and a further appeal was expected. New York Times, October 16, 1987.

This issue would be relevant if the test was taken in a program receiving federal funds. See 42 U.S.C. 247c(e)(5)("All information obtained in connection with the examination, care or treatment of any individual under any program which is being carried out with a grant made under this section shall not, without such individual's consent, be disclosed except as may ... be required by a law of a State ....")

29. See Schmerber v. California, 384 U.S. 757, 770, 86 S. Ct. 1826, 1835-36 (1966). Attempts by the prosecution to obtain a warrant to compel the defendant to submit to an antibody test may be blocked by laws forbidding mandatory testing. This was the result in People v. Barlow, a now unpublished opinion in which a Court of Appeal held that the California AIDS confidentiality law applied to a criminal proceeding in which the prosecution wanted to test the defendant's blood for HIV antibodies. In addition, testing may be objected to on the basis of relevancy. The fact that AIDS is not spread by biting, spitting, sex with a condom, or oral sex may demonstrate the lack of relevancy of seropositivity. In addition, evidence of seropositivity may be irrelevant without evidence that the defendant knew of this condition. Privacy concerns should also be raised in opposing forced testing in criminal proceedings.

30. See Boose v. Bussey, 573 F.2d 548, 550 (9th Cir. 1977)(Schmerber does not justify the warrantless seizure of pubic hairs because of the lack of danger that such evidence would be destroyed before a warrant could be obtained).

Appendix

The choice of a strategy for jury voir dire is extremely complicated. The nature of the charges, community attitudes about AIDS, the attitudes conveyed by the judge and opposing counsel and the degree of illness manifested by the defendant are just some of the factors to be considered. In some cases, counsel may wish to avoid all questions relating to homosexuality, for example, in order not to encourage peremptory challenges to jurors who reveal a sympathetic attitude. In other cases, questions on this subject may be desirable to set a tone or educate the jurors. The questions below are not intended to be an exhaustive list but are designed to raise various possible areas of inquiry which may be appropriate for the strategy in a particular case.

A. GAY-RELATED QUESTIONS.

1. Do you know anyone who is gay?
   a. How well do you know them?
   b. Describe them.
   c. When did you first find out they were gay?
   d. How did you find out?

2. Name three traits which you feel describe gay men in general.

3. Have you ever been surprised to find out that someone you know is gay?
   a. Why did this surprise you?
   b. What was it about them that made you think they weren't gay to begin with?
   c. Have you ever known anyone that was married who was gay?

4. How would you react if you found out your son/daughter was gay/lesbian?

5. Do you know the differences between being gay and being bisexual? What is the difference?

6. How do you feel about "gay rights," in general?

    a. Did you see any of the news media's coverage of _____? [Name a specific recent gay or lesbian event, such as the March on Washington, D.C., in the Fall of 1987.]

    b. What did you think about it? Did anything in particular strike you about it?

7. Have you heard of _____? [Name local/regional/national gay/lesbian activist group.]

    a. What do you know about their work?

    b. What do you think about their work?

    c. Have you ever donated money to them?

8. Do you follow a particular religious teaching or practice?

    a. How strongly do you hold and espouse your religion?

    b. What does that religion teach concerning homosexuality? How do you feel about this teaching?

    c. Do you think being gay is a sin? Do you think it should be illegal?

9. Do you think AIDS is the inevitable result of a gay lifestyle?

10. Do you think it is natural for two men or two women to be in an intimate relationship? Why or why not? Do you think that two people should have the right to do whatever they want in their own home, so long as it doesn't hurt anyone else?

11. Have you ever read _____ ? [Name gay or lesbian publications in the area.] How frequently?

12. Do you think gay people still experience any form of discrimination? Why or why not?

13. Have you heard of any incidents in which gay men or lesbians have been the victims of violent attacks?

14. In what area/district/neighborhood do you live?

15. In what areas/districts/neighborhoods do you normally shop or go to for meals or entertainment?

16. Have you ever gone down to the _____ ? [Name district/ neighborhood known to have a heavy concentration of gay men.]

    a. When was the last time you were there?

    b. What do you think of that area?

    c. Do you think that area has improved or declined within the past five (5) years?

17. What is your understanding about whether gay people are protected by civil rights laws of this country/state/city?

    a. Do you think they should be? Why or why not?

    b. What rights do you think gay men and lesbians should have?

B. AIDS-RELATED QUESTIONS.

1. If you had a friend whose roommate had AIDS, how would you feel about visiting at their home? How would you feel about getting together with your friend elsewhere?

2. Do you know what it means to be "seropositive?"

    a. Do you know what "HIV" stands for?

    b. Do you know what it means to have AIDS?

    c. Do you know the difference between being seropositive and having AIDS? Please explain.

3. From what you have read or heard, what do you think causes AIDS?

4. Do you think you can contract the AIDS virus by being in the same room as someone who has the disease?

    -- by hugging someone?

    -- by drinking out of the same glass?

    -- by socially kissing someone?

    -- by shaking their hand?

Do you know the ways that one can contract the AIDS virus?

5. There has been some publicity about physicians, dentists and other health care providers who refuse to treat people with AIDS. What do you think about this?

6. How do you think the police should treat someone they arrest who has AIDS?

    -- Do you think police should wear protective gear when dealing with people known to have or suspected of having AIDS?

7. What problems do you think people with AIDS face?

    -- ability to obtain health care

    -- loss of jobs and income

    -- loss of homes

    -- social stigma

8. Do you feel that gay men are more susceptible to contracting the disease than straight men? Why or why not?

9. How has the onset of the AIDS crisis affected your life?
   a. What changes have you made in your lifestyle in the past three years that are at least partially affected by the AIDS situation?
   b. Have you read the Surgeon General's (C. Everett Koop's) report on AIDS, or any part of it?
   c. Have you read any journal articles about AIDS?
      i. Which ones?
      ii. What did you learn from them?
   d. In the past three years, have you attended any workshops or gatherings dealing with issues concerning AIDS?
      i. What were the workshops about?
      ii. Who sponsored them?
      iii. What did you learn from them?
      iv. Did they confirm/disaffirm any beliefs you held?

10. How would you rank the following issues in terms of how important they should be on the country's list of priorities:
   Aid for the homeless
   AIDS
   Crime prevention
   National Budget/Deficit
   U.S.-Soviet Relations

11. Whom, if anyone, do you feel is responsible for causing the AIDS crisis? Why are they responsible?

12. What responsibility do you think our society has for the care and treatment of people with AIDS?

13. There has been a lot of controversy over the amount of funding the federal government has provided for research on AIDS. What do you think about this?

14. How do you feel our Government has responded to the AIDS situation? Appropriately? Inappropriately?

15. What do you think are the best things that have resulted from the AIDS crisis? What are the worst?

16. Do you feel the life of someone who is seropositive (or who has AIDS) is worth less or more than someone who has not been exposed to the virus?

17. Do you donate blood? Why or why not? If you were going to have an operation which required blood donations, how would you feel about receiving those donations?

18. Do you believe in the theory of "divine retribution?"

19. Why do you think people get AIDS?

20. Have you ever personally known anyone who has AIDS? Have you ever known anyone who is seropositive?
   a. Has anyone you know died of AIDS?
      i. Who were they?
      ii. How did you know them?
      iii. Did you see them the last few months of their lives? How often?
      iv. What was it like for them in the last few months of their lives?
      v. How did you feel when you knew they were going to die from the disease? How did they feel?

21. Do you think that being seropositive or having AIDS affects the way one thinks? How? Do you think it affects one's judgment?

22. Have you ever seen someone react differently than they normally react because they're in a stressful situation, such as when they witness a traumatic event or when they have a big fight with their husband/wife/boyfriend/girlfriend?
   a. Do you react differently when you're under stress? How does it affect you?
   b. Have you ever seen stress cause someone to do something irrational or unexplainable? Tell me about it.

23. Do you believe AIDS can cause permanent damage to one's brain?

24. Do you think the fear of contracting or passing the AIDS virus can cause someone to alter their behavior either consciously or subconsciously? How? Give me an example.

25. Do you believe that having AIDS or being seropositive would cause someone to lie? -- to forget?
   a. Do you think someone who is seropositive or who has AIDS would be more likely or less likely to tell the truth?
   -- more likely or less likely to remember events as they actually happened?
   b. Do you think having AIDS or being seropositive

could cause someone to misunderstand or disregard their obligation to tell the truth when they are under oath?

26. What do you think is a bigger worry for people who are seropositive but who have not yet contracted AIDS: the worry that they'll come down with the disease of the worry that they'll convey the virus to someone else?

27. Do you know what the term "dementia" means? What does it mean?

28. Have you ever known anyone who has had cancer or some mental disease?
    a. Did you know them before they had the disease?
    b. What differences did you notice in them before and after they contracted the illness?
    c. What do you think caused these differences?
    d. What differences did you notice in yourself before and after you knew about their disease?
    e. What did you learn about their disease?
    f. What differences did you notice in others before and after? What do you think caused these differences? Do you feel these differences were justified?

29. What is the most important realization about society that you have had as a result of the AIDS crisis?

30. What is the most important thing people can do to help stop the AIDS epidemic?

AIDS IN PRISONS AND JAILS

Anita P. Arriola

AIDS presents serious legal and administrative problems in the correctional setting, whether a county jail or a major prison system. Decisions concerning prevention, housing, and the delivery of medical care are frequently complicated because of the potential for a high concentration of individuals at risk for the disease and institutional constraints of overcrowding and limited budgets.

Unfortunately, many institutions have dealt with these issues in an ill-informed and haphazard manner, conducting HIV antibody testing and needlessly segregating seropositive prisoners and prisoners with AIDS or ARC under inhuman conditions of confinement. Such policies reflect both a lack of AIDS awareness on the part of prison administrators and an overriding concern for maintaining security and order. And, unfortunately, public hysteria and misinformation about the disease have brought political pressure to bear on an essentially medical question, with the result that mandatory HIV antibody testing of prisoners and other "hard-line" measures are being introduced in legislatures around the country.

Prisoners with AIDS or ARC or who are seropositive face special medical problems. When ill, they are often in need of acute medical care which frequently is not available in a prison hospital. Even when asymptomatic, it may be necessary for them to take AZT or another drug which can retard the development of opportunistic infections but is not available to them in prison. Prisoners who are dying need the comfort and support of friends and families, yet they are often denied visitation "privileges."

Anita Arriola is an attorney at Public Advocates, Inc., a non-profit public interest law firm located in San Francisco, California. She represents male inmates at San Quentin, Folsom, Deuel Vocational Institution and Soledad prisons; pregnant and postpartum inmates at the Santa Rita Rehabilitation Center; and inmates confined in the AIDS wings at the California Medical Facility - Vacaville.

This chapter addresses the legal aspects of AIDS-related measures in correctional institutions. It is worth noting at the outset that, with respect to federal constitutional law, the United States Supreme Court has been granting ever broader discretion to prison administrators on matters relating to institutional security. This can make challenges to correctional policies difficult. Great caution should therefore be exercised before the filing of an action.[1]

Nonetheless, the resolution of some AIDS-related prison cases has resulted in beneficial changes of policy and there are numerous instances in which the legal and policy arguments set forth in this chapter can be used without the necessity of filing a suit. In systems where an ill-informed policy exists, for example, confronting the administration with medical, public health and ethical arguments may prove effective. In addition, advocates may raise these issues on behalf of individual clients in criminal matters, habeas corpus proceedings, motions for sentence modification or in opposition to actions to compel testing.

With these caveats in mind, we now address the legal implications of policies and practices in correctional systems concerning AIDS. In particular, the following topics will be addressed: (1) testing (mandatory and voluntary testing; confidentiality of test results); (2) the quarantine or segregation of prisoners with AIDS, ARC or who are seropositive and the conditions of confinement (overcrowding, general sanitation, exercise, visitation, legal research materials, etc.); (3) quality of medical care and (4) early release.

I. HIV ANTIBODY TESTING OF PRISONERS

The HIV antibody testing of prisoners arises in a variety of contexts. Presently, mass screening is conducted in the federal system and some state and county systems of all new prisoners and prisoners being released. Some systems have tested all prisoners, while others screen only members of certain groups, such as gay men, IV drug users, female prostitutes, pregnant women, inmates with clinical indications of HIV infections, or "in response to incidents."[2] In other systems, testing is conducted on a voluntary basis or on request.

The key issues are whether such HIV antibody testing is legal and whether there is a right of refusal based on law, policy or ethical considerations. It may be argued that because of the potentially very serious negative effects of test results, medical ethics requires that there be a right of refusal, regardless of law or policy. For example, this may be likened to a patient's right to refuse a potentially risky surgical procedure, such as open heart surgery. With respect to the law, testing can be challenged as a violation of both federal and state constitutional privacy rights as well as a violation of state statutes. We turn to a discussion of these rights.

A. Constitutional protection of the right to privacy.

It is well settled that prisoners maintain civil rights under the United States Constitution.[3] Convicted prisoners are to be accorded those rights not fundamentally inconsistent with prisoner status or incompatible with the legitimate objectives of incarceration.[4] Consequently, courts, although reluctant to interfere with the internal administration of prisons, will intervene to remedy violations of those rights retained by prisoners.[5]

Prisoners retain some fundamental rights of personal privacy.[6] We shall examine this right with respect to mandatory HIV antibody testing under (1) the fourth amendment protection against unreasonable searches and (2) the generalized right to privacy. Both of these rights apply to state prisoners under the fourteenth amendment's due process clause and they may be asserted as the basis for a claim for damages or equitable relief under the federal civil rights statute (42 USC 1983).[7] They may also be raised in a petition for writ of habeas corpus[8] to challenge segregation based on seropositive test results. Or they may be raised as a defense in a criminal or civil proceeding where testing is sought.

1. The Fourth Amendment.

The fourth amendment of the United States Constitution states:

"The right of the people to be secure in their persons, houses, papers and effects, against unreasonable searches and seizures, shall not be violated . . ."

The Supreme Court has recently reaffirmed the principle that "the overriding function of the fourth amendment is to protect personal privacy and dignity against unwarranted intrusion by the State."[9] The Court has noted that such intrusions are restricted through imposition of "a standard of reasonableness upon the exercise of discretion by government officials."[10]

In the prison context, a fourth amendment violation may occur when the bodily integrity of a prisoner is invaded.[11] Courts will closely scrutinize the reasonableness of strip searches or body cavity searches.[12] The constitutionality of these searches will be determined by balancing the state's need for the particular search against the extent of the invasion suffered by the prisoner.[13] It may be argued that mandatory testing programs are an unreasonable intrusion upon the privacy rights of prisoners, thus constituting both a search and a seizure under the fourth amendment.[14]

In this regard, mandatory testing programs may be likened to compulsory drug testing by urinalysis, which courts have held with singular unanimity to constitute a fourth amendment search or seizure.[15] In order to establish a claim under the fourth amendment, mandatory testing programs must be shown to constitute an "unreasonable" search and seizure. The benchmark of a search which is "reasonable" under the fourth amendment is a warrant based on probable cause. Katz v. United States, 389 U.S. 347, 357 (1967). The fourth amendment warrant and probable clause requirements will be abandoned "only in those exceptional circumstances in which special needs, beyond the need for law enforcement, make the warrant and probable cause impracticable." New Jersey v. T.L.O., 469 U.S. 325, 340-1 (1985) (Blackmun J., concurring); O'Conner v. Ortega, 107 S. Ct. 1492, 1500, 94 L. Ed.2d 714, 725 (1987). Absent the "exceptional circumstances," even a compelling governmental interest will not justify departure from the customary requirements of prior judicial approval for a government search or seizure. United States v. U.S. District Court, 407 U.S. 297, 321 (1972).

The Supreme Court has limited prisoners' privacy rights under the fourth amendment in certain circumstances. In Hudson v. Palmer,[16] the Court ruled that the fourth amendment does not prohibit prison officials from conducting random searches of prisoners' cells. However, in Bell v. Wolfish, 441 U.S. 520, 560, 99 S. Ct. 1861, 1884 (1979), the Court applied a test for security-related body cavity searches of prisoners which balanced "the need for the particular search against the invasion of personal rights that the search entails." Factors to be considered include "the scope of the particular intrusion, the manner in which it is conducted, the justification for initiating it, and the place in which it is conducted." Thus, in the balancing analysis, it has been noted that "the greater the intrusion, the greater must be the reason for conducting a search" and that the government must demonstrate not only a legitimate need to conduct the body cavity search but also "that less intrusive measures would not satisfy that need." See Levoy v. Mills, 788 F.2d 1437, 1439 (10th Cir. 1986).

In applying the Bell test to body cavity searches in prisons, courts have considered such factors as whether the search involves physical contact, whether the searches are conducted by police officers instead of medical personnel, whether the search is conducted in a private area and in a hygienic manner, and the genuineness of the alleged security threat. These factors clearly determine the extent of the invasion suffered by the prisoner.[17]

The Bell standard has also been applied by several courts to the random urine testing of prisoners for drugs.[18] Under existing case law, however, it may be argued that prisoners should have greater protection from mandatory HIV antibody testing. Cases involving the Fourth Amendment rights of prisoners to date involve either (1) blood or urine testing designed to detect inmate drug use or (2) body cavity searches or cell searches to detect the smuggle or presence of money, drugs, weapons or other contraband. In both instances, the courts have upheld such practices where the level of intrusion on prisoners' privacy rights has been minimal and where prison administrators have demonstrated that the practices are necessary to maintain institutional security and to preserve internal order and discipline. Mandatory HIV testing programs are distinguishable in that they are not designed to detect or deter criminal activity or misconduct in prison, they involve a substantial infringement on prisoners' reasonable expectations of privacy, and they are not necessary to maintain internal security in prisons.

Whether Bell or a more stringent standard is applied, it will be necessary for a prisoner challenging a testing program to substantiate the high level of intrusion caused by the HIV antibody test, the unreasonableness of the search, the alternatives available to the prison administration to deal with the problems posed by AIDS, and the problems associated with the administration and reliability of the test.[19]

1. There is no question that the level of intrusion of HIV antibody testing on the personal privacy of prisoners is great. It involves a forced penetration of body tissues and an involuntary extraction of body fluids. Apart from the physical act of drawing blood, the psychological impact of learning that one is seropositive has been compared to receiving a death sentence. Because of the consequences of a positive test result, the testing process produces enormous anxiety and, for seropositive prisoners, can result in severe psychological trauma, including depression, rage reactions and severe social withdrawal.[20]

HIV antibody testing can affect additional privacy interests because of the enormous stigma attached to seropositivity and AIDS. Disruption of family relationships[21] due to rejection or visiting restrictions is a frequent occurrence. In addition, the privacy right of confidentiality in medical records may be violated[22] if the test results are kept in a manner in which they may be made known to staff or inmates. This can result in severe consequences, including the enmity of staff and other prisoners, isolation in housing units with loss of access to prison programs or privileges, and discrimination in housing, employment and insurability after discharge.

The magnitude of these dire consequences is increased by the fact that there is currently no treatment available for most asymptomatic seropositive persons. Under all these circumstances, it is clear that the level of physical and psychological trauma associated with a mandatory testing program is great and that mandatory HIV testing involves a type of search that offends "human dignity and privacy"[23] to a much greater degree than urinalyses or body cavity searches.

2. The key element in the Bell balancing test is the need for a particular search. In contrast to the dire consequences of mandatory HIV antibody testing of prisoners, official justifications for the need for such testing are weak. The primary reasons advanced for mandatory HIV testing programs are: (1) identification of seropositive inmates is necessary to prevent transmission of the disease within the prison (and therefore provide effective medical care and treatment); (2) providing seropositive inmates with special housing and programming is necessary to maintain institutional security and order; and (3) identifying and segregating seropositive prisoners is necessary to provide a safe working environment for correctional staff and to protect those prisoners from abuse or violence by other inmates.

These arguments are without medical or legal basis. First, testing to identify and segregate asymptomatic seropositive inmates will not prevent the spread of AIDS. Second, there is no evidence that seropositive prisoners are more likely than others to engage in misconduct or criminal activity, thereby justifying segregated housing for them. Indeed, segregation may actually create more problems of institutional security and order because prison systems may be unable to meet demands for more housing where there are large numbers of prisoners. Third, rather than protecting them, segregation of seropositive inmates may stigmatize them, subjecting them to intimidation, threats or actual violence from others concerned about the possible spread of AIDS. Indeed, segregation of all seropositive prisoners in an environment with the likelihood of repeated exposure to the virus and in unhealthy living conditions may actually pose a significantly increased health hazard. Finally, staff and prisoners must be educated about the dangers of AIDS and must take precautions in dealing with blood or other body fluids regardless of the antibody status of an inmate. Thus, widespread testing might lull seronegative inmates and those dealing with them into a false sense of security and undermine the important educational message that everyone needs to be very careful about behaviors known to be associated with transmitting the AIDS virus.

Additional arguments against the use of testing include the absence of proof of high rates of AIDS transmission in prison and therefore the need to screen.[24] Testing also undermines education and prevention programs by needlessly dividing the inmate population into a stigmatized class and a "safe" class, thus weakening the important educational message that everyone should be careful.[25]

3. There are alternatives available to correctional systems that are both more effective and avoid the negative consequences of mass screening. These alternatives include astute medical surveillance, blind (anonymous) testing, creative diagnostic procedures and carefully designed epidemiological studies. These alternatives can help correctional administrators assess the prevalence of seropositivity and project future incidence of AIDS and ARC for budgeting and treatment purposes.

Because there is presently no cure for the disease, leaders of the scientific community are united in their insistence that broad educational programs are the key in dealing with AIDS.[26] The report of the National Institute of Justice has emphasized the importance of on-going educational programs for both inmates and staff.[27] Instead of utilizing scarce prison resources to detect who is seropositive and who is not, more effective public health policies would stress educational efforts designed to inform inmates about preventive and risk behaviors, such

as unsafe sex, forced sexual acts or intravenous drug use. Moreover, an education program does not harm the civil liberties interests of inmates discussed above. For this reason, a prison system which engages in mandatory testing without implementation of a thorough educational program is not using the least restrictive alternative in dealing with the problem.[28]

Another alternative is to adopt a safe and rational policy of treating every individual as if he or she were at risk for AIDS. The Centers for Disease Control has issued excellent recommendations for correctional practice in several precautionary areas and these should be followed by staff in all situations in which there is a potential for HIV transmission, not just when dealing with inmates or staff members who have been identified as seropositive.[29] Similarly, the U.S. Department of Labor has recently issued detailed guidelines for protection of health workers against the HIV.[30] These guidelines call for employer training in the modes of transmission, recognition of which procedures are dangerous and the types of protections an employee should utilize. Protective clothing and equipment is specified.[31] Implementation of these procedures in the prison setting is necessary and appropriate and would help to diminish fear and anxiety on the part of prison staff.

4. Details of the testing procedures should also be examined to determine if they are being conducted in the least intrusive manner. Even if a court finds that the justifications for a mandatory testing program are reasonable, a prisoner's rights may still be violated if the manner in which it is carried out is unreasonable.[32] Factors to be considered include:

(a) Are the tests being conducted in a manner to minimize the number of false positives? Studies have demonstrated a wide range in accuracy among various laboratories.[33] In light of the drastic consequences of a false positive to an inmate, the laboratories used should be monitored by the prison to insure the accuracy and reliability of the test.

(b) No testing program should occur without psychological counseling for each individual tested. Counseling of seronegative persons is important to ensure that they do not interpret their test result as an indication that they can engage in unsafe practices. On-going (and not simply post-test) counseling of seropositive persons is needed to help them deal with the psychological traumas and devastation often stemming from this diagnosis. Counseling should be done by professional counselors in light of the serious repercussions of the test, and is an expensive component of the testing process. However, any testing program which ignores it is magnifying both the problem of AIDS in prison and the trauma associated with the invasion of prisoners' privacy rights.

(c) Closely related to the accuracy of the antibody test is the sensitive issue of confidentiality of test results. One of the negative consequences of mandatory testing is the lack of confidentiality of prison medical records. As mentioned above, the right to privacy encompasses the confidentiality of medical information, so this inquiry is both relevant to a least restrictive alternative analysis as well as to a violation of this right itself.[34]

Most correctional systems have general or specific confidentiality policies or laws regarding who should receive HIV antibody test results and who should be notified regarding diagnoses of AIDS or ARC. In some states, such as California and Wisconsin,[35] there are very restrictive laws governing disclosure of HIV antibody test results. In other states, the laws require that correctional authorities be notified of the results of the antibody test, but prohibit notification of the inmate.[36] Other systems routinely notify public health agencies when an inmate is diagnosed as having AIDS or ARC or when such an inmate is released.[37] The laws in each jurisdiction, as well as the correctional system's own policies and rules, should be consulted in order to challenge the disclosure of any antibody test results.

(d) The manner in which prisoners are selected for testing is also relevant. If only certain prisoners are tested, then the criteria for selection of inmates should be examined both for rationality and for whether its implementation may lead to harassment. One court voided a "random" drug testing program because guards knew the identity of the inmates being selected. The court held that the selection must be "truly random."[38]

If tests are given to inmates described as "homosexuals" or "IV drug users," then the criteria for identifying these inmates should be examined. Similarly, a rule that calls for tests in response to "an incident" may be particularly vulnerable to attack since individual motives of staff members may come into play. A Massachusetts court refused to order HIV testing of a prisoner who scratched a guard on the grounds that the tests would constitute a deprivation of the inmate's civil rights.[39]

(3) In voluntary programs, the correctional system may request all or certain inmates to be tested, but cannot or will not compel cooperation. In Montgomery County, Maryland, for example, all members of known high-risk groups are requested to submit to the antibody test, but no testing is performed without informed consent.[40]

The legal issue involved here is whether certain forms of coercion, such as threats of segregation or loss of privileges, may be applied in ostensibly voluntary testing programs. In addition to all of the possible theories mentioned above, it is also possible to challenge the "consent" as being given under duress, fraud or coercion. Further, an inmate's consent may be challenged under various rules and regulations governing the correctional institution, which prohibit coercion or intimidation of inmates.

In conclusion, a Fourth Amendment challenge to HIV antibody testing of prisoners should be considered by prisoner advocates. As shown below, many of the issues raised in a Fourth Amendment claim are equally applicable to other constitutional and statutory challenges to the testing of prisoners.

2. Federal and State Rights to Privacy.

While the U.S. Constitution does not explicitly mention any right of privacy, the United States Supreme Court has recognized that a right of personal privacy, or a guarantee of certain areas or zones of privacy, does exist under the Constitution. In various decisions[41] the Court has made it clear that only personal rights that can be deemed "fundamental" or "implicit in the concept of ordered liberty"[42] are included in this guarantee of personal privacy. From each or all of these cases it may be argued that mandatory HIV antibody testing programs intrude upon prisoners' basic right to privacy. It is the "right to be left alone"[43] that is paramount.

Most prison cases involving this right to privacy have concerned intimate physical contact between inmates and staff or viewing of prisoners by guards of the opposite sex. In approaching these cases, the courts have examined in great detail the extent and nature of the intrusion, the need for such intrusion and possible alternative procedures.[44] Some courts have fashioned detailed orders specifying with particularity when a guard may view inmates or regulating the ability of inmates to shield their cells or their bodies from view.[45]

The Supreme Court has recognized that prisoners have the right to privacy. In the recent case of Turner v. Safley, 107 S. Ct. 2254 (1987), the Court struck down a restriction on the ability of prisoners to marry. In doing so, the Court held that a regulation which impinges on inmates' constitutional rights must be "reasonably related to legitimate penological interests." First, there must be a valid, rational connection between the regulation and the governmental interest asserted to justify it. Id. at 2262. Second, in determining the reasonableness of a prison restriction, it is important to inquire whether there are alternative means of exercising the prisoners' rights. A third consideration is "the impact accommodation of the asserted constitutional right will have on guards and other inmates, and on the allocation of resources generally." Finally, the absence of ready alternatives is evidence of the reasonableness of a prison regulation. Id.

Application of the Turner "reasonable relationship" standard to HIV testing of prisoners raises many of the same issues discussed in the previous section. The lack of a reasonable relationship between testing and penological interests, the lack of an adverse impact on guards and inmates in abandoning testing, the better use of funds in AIDS-related educational programs, and the existence of other alternatives all can be advanced to demonstrate that the program violates constitutionally protected privacy rights of prisoners.

Some state constitutions also afford a right to privacy.[46] In California, for example, the right to privacy under Article I, section 1, is explicit. That section protects two types of privacy rights: substantive and informational. Like the right to be left alone under the federal constitution, Article I protects substantive rights such as the right to procreative choice[47] and the right to live in a household with unrelated individuals.[48] The second aspect protected by the Constitution is informational privacy; accordingly, Article I, section 1 has been held to protect medical records against disclosure absent a narrowly-tailored compelling interest.[49] Prisoners retain their right to privacy under the California constitution.[50]

B. State and local laws.

Mandatory testing programs may be challenged under existing laws or policies in some jurisdictions. For example, recently passed laws in California and Wisconsin prohibit HIV antibody testing without the informed consent of the subject. As a matter of policy, Louisiana and Montgomery, Maryland do no testing without informed consent. In addition, a number of other states prohibit drawing blood for any purpose without informed consent.[51] Such laws or policies may conflict with mandatory testing and should be consulted.

II. CONDITIONS OF CONFINEMENT

Correctional systems have adopted various housing policies once an inmate has been tested and identified as being seropositive or having ARC or AIDS. Routinely, jurisdictions segregate or quarantine the inmates from the rest of the general population indefinitely and under more restrictive conditions of confinement.[52] Often, they are deprived of numerous programs and services such as visitation,[53] exercise, access to legal research materials, the telephone, written correspondence, medical care and religious services.[54] These programs are vitally important to the emotional and physical well-being of inmates.[55]

Challenges to the quarantine or segregation of inmates based on their medical status (seropositivity, AIDS or ARC) and the conditions under which they are housed may be brought on the basis of federal or state constitutional standards, federal and state statutes or common law. We discuss below several of these claims and also the feasibility of raising them by means of a writ of habeas corpus.

1. Equal Protection.

In cases invoking the equal protection clause, courts have traditionally employed a strict scrutiny analysis in a limited category of cases where a statute or regulation singles out a "suspect class" for special treatment, or when the challenged law infringes upon a fundamental right.[56] Suspect classes have been generally limited to race, alienage, or national origin.[57] While classifications based on sex and illegitimacy have not been held to be suspect, they have nonetheless been subjected to heightened scrutiny.[58] Suspect classification status has not been granted to the aged or to the mentally retarded.[59] It is unlikely, therefore, that the Supreme Court would consider gays, hemophiliacs or intravenous drug users (members of the groups considered at high-risk for contracting AIDS) or prisoners to be members of a suspect classification.[60]

Denial of equal protection under the Fourteenth Amendment has been a basis for a number of suits brought by inmates who have been segregated or denied access to programs because of seropositivity or a diagnosis of AIDS or ARC. In general, courts have upheld unequal treatment of these prisoners so long as there exists a rational basis for such treatment.[61]

Prison officials have advanced both security and medical reasons to justify segregation or denial of access to programs. Medical justifications have focused on the desire to limit the spread of the disease,[62] while security reasons have dealt with protection of seropositive prisoners and prisoners with AIDS from the tensions and harm that could result from the fears of other prisoners.[63]

The courts have upheld the prison administration in all these cases. In part, these decisions reflect the deference which the Supreme Court has insisted be paid to prison administrators in matters relating to security. When medical justifications are advanced, however, the usual deference is less,[64] and the asserted justifications can be attacked with expert witnesses and evidence showing that there is no rational basis for a particular policy or program. In such cases, the courts must determine, for example, whether it is medically rational to restrict access of seropositive inmates to programs. In this regard, prison officials' concern about preventing spread of the virus through casual contact are not advancing sound medical arguments.[65]

On the other hand, prison officials should conduct AIDS educational programs in order to end fears justifying segregation. It was not an idle comment that one court noted in upholding a segregation policy that it was rational "at least until some better system is developed" and that the prison authorities were changing their programs as they worked "to improve their ability to cope with the needs of prisoners with AIDS."[66]

2. The Eighth Amendment.

The eighth amendment prohibits the infliction of "cruel and unusual punishment." For convicted persons,[67] it is necessary to demonstrate that conditions violate the eighth amendment in that they constitute "the wanton and unnecessary infliction of pain" or are "grossly disproportionate to the severity of the crime warranting imprisonment." Rhodes v. Chapman, 452 U.S. 337 (1981).

The Supreme Court has described cruel and unusual punishment as treatment that is incompatible with evolving standards of decency or that involves unnecessary, wanton infliction of pain. Id. at 346. In determining whether the actions of prison officials constitute cruel and unusual punishment, courts will consider whether those actions further legitimate penal interests. Id. Not every hardship, therefore, will constitute cruel and unusual punishment.

Id. at 347. The eighth amendment also places certain affirmative duties on prison officials. Failure to provide adequate medical care amounting to "deliberate indifference" to prisoners' needs violates the eighth amendment.[68]

Each or all of the following conditions of confinement may be challenged by inmates who are quarantined or isolated based on their medical status: the size of the cells; double-celling of inmates;[69] heating and ventilation; lighting; noise; plumbing, electrical systems; fire safety; earthquake safety; clothing, laundry and bedding; personal hygiene; general sanitation; pests; food; exercises; visitation; idleness (no opportunity or access to work, educational or vocational programs); protection of inmates from constant threats of violence by other inmates or staff; and overcrowding. In addition, the length of time of the deprivations is relevant.[70]

To challenge conditions of confinement, the so-called "totality of circumstances" test is applicable; i.e., whether taken as a whole, conditions violate the prohibition against cruel and unusual punishment. Id. at 362-63. Virtually every lower federal court has utilized this test, with the notable exception of the Ninth Circuit, which has rejected the totality approach and has stated: ". . . the court must consider the effect of each condition in the context of the prison environment, especially where the ill effects of particular conditions are exacerbated by other related conditions." Wright v. Rushen, 642 F.2d 1129, 1133 (9th Cir. 1981)(emphasis added).[71]

3. Other constitutional grounds.

In addition to the equal protection and eighth amendment grounds, particular correctional practices or conditions may also be struck down on the ground that they violate the more specific guarantees of the first, fourth, sixth amendments, as well as the guarantees of procedural due process and equal protection.[72] The due process clauses of the fifth and fourteenth amendments mandate that prisoners may not be deprived of life, liberty, or property without a meaningful opportunity to be heard.[73] The touchstone of due process is protection of the individual against arbitrary governmental action.[74] The threshold question in determining whether due process has been denied is whether the individual's claim represents a liberty interest protected under the due process clause.[75] Liberty interests may be created by the Constitution or court order, or by the states through statutes, regulations, or standard practices, policies or customs.[76] After establishing that a protected liberty interest is involved, courts must determine the adequacy of the process provided.[77] In doing so, courts weigh the private interest affected, the risk of erroneous deprivation of the interest through the procedures used, and the government's interest.[78]

Suits have been successfully settled with respect to restrictions on access to law libraries and religious services.[79] If access to legal research materials is limited, a claim founded on the requirements of due process can be raised. Due process requires that prison authorities must assist inmates in the preparation and filing of meaningful legal papers by providing prisoners with either access to adequate law libraries or adequate assistance from persons trained in the law. Bounds v. Smith, 430 U.S. 817 (1977). Due process also requires that the libraries available to inmates be "adequate" and that regulations governing inmate use of the library permit the meaningful use of the library. Ramos v. Lamm, 639 F.2d 559, 582-83 (10th Cir. 1980), cert. denied, 101 S. Ct. 1759 (1981).

4. The Rehabilitation Act of 1973.

Section 504 of the Rehabilitation Act of 1973 (29 U.S.C. sec. 794) forbids discrimination against handicapped individuals in any program which receives federal funds. This Act may apply if a prisoner with AIDS or ARC or who is seropositive is being denied access to a particular program that is funded in part by federal monies. It is not enough that the institution receive federal funds for another program (see Doe v. Coughlin, 509 N.Y.S.2d at 212), although a bill passed by the U.S. Senate at the time of publication would amend the law to provide coverage for all programs of an institution receiving federal funds.

Once it is determined that a program receives federal funds, the next question is whether a person with AIDS, ARC or who is seropositive is "handicapped" under the terms of the Act. The Supreme Court recently held that a person with tuberculosis, a communicable disease, was covered by the Act and that the legislative history of the bill demonstrates that "Congress was as concerned about the effect of an impairment on others as it was about its effect on the individual."[80] In light of this recent decision and the justification advanced by prison authorities that seropositive inmates must be segregated because of the fears the condition generates in other prisoners, a strong argument can be made that the Act covers both seropositive prisoners and prisoners with AIDS.

Finally, prison authorities must demonstrate that there is a rational reason why the prisoner is not "otherwise qualified" to participate in the program. In this regard, they may assert that the restrictions are necessary for medical reasons; that is, to halt the spread of the disease.[81] However, as discussed above, a prisoner's claims have a greater likelihood of success when the prison advances a medical justification, rather than one based on security because the degree of deference is less.[82]

5. Writs of Habeas Corpus.

A writ of habeas corpus is an order, signed by a judge, mandating the person in charge of a prison or jail (such as a Warden or Sheriff) to bring a prisoner in his or her custody to court. The traditional purpose of the writ is to secure the release of a defendant from illegal incarceration or illegal restraint of any kind. Prisoners may seek writs of habeas corpus to challenge both the conditions of their confinement as well as the illegality of confinement. For example, the eighth amendment may be used as grounds for a writ. The conditions in which prisoners with AIDS are confined present a number of possibilities for bringing a writ of habeas corpus. These include mandatory segregation without demonstrated medical necessity, lack of access to law libraries, poor food, inadequate health care, and restrictions on the use of prison facilities, such as exercise yards.

While some courts have found that conditions of confinement may be litigated pursuant to the federal habeas corpus statutes,[83] this is not preferable since the litigator will be burdened with the requirement of exhaustion of state remedies[84] and with other rules limiting the usefulness of this remedy.[85] In some states, habeas corpus is an appropriate vehicle for litigating conditions of confinement and obtaining broad relief. The writ may be used to "obtain declaration and enforcement of prisoner's rights in confinement."[86]

Constitutional rights of prisoners may also be enforced through state writs of habeas corpus. In California, the courts have held that prisoners may obtain release on habeas corpus because of cruel, inhuman, or excessive punishment in prison.[87] Cruel and excessive punishment often focuses on restrictions on prisoners, as well as excessively poor conditions in the prisons. For prisoners with AIDS, the restrictions and conditions they face are extremely severe. Segregation with other persons who may have opportunistic infections, lack of exercise, and inadequate nutrition create life-threatening situations for these prisoners.

III. QUALITY OF MEDICAL CARE

The most pressing issue faced by prisoners with AIDS, ARC or who are seropositive is access to and availability of adequate medical care. This is because many prison medical personnel are ill-informed about AIDS and about the specific clinical manifestations and treatment options for the disease; prison infirmaries are poorly equipped to provide decent medical care; and prison medical facilities are woefully understaffed. Conditions in a California prison were so bad in 1987 that even the U.S Justice Department found that the medical care provided constituted cruel and unusual punishment.[88]

Suits on the quality of correctional medical care may be brought on the basis of federal constitutional standards, state law, or common law. We discuss below these issues with respect to the eighth amendment and state provisions.[89]

1. The Eighth Amendment.

The eighth amendment proscription against "cruel and unusual punishment" requires that prison authorities provide adequate medical care to inmates. The eighth amendment is violated when, by act or omission, authorities demonstrate "deliberate indifference to serious medical needs." Estelle v. Gamble, 429 U.S. 97, 106, 97 S. Ct. 285, 290-91 (1976). In discussing this standard, the Court noted that:

> "An inmate must rely on prison authorities to treat his medical needs; if the authorities fail to do so, those needs will not be met. In the worst cases, such a failure may actually produce physical 'torture or a lingering death,' ... the evils of most immediate concern to the drafters of the Amendment. In less serious cases, denial of medical care may result in pain and suffering which no one suggests would serve any penological purpose.... The infliction of such unnecessary suffering is inconsistent with contemporary standards of decency as manifested in modern legislation codifying the common law view that '[i]t is but just that the public be required to care for the prisoner, who cannot by reason of the deprivation of his liberty care for himself.'"

Id. (citations omitted).

In applying this standard to medical treatment of prisoners with AIDS or ARC or who are seropositive, the following factors are noteworthy:

- The Supreme Court recently noted that the delivery of adequate medical care to prisoners does not "ordinarily clash" with other responsibilities of prison authorities. Therefore, the existence of deliberate indifference to a prisoner's serious medical illness can "typically be established or disproved without the necessity of balancing competing institutional concerns for the safety of prison staff or other inmates." Whitley v. Albers, 475 U.S. 312, 106 S. Ct. 1078, 1086 (1986). Courts are less willing to take "a broad hands-off attitude towards the daily problems of prison administration ... when matters of medical care are involved, as opposed to matters of prison discipline and security." Guglielmoni v. Alexander, 583 F. Supp. 821, 827 (D. Conn. 1984).[90] Under this standard, courts are therefore less willing to defer to prison officials' actions relating to the medical care and treatment of prisoners.

- Deliberate indifference to the serious medical needs of inmates can be demonstrated either by (1) a showing of a pattern of individual incidents involving inadequate medical care; or (2) pointing to systemic deficiencies in the delivery of medical care which make unnecessary suffering inevitable.[91]

- The standard for evaluating the adequacy of care is not static but reflects "the evolving standards of decency that mark the progress of a maturing society." Estelle v. Gamble, 429 U.S. at 103, 97 S. Ct. at 290.

- The requirements of adequate medical care apply equally to psychiatric care. The high salaries earned by psychiatrists are not a justification for not providing such treatment.[92]

Applying the foregoing standards to prisoners with AIDS, ARC or who are seropositive, each or all of the following may be asserted as bases for an eighth amendment claim: intentional interference with treatment or intentional misdiagnosis;[93] refusal to treat ailments or ignoring complaints;[94] deliberate refusal to provide medical therapy and pain-killers;[95] allegation that official knew of prisoner's pain from tooth infection but refused to allow prisoner to see dentist;[96] inadequate access to medical care in isolation cells which deprived inmate of nearly all fresh air and light;[97] and, that prison officials knowingly denied medical attention for a chronic disease.[98]

2. State laws.

There are also a variety of state laws that are relevant to the delivery of medical care to prisoners. Most states have legislation that sets forth a general standard of care or that specifies duties of prison officials. See Comment, Medical Rights of Prisoners, 42 Univ. of Chicago L. Rev. 705, 707 (1975) for statutory listing. The Comment notes that these statutes can be difficult to rely upon in litigation because many of them are broadly worded, they are generally silent on the issue of enforcement, and their purpose may not be to create a right of action.

In some states, correctional medical care may be subject to suits for common law torts, such as negligence. Medical malpractice suits are also a possibility. See, e.g., Church v. Hegstrom, 416 F.2d 449, 451 n.1 (2d Cir. 1969)(Connecticut statute provides a method for obtaining monetary damages in cases of official negligence).

In addition, medical care in correctional institutions is usually governed by the state laws (e.g., Medical Practice and Nursing Practice Acts) that apply to the standard and quality of care in the community at large. However, inmates are not necessarily entitled to all aspects of medical care available in the community at large -- for example, the right to choose one's own physician and the right to a second medical opinion.[99]

IV. EARLY RELEASE OF PRISONERS WITH AIDS OR ARC

As discussed above, prisoners dying of AIDS or severe ARC have a multitude of medical needs which frequently cannot be met in the prison setting. In addition, these dying people are deprived of psycho-social support services in the community and have sharply restricted access to their families. The early release of prisoners who are seriously ill with AIDS or ARC may be obtained through pardon, parole or sentence modification. Prisoner advocates can help effect the release of sick prisoners by preparing the prisoner's application for release. The following discussion covers only the general characteristics of each option, as the specifics are governed by state and federal statutory schemes.

A. Parole

Most jurisdictions will grant parole to prisoners who are statutorily eligible if they are likely to abide by the law

and if their release will not disturb societal welfare.[100] Parole is not a sentence modification but rather an integral part of the inmate's sentence. Inmates released on parole continue to be supervised for the duration of their sentences.[101]

In most jurisdictions, the prisoner must serve a minimum sentence before being considered for parole. In California, for example, prisoners may be paroled once they have served the minimum term prescribed by law for their crime if their parole is approved by the Board of Prison Terms.[102] Prisoners may also have to meet other statutory eligibility requirements to qualify for parole; some states stipulate that prisoners previously convicted of a felony or serving a life sentence may not be eligible for parole.[103]

In some jurisdictions, prisoners will automatically come before the parole board for consideration, while others require prisoners to file an application when they become eligible.[104] In New York State, approximately 50 inmates with AIDS have been paroled in the past two years if they have suffered at least one of the opportunistic infections associated with the virus and if they are considered no danger to the community.[105]

B. Sentence Modification

Sentence modification is probably the most feasible way to obtain early release for a prisoner with AIDS if the jurisdiction has a sentence modification statute. Whereas early paroles must be granted by the parole board, sentences may only be modified by the sentencing court.

In most states, the sentencing court may only modify a sentence on a defendant's motion during a specified period of time after its pronouncement. For example, the time limit in California is 120 days. In a small number of states, sentencing courts maintain jurisdiction to reduce or modify a sentence "at any time."[106] A court rule in New Jersey permits a prisoner at any time to make a motion to reduce a sentence based on existence of a serious illness and the deleterious effect of incarceration on the prisoner's health.[107]

The American Bar Association has recommended continuing jurisdiction over sentences by the trial court on motion of the correction or releasing authorities.[108] California has such a system[109] whereby the court may modify a sentence on the recommendation of either the Director of the Department of Corrections or the Board of Prison Terms. At the federal level, a prisoner must apply to the Bureau of Prisons which in turn files a motion with the sentencing court for sentence modification. The court may act on the motion at any time and is authorized to reduce the prisoner's sentence to the time already served.[110] Similarly, under Rule 35 of the Federal Rules of Criminal Procedure, a defendant may make a motion to reduce his or her sentence or the court may reduce a sentence without motion, within 120 days after the sentence is imposed or probation is revoked.[111] The obvious advantage of this provision over a parole application is that the prisoner may file an application for sentence modification long before he or she is eligible for parole.

In states such as California where two mechanisms exist for a sentencing court to modify a sentence, the prisoner should file an application for resentencing with either the Director of Corrections or the Bureau of Prison Terms or request the sentencing court to resentence within the 120 day period. Unfortunately, some jurisdictions (notably, New York State) do not have resentencing provisions. In those jurisdictions the prisoner will have to rely on early parole statutes or clemency provisions.

C. Pardon

In contrast to sentence modifications or parole, applications for reprieve or pardon are probably the least likely to be granted. Under the United States Constitution, the President has the power to grant pardons for offenses against the United States. Most state constitutions confer the power to pardon on the Governor, with some states creating a pardon board and others vesting the power to pardon exclusively with the Governor. The power to pardon traditionally rests in the executive branch and is probably not subject to judicial review.[112]

The executive may exercise the power to pardon when a pardon will promote the public good[113] or to mitigate the unduly harsh effects of enforcing criminal law in a specific case.[114] A Mississippi case specifically notes that a prisoner's health is an appropriate factor to consider when deciding whether to grant a pardon.[115] Historically, the governor's clemency power has been exercised under subjective standards, unbounded by precedent and under procedures which need not comply with even minimal standards of due process.[116]

Some states have specific statutory regulations regarding how and when an application for pardon must be filed, while in other states the prisoner simply files the petition with the Governor.[117] In any case, the petition should describe the inmate's medical condition and describe any other factors that are pertinent to an application for pardon in that jurisdiction.

CONCLUSION

The decision to impose mass screening and segregation of prisoners raises the question of why correctional systems are adopting measures not being adopted in the community at large to deal with the AIDS epidemic. In large part, this is due to the political impotence of prisoners, who, historically, have been easy targets of measures that severely restrict their civil rights. The real question, however, is whether screening and segregation are effective public health measures and whether there are less restrictive, more effective measures available.

Mandatory screening and segregation in prison facilities create the damaging impression that prisoners are to be treated as modern day lepers and that, like gay men and drug users, they are to be stigmatized as HIV carriers. The creation of AIDS wings or AIDS prisons also conveys a harmful message that will affect public perception about the nature of the disease and how to deal with it. Finally, such policies entail a massive expenditure of limited resources on measures that are unnecessary, unmanageable and ineffective in halting the spread of the disease.

The primary right of all prisoners is the right to a healthy and safe environment. It is critical that prisoner advocates explore both well-established precedent and creative theories to challenge AIDS-related policies that undermine that right.

Notes

1. The National Prison Project of the ACLU has recently developed an AIDS program and can be consulted for the latest information about cases and technical assistance. The Project is located at 1616 P Street NW, Washington, DC 20036 ((202) 331-0500). The Practice Manual editors and the author of this article are also available for assistance.

2. Hammett, AIDS in Correctional Facilities: Issues and Options xx-xxi (1987)(sponsored by the National Institute of Justice) [hereafter cited as "NIJ Study"].

3. See generally Project: Criminal Procedure, "Prisoners' Rights," 74 Geo. L.J. 973 (1986); Rudovsky, Bronstein & Koren, The Rights of Prisoners, American Civil Liberties Union (1973).

4. See Hudson v. Palmer, 468 U.S. 517, 525, 104 S. Ct. 3194, 3199 (1984)(prisoners retain those rights consistent with imprisonment or compatible with objectives of incarceration); Meadows v. Hopkins, 713 F.2d 206, 209 (6th Cir. 1983)(prisoners not stripped

of all rights at prison gate). See also Bounds v. Smith, 430 U.S. 817 (1977)(prisoners retain right of access to courts); Estelle v. Gamble, 429 U.S. 97, 102-03 (1976)(prisoners retain right to freedom from cruel and unusual punishment); Wolff v. McDonnell, 418 U.S. 539, 556 (1974)(prisoners retain right to due process subject to restriction imposed by nature of penal system); Cruz v. Beto, 405 U.S. 319, 322 n.2 (1972)(per curiam)(prisoners retain limited first amendment right to free exercise of religion); Lee v. Washington, 390 U.S. 333, 333-34 (1968)(per curiam)(prisoners retain right to equal protection).

5. See, e.g., Hutto v. Finney, 437 U.S. 678, 687 (1978)(comprehensive district court order correcting many constitutional violations justified by inadequate compliance with prior court orders); Bounds v. Smith, 430 U.S. 817, 832-33 (1977)(affirming district court order requiring that inmates have access to legal research facilities).

6. See Hudson v. Palmer, 468 U.S. at 542, 104 S. Ct. at 3208 (Stevens, J., dissenting in part)(quoting Houchins v. KQED, 438 U.S. 1, 5 n.2 (1978)(Burger, C.J.)(plurality opinion)("It is true that inmates lose many rights when they are lawfully confined, but they do not lose all civil rights.... Inmates in jails, prisons or mental institutions retain certain fundamental rights of privacy ....").

7. The statute provides:

> Every person who, under color of any statute, ordinance, regulation, custom, or usage of any State, Territory, or the District of Columbia, subjects, or causes to be subjected, any citizen of the United States or other person within the jurisdiction thereof to the deprivation of any rights, privileges, or immunities secured by the Constitution and laws shall be liable to the party injured in an action at law, suit in equity, or the proper proceeding for redress. For the purposes of this section, any Act of Congress applicable exclusively to the District of Columbia shall be considered to be a statute of the District of Columbia.

For a comprehensive review of Sec. 1983 and other federal civil rights statutes, see Nahmond, Civil Rights and Civil Liberties Litigation (Shepard's 1979).

8. For federal habeas corpus practice, see Wright, Miller & Cooper, Jurisdiction, sec. 4261 et seq; see also State Bar of California, Standing Committee on Legal Services for Prisoners: Manual for Use of Habeas Corpus by California Prisoners (1982).

9. Winston v. Lee, 470 U.S. 753, 759-60 (1985)(quoting Schmerber v. California, 384 U.S. 757, 767 (1966)).

10. Delaware v. Prouse, 440 U.S. 648, 653-54, 99 S. Ct. 1391, 1396 (1979); Camara v. Muni. Court, 387 U.S. 523, 528, 87 S. Ct. 1727, 1730 (1967).

11. See McKinley v. Trattles, 732 F.2d 1320, 1325 (7th Cir. 1984)(upholding jury verdict against guard who allegedly subjected prisoner to anal cavity search in violation of prisoner's rights); Lee v. Winston, 717 F.2d 888, 900-01 (4th Cir. 1983)(requiring surgery to remove possibly incriminating bullet violates fourth amendment when surgery requires deep incision

and general anesthetic); cert. granted, 466 U.S. 935 (1984), cert. denied 466 U.S. 942 (1984), judgement aff'd, 470 U.S. 753 (1985); cf. United States v. Caldwell, 750 F.2d 341, 343 n.2 (5th Cir. 1984)(suggesting that Hudson may imply relaxed fourth amendment standard in context of body cavity searches performed in prison), cert. denied, 105 S. Ct. 1873 (1985).

12. See generally Note, Constitutional Limitations on Body Searches in Prisons, 82 Colum. L. Rev. 1033 (1982).

13. See Bell v. Wolfish, 441 U.S. 520, 559 (1979)(courts must consider "the scope of the particular intrusion, the manner in which it is conducted, the justification for initiating it and the place where it is conducted").

14. Caution is advised in presenting this claim, since no case has yet decided this and, as discussed below, the prerequisites for establishing a fourth amendment "search and seizure" claim are stringent.

15. National Treasury Employees Union v. Von Raab, 816 F.2d 170, 176 (5th Cir. 1987); McDonell v. Hunter, 809 F.2d 1302 (8th Cir. 1987); Shoemaker v. Handel, 795 F.2d 1136 (3rd Cir. 1986), cert. denied, 107 S. Ct. 577 (1986); Capua v. City of Plainfield, 643 F. Supp. 1507, 1514 (D.N.J. 1986). A very recently decided case, Amalgamated Transit Union, Local 1277 v. Sunline Transit Agency, No. CV086-827ORG(GX), slip op. at 10-19 (C.D. Cal. July 7, 1987), thoroughly analyzes the applicability of the fourth amendment to drug testing. Similarly, blood tests have been held to fall within the fourth amendment in Schmerber v. California, 384 U.S. 757, 767-68 (1966).

16. 468 U.S. 517, 104 S. Ct. 3194 (1984).

17. See Bonitz v. Fair, 804 F.2d 164, 172 (1st Cir. 1986); Blackburn v. Snow, 771 F.2d 556 (1st Cir. 1985); Arruda v. Fair, 710 F.2d 886, 888 (1st Cir. 1983) cert. denied 464 U.S. 999 (1983); Logan v. Shealy, 660 F.2d 1007, 1013 (4th Cir. 1981), cert. denied 455 U.S. 942 (1982); Hill v. Bogans, 735 F.2d 391, 394 (10th Cir. 1984); Frazier v. Ward, 528 F. Supp. 80, 83 (N.D.N.Y. 1981); Sims v. Brierton, 500 F. Supp. 813, 817 (N.D. Ill. 1980)(stating that the prison administration's "security concerns are excessive"); Hodges v. Klein, 412 F. Supp. 896 (D.N.J. 1976).

18. These cases have explicitly rejected the argument that the restrictive standard for random searches of cells under Hudson should apply to the forced extraction of body fluids. Storms v. Coughlin, 600 F. Supp. 1214 (S.D.N.Y. 1984); Tucker v. Dickey, 613 F. Supp. 1124 (D.C. Wis. 1985).

19. Information on these issues is contained in other sections of this Manual, including the chapter on medical issues (which contains a section on testing), the issue of The Exchange on mandatory testing which is a Manual Appendix, and the issue of this publication on prisons and jails which is attached to this article.

20. See The Exchange, August 1987, at 2 (reprinted in the appendix to this article).

21. The Supreme Court has noted the importance of family relationships to prisoners and found a "constitutionally protected marital relationship in the prison context." Turner v. Safley, 107

S. Ct. 2254, 2265 (1987).

22. See, e.g., Shoemaker v. Handel, 795 F.2d 1136, 1144 (3rd Cir. 1986) cert. denied 107 S. Ct. 577 (1986); U.S. v. Westinghouse Electric Corp., 638 F.2d 570, 577 (3rd Cir. 1980); Capua v. City of Plainfield, 643 F. Supp. 1507, 1515 (D.N.J. 1986).

23. See Schmerber v California, 348 U.S. at 770.

24. A survey of 58 federal, state and local prison systems conducted by the National Institute of Justice in 1986 found that AIDS cases were rising more slowly among prison inmates than in the population at large. New York Times, March 12, 1987, at 8.

25. For further discussion, see the excerpt from the article by Urvashi Vaid reprinted in the December 1986 issue of The Exchange.

26. An extremely authoritative source in this regard is the publication by the National Academy of Sciences, Confronting AIDS: Directions for Public Health, Health Care and Research (1986).

27. See NIJ Study, note 2 above, at xviii ("education and training must continue to be the cornerstone of the response to AIDS in correctional facilities, as in society at large.")

28. One court has, in fact, ordered the distribution of an AIDS brochure to all inmates at a New York prison. See LaRocca v. Dalsheim, 120 Misc. 2d 697, 707, 467 N.Y.S.2d 302, 310 (Sup. Ct. 1983).

29. See Centers for Disease Control, Recommendations for Preventing Transmission of Infection with Human T-Lymphotropic Virus Type III/Lymphadenopathy-Associated Virus in the Workplace, 34 MMWR 681 (Nov. 15, 1985).

30. Dep't. of Labor, Dep't of Health and Human Services, Joint Advisory Notice: Protection Against Occupational Exposure to Hepatitis B Virus (HBV and Human Immunodeficiency Virus (HIV), 52 Fed. Reg. 41818 (Oct. 30, 1987). For information, call the National OSHA Information Office at (202) 523-8148.

31. With regard to inmates, distribution of condoms would be another means of reducing the spread of HIV in prisons. Such a policy has been implemented in Vermont, Vermont Dept. of Corrections Medical Procedures 412 JJ (Addendum) and as part of a pilot program in certain city jails in New York. See New York Times, June 30, 1987. Texas is considering a measure similar to Vermont's. San Francisco Examiner, April 15, 1987.

32. See Tucker v. Dickey, 613 F. Supp. 1124, 1131 (D.C. Wis. 1985).

33. The Congressional Office of Technology Assessment conducted a study of the false positivity and negativity rates of approximately 700 U.S. laboratories. It found that some laboratories achieve performance standards close to the ideal of 0.5 percent false positives and 0.4 percent false negatives. Other laboratories had false positive rates greater than 4.7 percent and false negative rates greater than 9.3 percent. See Washington Post, October 27, 1987, at 5.

34. In New Jersey, inmates have filed suit seeking strict confidentiality of all AIDS-related medical records. Sheridan v. Fauver, No. 85-3042 (U.S.D.C. N.J. filed Aug. 1985).

35. In California, only the subject may receive the results of the test unless he or she gives written authorization for others to receive it. Written consent is required for each separate disclosure. Cal. Health & Safety Code sec. 199.21. In Wisconsin, the only legal recipients of test results are the subject, the subject's health-care provider, laboratory personnel and other staff of health-care facilities, and the state epidemiologist. Any disclosure to others requires a court order. Wisc. Stat. Ann. sec. 146.025 (West Supp. 1986).

36. NIJ Study, note 2 above, at 58.

37. Id.

38. Storms v. Coughlin, 600 F. Supp. at 1223.

39. Dean v. Bowie, No. 87-4745 (Suffolk Super. Ct. filed Aug. 27, 1987).

40. NIJ Study, note 2 above, at 42.

41. The court has found the roots of that right to privacy in the first amendment, Stanley v. Georgia, 394 U.S. 557 (1969) in the fourth and fifth amendments, Terry v. Ohio, 392 U.S. 1 (1969), in the penumbra of the Bill of Rights, Griswold v. Connecticut, 381 U.S. 479 (1965) and in the ninth amendment, id., or in the concept of liberty guaranteed by the first section of the fourteenth amendment. Meyer v. Nebraska, 262 U.S. 390 (1923).

42. Roe v. Wade, 410 U.S. 113, 152 (1973) citing Palko v. Conn., 302 U.S. 319, 325 (1937).

43. Olmstead v. United States, 277 U.S. 438, 478 (1928) (Brandeis, J., dissenting).

44. Grummett v. Rushen, 779 F.2d 491 (9th Cir. 1985); Cumbey v. Meachum, 684 F.2d 712 (10th Cir. 1982); Dawson v. Kendrick, 527 F. Supp. 1252, 1316-17 (E.D.W. Va. 1981); Bowling v. Enomoto, 514 F. Supp. 201 (N.D. Cal. 1980).

45. Forts v. Ward, 471 F. Supp. 1095 (S.D.N.Y. 1979) vacated in part 621 F.2d 1210 (2d Cir. 1980); Hudson v. Goodlander, 494 F. Supp. 890, 894-95 (D. Md. 1980).

46. The constitutions of the states of Alaska, Arizona, California, Florida, Hawaii, Illinois, Louisiana, Montana, South Carolina and Washington contain privacy provisions. In some other states (including Georgia, Idaho and Massachusetts), the right to privacy has been judicially recognized. See also 1987 Lesbian/Gay Law Notes 1 (Minnesota); 1986 Lesbian/Gay Law Notes 71 (Kentucky).

47. Committee to Defend Reproductive Rights v. Meyers, 29 Cal.3d 252 (1981).

48. City of Santa Barbara v. Adamson, 27 Cal. 3d 123 (1980).

49. Board of Medical Quality Assurance v. Gherardini, 93 Cal. App. 3d 669 (1979).

50. See In re Long, 127 Cal. Rptr. 732 (App. 1976). See also Sterling v. Cupp, 625 P.2d 123 (Or. 1981)(prisoners' privacy protected under Oregon constitution).

51. NIJ Study, note 2 above, at 41.

52. The NIJ Study revealed that 27 percent of responding jail systems segregate all seropositive inmates and an additional 30 percent make case-by-case determinations. The incidence of segregation of prisoners with AIDS or ARC is still higher. See NIJ Study, note 2 above, at xxii. The study notes that the 27 percent figure is a decrease from 41 percent the previous year.

53. In one case, conjugal visits were denied. See Doe v. Coughlin, 125 A.D.2d 783, 509 N.Y.S.2d 209 (1986), affd, 56 U.S.L.W. 2330 (1987).

54. In Jones v. North Carolina Prisoners' Labor Union, 433 U.S. 119 (1977), the court held that prison administrators were justified in restricting the right to group worship.

55. On the other hand, some inmates have filed actions seeking separate housing for those who test positive (see La Rocca v. Dalsheim, 120 Misc. 2d 697, 467 N.Y.S.2d 302 (N.Y. Sup. 1983); Herring v. Keeney, (U.S.D.C. Or., filed Sept. 17, 1985); Sheppard v. Keeney, (U.S.D.C. Or. filed Oct. 7, 1985); Malport v. Keeney, (U.S.D.C. Or. filed Oct. 11, 1985); Telepo v. Fauver, No. 85-1742A (U.S.D.C. N.J. filed April 15, 1985)) or seeking mass screening of inmates, Potter v. Wainwright, No. 85-1616-CIV-T15 (U.S.D.C. Fla. Mid. D.). Other inmates have filed suit to prevent homosexuals from working in the prison food service and to obtain protection against homosexuals spreading HIV infection through assaultive and consensual acts. Stalling v. Cane, (Fla. 2d Cir., DeLeon County). Finally, one inmate has claimed severe emotional distress as a result of being housed in the same unit with ARC inmates. Yates v. Lewis, No. CIV-86-1538-PHX (U.S.D.C. Ariz.). See also Foy v. Owens, No. 85-6909, slip. op. (E.D. Pa. Mar. 19, 1986)(inmate claimed right to be free from exposure to AIDS but court dismissed claim as frivolous).

56. See San Antonio Independent School District v. Rodriguez, 411 U.S. 1, 4-5, 9-10 (1973)(strict scrutiny applied to constitutional claims brought under equal protection clauses by class of poor families challenging state system for financing public education based on local property tax).

57. See Graham v. Richardson, 403 U.S. 365, 376 (1971)(statutes providing different welfare benefits to aliens and non-aliens subject to strict scrutiny under equal protection clause); McLaughlin v. Florida, 379 U.S. 184, 196 (1964)(state statute prohibiting co-habitation of whites and blacks to be invalid subject to strict scrutiny by court).

58. See Mississippi University for Women v. Hogan, 458 U.S. 718, 723-27 (1982)(court found discriminatory admissions practice unconstitutional where male sought admissions to all female university nursing school, applying heightened standard of review); Gomez v. Perez, 409 U.S. 535 (1973)(state classification providing that only legitimate children had judicially enforceable rights to support from natural fathers struck down under middle tier standard of review).

59. See Massachusetts Board of Retirement v. Murgia, 427 U.S. 307, 312 (1976)(age classification subject to rational basis test); see also City of Cleburne v. Cleburne Living Center, 105 S. Ct. 3249, 3255-58 (1985)(mentally retarded not a suspect class).

60. See Bowers v. Hardwick, 106 S. Ct. 2841, 2844 (1986)(denying that right to engage in homosexual sodomy is fundamental); see also Cordero v. Coughlin, 607 F. Supp. 9, 10 (S.D.N.Y. 1984)(persons with AIDS not a "suspect class").

61. See Cordero v. Coughlin, 607 F. Supp. (segregation of prisoners with AIDS bears rational relation to legitimate governmental objectives of safeguarding them from threats and violence and similarly protecting others).

62. See Judd v. Packard, 669 F. Supp. 741 (D. Md. 1987)(segregation justified as part of a "program of AIDS prevention"); Doe v. Coughlin, note 53 above (denial of access to conjugal visit program rational as a means of preventing the transmission of AIDS); NIJ Study, note 2 above, at xxiv.

63. See Cordero v. Coughlin, note 60 above; Powell v. Department of Corrections, 647 F. Supp. 968 (N.D. Okla. 1986) (court dismissed seropositive inmates's 14th Amendment claim challenging his segregation from the general prison population, citing protection of other inmates from spread of the disease).

64. See Wellman v. Faulkner, 715 F.2d 269, 272 (7th Cir. 1983) cert. denied, 468 U.S. 1217 (1984); Todaro v. Ward, 565 F.2d 48, 54 (2d Cir. 1977)("policy of deference to state officials is less substantial when ... matters of prison discipline and security are not at issue"); Burks v. Teasdale, 492 F. Supp. 650, 655 (W.D. Mo. 1980); Guglielmoni v. Alexander, 583 F. Supp. 821, 826-27 (D. Conn. 1984). See also Whitley v. Albers, 106 S. Ct. 1078, 1084-86 (1986)(discussed below in medical section). Although these cases all deal with the right to medical treatment, it is arguable that less deference would also be paid when a medical justification is given for housing or program denial.

65. Nonetheless, such an argument was accepted by one court in approving a ban on conjugal visits by prisoners with AIDS because "the possible risk of transmission from close contact with an AIDS sufferer remains an unresolved question of great concern." Doe v. Coughlin, 509 N.Y.S.2d at 212.

66. Cordero v. Coughlin, 607 F. Supp. at 10. If sex among inmates is raised by the administration as a rationale for segregating seropositive inmates, see LaRocca v. Dalsheim, note 28 above, at 702(court orders distribution of AIDS brochure noting that "the dissemination of information among inmates may reduce the incidence of prison sex").

67. This section focuses solely on the rights of convicted persons. For pre-trial detainees, it must be established that the conditions of confinement deny substantive due process by subjecting such prisoners to "genuine privation and hardships over an extended period of time" or to restrictions or conditions which are not "reasonably related to a legitimate goal." Bell v. Wolfish, 441 U.S. 520 (1979).

68. Estelle v. Gamble, 429 U.S. 97, 104 (1976), reh'g denied, 429 U.S. 1066 (1977). See section III on medical care below.

69. Double-celling of prisoners alone, however, does not make prison conditions cruel or unusual. Rhodes v. Chapman, 452 U.S. at 347-49.

70. See Spain v. Procunier, 600 F.2d 189, 199-200 (9th Cir. 1979).

71. See also Hoptowit v. Spellman, 753 F.2d 779, 783 (9th Cir. 1985)(district court must consider and decide whether each condition amounts to unnecessary and wanton infliction of pain).

72. See, e.g., Bell v. Wolfish, 441 U.S. 520 (1979) (first and fourth amendments, due process claims); Kincaid v. Rusk, 670 F.2d 737 (7th Cir. 1982) (first amendment claim); Smith v. Jordan, 527 F. Supp. 167 (S.D. Ohio 1981) (fourth amendment claim); Dawson v. Kendrick, 527 F. Supp. 1252 (S.D.W. Va. 1981) (procedural due process, sixth amendment, equal protection claims). But see Hewitt v. Helms, 459 U.S. 460, 103 S. Ct. 864, 869-70 (1983)("the transfer of an inmate to less amenable and more restrictive quarters for nonpunitive reasons is well within the terms of confinement ordinarily contemplated by a prison sentence") and Turner v. Safley, discussed in sec. IA(2) above (limited test for correspondence).

73. Parratt v. Taylor, 451 U.S. 527, 540 (1981).

74. Wolff v. McDonnell, 418 U.S. 539, 558 (1974).

75. Meachum v. Fano, 427 U.S. 215, 223-24 (1976).

76. See generally Project: Criminal Procedure, note 3 above, at 983-84.

77. Quick v. Jones, 754 F.2d 1521, 1523 (9th Cir. 1985).

78. See Mathews v. Eldridge, 424 U.S. 319, 334-35 (1976).

79. See NIJ Study, note 2 above, at xxiv.

80. School Board of Nassau County v. Arline, 478 U.S. ___, 107 S. Ct. 1123, 94 L. Ed. 2d 307 (1987).

81. See Doe v. Coughlin, 509 N.Y.S.2d at 212.

82. See discussion accompanying note 64 above.

83. Roba v. United States, 604 F.2d 215 (2d Cir. 1979); Knell v. Bensinger, 522 F.2d 720 (7th Cir. 1975).

84. Harris v. McDonald, 555 F.Supp. 137 (N.D. Ill. 1982).

85. See, e.g., United States ex rel. Hoover v. Franzen, 669 F.2d 433 (7th Cir. 1982)(pendent jurisdiction not available under habeas corpus statutes).

86. In re Davis, 25 Cal. 3d 384, 158 Cal. Rptr. 384 (1979)(detention of prisoners in administrative segregation without a hearing violates their due process rights; writ of habeas corpus is proper method to enforce their rights).

87. See, e.g., In re Riddle, 57 Cal. 2d 848, 22 Cal. Rptr. 472 (1962).

88. San Francisco Chronicle, June 14, 1987, at 1 (medical and psychiatric care at the California Medical Facility at Vacaville violates inmates' constitutional rights "to be free from deliberate indifference to their serious medical needs" stated Assistant U.S. Attorney General William Bradford Reynolds in a letter to California Governor George Deukmejian).

89. Claims relating to the denial of medical care as a violation of the equal protection clause were discussed in the previous section.

90. See also Burks v. Teasdale, 492 F. Supp. 650, 655 (W.D. Mo. 1980).

91. See Ruiz v. Estelle, 503 F. Supp. 1265 (S.D. Tex. 1980), aff. in part, rev. in part, 679 F.2d 1115 (5th Cir.), amended in part, vacated in part, 688 F.2d 266, cert. denied, 460 U.S. 1042 (1983).

92. Wellman v. Falkner, note 64 above, at 273 (weighs against the state the facts that a psychiatric position remained vacant for two years and the authorized salary was "woefully inadequate"). 'See also Guglielmoni v. Alexander, 583 F. Supp. at 826-28.

93. Benson v. Cady, 761 F.2d 335, 340-41 (7th Cir. 1985).

94. Johnson v. Treen, 759 F.2d 1236, 1238 (5th Cir. 1985).

95. McCarthy v. Weinberg, 753 F.2d 836, 839 (10th Cir. 1985).

96. Fields v. Gander, 734 F.2d 1313, 1314-15 (8th Cir. 1984).

97. Hoptowit v. Ray, 682 F.2d 1237, 1257-58 (9th Cir. 1982).

98. Williams v. Treen, 671 F.2d 892, 901 (5th Cir. 1982).

99. However, in some jurisdictions, including California, certain statutes allow for the ability of an inmate to see a physician of his or her own choice or to obtain a second medical opinion. See Cal. Civ. Code sec. 3354(b). These statutes and their implementing rules and regulations should be consulted and often provide a solution for those inmates in need of immediate transfer to an outside physician or hospital.

100. Lewis v. Rockefeller, 305 F. Supp. 258, 259, aff'd, 431 F.2d 368 (2d Cir. 1970).

101. Geraghty v. U.S. Parole Commission, 429 F. Supp. 737, 741 (M.D. Pa. 1977), aff'd, 719 F.2d 1199 (3d Cir. 1983) cert. denied, 465 U.S. 1103 (1984).

102. California Penal Code secs. 3040, 3049.

103. See Commonwealth ex rel. Banks v. Cain, 345 Pa. 581, 28 A.2d 897, 143 A.L.R. 1473 (1942); Eisentrager v. State Board of Parole Commissioners, 85 Nev. 672, 462 P.2d 40 (1969).

104. Federal prisoners must file such an application, for example. 28 CFR 2.11 (1987).

105. N.Y. Times, March 7, 1987, at 1.

106. These jurisdictions include New Jersey, Wisconsin, Kansas and District of Columbia. See Note, Survey of Criminal Proce-

dure, note 3 above. Statutes and caselaw in various states relevant to sentence modification are set forth in an appendix to this article.

107. Court Rule 3:21-10(b)(2). See State v. Priester, 99 N.J. 123, 491 A.2d 650 (1985).

108. ABA Comm. on Minimum Standards for Administration of Criminal Justice, Standards Relating to Sentencing Alternatives and Procedures, sec. 6.2 (Approved Draft 1968).

109. California Penal Code sec. 1170(d).

110. 18 U.S.C. 4205(g)(1976)("At any time upon motion of the Bureau of Prisons, the court may reduce any minimum term to the time the defendant has served.")

111. This provision also applies within 120 days after affirmance of the judgment or dismissal of the appeal, or within 120 days after entry of any order or judgment of the Supreme Court denying review of or upholding a conviction or probation revocation.

112. Solesbee v. Balkcom, 339 U.S. 926, 70 S. Ct. 618 (1950).

113. Moore v. Lawrence, 192 Ga. 441, 15 S.E.2d 519, 521 (1941).

114. Egan v. United States, 268 F.2d 820, 824, cert. denied 361 U.S. 868 (1959).

115. Ex Parte Chain, 210 Miss. 415, 49 So. 2d 722, 725 (1951) ("the responsibility for determining whether the petitioner is a fit subject for clemency, whether because of the condition of his health he should be pardoned ... is a responsibility that rests upon the governor.")

116. See Note, Survey of Criminal Procedure - Modification of Sentences, 30 Rutgers L. Rev. 657, 672-73 (1977)(citing Goldfarb & Singer, After Conviction 330, 340 (1973)).

117. See, e.g., Cal. Penal Code sec. 4852.01 et seq.

Appendices

1. Reduction or Change of Sentence.

2. AIDS in Jails and Prisons, The Exchange (National Lawyers Guild AIDS Network, Dec. 1986).

APPENDIX 1

Wisconsin, Kansas, and the District of Columbia allow reduction or change of sentence "at any time" in specified circumstances. See State v. Wuensch, 69 Wis. 2d 467, 480, 230 N.W.2d 665, 671-72 (1975)(modification on application of the defendant based on new factors or an abuse of discretion); Kutchera v. State, 69 Wis. 2d 534, 552-53, 230 N.W.2d 750, 760 (1975)(modification

because of change of law); D.C. Code sec. 24201(c)(1967)(modification of minimum sentence to time served on application of correctional authorities, except for conviction of assault with intent to rape or armed robbery after prior conviction for crime of violence); Kansas Stat. sec. 21-4603 (Supp. 1975)(modification of minimum sentence to time served on recommendation of Secretary of Corrections).

Most jurisdictions allowing reduction or change of sentence provide a specific time period within which such change may occur. ABA Comm. on Minimum Standards for Administration of Criminal Justice, Standards Relating to Sentencing Alternatives and Procedures, sec. 6.1(a) commentary (Approved Draft 1968). See, e.g., Ariz. Rev. Stat. ch. 17, sec 24.3 (1973)(within 60 days after entry of judgment but before appeal filed); Ill. Ann. Stat. ch. 38, sec. 1005-8-1(d)(Smith-Hurd 1973)(within 30 days after imposition of sentence); Fed. R. Crim. Pro. 35 (within 120 days of imposition of sentence or resolution of appeal); Fla. R. Crim. Pro. 3.800 (within longer of the same term of court or 60 days from imposition or resolution of appeal).

Some jurisdictions follow the old common law rule, allowing change of sentence only during the term of court, until service of sentence has begun. See, e.g., Mich. Stat. Ann. sec. 28.1097 (1972); People v. Fox, 312 Mich. 577, 581, 20 N.W.2d 732, 733 (Sup. Ct. 1945). Some jurisdictions allow no change of sentence other than to correct error. See, e.g., Vt. R. Crim. Pro. 36 (change only to correct clerical error).

The constitutionality of the "at any time" provisions of the New Jersey motion to reduce sentence has been upheld. State v. Robinson, No. A-2669-75 (N.J. Super. Ct. App. Div. Mar. 17, 1977), rev'g 140 N.J. Super. 459, 356 A.2d 449 (Law Div. 1976).

IDS NETWORK

THE EXCHANGE

Issue 2 December 1986

AIDS in Jails and Prisons:
What We Can Do.

This issue of **The Exchange** focuses on AIDS in jails and prisons. With the spread of the disease, jail and prison administrators in all regions are facing the AIDS-related issues of housing, prisoner and guard education, testing, condom distribution, medical care and confidentiality of medical records. In many cases, they have dealt with these issues badly or haphazardly, failing to formulate policies in advance, acting out of ignorance, reacting to the fears of guards and prisoners. The development of reasoned, safe and humane policies for the treatment of prisoners with AIDS and related conditions is critical. We feel that strong progressive input into the policy-making process is essential and urge our members to contribute to it. The following article is written by Paul Albert, a member of our Editorial Board. This is a second printing of this issue which is somewhat abbreviated from the original.

The issue of AIDS in jails and prisons has received little media coverage and inadequate attention within the penal system. Most jails and prisons currently have only rudimentary policies which often are based on misinformation and generally involve segregation and discrimination.   An example of such a policy is described in the accompanying article about a Florida jail in which asymptomatic inmates testing positive for the AIDS antibodies ("seropositive inmates") are segregated under terrible conditions.

Segregated inmates in longer-term prisons face similar deprivations, including lack of access to work programs, education,
the law library, religious services, and counseling, and greatly restricted visits with family and friends. Many prisoners with AIDS face being locked in a cell for the rest of their lives.

Surveys show that this type of segregation is common: 41% of city and county jails in a recent study segregate all seropositive inmates and an additional 30% make case-by-case determinations. The incidence of segregation of prisoners with AIDS or ARC is still higher. See the National Institute of Justice (NIJ) study listed in our Resource Section.

There is no medical reason to segregate prisoners with
AIDS except during periods when they need hospitalization. As discussed in the accompanying article by attorney Urvashi Vaid, blanket administrative segregation is also unjustifiable in most cases.

The policy of segregating people with AIDS and related conditions is essentially a knee-jerk reaction by administrators accustomed to using lock-up as an easy means of handling difficult situations. As the Florida jail administrator states: "We didn't know anything about AIDS. We were just locking them down."

This statement summarizes the importance of administration and staff education in the development of

National Lawyers Guild AIDS Network
11 Gough Street Third Floor   San Francisco CA 94102   415 861-8884

AIDS policies. The NIJ study uncovered widespread fear among guards of catching AIDS through casual contact with prisoners with AIDS or ARC. As a result, guards in many systems have demanded segregation policies and the mass testing of inmates to identify those who are seropositive. AFSCME, a prominent union representing guards, has passed a national resolution in favor of mandatory testing and lobbied for legislation to this effect in New York state. Policy reasons against testing are discussed in the Vaid article.

Demands for the segregation of people with AIDS have also come from inmates. There is a great deal of misinformation and anxiety about AIDS among prisoners, which has resulted in hostility, physical threats and even assaults against persons suspected of having the disease. Prisoner education aimed at calming these fears is essential if people with AIDS are to live in the general prison population.

It is also important that education promote safe sex and needle practices. Consensual and forced sex are common in prison, as are intravenous drug use and tattooing. Education of prisoners provides an opportunity to reach an at-risk segment of the population which is difficult to reach on the streets and likely to spread the disease into the heterosexual community at large. Many women in jails are prostitutes as well as drug users, and most

men who engage in homosexual sex in prison are basically heterosexuals.

In spite of these factors and the growing public support for AIDS education, most prison officials resist meaningful safe sex and needle educational programs out of fear of appearing to acquiesce in these practices. As a result, most AIDS educational programs which do exist are ineffective and do not take into account the prison environment. For example, all of the inmate training materials reproduced as models in the NIJ study urge prisoners to avoid all sexual conduct but do not mention anal intercourse or attempt to distinguish between safe and unsafe sexual practices. The word "tattoo" is not mentioned at all.

Because this is a difficult issue for prison administrators, Vaid recommends that prisoner education be run by outside agencies. In this way, administrators do not have to become personally involved in approving the details of the program. In addition, outside persons are more apt to be believed by inmates than prison staff.

The staff of the San Francisco Sheriff's office opposes this position, however, and feels that it is preferable to work to win the support of administrators and medical personnel for an effective program and then involve them in all of its aspects. It has developed posters against tattooing, needle sharing and unsafe sex and distributed

wallet cards with safe practice information. Its training materials are available to other law enforcement agencies. See the Resource Section.

In addition to education, it is also desirable to promote safe sex by distributing condoms to prisoners. Condoms have been distributed in penal institutions in New South Wales, Australia, according to Vaid. In jurisdictions in which sex among prisoners is illegal, such a policy probably could not be implemented. However, it is vital that condoms be distributed in conjunction with conjugal visits, and the lack of condoms should in any case not deter a meaningful safe sex educational program.

Medical care and confidentiality of records are also important issues. In addition to medical treatment it is important to emphasize that prisoners with AIDS or related conditions greatly need counseling, both for their own mental health and to minimize the likelihood that they will spread the disease. The low standard of medical care required by law is discussed in Vaid's article.

Until effective inmate and guard educational programs are implemented, confidentiality of medical records is essential to the safety of prisoners with AIDS and related conditions within the general prison population. It is difficult to guarantee confidentiality in most systems, however, because guards and prisoner clerks have access to medical files. In order to deal with this problem, doctors in some New York prisons couch their written records in terms which do not explicitly mention AIDS and the San Francisco jail medical records are kept completely confidential and not revealed to the jail administration. However, in some jurisdictions, there may be labor agreements which affect the ability of the administration to keep test results confidential. See Delaware Dept. of Corrections, 86 Lab.Arb.Rpts. 849 (BNA 1986).

Conclusions: AIDS poses enormous problems within the penal system, problems which are likely to escalate in the coming years unless rational and humane policies are established. However, it is not easy to develop such policies within the violent and punitive context of prisons and jails. Nonetheless, it is clear that the establishment of an on-going, effective educational program is the crucial first step and that persistent outside pressure is needed in most jurisdictions to make this a reality. It is also clear that prisoners with AIDS and related conditions urgently need advocates to support them. We urge Network members to become involved in this process.

Resources:

ACLU National Prison Project Journal published articles on AIDS in prison by Urvashi Vaid in issues number 6 and 7 (Winter 1985, Spring 1986). 1616 P St. NW, #340, Washington, DC 20036. 202/331-0500.

AIDS in Correctional Facilities: Issues and Options, by Theodore Hammer, published by the National Institute of Justice (1987). 217 pages with appendices. $24.95. 202/334-2000.

The San Francisco Sheriff's Office has developed AIDS training materials for the education of law enforcement officials. They are available free to law enforcement agencies. Contact Lt. Jan Dempsy, 415/558-3127.

What you can do on a local level.

Urge jail administrators to be formulate thoughtful AIDS policies now. Even if there are currently no AIDS cases, if an administration waits until the arrival of the first prisoner with AIDS to adopt a policy, it will inevitably adopt a reactionary one reflecting panic among the staff and other prisoners.

Work with the local medical community. It is usually best if a medical person is the chief spokesperson in dealing with jail administrators in order to minimize adversarial overtones.

Stress to prison officials that AIDS education needs to be provided on an on-going basis.

AIDS virus inmates in 'leper' cell

By BOB LOWE
Herald Staff Writer

At the end of a long, dingy corridor in the Dade County Jail, past the cell filled with prisoners who have diabetes, broken legs and bad kidneys, live a group of men who call themselves "the leper colony."

Their 15- by 40-foot home is officially called "1-A," but most people in the jail know it as the AIDS cell. A majority of the men inside are charged with theft or drug possession. Two await trial for murder. A male prostitute bonded out last month.

All of the prisoners have been diagnosed as having the AIDS virus, known in medical parlance as HTLV-3. In other ways they are perfectly healthy. They don't have AIDS itself and most of them probably never will. But their blood tests showed positive, their jail cards have been red-stamped "priority," and so they live together in isolation.

Because of the sheer number of cases and the unusual pressures of prison existence, the jail is adapting to AIDS a step ahead of other institutions. Life in cell 1-A provides an early glimpse at how society is learning to live with the deadly disease.

It's a life of uncertainty and what the inmates describe as jailhouse double standards. Because judges and lawyers don't want them around, they're not always permitted to attend their own court hearings.

Until they complained last spring, the inmates of 1-A had no regular exercise. Since then they've often missed their weekly hour in the jail yard and spent nearly all of June without seeing daylight.

For some, the uncertainty is the worst of all. They aren't completely sure they have the AIDS virus because their blood tests so often prove wrong. A medical expert said one test used by the jail is useless for detecting the virus.

Health authorities say there are no proven cases of the AIDS virus being transmitted by casual contact. The virus is spread through sexual intercourse and the exchange of infected body fluids, particularly blood. But such subtleties are lost in the jail.

There is camaraderie among the 18 men in cell 1-A, but there is also fear and anger. Fear of the virus that can haunt them for the rest of their lives. Anger at being ostracized by the guards, by the courts and by their fellow inmates, who would rather kill than live with a man carrying AIDS.

★ ★ ★

Charles Silas, 33, a drug user diagnosed as having the AIDS virus in March, has been in and out of the jail for the past six months. He is serving a one-year sentence for theft:

"They didn't ask me anything. They just took my blood and three or four weeks later said, 'You've got AIDS. Pack your things. You're coming with us.'

"They weren't sure what they wanted to do with us. I was a trusty on the third floor. I freaked. I've lived with the fact that I might die.

"News travels fast from here to the street and from the street to here. When I got out of here, no one wanted to be near me. Someone in the captain's office told my fiance that I had AIDS. She came for a contact visit and they just said, 'He's in the AIDS cell.' It caused her to trip out. I was screwed up in the head after that. I was

arrested for anything. The last time I reached through a fence and picked up a staple gun.

"When I was a trusty I began pushing a food cart. Then I was a cook. You get to move around and earn 'gain time' so you get out sooner.

"Here, you're just lying in a cell. Lying in a cell for 364 days. Can you imagine that? I do the laundry for everyone. I get out once a week to do that. I look forward to that every week.

"We've had guys who came back and they didn't even tell them they had the AIDS virus. We've had guys who wanted to fight and guys who just wouldn't talk. We had one guy who didn't want to eat and didn't want anyone talking to him.

"We educated ourselves. We had to. I never talked to a doctor or a counselor. Ron Brooks [a cellmate] got some pamphlets and we dug through those and so forth. They talked a lot about vitamins, exercises, things to watch for. A lot of things we can't get here.

"We had to raise hell to get basic things. Cleanliness is important for infection. We took it upon ourselves to keep everything clean. We had to fight and complain to get the stuff we needed. There was something about keeping bleach in the cell.

"We feel like we have the plague and aren't to be touched. Nobody gives a damn. They put us where we'd be out of the way. They're afraid. I don't take it personally. They don't have the knowledge of what we have.

★ ★ ★

Day never ends in cell 1-A. The lights are always on, the television and noise level always turned up. Inmates develop different sleep cycles — some rest at night and others during the day.

Two rows of bunkbeds line most of the cell, with space in the middle to walk through. Torn sheets form makeshift clotheslines from which towels and underwear hang. At one end are a few tables and chairs as well as the shower, toilet and sink.

The inmates in 1-A don't leave their cell. The best gauge of time is the arrival of meals three times a day on plastic plates painted silver to separate them from the rest. The jail eats early — breakfast by 4 a.m. — so that everyone's available for court.

Early this year, when the Dade County Jail decided it could no longer just release inmates with AIDS or HTLV-3 by sending them to hospitals, cell 1-A gained its special status.

"We didn't know anything about AIDS," said Cpl. Armando Quinoa, administrative assistant to the jail supervisor. "We were just locking them down."

"It went back to the old stereotype," said Russell Buckhalt, assistant director of Social Services at the jail. "Isolate them and forget about them. It's been very difficult to break the old habits."

In the jail, recreation time — a chance to leave the cell and walk outside in the fresh air, sun and open space — is like gold. And at first the inmates in 1-A couldn't count on any of it.

They complained and in March the jail began opening the jail yard on weekends so that 1-A could get an hour of recreation each Sunday. That's half the recreation time required by state guidelines, but the same as

other inmates get in the overcrowded jail.

Because of rain and staff shortages, however, the inmates in 1-A still spend many Sundays without seeing daylight. They question whether 30-minute cloudbursts have become excuses for guards who would rather have nothing to do with them. Last week, jail officials said they would increase the recreation time to three hours.

Jail inmates normally attend their arraignments and bond hearings. But many of the men in 1-A have missed those court appearances, even in some cases where records indicate they attended. They say the problem persists despite efforts by jail officials to get them to the hearings.

"When the bailiffs saw a person was in 1-A, they were going to the judges and saying this person's a positive and not taking them over," said Buckhalt.

"Many judges have told the bailiffs not to bring them to their courtrooms. It's been very difficult to get public defenders to come over, too. The inmate doesn't know what's going on with his case."

"The judges do what they want individually," said Dade Circuit Court Judge Gerald Kogan, administrative judge for the criminal division. "There's no policy."

"There was some concern initially about dealing with people who have AIDS," said Dade Public Defender Bennett Brummer. "I think that's been eliminated."

An AIDS task force at the jail would like to see inmates with the virus eventually merge with the regular jail population. But Buckhalt, who heads the group, doubts whether that will work. In the jail, it's virtually impossible to keep secret an inmate's health problems.

"The inmates know if they bang the guy up, he'll be moved and they won't hesitate to do that," said Buckhalt. "I don't want to put somebody's life in jeopardy."

★ ★ ★

Corrections Officer Armando "Al" Quinoa, 36, is the father of a 7-month-old daughter:

"The first thing my wife asks me when I

Quinoa

go home is whether I was in the AIDS area. She won't let me touch the baby until I've taken a shower. We have to worry about other things, too, like hepatitis. I spend most of my time in an office but I never wear anything twice. My cleaning bill is $24 a week.

"One inmate was with a group of guys in the shower and someone noticed a rash on his legs. One guy said, 'He's got AIDS' and everyone was saying he has AIDS. They were ready to kill him. We had to take him out and put him somewhere else. And he tested negative."

Mary is one of two corrections officer-counselors who volunteered to work with the inmates in 1-A:

"At first everyone was afraid, including myself. We had no definite knowledge about AIDS. I didn't want to work with these people. I transferred from my floor so I wouldn't have to deal with them.

"Then I reconsidered. Somebody had to do it. Why not me?

"At first I thought I might contract the disease. I didn't want them to touch me or my clothing. As I've learned a little more, now I touch them and their clothing as long as there's no blood or feces. I go in the cell sometimes. I didn't do that before. We hold hands and have prayer.

"They had a gripe as far as feeling ostracized, but not any longer. They get a telephone 24 hours a day compared to four hours in some of the other cells. They get better visiting hours now. They are really pampered to a certain degree.

"Most of my children are grown. They don't know I work back there. I would never discuss it with my children. I wouldn't want them to know."

★   ★   ★

Ron Brooks, 39, is completing a one-year sentence for cocaine possession. Self-educated, his talk drifts easily from medical tests to politics to complicated legal questions.

"We are treated like pariahs, lepers back here," says Brooks. "Very few people will come back to deal with us, even among the medical people."

When Brooks is mentioned, those who work at the jail tend to roll their eyes and use words like "con man" and "troublemaker." He is the kind of guy, they say, who has spent most of his life in institutions and knows how to manipulate them for personal gain.

In the eight months that he's been in 1-A, Brooks has complained, cajoled and pressured jail officials to change how they deal with inmates who have AIDS and the HTLV-3 virus. He has pushed, often successfully, for better tests, access to court hearings, regular recreation, gain time and different attitudes.

His activism has earned him the enmity of some of his cellmates.

After Brooks returned from one recent meeting with the promise of more recreation time, he got into a fight when the extra sessions didn't materialize the next week.

"They thought I was lying," Brooks said.

"Some cats like him and other cats don't," said Wendell Levarity, an accused murderer. "He interferes with things."

But when a new inmate arrives in panic or anger, adds Levarity, it's usually Brooks who explains why he's there.

"They hit that door saying, 'I'm going to die. Oh, I got to get out of here.' Brooks let's them know what's going on." Jail officials acknowledge Brooks' role as counselor and resident medical expert.

"What I'm doing is to help alleviate things here and shed some light on what's going on," said Brooks. "If it shows something in me worth rehabilitating as a result of this, I don't see anything wrong with that. I don't have any job. I don't have any family or money. What would you do?"

★   ★   ★

Balanced Response Needed to AIDS in Prison
By Urvashi Vaid

Should Prisoners Be Screened for the HTLV-III Antibody?

Why is it important to determine the antibody status of all prisoners? Will testing and segregation actually have an impact on the transmission of virus among prisoners? Do mandatory testing and the segregation of seropositive persons violate the due process or Eighth Amendment rights of prisoners? Although these fundamental questions have yet to be answered by the courts, mass testing has already become the reality in five states and in the Federal Bureau of Prisons (all pregnant women inmates are tested).

Calls for the mandatory testing of inmates for HTLV-III antibody are medically unwarranted and legally impermissible. Indeed, in January of 1986, the National Association of State Corrections Administrators voted against mandatory testing. When fears about AIDS are set aside, two facts remain: first, the HTLV-III virus is not spread by casual contact; and second, testing for antibodies to the virus will not halt its spread even if all seropositive prisoners are segregated.

A recent study has shown that persons in very close, day-to-day contact with persons with AIDS did not "catch" the virus. Those studied shared houses, dishes, beds, meals, even toothbrushes with diagnosed AIDS patients and did not seroconvert from antibody negative to positive.[16] Since the HTLV-III virus cannot be spread through casual day-to-day contact, the public health justification for screening all inmates at intake or while they are incarcerated is questionable. Unlike tuberculosis, which can be airborne, or hepatitis B which can be transmitted through saliva, the HTLV-III virus has only been shown to be transmissible through blood products and semen. Intake screening would only serve to create a class of persons stigmatized throughout their incarceration by their antibody status.

Mandatory testing will not halt the spread of AIDS in prison. There is a continuing risk that the virus may be passed along even if all confirmed seropositive inmates are separated from the general population, given the significant number of false negatives and false positives engendered by the ELISA test; given the fact that there is a gestation period between infection with the virus and the generation of antibodies; and, given the fact that seronegative persons who assume that they are "safe" will continue to engage in high-risk activities. A credible argument can also be made that mandatory testing will increase the development of AIDS among prisoners who are confirmed to be seropositive and housed with other seropositive people. The current medical evidence indicates that while a single exposure to the HTLV-III virus does not result in infection, multiple exposures enormously increase the chance of a person getting the virus. By housing all antibody positive prisoners together, prisons only increase the chance that these inmates will be exposed to the virus.

Proponents of mandatory antibody testing are motivated largely by the fact that sexual activity, both consensual and forced, does take place in prison. The argument is made that since prison systems have been notoriously unable to control sexual assault, much less consensual sex, mass antibody testing and segregation of all seropositives would at least help assure that no prisoner involuntarily acquired HTLV-III infection.

The fundamental problem with mandatory testing is that it will have little impact upon the incidence of either consensual sexual activity or sexual assault. Administrators concerned about the spread of HTLV-III infection through consensual sex would be better served by initiating well-designed, on-going educational campaigns geared at informing inmates about how the virus is transmitted.[17] Given the great concern most feel about contracting AIDS, there is every reason to believe educating prisoners about safe sex practices would have an impact on their behavior.

Sadly, the real obstacle to the distribution of risk-reduction materials in prison lies not with their lack of effectiveness, but with a dilemma peculiar to prisons. Many states have criminalized any sexual activity among prisoners. In other states, sodomy itself is a crime. Prison officials interested in disseminating safe-sex or risk-reduction information may find themselves in the awkward position of discussing practices which they are supposed to punish. By asking state health agencies or outside groups to produce and conduct educational sessions, officials may be able to ease their dilemma. In any event, the discomfort of prison officials should not be the deciding factor in the availability of invaluable educational information. The reality of long term incarceration is that some prisoners will have consensual sex. At a minimum, the prison has an obligation to inform inmates how the AIDS virus is and is not transmitted.

Prison rape is a by-product of the inhumanity and perversity endemic to our prison system's treatment of prisoners' sexual needs. This underlying and largely unaddressed problem has been given a new dimension by the fact that AIDS is sexually transmitted. The American prison system has helped institutionalize the phenomenon of prison rape by: prohibiting prisoners from conjugal visits with their loved ones; prohibiting even basic contact visits; by banning and criminalizing consensual sex; and enshrining the values of total domination and control. Mandatory screening for the HTLV-III antibody will not decrease prison rape, nor will it eliminate the possibility that a victim of sexual assault might be infected. The flaws inherent in the antibody test suggest that prisoners with the virus will escape detection and could continue to spread the virus to others. A proper classification system ought to identify violent inmates and house them accordingly, rather than penalizing all inmates who happen to be seropositive.

Increased staffing, the isolation of violent offenders, the elimination of unsupervised dormitory housing, and an unhesitating commitment by security staff to not tolerate rape are among the solutions prison officials must implement. One of many ironies of prison life is that weaker inmates are identified and separated into more restrictive custody settings, while predatory and more traditionally macho inmates remain in general population, with even greater freedom to coerce sexual favors. If prisons are concerned about seroconversion among previously seronegative inmates, the policy of testing victims of sexual assault after an attack would be a far less intrusive option to mandatory testing.

Mandatory testing represents an overreaction on the part of correctional administrators who are quite reasonably concerned about the disease. It represents precisely the kind of inappropriate and irrational response to otherwise legitimate penological objectives which the Supreme Court noted in *Bell v. Wolfish*[18] would violate the due process clause. Most of the concerns voiced by proponents of testing could be adequately dealt with through the development of educational programs and materials aimed at changing an inmate's behavior. The concern most prisoners have about contracting AIDS would only serve to augment the effectiveness of such educational programs.

Segregation of Inmates

The only medical basis justifying the segregation of inmates with AIDS, ARC or HTLV-III seropositivity, would be if the individual prisoner's condition medically warranted such isolation (if he or she could not control bodily secretions or was so weakened as to require intensive care). Since the virus cannot be transmitted through casual contact, prisoners who encounter either seropositive inmates or those with ARC or AIDS in the general population are not at any extra risk of contracting the virus.

Nevertheless, segregation of all three categories of inmates is common among state systems. Segregation of inmates with AIDS is the policy of 42% of the state and federal systems (21 out of 51). Of these 21 systems, 18 (36%) also segregate inmates with ARC, and another 8 (16%) segregate seropositive inmates as well.[19] Only two states reported that they do not segregate any inmates because of AIDS or AIDS-related conditions.

The primary justification offered for the isolation of these inmates is that they might be assaulted in general population. This argument for segregation stems from the fact that there is no confidentiality of medical information in most prisons. Corrections staff and inmates are very likely to be aware of which persons are seropositive, or have ARC. Invariably, rumors (both true and false) will circulate about a prisoner's illness being AIDS-related, and that individual may become the target of threats and serious attacks. Certainly prison administrators would be justified in removing an individual who is being threatened from general population. But selectively placing individuals on protective custody status is markedly different from a policy of wholesale segregation of all prisoners with AIDS-related conditions.

A number of states, including Nevada which has tested all its inmates, house seropositive inmates in general population, unless their condition medically warrants another type of confinement. The threat to the welfare of seropositive inmates is likely to be related to the amount and quality of education a prison system provides. New York State, for example, which has had the highest number of prisoners with AIDS, does not segregate prisoners diagnosed with ARC.

To date, only a handful of lawsuits have been filed to challenge prison policies regarding the segregation of inmates with AIDS-related conditions. *Cordero v. Coughlin*,[20] which was discussed at length in the last issue of the *JOURNAL*, involved a challenge to New York's policy of segregating inmates with AIDS. The court held that such segregation was reasonable and that the conditions of confinement did not violate prisoners' Eighth Amendment rights. More recently, at least two cases have been filed by asymptomatic prisoners who are antibody-positive and are being segregated under allegedly unconstitutional conditions.[21] The evidence gathered by the National Prison Project about the conditions under which most inmates with AIDS and AIDS-related illnesses are being confined suggests that many more lawsuits addressing conditions will be forthcoming. Prison officials should remember that while the decision to segregate may be reasonable under the circumstances, conditions of confinement in segregation must be constitutionally adequate.

It is the Prison Project's position that if segregation is imposed, it must be akin to protective custody, and not punitive or administrative detention. Like protective custody inmates, prisoners segregated because of AIDS-related conditions must be provided access to programs, jobs, recreation, visits, exercise and adequate out-of-cell time.[22]

Medical and Mental Health Care

Potentially the most litigation-prone area involving prisoners with AIDS-related conditions involves the provision of medical and mental health care. While there is no cure for the underlying immune deficiency caused by infection with the HTLV-III virus, medical treatment for many of the opportunistic infections experienced by AIDS patients is available. Neither the NPP survey nor the NIJ/ACA study evaluated the nature and quality of the medical care that is being provided to prisoners with AIDS and ARC. The anecdotal information we have gathered through inmate correspondence and our general experience with medical care in prison suggests that serious shortfalls are likely to exist.

Medical care of prisoners with AIDS-related conditions must meet the standard set forth in *Estelle v. Gamble*, and subsequent cases. The *Estelle* court concluded that "deliberate indifference to serious medical needs of prisoners constitutes the 'unnecessary and wanton infliction of pain', . . . proscribed by the Eighth Amendment."[23] The Eighth Amendment requires that prison officials provide a system of ready access to adequate medical, mental health and dental care with competent staff. Reasonable and speedy access to outside facilities must also be available for services not provided within the prison. Inmates must be able to make their problems known to medical staff. Adequate facilities and staff to handle medical emergencies must be provided.[24] Mental health counseling is especially important to deal with an inmate's reaction to a diagnosis of AIDS or a positive antibody test.

Conclusion

It is critical that prisoners' rights advocates do not accept at face value the justifications for mandatory screening and wholesale segregation put forward by some in the corrections community. Alternative remedies must be developed which protect inmate and staff health and also protect prisoners' rights to privacy, due process and freedom from cruel and unusual punishment. ∎

INSURANCE

PART I

INSURANCE AND AIDS-RELATED ISSUES

Mark Scherzer

The spread of AIDS has raised numerous insurance-related problems not only for persons with the disease but also for members of so-called "at risk" groups. This chapter will focus on the insurance problems of people with AIDS and gay men.

AIDS is not the first epidemic to present problems for gay people in obtaining insurance. It was preceded by an epidemic of ignorance and stereotyping which for decades made it difficult for any openly gay male or lesbian to obtain insurance.

In the early part of this century, insurance company medical directors were advised to be wary of issuing insurance to "sexual inverts" because they were given to excessive use of drug and alcohol, their lives were often shortened by suicide, and because the male inverts, with a feminine aversion to muscular exercise, became fat and flabby by the age of 40.[1] It appears that insurance companies throughout

Mark Scherzer is a partner in the New York City law firm of Scherzer & Palella and is experienced in insurance policy litigation. This chapter is an adaptation of an article originally published in Sexual Orientation and the Law, produced by the Anti-Sexism Committee of the San Francisco Chapter of the National Lawyers Guild and published by Clark Boardman Company. We are grateful for their permission to republish it.

most of the succeeding decades considered homosexuality to be an impairment of habits or morals which, if disclosed or suspected, would be a factor weighing against issuance of insurance policies to lesbians and gay males. Even after 1973, when the American Psychiatric Association determined that homosexuality was no longer considered to be a mental illness, the underwriting manuals of some insurance companies continued to list homosexuality as an impairment of habits or morals. Even if these standards came to be used infrequently, their presence in the internal publications of some insurers gave an official imprimatur to homophobic bias in insurance underwriting.

For persons with AIDS, and for the gay men from whose ranks the overwhelming majority of Americans diagnosed with AIDS have come,[2] the stereotyping and homophobia which has affected the issuance of insurance to gay people is not merely a vestigial fact of social history. Gay men as a class are again being perceived as poor insurance risks, and are at times even being denied insurance benefits to which they have contractual rights. This is a significant threat to the well-being of all gay men, regardless of whether they are at risk for AIDS.

Health insurance is an important institution which is the only means most Americans have to provide themselves with quality health care. Our health care system has been described as an increasingly industrialized and privatized system in which care is more often provided by richly capitalized, for-profit corporations. Health care is expensive, and for any significant disease or injury, care might be unavailable in the absence of public or private insurance. Similarly, disability insurance is one of the few ways in which meaningful welfare benefits (beyond the minimal provisions of public benefit programs) are provided to those unable to work. Life insurance is a mechanism for avoiding impoverishment of families (be they traditional or unorthodox) deprived of their breadwinners or whose resources have been depleted by caring for the terminally ill.

The vast majority of Americans who have private health insurance are covered by employer-provided group insurance plans. Host employers, however, appear no longer to be purchasing insurance through insurance companies, but rather are funding their own coverage, either through internal "insurance" plans or through multi-employer groups.[3] By doing so, these employers not only maintain control over the money they would be paying in premiums, they also are able to circumvent at least some of the laws which regulate insurance plans.

Whether covered through traditional employee group plans or through the self-funded, so-called ERISA plans (regulated under the federal Employee Retirement Income Security Act), a key element of such employee coverage is that, in large groups (generally those consisting of over ten members), there is rarely individual underwriting of insurance. Actively employed people are traditionally considered among the healthiest, and with large groups of them there is considered to be an adequate pool in which to spread risk, so that employment alone is generally sufficient to qualify one for the group's insurance.[4] The practitioner who is consulted by a gay man or a person with AIDS covered by this sort of insurance is usually dealing with ways in which benefits have been limited, denied or terminated, rather than with refusals to offer insurance coverage.

With respect to those not covered through large groups, the situation is markedly different. Insurance companies will generally not issue policies covering any members of a small employee group who do not meet individual underwriting criteria. Both individuals and employees in small groups must generally satisfy insurers that their health is sufficiently good so as not to present an unduly high risk to the insurer. With respect to such policies, attorneys with gay clients are likely to be consulted about the propriety of questions asked in the application process, with respect to refusals to offer coverage, and with respect to denials of claims on grounds associated with misrepresentations by the insurers in the process of applying for insurance. There is reason to believe that the proportion of gay people in small groups or with individual health insurance coverage is higher than the proportion of people so covered in the nation as a whole; gay people who have not had protection from employment discrimination in most American jurisdictions may well have a disproportionately high rate of self-employment.

With respect to life insurance, too, practitioners will most likely confront questions regarding denials of applications for insurance, improper underwriting questions, and claims that the insured have misrepresented their health in applying for insurance. While many Americans have life insurance through their employer or other group insurance arrangements, the greatest dollar value of life insurance is by far in individually purchased policies.[5]

This chapter will focus on the issues which will most likely be confronted by a client with AIDS, or by any gay male in the era of AIDS, in obtaining, maintaining, and receiving benefits from private insurance coverage. Because insurance regulation is largely in the control of the individual states, the practitioner is strongly urged to consult the insurance law and regulations of his or her own state for guidance with respect to any particular problem. In addition, treatises which are national in scope[6] are highly recommended as comprehensive compendia of cases involving the areas of insurance law most regularly litigated.

In addition to general materials on insurance law, there is an increasing volume of literature specifically dealing with AIDS and insurance. This literature is extremely useful for background in the broad policy issues of anti-gay discrimination and HIV antibody testing. See Schatz, The AIDS Insurance Crisis: Underwriting or Overreaching? 100 Harv. L. Rev. 1782 (1987); Clifford and Iuculano, AIDS and Insurance: The Rationale for AIDS-related Testing, 100 Harv. L. Rev. 1806 (1987); Hoffman and Kincaid, AIDS: The Challenge of Life and Health Insurers' Freedom of Contract, 35 Drake L. Rev. 710 (1986-87), Hammond and Shapiro, AIDS and the Limits of Insurability, 64 Milbank Quarterly Supp. 1, 145 (1986); Oppenheimer and Padgog, AIDS: The Risk to Insurers, the Threat to Equity, Hastings Center Report (18 October, 1986); American Academy of Actuaries, Risk Classifications and AIDS (1986). None of these papers purports to give practical advice, and most of them are written from an insurance industry perspective. The law review articles do, however, contain surveys of the laws and regulations of major American jurisdictions, while the other articles examine the economic effects of various approaches to underwriting.

Insurance Problems of Persons with AIDS

1. Obtaining Insurance Coverage

Persons with AIDS or ARC who do not have private insurance coverage at the time of their diagnosis have limited options for obtaining such insurance. If they are able to work, they should be encouraged to obtain employment in which a large group will cover them without reference to their individual insurability (although such plans may still exclude payments for "pre-existing conditions"). If they are unable to work, they may be able to benefit from open enrollment periods which some local Blue Cross/Blue Shield groups may offer to anyone who registers for coverage and pays premiums, again without regard to individual insurability. Otherwise, they are relegated to applying to private insurers for individual life and health insurance, which may be an almost hopeless endeavor.

Application forms for insurance generally must be submitted for approval to the state agencies which regulate insurance companies. The state insurance departments usually judge those forms by a number of criteria, including whether the questions therein are fair, and whether they would mislead the public. Almost universally in individual application forms there will be questions regarding the applicant's health history, which may include not only questions regarding treatment for specific diseases or conditions, but also regarding any consultations with doctors (other than regular check-ups) within a period of years preceding the application. If the applicant with AIDS or ARC answers the questions truthfully, the diagnosis will almost inevitably be disclosed, and the insurance company will not issue the policy.

Insurers who do not wish to rely upon general health questions for screening out people with AIDS or ARC have developed questions specifically designed to determine whether the applicant has been diagnosed with AIDS or ARC. One of the first insurers to do so, the reinsurance company Lincoln National Life Insurance Company of Fort Wayne, Indiana, had received permission to ask questions regarding AIDS from 10 states, including its home state of Indiana, by September 1985. At about the same time, Northwestern Mutual Life Insurance Company was seeking permission in every state to ask questions regarding AIDS, and had received permission in 16 states.[7] In response to numerous requests from insurers, the Department of Insurance in New Jersey issued guidelines for the types of questions which will be approved for insurers who wish to inquire about AIDS. The guidelines suggested that the Department would approve questions regarding whether applicants had received treatment from a member of the medical profession for AIDS or ARC, but not questions regarding whether applicants had reason to suspect they had AIDS, or whether they had any symptoms of AIDS.[8]

Practitioners who believe that questions on insurance applications regarding AIDS may be unfair or misleading should contact their state insurance departments to determine whether the questions have been approved. If questions regarding AIDS or ARC which do not appear on application forms are asked of their clients orally, there may be grounds for complaint of unfair practices by the company or agency involved. The likelihood is, however, that insurance companies will be allowed a relatively free reign to ask proper questions about actual diagnoses or treatments for AIDS or ARC.

2. Maintaining Insurance Coverage

Clients will frequently ask their attorneys whether their diagnosis of AIDS affords their insurance company a basis for cancelling their policies. There appears to be a common belief that such cancellations take place. Clients should be reassured that a diagnosis is not a legitimate basis for cancellation of a policy. The policy should continue according to its terms as long as premiums are paid when due and the other terms of the policy are complied with. The insurance industry has emphasized in its public relations materials that existing insurance contracts will cover many if not most of those who are currently being diagnosed with AIDS.[9]

Of course, some insurance policies (called term policies) are issued only for a limited period of time. Unless the right to renew them is guaranteed by the insurance company in the insurance contract, the policies may expire and replacement policies may not be available without a new application and proof of good health. More important, and particularly significant for persons with AIDS, eligibility for continued coverage by group insurance may terminate when someone is no longer a member of the group. Thus, the almost inevitable departure from employment by a person with AIDS may precipitate a loss of insurance coverage.

There are safeguards against loss of coverage. Many policies contain contractual provisions, some of which are required by law, for individuals to convert from group to individual coverage at the termination of their membership in the group. The attorney advising a person who left employment should pay particular attention to the deadlines imposed by the policy or by local law for conversion options to be exercised. In New York, for example, an insured person has the right to convert from certain group life and health insurance policies to individual policies, but must exercise the option within a short period after termination of coverage. The period may be extended if the group member is not given notice of the right to convert to a group health policy, but if the group member is given no notice at all the right to convert to an individual health policy expires within 90 days of termination of membership in the group.[10] The insured who does not exercise the conversion right may only be left with a claim of dubious value against the employer for failure to give the required notice.

Even when conversion appears to be mandated, it may, for technical reasons, be unavailable. Employers of small groups who offer insurance will frequently purchase policies which are held by trusts established by major insurance companies. The policies held by the trusts may benefit a multitude of small employers, and the trusts are often domiciled in states such as Rhode Island and Missouri, in which the restrictions on the types of group insurance which can be held by trusts are minimal, and in which conversion options may not be mandated. Thus, although most states mandate conversion options on group health coverage, local employers in those states may have obtained coverage under group plans in states where conversion is not mandated. Whether conversion will have to be offered in those circumstances may raise interesting questions regarding the applicability of local laws.[11] In any event, multistate employers whose headquarters are in states which do not mandate conversion, and who have group policies covering all their employees, will almost certainly not be required to offer conversion policies.

Nor is conversion, when available, a panacea. Conversion policies often offer benefits which are meager compared to the group policies under which the person with AIDS was formerly insured, and the premium rates are often very high. Still, if the person can afford the premiums,[12] the conversion benefit is a right worth fighting for; when facing an illness like AIDS, even partially comprehensive insurance is better than none at all. If an insurance company resists conversion because of fear of the costs associated with AIDS, one may have both a breach of contract remedy and an administrative remedy. In July, 1986, an administrative complaint by National Gay Rights Advocates was filed with the California Department of Insurance against Sentry Life Insurance of Wisconsin, alleging that the insurance company had repeatedly ignored requests for conversion.[13] As a result of the complaint, the respondent agreed to afford coverage to the claimant.

Employers who self-insure under ERISA plans will generally not be required by state laws to offer conversion policies; the laws generally apply only to policies of insurance issued by insurance companies. A new federal law known as "COBRA", however, offers assistance to insurers under both ERISA plans and group insurance plans involving 20 or more employees, by requiring a terminated employee to be offered a continuation of group coverage (as opposed to conversion to an individual policy) at the group rate, paid by the terminated employee's contribution,

for up to 18 months.[14] Some states have mandated similar extensions of coverage for persons who are terminated from groups.[15] The attorney representing the person with AIDS may have to bring these recently enacted laws to the attention of employers to make sure that benefits are extended. For more information on COBRA, see the second section of this chapter.

In the case of individual policies, a key element in maintaining coverage is continued payment of premiums. As noted above, in some cases there may be public funds available to assume such payments. In cases where there are not such funds available, there still may be ways to relieve the person with AIDS from the burden of paying the premiums. Some policies have waivers of premiums in the event of disability of the insured. The attorney should examine the policy and, if there is such a provision, submit due proof of the disability to the insurance company in a timely fashion, so that coverage may be continued without payment of premiums.

If there is a lapse of payment in premiums, vigilance is required. After a grace period for payment which is generally provided by contract, some insurers will offer reinstatement of the insurance contract. But if the reinstatement offer includes a requirement for new representations as to health, it may effectively preclude the person with AIDS from reinstating the policy.

3. Obtaining Payment of Claims

There is some anecdotal evidence that some insurance companies have "resisted" AIDS claims by failing to respond to them (perhaps motivated in part by fear on the part of claims examiners of handling claim papers submitted by persons with AIDS). In the event that claims are not handled properly, the insurance laws of some states provide a remedy by prohibiting unfair claims settlement practices. Connecticut, for example, requires that insurance companies have a general business practice which includes, among other things, acknowledging communications, investigating and affirming or denying claims with reasonable promptness, not misrepresenting facts or provisions of insurance policies, not refusing to pay claims without adequate investigation, and not compelling insurers to institute litigation to recover amounts due.[16] While remedies for violations of such statutes will in some jurisdictions be by direct suit against the insurance company, in most cases there will be jurisdiction in the state insurance departments to obtain redress.

Problems in obtaining payment of the medical costs of persons with AIDS are most likely to involve issues of what is a covered expense under the policies. Examples of likely difficulties include:

a. Experimental Treatments

Many health insurance policies exclude coverage for experimental treatments. Many treatments for AIDS are experimental. The point at which each treatment ceases to be deemed experimental and rather becomes an accepted mode of treatment may have to be resolved on a case-by-case basis.

b. Home Health Care

Some health insurance plans exclude coverage for home health care. Some states, such as New York, now mandate that such coverage be offered.[17] The practitioner should check the language of the policy and local law in order to advise the client about the relative costs of inpatient and outpatient care.

c. Exclusion of AIDS from Coverage

There have been scattered reports of standard group or individual insurance policies which exclude AIDS as a covered condition. One state Blue Cross (California) requested permission, at the behest of an employer for whom it administered a group plan, to exclude sexually-transmitted AIDS and other sexually transmitted diseases (but not AIDS transmitted by blood transfusion), which request was denied.[18] National Gay Rights Advocates has filed a complaint with the Texas State Board of Insurance against Texas Bankers Life and Loan Insurance Company, which has announced a similar AIDS exclusion. According to NGRA, at least 18 state insurance departments (Arizona, California, Colorado, Delaware, Florida, Kansas, Maryland, Massachusetts, Michigan, Minnesota, Missouri, New York, North Carolina, Oregon, Pennsylvania, South Dakota, Tennessee and Wisconsin) have indicated that they will not allow insurance companies to exclude or severely limit health insurance coverage for AIDS.

There are strong arguments to be made that such exclusion should not be permitted. With respect to urban gay men, health insurance coverage which excluded coverage for AIDS could be held to be so limited in scope as to be of no substantial value to the policy holders. In New York, at least, the insurance commissioner is charged with regulat-

ing the insurance industry so as to prevent from being sold policies without substantial benefit to the policy holders.[19]

With respect to ERISA plans, however, there have been attempted exclusions of coverage for AIDS. These exclusions raise complex problems with respect to the regulations to which those plans may be subjected. In ACLU of Oregon v. Beaverton Datsun and N.F. Falta & Associates, a complaint filed with the Equal Employment Opportunity Commission, an anonymous complainant is asserting that exclusion of AIDS as a covered condition in a multi-employer welfare association ERISA plan violates federal sex discrimination laws because of its disparate impact on male employees. A concurrent complaint was successfully filed with the Oregon Department of Labor alleging violations of both sex and handicap discrimination provisions of state law.[20] At issue in these complaints is the extent to which ERISA plans may be subject to state insurance laws as well as general state anti-discrimination laws.

d. Pre-existing Condition Exclusions

Many health and disability and some life insurance policies contain exclusions from coverage for claims arising from conditions which the insured had at the time of inception of the policy. The exclusion may be perpetual, or (for health insurance particularly) it may only apply to claims made within the first months or years the policy is in effect. Persons with AIDS whose coverage started within a short time prior to their diagnosis frequently face denials of their claims by insurers who rely on the pre-existing condition exclusion. Although the usual rule in construing insurance policies is to interpret them broadly in favor of coverage, the rule does not always apply when the pre-existing condition exclusion is asserted by a non-profit hospital plan.[21] In fact, there is authority that the burden of proof is on the insured to establish that the condition is not pre-existing.[22]

In order for a condition to be pre-existing, however, the general rule is that it must be manifest, not latent, at the time of inception of the policy. At the least, this means that symptoms must be present from which the condition can be diagnosed with reasonable accuracy.[23] It has been held that when symptoms are compatible with but not diagnostic of a particular condition, then the condition will not be considered pre-existing based on such generalized symptoms alone.[24] If a symptom present before the inception of the policy can derive from any number of causes, the jury might properly determine that the condition for which coverage is claimed was not the cause, and was not, therefore, a pre-existing condition.[25]

Applying these principles to the situations faced by persons with AIDS, one can imagine a whole range of facts which may be used as bases for applying the pre-existing condition exclusion. Perhaps the easiest to overcome is the claim of pre-existing condition asserted against a person who was completely asymptomatic at the time of inception of the policy, but who was seropositive for HIV antibodies. Of course, while HIV infection is clearly associated in some manner with AIDS, the disease is apparently not the inevitable outcome of infection, at least without the operation of some as yet undiscovered "cofactors." Even if there were a direct cause and effect relationship between exposure and disease, asymptomatic infection would be a clear example of a latent, rather than a manifest, condition which would not be the proper subject of a pre-existing condition exclusion. The New York Insurance Department has explicitly recognized this in an advisory letter to the state's AIDS Institute.[26]

Perhaps slightly more difficult is the case of a client who complained of fatigue and malaise or who had some minimal lymphadenopathy at the time of the inception of the policy. These are symptoms for which it might be reasonable not to seek treatment, and they are certainly referable to conditions other than AIDS. One would have a strong argument that these symptoms do not constitute pre-existing conditions for AIDS.

More difficult yet is the client with sudden dramatic weight loss or inexplicable oral thrush at the time of inception of the policy. The question for the jury would be whether those symptoms were possibly attributable to other causes, or were sufficient, if inquiry had been made to a physician and appropriate tests performed, to diagnose ARC (assuming that ARC would be considered a pre-existing condition for AIDS, a conclusion which is not foregone but may be likely).

Most difficult is the client who had lesions of Kaposi's sarcoma (an AIDS-related cancer) at the time of inception of the policy but who is later hospitalized for pneumocystis carinii pneumonia (an entirely different AIDS-related illness). While one could certainly make the argument that neither condition is a pre-existing one for the other, since many persons with AIDS have only one of these conditions and never develop the other, the tendency of the court may be to consider the real ailment to be the underlying immunodeficiency syndrome, and each disease to be a manifestation of a single pre-existing condition. Only great strides in our understanding of the etiology of these diseases will enable us to argue with conviction that one condition which is considered diagnostic for AIDS should not be considered a pre-existing condition for other such conditions.

The pre-existing condition exclusion is one of the most frequently invoked limitations on coverage. While the science of AIDS is still in its infancy, certainly there is sufficient information available to contest those invocations of the exclusion which overreach its legitimate bounds.

4. Resisting Rescission Policy

Some insurance companies are convinced that persons who know they are likely to contract AIDS have embarked on a campaign to purchase insurance which they should not qualify for. General Reassurance Company of Stamford, Connecticut, reported that in 1984 its average payment of claims in AIDS-related cares was four times that of the average of all claims paid,[27] and insurance company spokespersons have cited such statistics as indications that those at high risk are "loading up" on insurance.

One of the major defenses for insurance companies against such "loading up" is rescission, if the person materially misrepresented his or her health or qualifications for insurance in applying for the policy. Insurance companies do this with some frequency, and there have been numerous claims by insurance companies that policies issued to people who have contracted or died of AIDS are subject to rescission.[28]

Almost universally, states have statutes which prevent rescission of life insurance policies if the policy has been in force (and the insured has lived) for two years from the date of issuance or the policy. At that point, the policy has become "incontestable," if the insured dies within that initial two years and claim is made, depending upon the wording of the policy's incontestability provision and local decisional law, the statute of limitations may be tolled and the insurer's time in which to rescind may be extended. With respect to health and disability insurance policies, the provisions of law vary far more from state to state, and some such policies may have no incontestability provisions.

If a policy is still contestable, an insurance company which perceives a basis for rescission will generally tender a check to the insured or the beneficiary for all premiums paid under the contract. If that tender of rescission is not accepted, then litigation may result, initiated by either party: the insurer seeking the equitable relief of rescission, and/or the insured or his or her beneficiaries seeking damages for failure to pay the policy proceeds.

In undertaking such litigation, the practitioner should avoid assuming that rules of law applicable to other types of contracts will automatically apply to insurance contracts. Frequently, for example, clients will advise their attorney that although facts were left off the application form, the insurance agent who sold the policy knew the facts and advised against recording them. One's instinct might be automatically to pursue a claim of waiver or estoppel, but one should do some careful research first. In many states, there is case law which holds that the knowledge of an insurance agent will not bind the company he or she represents. On the other hand, there may be special provisions of law which make it more difficult for the insurance company to rely upon the misrepresentations. While actual fraudulent misrepresentation might be a valid ground for rescinding some contracts, in New York an insurance company can only rely on representations contained in the application if those representations are contained in a copy of the application attached to the policy at issuance.[29]

Obviously, the critical issues in material misrepresentation cases are likely to be whether the insured made misrepresentations and whether the false or undisclosed information is material. But the battle will focus on different kinds of facts in different jurisdictions, and under insurance policies with different provisions. The major issues include:

a. Intent

In some cases, statutes have been interpreted to require that misrepresentation must have been made with fraudulent intent in order to void a policy.[30] In others, the insured's intentions are not relevant, so long as a material fact was not disclosed.[31] Some cases hold that if an insured had material information but did not fully understand its import, he or she is excused from not having disclosed, whereas in other cases the insured's understanding of his or her condition is deemed less significant.[32]

b Materiality of Undisclosed Facts

In some states, an undisclosed fact will not be considered material unless it contributed to the condition which gave rise to the claim,[33] so that a failure to disclose a heart condition would not be a material misrepresentation if a person died of AIDS. In other states, undisclosed facts are considered material if the particular insurance company involved would not have issued a policy, or would have issued a materially different policy, had it known of the facts not disclosed.[34] There, the policy of a person who died of AIDS might be subject to rescission if he or she had failed to disclose a gall bladder problem. Cases differ too on whether materiality of the undisclosed fact will be determined according to what a reasonable insurer would have done with the information or according to what the particu-

lar insurer involved in the case would have done. Obviously, choice of law questions may be important in determining the outcome of cases, and the practitioner will do well to pay attention to the insured's domicile at the time the policy is purchased as well as at the time the claim is made, along with other factors relevant to choice of law, in order to make use of the most advantageous legal standard.

In some cases, one may find that had a condition been disclosed to the insurance company, the company would have issued a policy but charged a higher premium or imposed other special terms. In most states, it is deemed appropriate to order rescission of the policy because the precise policy which was issued would not have been issued.[35] Under the language of certain policies, though, the insurer may be relegated to being awarded the higher premiums it would have charged had it known of the facts not disclosed.[36]

While in some cases courts will find that misrepresentations are material as a matter of law, there is substantial authority that materiality of misrepresentation is for the jury to decide. In order to withstand summary judgment, the practitioner may well have to undertake extensive discovery into the underwriting practices of the insurance company in order to demonstrate that, notwithstanding an insurance company's assertions that it would not have issued a policy, the conditions which the insurance company claims would have been material were in fact not material. Examination of underwriting manuals, the internal guidelines insurance underwriters use in determining whether to issue policies, may give some idea of what the company's standards actually are. In addition, however, one may have to examine the applications of others to whom insurance was issued, to see whether those who disclosed conditions similar to the ones claimed to be material were issued insurance. If the insurance company issued policies to other applicants similarly situated it would certainly be compelling evidence that the condition was not material as a matter of law.[37]

Particularly with respect to AIDS, a disease about which both medical knowledge and underwriting standards are rapidly changing, there may be no clear written standards in insurance company underwriting manuals. Discovery will undoubtedly have to delve into the knowledge of underwriters about the disease at the time they considered the representations made by insurers, and the degree to which they had realized the association with AIDS of various conditions which may have been present in the applicant's medical history. As discussed in the following section, the insurance industry has recently reacted to the AIDS crisis by adopting numerous techniques to screen applicants. However, this reaction comes several years behind the development of the disease in the population and, particularly for policies issued before 1984, neither insureds nor insurers should be assumed to have given significance to medical facts which the general public might now associate with AIDS.

Insurance Problems of Healthy Gay Men

Because gay men have been disproportionately affected by AIDS in the United States, they are frequently referred to as a "high risk group." This seemingly innocuous term has serious ramifications for those to whom it is applied. As with any label, the term contains a kernel of truth. in the United States, gay men at this time are more likely to contract AIDS than are most other people, and in some cities a devastating proportion of them have succumbed to the disease. Further, in some locations a majority of gay men may be seropositive for HIV antibodies, a status which is at least associated with risk of AIDS.

At the same time, the use of the label "high risk group" is deceptive. An insurer which concentrated on weeding out the gay men from its pool of insurers would in one sense be acting rationally by eliminating from coverage a high risk group. But by doing so it would also simultaneously be eliminating many healthy men from the risk pool, and, if it were preoccupied with eliminating the high risk group rather than the risk itself, would be insuring significant numbers of people who are at equal or greater risk for AIDS than gay men. In this section, the problems of those who are in the risk group, but not necessarily at high risk, will be examined. As the reader will see, the major legal battles between insurers and lesbian and gay rights advocates focus on both the extent to which insurers can screen for risk factors for AIDS (which will tend to exclude many gay men from insurability), and the extent to which they may use indicia of risk group membership itself as an element in the screening process.

1. Antibody Screening

The issue which has been the most sensitive has been the use of HIV antibody tests as a screening mechanism. It has probably been the most sensitive because of the medical facts which point consistently to some association, as yet incompletely understood, between HIV infection and development of AIDS. Upon incomplete information, HIV antibody testing appears to be a rational way to exclude from coverage a group of people (seropositive people) who are statistically more likely to develop AIDS than their seronegative peers.

a. As a Condition in Applying for Insurance

When a client calls to say that he or she has been asked to take an antibody test as a condition of applying for insurance, what can the lawyer do? If the client lives or makes the insurance application in California or the District of Columbia, the answer is easiest. In those jurisdictions, legislation has been adopted which restricts the use of the antibody test by insurers, among others.[38] The client should be instructed to decline to take the test and the attorney seek intervention of the local insurance regulators should the insurer refuse to consider the client's application without the test.

The legislation is controversial and is under attack by the insurance industry. In Maine, a ban on inquiries regarding testing expires by the terms of the statute on October 1, 1988. In Wisconsin, the legislature banned antibody testing until the state epidemiologist certified that the antibody test was medically significant and sufficiently reliable for detection of HIV antibodies, and the state insurance commissioner certified that it was sufficiently reliable for use in underwriting. Those certifications having been made,[39] all that remains of the restriction is a ban use of the test for group insurance.

In the District of Columbia, where the ban on testing is sweeping, the insurance industry undertook a court challenge to the constitutionality of the legislation.[40] In that action, it was alleged that the law is unconstitutional as a deprivation of property; it was asserted that the ban on testing is an irrational and arbitrary legislative act. The district court rejected that argument and dismissed the action, finding that the law is rationally related to a legitimate governmental purpose.[41] As of this writing, however, the D.C. City Council is under increasing pressure to weaken or revoke the law.

Where there is no protective legislation, there may, in some jurisdictions, be administrative guidelines which will have at least persuasive effect on insurance companies. In New York and Massachusetts, state insurance departments have promulgated regulations which prohibit use of the test by health insurers. In both states, the insurance industry has challenged the regulations in court, and has succeeded in staying their implementation. See Matter of Health Insurance Association of America, et al., v. James P. Corcoran, Sup't of Insurance (Sup. Ct., Albany Co., Index No. 7970-87, Aug 19, 1987 (Prior J.)) and Life Insurance Association of Massachusetts v. Singer (Mass. Super. Ct., Suffolk Cty., Case No. 87-5321, Oct 2, 1987 (Steadman, J.)).

New Jersey guidelines suggest that antibody tests may not be used for health or disability policies unless there is medical evidence in the applicant's history which would justify the use of the test. For life insurance policies, the test is more broadly authorized, but it still may not be required based upon lifestyle (presumably, sexual orientation) alone.[42] In Connecticut, in a regulatory move of uncertain import in July 1986, the Insurance Commissioner prohibited insurers from questioning applicants regarding HIV antibody test results, although he had authorized such questions regarding a specific sequence of tests only two weeks earlier.[43] Many other states may issue guidelines pursuant to recommendations made by the National Association of Insurance Commissioners. See text accompanying note 62.

Complaints have been made to a number of state insurance departments when antibody testing has been sought by insurers. They have been made in states with protective legislation (California), in states with regulatory guidelines (New York, New Jersey, Oregon), and in states with no formal position opposed to use of the antibody test (Ohio).[44] In no state has such a complaint led to a formal administrative finding. In New York and California, complaints have led the respondent insurers to consider applications for insurance without requiring antibody testing.

In the states without formal restrictions on testing, the theory of the complaints has been that the use of the antibody test is an unfair practice under the state's insurance laws. Under the insurance laws of most states, there are general prohibitions against discrimination among individuals of the same class and equal life expectancy or who present the same hazard. If the insurer requires primarily gay men to take the antibody test, then there is a strong argument that it is treating some people who are seropositive (the untested heterosexuals and lesbians) differently from others (the tested gay men). While perhaps counterproductive in encouraging wide use of a test which will exclude people from the insurance pool, the argument has force.

If the insurer uses the test as a general screening device, then the argument against it is a much more difficult one. One must base one's opposition on the uncertain meaning of the test and its inability to predict disease, hence arguing that seropositivity alone does not place one in a different risk class. At least at this stage in our scientific understanding of AIDS, it may be unfair to use the test to distinguish among candidates for insurance.

This argument against the antibody test is difficult because seropositivity obviously does have some relationship to development of the disease. Insurers assert that the seropositivity, statistically, presents a risk of mortality well over five times the normal risk in 30 year old men.[45] The insurance industry, has, of course, focused on some of the more pessimistic statistical data, and focused on an age group with normally very low mortality, to present seropositivity as an uninsurable risk.[46] But even if the industry's data were unassailable, there would be reasons to distinguish seropositivity from the situations which the industry claims to be analogous -- e.g., blood cholesterol as a risk factor for heart disease. Some researchers believe that there are seropositive people who have antibodies which are effective at fighting the viral causes of AIDS, which means that those seropositive people may be at less risk for AIDS than those who have not been exposed at all to HIV virus.[47] Scientists have not yet been able to distinguish the effective antibodies from the ineffective ones but, if the theory is correct, then those who are eminently insurable will be systematically denied insurance by antibody screening. Since not all seropositive people have become (or are even predicted to become) ill, and development of the disease must be caused by some as yet unidentified other factors, the argument must be that until the disease mechanisms of AIDS are better understood, it is unfair to use seropositivity as a screen -- particularly when the screen will effectively limit participation by a whole class of people in the insurance pool and in all the economic activities and benefits which depend upon participation in that pool.

The filing of administrative complaints with respect to blood test requirements may be efficacious in individual cases, but it is unlikely that a significant proportion of those who are asked to take antibody tests will seek the assistance of a lawyer before submitting to the test. More frequently, the attorney is likely to be consulted after the testing has been done and the person has been denied insurance. The remedies available in such cases will depend in large part upon whether the person consented to the test and upon how the results were used.

b. Nonconsensual or Without Adequate Information

The ability of an insurer to use HIV antibody tests may depend in part upon how it obtains consent for the tests. In 1987, The Prudential Insurance Company and Lambda Legal Defense and Education Fund announced an out of court settlement of a suit brought by "John Doe", a life insurance applicant who was not issued an insurance policy following a positive result on an HIV antibody blood test protocol.

Doe, who stressed that he did not know his antibody status

before Prudential tested him, alleged that he did not consent to have his blood screened for HIV antibodies; that Prudential violated its obligations to keep his test results confidential when an underwriter disclosed the results to a nonemployee of Prudential; and that Prudential transmitted the antibody test results to him directly although he requested they be sent to his physician. Prudential emphasized that its willingness to settle did not signify it admitted any of Doe's allegations.

Prudential agreed to strengthen its existing procedures for obtaining informed consent for antibody testing, and to require signed consent from all applicants after they have been clearly informed that their blood will be tested for HIV antibodies. Prudential agreed to reinforce among its employees its existing policy on confidentiality with an emphasis on the sensitivity of AIDS related information, and to clarify its existing policy on communicating blood test results to applicants and on giving those applicants who so elect the opportunity to have the results conveyed to their physician, who can counsel them regarding the results. In addition, Prudential made a financial settlement with Doe. The parties agreed to keep the details of the settlement confidential.

If antibody tests are performed without the consent of the applicant for insurance, or if the tests were misrepresented to the applicant as "routine" blood tests (which has happened), the person may have a claim for battery against the insurance company and the medical personnel who performed the test. In a number of states, the facts which must be disclosed to a person taking an HIV antibody test in order to constitute informed consent are set out in laws or regulations regarding the test,[48] and if those facts are not disclosed, a claim not only of battery but also of medical malpractice against the medical personnel administering the test may be established. (Proving damages in such cases may raise more difficult issues. Aside from the emotional distress which may ensue from knowledge of seropositivity, what are the actual damages? May damages be measured by the value of the insurance policy for which the plaintiff applied?)

Where there are statutes regulating the use of the test, there are often statutory penalties for use of the test without informed consent or for unpermitted purposes. The plaintiff's attorney in those jurisdictions is likely to face the issue whether the statutory remedies were intended to supplant traditional tort remedies which might be available to plaintiffs. Some of those issues may be litigated in Wisconsin, where there is currently an action for invasion of privacy and other torts, as well as violations of Wisconsin's law regarding HIV antibody testing, pending

against an insurer and laboratory which allegedly performed T-cell subset tests and an HIV antibody test after the applicant crossed out those tests on the consent card. See Murray v. Bander's Life Company and Home Office Reference Laboratory, Milwaukee County Circuit Court, Case No. 736-495.

Even if the client consented to the antibody test, there still may be questions as to whether the client was adequately informed of the risks and benefits of the test, as required by specific regulatory statutes or under the common law. In states where there is no specific statutory remedy, there may be, in addition to tort remedies, a claim that the use of the test constituted an unfair insurance practice under the general provisions of the state insurance code. The extent to which courts will entertain private claims under such regulatory statutes will also vary from jurisdiction to jurisdiction.[49]

c. Limiting the Damage from a Positive Test Result

The most important task after a test has been administered may be to limit the damage from a positive test result. If test results are disclosed to those outside the insurance company, there may be significant damage to the seropositive person, including loss of employment. There may be claims against the company for breach of fiduciary or implied contractual duties to protect confidentiality, similar to the duties of physicians entrusted with confidential information. There may also be claims in tort. In California, a worker's compensation insurer has been sued for the unauthorized disclosure by one of its examining doctors for an unrelated condition. Urbaniak v. Newton, No. 87-0679 (Super. Ct. San Fran. Co.).

Further, the seropositive person who is recorded as such will have future problems in obtaining insurance with other companies. Insurance companies typically ask whether applicants have previously been denied insurance by other companies. In addition, through Medical Information Bureau, Inc. (M.I.B.), most insurers have access to a bank of computerized information about health conditions of insurance applicants disclosed and evaluated in the process of underwriting their applications. Member insurers are required to submit information about numerous different health conditions and some nonmedical information, such as reckless driving histories. The applicant for insurance usually authorizes the insurance company to examine his or her M.I.B. file. If a coded condition appears with reference to the applicant's previous insurance applications, the company will be prompted to ask specific questions of the applicant regarding the history which relates to the code.[50]

The M.I.B. formerly established four AIDS-related codes for recording information, encompassing clear-cut AIDS or ARC, HIV seropositivity as measured by two or more types of antibody tests, unexplained prodromal symptoms such as weight loss or diarrhea, and abnormal T-cell ratios.[51] Subsequently, the M.I.B. revised its coding system, and now includes all persons testing HIV antibody positive in a broader category of persons who have "abnormal" blood test results. Nonetheless, once a person has been recorded in this system as having a blood disorder, it is apparent that any future insurance applications will come under extremely close scrutiny. This may be so even if the person who has been coded for HIV seropositivity is living in a state where antibody testing as a condition of insurance is prohibited. The insurer will not use the information contained in the M.I.B. system as a basis for underwriting; it will, rather, use it as a basis for further close inquiry.

How can the damage be limited? There is one limitation inherent in the system. All records are removed after seven years.[52] The person who knows there is an AIDS-related code in M.I.B. should not continue to apply for insurance and thereby perpetuate the adverse coding. More active forms of limitation of damage are also possible, however. One may request the examination of one's M.I.B. file. The medical information in it will be sent to a physician designated by the consumer. One may seek correction of the file, and there may be numerous ways in which the coding or the information is inaccurate. One might argue, for example, if one was classified as seropositive based upon only a single ELISA test, without confirmatory tests being performed, that this was an insufficient basis for the classification.

Aside from the disclosure rights one has with respect to one's M.I.B. records under Federal Trade Commission regulation, there are also some rights of access to reports and records in the hands of individual insurance companies. To the extent that insurance companies commission reports of investigations into the prospective policyholder's characteristics or mode of living, such reports may be subject to disclosure to the consumer under the federal Fair Credit Reporting Act, 15 U.S.C. Sects. 1681 et seq.[53] This may be of particular use when insurance companies make questionable inquiries into sexual orientation or other aspects of a person's lifestyle,[54] a not infrequent subject of questions to one's neighbors and business associates. Further, one may have rights under the laws of states such as Connecticut, which has enacted an Insurance Information and Privacy Protection Act.[55] The Act provides mechanisms for discovery of and correction of an individual's insurance company records.

In most jurisdictions, insurers will be able to use antibody screening. In the absence of specific regulations or legislation, it will be difficult to argue that antibody testing is unlawful. Discriminatory use of the test, however, may well be subject to attack, as will use of the test without informed consent, sloppy testing procedures, and misuse of the information obtained through the test. The practitioner should examine each step of the process to make sure that his or her client has been fully informed of the use and meaning of the test and fully protected from disclosure to persons other than the underwriters who have used the test for underwriting purposes.

2. Demographic Screenings

Antibody testing is just one way in which insurers have sought to prevent those at high risk for AIDS from obtaining insurance policies. They have also engaged in what their opponents have called a form of redlining, in which unmarried men aged 20 through 45 have come under close scrutiny in applying for insurance. These are demographic markers for gay males. The insurers will look particularly closely at applicants who name "unusual" beneficiaries, such as roommates or friends, as well as at those whose medical histories include such incidents as rectal gonorrhea. They may even make judgments based upon profession. Those in stereotypically gay male businesses -- florists, interior decorators, etc.-- are assumed to be gay, therefore subject to cautious underwriting.[56]

Some of these concerns, such as the concern with beneficiaries, are not new to lesbians and gay men. Many insurance companies have, as a matter of internal policy and as a means of avoiding the underwriting of particularly risky policies, long ago developed guidelines which require that even when a person is buying insurance on his or her own life (in which there is always an insurable interest), the beneficiary to be named in the policy have an insurable interest as well. For many years, lesbians and gay men have been instructed by their insurance professionals to name their parents or their estates as beneficiaries when applying for insurance, and to change the beneficiary designation for the benefit of their lover later on, after the policy is issued. If there is no pecuniary interest such as a joint business interest or real property ownership or joint debt, then there is no interest the insurance company will recognize, and one may be barred from buying insurance for lack of a qualified beneficiary.

The advisor to a gay man today might well give the same advice, except that insurance companies are screening for single men who name their mothers or siblings as beneficiaries as well. The fear of underwriting AIDS has made suspect some of the beneficiary designations which were for many years the standard designations of single men, either gay or straight.[57] Perhaps the better advice today is to be ready to substantiate the pecuniary interest of a lover.[58] (Is there a cohabitation agreement providing obligations of continuing support? Are they both signatories to a lease which may give rise to joint and several liability? Are they co-parenting a child?) If the health of the men is good, and if they are refused insurance based upon what is apparently a lifestyle bias, there may be a number of remedies.

In Washington, D.C., which bars discrimination based upon sexual orientation, insurance is defined as a public accommodation; therefore, one may make a direct claim for anti-gay discrimination.[59] In other states, as New York's Superintendent of Insurance has publicly proclaimed, discrimination based upon sexual orientation would violate the fair trade laws.[60] In California, there may be a claim for such discrimination under the Unruh Civil Rights Act. Such a claim has withstood a motion to dismiss in NGRA & Hurlburt v. Great Republic Life Insurance Company.[61]

Also helpful is a model regulatory bulletin adopted by the National Association of Insurance Commissioners in December 1986, which forbids health and life insurers to inquire into an applicant's sexual orientation or to use such information in the underwriting process.[62] (See appendix at end of article.) The bulletin also bars the use of information about gender, marital status, living arrangements, occupation, medical history, beneficiaries, and zip codes or other territorial classifications to determine an applicant's sexual orientation. The guidelines have been incorporated into regulations in several states, and should be persuasive to both regulators and insurers in other jurisdictions.

In addition to claims that discrimination based upon sexual orientation violates the law, where the insurer has used other demographic criteria as markers for sexual orientation, there may be claims based on the use of those markers alone, in New York for example, to treat single men differently from married men may violate the statutory prohibitions on marital status discrimination, which have been found to be violated when "mode of life" judgments were made by insurers (distinguishing heterosexual couples merely living together from those who are married).[63] To treat men in certain cities, such as New York and San Francisco, differently from men in other cities, such as Albany and Sacramento, might be determined to violate the general proscriptions under the insurance law, or to constitute unfair discrimination. It is exposure to the causative

agents of AIDS, not residence in any particular city, which places one at risk.

When a client is refused insurance, and the practitioner suspects that impermissible factors were used in underwriting, it will obviously be essential to obtain as much information as possible about how the refusal came about. But aside from looking at how specific anti-discrimination laws may apply to the facts presented, the attorney should also have a firm grasp of the policy reasons which support restrictions on screening.

AIDS is not likely to bankrupt our vast private insurance system, on which many depend for decent health care and on which many depend for access to home ownership (where mortgage insurance is required) or employment (where insurability either for key person insurance or for group health coverage may be a criterion). The systematic exclusion of gay men from the private insurance system may, on the other hand, rupture and polarize society in serious ways. We have, by legislative act, prohibited the use of numerous facts of actuarial significance in the underwriting of insurance -- race, marital status, handicap -- undoubtedly because the social cost of using those facts outweighed the benefit to the private insurance system. While not understating the severity of the AIDS epidemic, we must assert that the same analysis applies here and that, as long as adequate public health and welfare systems are not in place, it must be a social priority to maintain insurance coverage for a social group which already has suffered inordinate discrimination.

Notes

[1] W.L. Howard, The Sexual Pervert in Life Insurance, 16 Med. Examiner 206-07 (July 1906), as summarized in J.N. Katz, Gay/Lesbian Almanac 319-20 (1983).

[2] Centers for Disease Control, Update: Acquired Immunodeficiency Syndrome--Limited States 35 MMWR No.2 (Jan. 17, 1986).

[3] D.A. Rublee, Self-Funded Health Benefit Plans: Trends, Legal Environment, and Policy Issues, 255 J.A.M.A. (1986).

[4] American Academy of Actuaries, Risk Classification and AIDS (May 1986).

[5] American Council on Life Insurance, Life Insurance Fact Book (1986) (not in print at time of this publication).

[6] See, e.g., G.J. Couch, Cyclopedia of Insurance Law (2d ed. 1959); Appleman, Insurance Law and Practice (1941-48).

[7] J. Barron, Insurers Study Screening for AIDS, New York

Times, Sept. 26, 1985, at B12, col.4; AIDS Costs: The Price Business Is Paying, Wall St. J., Oct.18, 1985, at 12, col.1.

8 State of New Jersey, Department of Insurance, Bulletin #85-3 (1985).

9 American Council of Life Ins. & Health Ins. Ass'n of America, White Paper: The Acquired Immunodeficiency Syndrome & HTLV-III Antibody Testing (1986).

10 N.Y. Ins. Law sec. 3220(a)(6)(31 days to convert from group life insurance); see also id. sec. 3221(e)(1),(e)(8)(45 days to convert from group health insurance, but not longer than 90 days if no notice is given).

11 Cf. Cross v. Mutual Benefit Life Ins. Co., 173 Cal. 3d 821, 219 Cal. Rptr. 305 (1985). See Failure to Convert Group Insurance Coverage Challenged AIDS Policy & L. (BNA), July 16, 1986, at 2.

12 It may be useful to explore programs which will assist the person with AIDS to pay for the insurance. Medicaid will assume third party health insurance premium payments in some localities.

13 Rick v. Sentry Life Ins. of Wis. (administrative complaint before Cal. Dep't of Insurance), AIDS Policy & L. (BNA), July 16, 1986, at 2.

14 Pub. L. No. 99-272 (April 7, 1986).

15 E.g., N.Y. Ins. L. sec. 3221(m).

16 Conn. Gen. Stat. Ann. sec. 38-61(6).

17 N.Y. Ins. L. sec. 3216(j)(2), 3221(k)(1)(A)

18 AIDS Costs: The Price Business Is Paying. Wall St. J., Oct. 18, 1985, at 12, col.4.

19 N.Y. Ins. L. sec. 3217(b)(5).

20 The Department ruled in favor of plaintiff on the sex discrimination claim, but ruled that claims of handicap discrimination are pre-empted by federal law under Shaw v. Delta Airlines, 463 U.S. 86 (1983).

21 See Moeller v. Associated Hosp. Serv., 304 N.Y. 73, 106 N.E. 2d 16 (1952), which recognized the general rule that policies should be strictly construed in favor of insureds, but did not apply that rule when the insurer was a nonprofit hospital plan.

22 Klar v. Associated Hosp. Serv., 211 N.Y.S.2d 538 (N.Y.C. Mun. Ct. 1959); Society of New York Hosp. v. Burstein, 253 N.Y.S.2d 753 (App. Div. 1964).

23 94 A.L.R.3d 990, 998; Couch, supra note 6, at sec. 41:814. Regulations adopted in New York make this requirement ex-plicit, by defining pre-existing condition as "the existence of symptoms which would ordinarily cause a prudent person to seek diagnosis, care or treatment within a two-year period preceding the effective date of the coverage of the insured person, or a condition for which medical advice or treatment was recommended by a physician or received from a physician within a two-year period preceding the effective date of coverage of the insured person."

24 Abernathy v. Hospital Care Ass'n, 254 N.C. 346, 119 S.E.2d 1 (1961).

25 Smith v. Industrial Hosp. Ass'n, 194 Or. 525, 242 P.2nd 592 (1952).

26 Letter dated August 22, 1984, from Alan Rachlin, Associate Attorney, New York Ins. Dep't, to Mel Rosen, C.S.W., New York State AIDS Institute. While the reasoning of the letter is not entirely clear, leaving open the possibility that seropositivity could be considered a pre-existing condition if the antibody were ever found to be an "indicator or a cause of AIDS," the result is clearly the correct one under the applicable principles of law.

27 J. Barron, Insurers Study Screening for AIDS, supra note 7.

28 See e.g., Kentucky Central Life Insurance Company v. Webster, 651 F. Supp. (N.D. Ala 1986), in which an insurer was held obligated to pay the proceeds of a policy on the life of a person who failed to disclose various dermatological conditions and later developed AIDS. The Court held that the dermatological conditions were not material to the risk. And, compare Zachary Trading, Inc. v. Northwestern Mutual Life Insurance Co., 668 F. Supp. 242 (S.D. N.Y. 1987), in which undisclosed severe anemia and generalized enlarged lymph glands were held sufficient to grant summary judgment for rescission, with Northwestern Mutual Life Insurance Company v. Barth 85 Civ. 8360 (GLG)(U.S.D.C., S.D.N.Y., May 11, 1986)(Goettel, J.), in which an insurer sought rescission of policies issued to a man who died of AIDS. In Barth, the court found that whether an undisclosed health history including lymphadenopathy, low T-cell ratios, oral thrush, and anergy would have been material to the insurer, was a question of fact for the jury. In light of the insurer's issuance of policies to some persons with lymphadenopathy and in light of the insurer having ignored numerous disclosed risk factors for AIDS in the application, it could not be said that the nondisclosure was material as a matter of law.

29 N.Y. Ins. Law sec. 3204(2).

30 See e.g., Metropolitan Life Ins. Co. v. Burno, 309 Mass. 7, 33 N.E. 2d 519 (1941), and discussion in Keeton, Insurance Law: Rights at Variance with Policy Provisions, Part II, 83 Harv. L. Rev. 1281, 1292-94 (1970). See also Levin v. Metropolitan Life Ins. Co., 381 Pa. 615, 114 A. 2d 330 (1955).

31 See Note, Misrepresentation by Insured Under the New York Insurance Law, 44 Colum. L. Rev. 241 (1944).

[32] Compare Thompson v. Occidental Life Ins. Co., 9 Cal. 3d 904, 513 P. 2d 353 (1973), in which the beneficiaries recovered although the insured did not disclose the existence of a condition, because he failed to appreciate the significance of medical facts related to him by his physicians, with Minnesota Mutual Life Ins. Co. v. Camdelore, 416 So. 2d 1149 (Fla. 1982), in which the beneficiaries did not recover, although the insured, in doctor visits he did not disclose, was told that he had normal findings, but the symptoms for which he sought treatment in fact were precursors of a deadly disease.

[33] National Old Line Ins. Co. v. People, 256 Ark. 137, 506 S.W.2d 128 (1974); Hawkins v. New York Life Ins. Co., 176 Kan. 24, 269 P.2d 389 (1954); R.I. Gen. Laws sec. 27-4-10 (1979).

[34] Formosa v. Equitable Life Assurance Soc'y, 166 N.J. Super. 8, 398 A.2d 1301 (App. Div. 1979).

[35] Barrett v. State Mut. Life Assurance Co., 58 A.D.2d 320, 396 N.Y.S.2d 848 (1977), aff'd mem, 44 N.Y.2d 872, 373 N.Y.S.2d 1000, cert. denied 440 U.S. 912 (1978).

[36] Wiedmayer v. Midland Mut, Life Ins. Co., 108 Mich. App. 96, 310 N.W.2d 285 (1981).

[37] In Pinney v. Aetna Life Assurance and Annuity Company, (Supreme Ct., N.Y. Co., Index No. 28283/86, June 24, 1987)(Sherman, J.), an action on a health insurance policy by a person with AIDS in which the insurer counterclaimed for rescission, the court denied the insurer's motion for a protective order against such discovery. Plaintiff sought to examine applications in which lymphadenopathy, amebiasis and other conditions frequently found in persons with AIDS were disclosed. The court ordered them to be produced, with personal identifying information deleted.

[38] Cal. Health & Safety Code secs. 199.20-23; D.C. Act 6-170 Laws 2367.

[39] In a memorandum dated Aug. 6, 1986 entitled Final Copy of HTLV-III Serologic Testing Paper Related to Wisconsin Statute 631.90 Pursuant to Underwriting Individual Insurance Policies, State Epidemiologist Dr. Jeffrey P. Davis determined the test sufficiently reliable, provided certain strict testing protocols were followed. Based on that determination, the Wisconsin Insurance Commission published a proposed rule on Dec. 15, 1986 to allow insurers to use HIV testing. Required are two positive ELISA tests, one on initial testing and the second on one of two repeat tests of the same specimen, plus a reactive Western blot.

[40] American Council of Life Ins. & Health Ins. Ass'n v. District of Columbia 645 F. Supp. 84 (D.D.C. Sept. 19, 1986).

[41] Id.

[42] N.J. Dep't of Ins. Bull. No. 86-1.

[43] Conn. Ins. Dep't., Bull. No. PF-16 (July 11, 1986; revised July 25, 1986).

[44] See 1 AIDS Policy & L. 3 (BNA) (Oct. 22, 1986), for reports on formal complaints filed against insurance companies: Miller against North American Life & Cas. Co. (Cal., filed by Nat'l Gay Rts. Advocates); Cornet against Bankers Security Life Ins. Co. (N.Y.); Ehlert against Aid Ass'n for Lutherans (N.J., filed Oct. 1, 1986 by Lambda Legal Defense & Education Fund); complaints filed anonymously against Minn. Life Ins. Co. (Ohio) and New Eng. Mut. Life Ins. Co. (Or.).

[45] Comm. on Risk Classification, American Soc'y of Actuaries, Risk Classifications and AIDS (May 1986).

[46] The American Academy of Actuaries' Units Report on Risk Classification and AIDS relied upon an assumption that between 8 percent and 34 percent of seropositive people will develop AIDS in a three-year period, citing J.J. Goedert et al., Three year Incidence of AIDS in Five Cohorts of HTLV-III-Infected Risk Group Members, 231 Science 992 (Feb. 28, 1986). Other longitudinal studies, however, show conversion from seropositivity to AIDS at a much slower pace -- closer to one to two percent per year. See H.W. Jaffee et al., The Acquired Immunodeficiency Syndrome in a Cohort of Homosexual Men: A Six-Year Follow-up Study, 103 Ann. Internal Med. 210-14 (1985). Obviously, the relative mortality statistics change dramatically depending upon which set of figures is used.

Further, the actuaries examine relative mortality for 30-year-olds. The relative effect of seropositivity on the mortality of 55-year-olds, who have a naturally higher death rate, is much less than it is for 30-year-olds. Although the mortality differential between seropositive and seronegative 55-year-old would be less than 500 percent (the cut-off point for insurability, say the actuaries), there has been no reported instance of an insurance company offering any insurance to a 55-year-old seropositive male, even at an increased premium.

[47] See M. Hunt, Teaming Up Against AIDS, New York Times Magazine, Mar. 2, 1986, at 46, col. 5, for a description of Harvard researchers Groopman and Essex pursuing this possibility.

[48] Both of the jurisdictions which have prohibited use of the tests has provided for civil penalties as well as claims for actual damages. But the District of Columbia law appears to make the remedies mutually exclusive, and in California, there may be an argument that the civil penalties are intended to supplant punitive damages which might otherwise be available.

[49] Under Massachusetts law, a court has decided that an insurance company did not violate the laws prohibiting invidious discrimination, without even questioning whether there was a

private cause of action for such discrimination. Sullivan v. Manhattan Life Ins. Co., 626 F.2d 1080 (1st Cir. 1980). Under New York law, courts have strongly suggested that there is no private cause of action for violation of the insurance regulatory statutes, although they have assumed arguendo that there was such a private right of action in finding against plaintiffs on the merits of their claims. See, e.g., Dano v. Royal Globe Ins. Co., 59 N.Y.2d 827, 451 N.E.2d 488 (1983).

[50] N.M. Day, MIB Fact Sheet, N.Y. State Bar J. (Nov. 1984), at 26, 27.

[51] National Ass'n of Ins. Comm'rs, Advisory Comm. on AIDS, Report to the Health Ins. & Life Ins. Comms. (Dec. 9, 1986).

[52] Day, supra note 50, at 27.

[53] See Houghton v. New Jersey Mfrs. Ins. Co., 615 F. Supp. 299 (E.D. Pa. 1985).

[54] Discussed at length in next section.

[55] Conn. Gen. Stat. secs. 35-500-23.

[56] See, e.g., Insurer Screening Unmarried Males New York Times, Oct. 7, 1985, at A28, col. 1, regarding Lincoln National Life Insurance Company.

[57] The Munich American Reassurance Company had singled out for special attention applicants who named parents or siblings as beneficiaries. The guidelines were modified after the California Insurance Department interceded. Gay Legal Organization Fights AIDS Insurance Bias, N.Y. Native, May 19, 1986, at p. 12.

[58] The correct designation of beneficiary is the issue being currently litigated in The New England Mutual Life Insurance Company v. Duke, Index No. 28359/87 (Supreme Court, New York County), pending in New York. In that case, an insurer is seeking to rescind a life insurance policy because the insured described his roommate, with whom he shared leasehold and consumer credit obligations, as a business partner. The insured is asserting, among other defenses, that the insurer's agent instructed him to describe the relationship in those terms, and that rescission on that ground would violate public policy and constitute an unfair and deceptive practice.

[59] D.C. Code Ann. sec. 1-2501-57.

[60] J.P. Corcoran, Superintendent of Insurance, Testimony Before the Subcomm. on Intergovernmental Relations & Hum. Resources of the U.S. House of Representatives (Sept. 1985). The extent to which such discrimination will be the subject of regulatory action may be revealed when the New York Insurance Department acts on a complaint filed in November 1987, by a hairdressing salon against The Guardian Life Insurance Company of America. The complaint charged that a recently instituted underwriting guideline under which hairdressing salons would no longer be issued group health insurance coverage constituted an unfair effort to avoid underwriting gay men.

[61] National Gay Rts. Advocates v. Great Rep. Life Ins. Co., No. 857323 (Cal. Super. Ct., San Francisco).

[62] National Association of Insurance Commissions, Advisory Committee on AIDS, Medical/Lifestyle Questions on Applications and Underwriting Guidelines Affecting AIDS and ARC (Dec. 11, 1986).

[63] 1976 Ops. Att'y Gen. 58 (Dec. 13, 1976)(opinion of Thomas A. Harnett, New York Superintendent of Insurance).

Appendix

National Association
of Insurance Commissioners

Guidelines on Underwriting for AIDS

Passed by NAIC, December 1986

PROPOSED BULLETIN

Subject: Medical/Lifestyle Questions or Applications and Underwriting Guidelines Affecting AIDS and ARC

(Recital of applicable authority if needed and purpose of bulletin. Issuance of bulletin is to assist insurers to formulate and design medical/lifestyle questions in applications for and underwriting standards affecting health and/ or life insurance coverage in conformity with the fair standards adopted by the NAIC at its December 1986 meeting.)

I. General Propositions

A. No inquiry in an application for health or life insurance coverage, or in an investigation conducted by an insurer or an insurance support organization on its behalf in connection with an application for such coverage, shall be directed toward determining the applicant's sexual orientation.

B. Sexual orientation may not be used in the underwriting process or in the determination of insurability.

C. Insurance support organizations shall be directed by insurers not to investigate, directly or indirectly, the sexual orientation of an applicant or a beneficiary.

II. Medical/Lifestyle Application Questions and Underwriting Standards

A. No question shall be used which is designed to establish the sexual orientation of the applicant.

B. Questions relating to the applicant having or having been diagnosed as having AIDS or ARC are permissible if they are factual and designed to establish the existence of the condition.
For example: Insurers should not ask "do you believe you may have ...?", but rather "do you know or have reasons to know ...?".

C. Questions relating to medical and other factual matters intending to reveal the possible existence of a medical condition are permissible if they are not used as a proxy to establish the sexual orientation of the applicant, and the applicant has been given an opportunity to provide an explanation for any affirmative answers given in the application.
For example: "Have you had chronic cough, significant weight loss, chronic fatigue, diarrhea, enlarged glands ...?". These type of questions should be related to a finite period of time preceding completion of the application and should be specific. All of the questions above should provide the applicant the opportunity to give a detailed explanation.

D. Questions relating to the applicant's having or having been diagnosed as having or having been advised to seek treatment for a sexually transmitted disease are permissible.

E. Neither the marital status, the "living arrangements", the occupation, the gender, the medical history, the beneficiary designation, nor the zip code or other territorial classification of an applicant may be used to establish, or aid in establishing, the applicant's sexual orientation.

F. For purposes of rating an applicant for health and life insurance, an insurer may impose territorial rates, but only if the rates are based on sound actuarial principles or are related to actual or reasonable anticipated experience.

G. No adverse underwriting decision shall be made because medical records or a report from an insurance support organization shows that the applicant has demonstrated AIDS-related concerns by seeking counseling from health care professionals. This sub-section does not apply to an applicant seeking treatment and/or diagnosis.

(Provision for States permitting testing)

H. Whenever an applicant is requested to take an AIDS-related test in connection with an application for insurance, the use of such a test must be revealed to the applicant and his or her written consent obtained. No adverse underwriting decision shall be made on the basis of such a positive AIDS-related test unless an established test protocol* has been followed.

I. Optional language to be considered by each State:

Alternative A: Insurers should not be permitted to ask an applicant if he or she has tested positive on an AIDS-related blood test.

Alternative B: Insurers should be permitted to ask an applicant if he or she has tested positive on an AIDS-related issue.

*Note: "Established test protocol" means the protocol adopted in a particular State. At a minimum, it requires two positive ELISA tests. In some States, it also includes one positive Western blot. It is anticipated that new and more effective AIDS-related tests will be developed which might replace those currently in use.

PART II

COBRA

Introduction

Benjamin Schatz

An extremely important body of insurance law for people with AIDS or ARC who are unable to continue working is the Consolidated Omnibus Budget Reconciliation Act, or COBRA. Under this Act, which was enacted in April 1986 (Pub. L. 99-272), an employee or beneficiary may elect to "continue" health (but not life) insurance coverage provided by an employer for 18 or 36 months, depending upon the "qualifying event." The Act applies whether the employer obtains coverage through an insurance company or is "self-insured," and covers medical, dental, vision and HMO plans.

The provisions of the Act are, unfortunately, very complex. The Memorandum below by Katherine Franke gives an overview of the regulations which govern it. The following points will be helpful:

Coverage is continued for 18 months if: an employee quits or is fired (except for "gross misconduct"); or, if an employee's hours are reduced so that he/she is no longer eligible for the health plan. (Note: This is the amount of time which will usually apply to clients who lose their jobs after they develop AIDS or ARC.)

Coverage is continued for 36 months: to the spouse or dependent of an employee who dies or is divorced; to dependent children who lose their dependent status, or to spouses or employees who become eligible for Medicare.

The premiums charged for continued coverage may not exceed 102% of the cost for active employees under the employer's plan. Costs may be charged to the employee/beneficiary.

The employee must be notified of his her right to continue

coverage within 44 days of the "qualifying event." The employee then has sixty days to elect continued coverage.

Employers who fail to notify can be penalized by loss of the company's tax deduction for any group health plan payments made that year, by a $100 per-day fine payable to the aggrieved employee, and by suits to force compliance.

All employers are affected except those with fewer than 20 employees, religious organizations, and the federal government.

COBRA coverage can be ended if premiums are not paid, the employee/ beneficiary is covered under any other group health plan or becomes eligible for Medicare, or if the employer drops its group health plan.

Memorandum

To: All Interested Parties
From: Katherine M. Franke
Re: A Guided Tour of COBRA
Date: August 19, 1987

The Treasury Department has at long last issued its proposed Consolidated Omnibus Budget Reconciliation Act (COBRA) regulations. They appear in Question and Answer form at 52 Fed. Reg. 22716 (June 15, 1987).

With this proposed COBRA interpretation, Treasury has, not surprisingly, taken a restrictive view of the scope of continuation benefits for workers who leave employment. Since an understanding of the intricacies of COBRA has become instrumental to representation of persons who encounter AIDS-related employment and insurance problems, I have prepared the following analysis of COBRA.

Benjamin Schatz is the Director of the AIDS Civil Rights Project of National Gay Rights Advocates in San Francisco.

Katherine Franke is an attorney with the AIDS Discrimination Unit of the New York City Human Rights Commission and a member of the Executive Committee of the National Lawyers Guild AIDS Network.

I. When must group health plans comply with COBRA?

The continuation coverage requirements for groups health plans were adopted as part of COBRA on April 7, 1986 (29 U.S.C. secs. 1161 et seq.). However there has been confusion concerning the effective date of COBRA for particular health plans.

a. Non-collectively bargained plans.

For non-collectively bargained health plans, the plan must comply with COBRA as of the first day of the first plan year beginning on or after July 1, 1986. Typically, employers enter into contracts with insurers on a yearly basis. Plan years are determined according to the date upon which the contract is renewed, not according to the date the member became eligible for coverage.

b. Collectively bargained plans.

For health plans "maintained pursuant to" a collective bargaining agreement, the plan must comply with COBRA as of the first day of the first plan year beginning on or after the later of (1) January 1, 1987, or (2) the date on which the last of the collective bargaining agreements relating to the plan terminates. Clearly, by this rule, organized workers are penalized for having bargained health care benefits. Unfortunately, this provision appeared in the statute, and is therefore not subject to agency discretion.

Note: Often, both exempt and non-exempt workers are covered under a health plan which was negotiated through the collective bargaining process. COBRA did not make clear whether the effective date of the exempt employees' conversion rights would be subject to the rule for collectively bargained or noncollectively bargained plans. The new regulations clarify how these two groups of employees are to be treated. Employees in the bargaining unit are determined to be receiving health coverage pursuant to a collectively bargained plan. Conversely, under the new rules, the exempt employees are deemed to be receiving benefits pursuant to a non-collectively bargained plan, even though their health coverage is provided by the same trust or fund as the organized employees. In these contexts, the arrangement consists of two separate health plans for the purposes of COBRA's effective date.

c. COBRA coverage where the qualifying event occurs prior to COBRA's effective date, but where coverage under the group plan ends after the effective date of COBRA.

It is quite common for a group health plan, either as a matter of contract or according to state law, to provide several weeks or even months of continuation coverage under the group plan to an employee when he or she leaves employment. This situation often poses a COBRA timing problem -- is the individual entitled to COBRA benefits where the loss of employment occurred prior to the effective date of COBRA, but where he or she does not lose group coverage until after the plan is subject to COBRA? For example, for a group plan which becomes subject to COBRA on January 1, 1987, if the employee leaves employment on September 30, 1986 and the group contract provides for six months of continued coverage subsequent to leaving work, does the individual have COBRA rights since he or she would actually lose group coverage after the group plan is subject to COBRA?

Unfortunately, the answer is no. A COBRA qualifying event is one which would result in the loss of coverage of a qualified beneficiary. 29 U.S.C. sec. 1163. It need not actually result in the loss of coverage at that time. Under the Treasury Department's reading of the Act, the qualifying event itself must have occurred after the effective date of COBRA. Accordingly, one may not bootstrap various extensions of coverage in order to achieve COBRA rights where the employee left work prior to the effective date of COBRA.

Treasury's reading of the timing aspects of the Act has resulted in a somewhat peculiar, or perhaps cruel, twist. Under the circumstances discussed above, where an employee leaves work prior to the effective date of COBRA but does not lose actual group coverage until after the plan is subject to COBRA, the employee's spouse or dependents may be able to acquire COBRA rights which are not available to the covered employee. If, in this example, the qualified beneficiary divorces his or her spouse sometime after January 1st, but before his or her extra-COBRA extension benefits expire in May 1987, the spouse will acquire COBRA rights at the time of the divorce, even though the covered employee will not. This is the case because the divorce of a covered employee from the employee's spouse is a qualifying event separate from the termination of the covered employee's employment. 29 U.S.C. sec. 1163(3).

The best way to avoid the COBRA timing problem, which operates as a penalty against employees who are afforded extra-COBRA extension benefits, is to negotiate some form of leave without pay for the period during which the individual would have received extension benefits under the contract, or, at a minimum, until the effective date of COBRA. Although this arrangement, technically, forestalls the happening of the qualifying event until the effective date of COBRA, it practically requires very little of the employer. Note, however, that placing an employee on leave will not delay the qualifying event if the employer shifts to the employee the responsibility to pay premiums. The qualifying event will not occur as the employee is treated the same as all other members of the group.

d. Notice to covered employees of COBRA rights.

At the time that COBRA becomes effective for a particular group health plan, the plan must provide written notice concerning COBRA rights to each covered employee and his or her spouse. 29 U.S.C. se. 1166(1).

II. Who must pay for COBRA benefits?

The statute states that the employer may require the qualified beneficiary to pay for COBRA premiums paid by the employer. 29 U.S.C. sec. 1162(3). Similarly, the proposed regulations state that a group health plan can require a qualified beneficiary to pay for COBRA coverage. 53 Fed. Reg. 22731, Answer 44. Most employers will, no doubt, elect to have the qualified beneficiary pay COBRA premiums. However, there is an argument that this need not be the case under all circumstances. I have on several occasions convinced employers to pay for COBRA benefits when the employer paid all or substantially all of the premiums while the employee was working.

The argument goes something like this: In general, Congress intended that COBRA benefits

> consist of coverage which, as of the time the coverage is being provided, is identical to the coverage provided under the plan to similarly situated beneficiaries under the plan...

29 U.S.C. sec. 1162(1)(emphasis added). Given this congressional purpose -- that individuals receiving COBRA benefits receive benefits on terms identical to those received by other employees -- it is preferable that the employer provide COBRA benefits to eligible individuals according to terms in effect at the time of the qualifying event. As applied to the payment of premiums, this means that where the employer was responsible for funding the group plan, under COBRA this responsibility would continue for the 18 or 36 months following the qualifying event. Similarly, where the employer and the employee shared proportionate contributions to the plan, they would continue to do so during the requisite period of COBRA benefits. Under this interpretation of COBRA, individuals receiving COBRA benefits would truly obtain benefits identical to similarly situated employed beneficiaries. The

statutory provisions permitting an employer to charge the qualified beneficiary for COBRA coverage merely allows the employer to do so in those circumstances where the covered employee was already paying premiums prior to the qualifying event. Accordingly, the 102% limit is viewed as a ceiling in the limited circumstances.

My comments on the proposed COBRA regulations suggested a clarification which would require employers to pay for COBRA benefits under the circumstances outline above. I seriously doubt that the IRS will adopt my interpretation, although the proposed rules do not foreclose my reading of Congress' intent.

III. What is a qualifying event?

In order for an event to trigger COBRA rights, three conditions must be met. First, it must be either i) the death of an employee covered by the group plan; ii) the termination (other than by reason of gross misconduct) or reduction of hours of a covered employee's employment; iii) the divorce or legal separation of a covered employee from the employee's spouse; iv) a covered employee becoming entitled to Medicare benefits; or v) a dependent child ceasing to be a dependent child of the covered employee.

Second, the event must, according to the terms of the group health plan, cause the covered employee, or the spouse or dependent, to lose coverage under the plan, or to cease to receive coverage according to terms and conditions as in effect immediately prior to the qualifying event.

Finally, the loss of coverage need not occur immediately after the qualifying event, rather, the event must merely trigger the loss of coverage at some time in the future. In other words, the fact that a group contract or local law provides for a period of extra-COBRA continuation coverage when an employee leaves the group does not mean that the termination from employment will result in the loss of coverage. As discussed above, in order that COBRA rights attach, the qualifying event must occur after the effective date of COBRA, notwithstanding the date upon which the individual actually loses coverage.

IV. When do COBRA benefits begin, and for how long do they run?

According to Treasury's interpretation for the Act, COBRA benefits are to begin running as of the date of the qualifying event. One may not piggyback contractual or statutory continuation coverage onto COBRA coverage in order to obtain more than 18 or 36 months of coverage mandated by COBRA. Accordingly, the length of COBRA benefits is measured from the date of the qualifying event even if the qualifying event does not result in a loss of coverage under the plan until some later date. If, however, the extra-COBRA continuation coverage does not satisfy all of the requirements for COBRA coverage, i.e.: it is not identical to coverage obtained prior to the qualifying event, the employee must be offered the opportunity to elect COBRA conversion coverage in lieu of the alternative continuation coverage. Should the employee elect the alternative coverage over the COBRA coverage, he or she need not be offered COBRA coverage at the end of the alternative coverage.

a. Who must notify the plan of a qualifying event?

The employer has 30 days to notify the plan administrator when a covered employee dies, is terminated, becomes entitled to Medicare benefits or the employer has begun bankruptcy proceedings, that is, when an employee gains COBRA rights pursuant to 29 U.S.C. sec. 1163 (1), (2), (4) and (6). On the other hand, it is the employee's duty to notify the plan administrator when she or he has been divorced, or when a dependent child has ceased to be a dependent child under the plan. In these 29 U.S.C. sec. 1163 (3) and (5) situations, the employee must notify the plan administrator of the qualifying event within 60 days after the later of i) the date of the qualifying event, or ii) the date that the qualified beneficiary would lose coverage on account of the qualifying event.

b. When must the covered employee or qualified beneficiary elect COBRA coverage?

The group plan may condition COBRA coverage upon a timely election of such coverage. The regulations set out rules for calculating the amount of time which must be afforded a covered employee or qualified beneficiary to elect such coverage. This time period must be provided at a minimum, and the employer may provide additional time if it so chooses. The election period must begin on the date of which coverage terminates under the plan by reason of the qualifying event, and ends 60 days after the later of i) the date that the qualified beneficiary would lose coverage on account of the qualifying event, or ii) the date that the qualified beneficiary is sent notice of his or her right to elect COBRA coverage. The election is considered to be made on the date that it is sent to the employer or plan administrator, and coverage must be provided retroactive to the date coverage would have otherwise been lost.

An example will make the calculation of the election period clearer. An employee leaves work on June 1, 1988, and the plan provides that employer-paid coverage ends immediately upon the termination of employment. The election period must begin on June 1, 1988 and must end not earlier than July 31, 1988. However, if notice of the right to elect COBRA coverage is not sent to the employee until June 15, 1988, the election period must not end earlier than August 14, 1988. Finally, if the plan provides for six months of employer-paid coverage subsequent to termination from employment, the employee does not lose coverage until December 1, 1988. The election period under this scenario may begin as late as December 1, 1988, and must not end earlier than January 30, 1989. If, however, the employer-paid extension coverage is not identical to the employee's coverage prior to the qualifying event, the election period begins on June 1, 1988 and must not end before July 31, 1988.

c. Can a qualified beneficiary waive his or her rights to COBRA coverage?

A qualified beneficiary who, during the election period, elects not to receive COBRA coverage can revoke that election at any time before the end of the election period. However, if an individual waives coverage and subsequently revokes that waiver, coverage need not be provided retroactive to the date of loss of coverage.

V. When do COBRA benefits end?

Covered employees who are terminated from employment are to receive COBRA benefits for 18 months from the date of the qualifying event. All other qualified beneficiaries must receive COBRA coverage for 36 months from the date of the qualifying event.

These 18 and 36 month periods can be discontinued under the happening of the following event:

> *The date upon which the employer ceases to provide any group health coverage to any employee. 29 U.S.C. sec. 1162(2)(B).

> *The date upon which the covered employee or qualified beneficiary fails to pay his or her premiums. Payments shall be considered timely if made within 30 days of the date due, or such longer period as is provided in the plan. 29 U.S.C. sec. 1162(2)(C).

*The date upon which the qualified beneficiary (except retirees and widows) first becomes eligible for Medicare benefits. 29 U.S.C. sec. 1162(2)(D)(ii).

*The date upon which the qualified beneficiary first becomes covered under any other group health plan, even if the other coverage is less valuable to the beneficiary than COBRA coverage due to pre-existing condition clauses. 29 U.S.C. se. 1162(2)(D)(i).

VI. Can a qualified beneficiary change his or her benefits after electing COBRA coverage?

By its terms, COBRA requires an employer to provide a qualified beneficiary or covered employee benefits identical to those he or she received prior to the qualifying event. As such, where the employer maintains more than one group health plan, one does not have the option to elect COBRA coverage different from the coverage he or she received prior to the qualifying event. This restriction presents potential difficulties for individuals who were receiving expensive group coverage and where the employer has made a less expensive plan available to its employees. It is also problematic for those employees who are covered by an HMO, and who are leaving the HMO's area of sevice at the time of the qualifying event (i.e., the divorced spouse chooses to leave the area after the divorce, the employee is leaving employment because of a move, or a disabled employee leaves work and the service area in order to live with his or her family elsewhere). Unlike national indemnity insurance plans, most HMO's limit coverage to individuals in its immediate service area. As such, COBRA HMO benefits are of little value to qualified beneficiaries who leave the service area at the time of the qualifying event.

The Treasury rules do provide a way in which a qualified beneficiary can change the type of coverage he or she receives under COBRA if the plan under which they are covered is too expensive, unavailable in their locality or inadequate for any other reason. Where the employer provides an annual open enrollment period to all similarly situated employees, during which time the plan participants are provided the opportunity to change plans or add beneficiaries without regard to pre-existing conditions or other limitations, the same open enrollment rights must be made available to individuals receiving COBRA coverage. Note, however, that a recipient of COBRA coverage may elect to change plans during the open enrollment period only if he

or she has made timely payment of premiums under the disfavored plan from the date of the qualifying event until the beginning of the open enrollment period.

The Treasury rules also provide that where a qualified beneficiary participated in an HMO that will not service his or her needs in the area to which he or she has relocated after the qualifying event, and the employer has employees in that area, the qualified beneficiary must be given an opportunity to elect alternative coverage if a similarly situated active employee who transfers to that new location while continuing to work for the employer would be given the opportunity to elect alternative coverage at the time of the transfer.

VII. Can a covered employee add new beneficiaries to his or her coverage at any time after the qualifying event?

Yes and no. The group of qualified beneficiaries entitled to elect COBRA coverage as a result of the qualifying event is closed as of the day before the qualifying event. As a result, COBRA rights are not afforded to the new spouse or child of a covered employee who gets married or has a child after the qualifying event. The only way in which a new beneficiary can receive coverage under the qualified beneficiary's COBRA coverage is to add said beneficiaries to the plan during the plan's open enrollment period. The beneficiary brought into the plan in this manner would not have COBRA rights should the covered employee die or divorce the new beneficiary during the period of the covered employee's COBRA coverage.

VIII. What happens at the end of COBRA coverage?

When a qualified beneficiary's COBRA coverage expires at the end of the 18 or 36 month period, the group plan must provide the qualified beneficiary the option of converting to an individual health plan if such an option is otherwise generally available to similarly situated active employees under the group plan. This conversion option must be made available to the qualified beneficiary during the 180 day period that ends on the expiration of COBRA coverage.

THE RIGHT TO NURSING HOME CARE FOR PERSONS WITH AIDS

David Piontkowsky and Michael J. Kowal

Introduction

Nursing home care is a vital concern of persons with AIDS/ARC. Many of these people do not require the complete medical care of a hospital and yet need the 24 hour support services typically provided in the nursing home setting. AIDS support organizations report, however, that few, if any, nursing homes are willing to admit persons with AIDS or ARC. Nursing home professionals fear that if they admit persons with AIDS/ARC, their staff and the other patients would object and it may cause some patients to refuse to stay in that home. This paper focuses on the legal right of persons with AIDS/ARC to nursing home care.

I. Federal law: Section 504 of the Rehabilitation Act of 1973.

A. Case in Chief

Section 504 of the Rehabilitation Act of 1973 prohibits handicap discrimination in any program, including health care, by any private entity receiving federal funds. Section 504 states that no person "shall, solely by reason of his [sic] handicap, be excluded from participation in, be denied the benefits of, or be subject to discrimination under any program or activity receiving federal financial assistance." 29 U.S.C. 794.

Success under Section 504 requires a showing that the plaintiff (1) is a handicapped individual; (2) is otherwise qualified for admission to the nursing home; (3) was

This article was written by David Piontkowsky of Pearlman & Piontkowsky, Ferndale, Michigan, former Legal Director of the Michigan Organization for Human Rights and member of the Governor's Task Force on AIDS, and Michael J. Kowal, University of Detroit School of Law -- Class of 1987, Legal Assistant, Pearlman & Piontkowsky.

denied admission or otherwise discriminated against; and (4) was denied or discriminated against solely because of the handicap. Each prong is addressed below.

1. Handicap

A handicapped individual is broadly defined under the Act to include

> [A]ny person who (i) has a physical or mental impairment which substantially limits one or more of such person's major life activities, (ii) has a record of such an impairment, or (iii) is regarded as having such an impairment. 29 U.S.C. Section 706(7)(B).

The definition is clear and, subsequent to School Board of Nassau County v. Arline, 107 S. Ct. 1123, 97 L. Ed. 2d 307, there can be no doubt that AIDS is a covered handicap. The Court's footnote 7 notwithstanding, the statutory language and rationale of Arline would also encompass all people infected with HIV within its protective reach.

2. Otherwise Qualified

To be otherwise qualified for admission, a nursing home applicant generally must not require special medical or surgical treatment at the time of admission. See. e.g., Mich. Comp. Laws Ann. 333.21727. Generally, the person with AIDS seeking nursing home admission has been discharged, or could be certified by her or his doctor as dischargeable to a nursing home facility. With a few exceptions, there is generally no greater care needed for a person with AIDS than that needed for other nursing home patients. Although some nursing homes may argue that a person with AIDS who is presently stable is likely to require increased medical attention in the future, this reasoning applies equally to many, if not most, nursing home patients.

3. Discrimination

The most common problem is denial of admission to the nursing home, although in other facilities, such as hospitals, discrimination in services or care has been noted. Such service discrimination by nursing homes may arise once the door to admission is opened. For the immediate future, however, proof of the third element, denial of admission, will usually not be difficult.

4. Sole Reason

It is not unusual for a nursing home to obscure the reason for its denial of admission. Section 504 requires a showing that the denial was based solely on AIDS. On occasion, the nursing home will give that reason; often, though, it must be proven using circumstantial evidence and overcoming defenses raised explicitly by the facility.

B. Defenses

The defenses which nursing homes may raise include the argument that there is no room at the home, that the home only accepts private pay patients, that the home is not covered by the Act because it does not accept funding for separate programming, and that the patient has other diseases that the facility is not prepared to treat. Each of these defenses can be overcome.

The arguments that there is no room in the facility or that the facility only accepts private pay patients are two sides of the same coin. Both seek to restrict access to the facility. After a complaint is filed in such a case, the normal discovery proceeding can determine if the facility has deviated from those practices in the past. Many nursing homes claim that they have a strict waiting list which is taken in first-come, first-serve order, which may, in fact, not be the case. Some homes which seek private pay patients will nonetheless keep a patient who becomes unable to pay after he or she is admitted and do in fact accept Medicaid funds.

Case law makes it clear that Medicare or Medicaid payments to an institution or individual practitioner constitute federal funding for application of Section 504. U.S. v. Baylor University Medical Center, 736 F.2d 1039 (5th Cir., 1984), cert. denied, 105 S. Ct. 958 (1984). Therefore, a nursing home which has patients receiving Medicare or Medicaid is covered by Section 504 regardless of whether the particular person with AIDS/ARC is receiving any federal aid. A federal cause of action may be filed to seek redress for exclusion of any potential patient from a nursing home. It is not a defense that the plaintiff is not a current patient at the facility. Furthermore, in some states, a physician who denies care to a person with AIDS or related conditions may be in violation of handicap discrimination provisions in state licencing codes. (See, e.g., Cal. Bus. & Prof. code 125-6) In such cases, charges should be filed before the state medical practices board.

Normally, the defense that a person with AIDS has diseases that the facility is unable to treat will not withstand scrutiny. With a few exceptions, the infections and cancers to which persons with AIDS may be susceptible are no different than those to which the normal nursing home patient would be susceptible. This is especially true of the patient who has been stabilized by the hospital and is ready for discharge. As noted earlier, the fact that a person with AIDS may be likely to require emergency attention in the future is not a valid defense, given the broad applicability of this argument to nursing home patients in general.

C. Litigation

Litigation under the Act on behalf of persons with AIDS seeking nursing home care has been sparse. A Texas District Court case, McEnany v. Four Seasons Nursing Centers, Inc. (No. 409241, Travis County, Texas), involves a person with AIDS who was denied admission to a nursing home which provided full-time nursing care. Fifteen other homes also refused care. The complaint alleges violation of Section 504 and Texas antidiscrimination laws (Tex. Hum. Res. Code Ann. Section 121.001 et seq. (Vernon 1980)). The case is continuing on behalf of the plaintiff who died before a preliminary injunction hearing was held. Complaints of handicap discrimination have also been filed with the Austin Human Relations Commission against four other homes.

In another case, the Minnesota Human Rights Department took action against sixteen nursing homes in northeastern Minnesota which allegedly refused to care for HIV-infected patients. (See AIDS Policy and Law [BNA], Sept. 23, 1987 at 3.) At least three of the homes subsequently agreed to open their doors to persons with AIDS or related conditions.

II. State Statutes

A. Handicap Discrimination Statutes

Similar to the federal legislation, many states prohibit discrimination against a person with a handicap in a wide range of areas, including public accommodation. These state statutes may be applied to redress injuries caused by nursing homes which deny admission to a person with AIDS/ARC.

A cursory survey indicates the following thirty-five jurisdictions provide such coverage:

Alabama, Alaska, Arizona, California, Colorado, Connecticut, District of Columbia, Idaho, Illinois, Iowa, Kansas, Kentucky, Louisiana, Maine, Maryland, Massachusetts, Michigan, Montana, Nevada, New Hampshire, New Jersey, New York, North Dakota, Ohio, Oklahoma, Oregon, Pennsylvania, Rhode Island, South Carolina, South Dakota, Tennessee, Texas, Washington, West Virginia, and Wisconsin.

Practitioners are advised to consult their local statutes for particulars. Several fairly typical statutes are briefly examined here.

California's Health and Safety Code states:

The purpose of this part is to insure that public accommodations or facilities constructed in this state with private funds adhere to the provisions of Chapter 7 (commencing with Section 4450) of Division 5 of Title 1 of the Government Code [dealing with access to building and facilities]. For the purposes of this part "public accommodation or facilities" means a building, structure, facility, complex, or improved area which is used by the general public and shall include ... hospitals.

As used in this section, "hospitals" includes, but is not limited to, hospitals, nursing homes, and convalescent homes. Cal. Health & Safety Code Section 19955(a)(West)(emphasis added).

The California Civil Code states:

(a) [P]hysically disabled persons shall be entitled to full and equal access, as other members of the general public, to accommodations, advantages, facilities of all ... hotels, lodging places, places of public accommodation, ... and other places to which the general public is invited, subject only to the conditions and limitations established by law, or state or fed-

eral regulation, and applicable alike to all persons.

(b)(1) [P]hysically disabled persons shall be entitled to full and equal access, as other members of the general public, to all housing accommodations offered for rent, lease, or compensation in this state[.]

(2) "Housing accommodations" means any real property, or portion thereof, which is used or occupied, or is intended, arranged, or designed to be used or occupied, as the home, residence, or sleeping place of one or more human beings[.] Cal. Civ. Code Sec. 54.1 (West).

Relief for a violation of the above provisions, pursuant to Section 54.3 of the California Civil Code, includes:

the actual damages and any amount as may be determined by a jury, or the court sitting without a jury, up to a maximum of three times the amount of actual damages but in no case less than two hundred fifty dollars ($250), and such attorney's fees as may be determined by the court in addition thereto, suffered by any person denied any of the rights provided in Sections 54, 54.1 and 54.2.

Injunctive relief is also available under Section 55 of the Civil Code.

The Michigan Handicapper's Act, Mich. Comp. Laws Ann. Section 37.1101 et seq. (West 1985), states at Section 37.1102(1):

The opportunity to ... full and equal utilization of public accommodations ... without discrimination because of a handicap is guaranteed by this act and is a civil right.

The Act defines "public accommodation" broadly:

business, educational institution, refreshment, entertainment, recreation, health or transportation facility of any kind whether licensed or not, whose goods, services, facilities, privileges, advantages, or accommodations are extended, offered, sold, or otherwise made available to the public. Mich. Comp. Laws Ann. Sec. 37.2301(a)(West 1987).

A person with AIDS/ARC seeking admission to a nursing home has a clear right to be free from discrimination.

The Act, similar to many others, provides a defense based on accommodation "which would impose an undue hardship." Mich. Com. Law Ann. Sec. 37.1102(2)(West 1985). Accommodation under Michigan law has not been explored outside of the employment context.

The Michigan statutory scheme allows a complainant to file a claim either with the Michigan Department of Civil Rights for investigation and action or in state court. Some states require exhaustion of administrative remedies prior to filing a lawsuit. In cases involving persons with AIDS, immediate needs of the patient favor a court action seeking injunctive relief where possible. The Michigan statute allows relief in the form of injunctive relief, compensatory damages, exemplary damages, costs and attorney fees.

Illinois defines "places of public accommodation" as:

> (1) ... a business, accommodation, refreshment, entertainment, recreation, or transportation facility of any kind, whether licensed or not, whose goods, services, facilities, privileges, advantages or accommodation are extended, offered, sold, or otherwise made available to the public. Ill. Ann. Stat. ch. 68, Sec. 5-101(A)(Smith-Hurd).

Section 5-102(A) expressly creates a civil rights violation to deny or refuse to another the full and equal enjoyment of the facilities and services of any public place of accommodation. The relief for any such violation includes: cease and desist orders, actual damages, admitting the complainant to the public accommodation, extending the full and equal enjoyment of the services, facilities, privileges, advantages, and costs and attorney fees. Ill. Ann. Stat. ch. 68, Sec. 8-108 (Smith-Hurd).

Illinois' "White Cane Law", Ill. Ann. Stat. ch. 23, Secs. 3361 et seq., provides an alternative remedy through criminal prosecution of those who would discriminate against the physically disable.

New York's Human Rights Law, N.Y. Exec. Laws Sec. 296(2)(a)(McKinney) states:

> It shall be an unlawful discriminatory practice for any person, being the owner, lessee, proprietor, manager, superintendent, agent or employee of any place of public accommodation, because of ... disability ... of any person, directly or indirectly, to refuse, withhold from or deny to such person any of the accommodations, advantages, facilities or privileges thereof, including the extension of credit, or, directly or indirectly, to publish, circulate, issue, display, post or mail any written or printed communication, notice or advertisement, to the effect that any of the accommodations, advantages, facilities, and privileges of any such place shall be refused, withheld from of denied to any person on account of ... disability ... or that the patronage or custom thereat of any person of or purporting to ... have a disability is unwelcome, objectionable or not acceptable, desired or solicitated.

Disability is defined as:

> [A] physical, mental or medical impairment resulting from anatomical, physiological or neurological conditions which prevents the exercise of a normal bodily function or is demonstrable by medically accepted clinical or laboratory diagnostic techniques or (b) a record of such an impairment or (c) a condition regarded by others as such an impairment, provided, however, that in all provisions of this article dealing with employment, the terms shall be limited to disabilities which do not prevent the complainant from performing in a reasonable manner the activities involved in the job or occupation sought or held. N.Y. Exec. Laws Sec. 292(21)(McKinney).

To date, no state has enacted any law specifically proscribing AIDS discrimination. The State of Washington's Human Rights Commission has adapted guidelines which address AIDS-based discrimination in several areas, including public accommodation, pursuant to the state handicap discrimination law. The guidelines begin by defining AIDS as a disability under state law. They go on to prohibit discrimination against an individual who has or is perceived to have AIDS. Application questions concerning AIDS or HIV seropositivity are forbidden in applications for credit or employment as well as in real property transactions and ban HIV testing as a condition for services or employment situations.

B. State Health Codes

Many states have, in their health code, provisions governing nursing home care. These statutes may require a nursing home to have a contagious disease plan and area for caring for such cases if patients with contagious diseases are admitted. The required plan must be approved by the state's department of health.

Michigan has a typical statute, Mich. Comp. Laws Ann. Sec. 333.21717 (West 1985), which states:

> An individual shall not be admitted or retained for care in a nursing home who requires special medical or surgical treatment, or treatment for ... communicable tuberculosis, or a communicable disease, unless the home is able to provide an area and a program for the care. The department shall approve both the area and the program[.]

The nursing homes may attempt to use these statutes as a shield against being required to treat persons with AIDS/ARC. The claim is that AIDS/ARC is a communicable disease and that the home does not have an adequate and approved plan or area set aside for care and that they do not have the facilities for the care needed.

This defense should fail for two reasons. First, the communicable disease provision should not be read as an exemption from having to care for persons with AIDS. The legislative intent was to require nursing homes to develop adequate responses to communicable diseases, not to ignore them. These sections can be used administratively by the Public Health Department to require nursing homes to develop appropriate care plans. The question for private practitioners is whether this requirement can be the basis for a civil action: If no plan has been adopted a private cause of action may be argued from the failure to act pursuant to the public health need for appropriate care.

Second, AIDS is unlikely to be considered "communicable" within the meaning of these statutes. The intent of such statutes is clearly to protect nursing home patients from being infected as a result of proximity to other patients with casually communicable conditions. Since AIDS is not casually communicable, the special requirement of these statutes may not apply. Indeed, many state health departments have deliberately chosen not to define AIDS as a contagious or communicable disease.

C. Sexual Orientation Nondiscrimination Statutes

The State of Wisconsin prohibits discrimination on the basis of sexual orientation. See Wis. Stat. Ann. Secs. 66.432, 66.433, 101.22, 111.31 (West). Michigan has similar protection in its nursing home provisions of the Public Health Code, the pertinent sections of which state:

> [A] licensee shall certify annually to the department, as part of its application for licensure and certification, that all phases of its operation, including its training program, are without discrimination against persons or groups of persons on the basis of race, religion, color, national origin, sex, age, handicap, marital status, sexual preference or the exercise of rights guaranteed by law, including freedom of speech and association. If the department finds a violation of rights enumerated in this section, the department shall direct the administrator of the nursing home to take the necessary action to assure that the nursing home is, in fact, operated in accordance with the rights listed in this section. Mich. Comp. Laws Ann. Sec. 333.21761 (West 1985).

An argument could be constructed to allow a civil action based on sexual orientation discrimination because approximately 70% of AIDS cases involve men who have engaged in homosexual behavior. This approach would be far less effective than a direct challenge based on handicap, but could be included as a secondary count in an appropriate complaint.

III. City Ordinances

At least nine cities have enacted ordinances prohibiting discrimination against those with AIDS and ARC, and against those who test positive to the HIV antibody: Austin, Texas; San Francisco, Los Angeles, Sacramento, Oakland, Berkeley, West Hollywood, Riverside and Hayward, California. Austin's ordinance makes it illegal for employers with 16 or more employees, labor organizations, and employment agencies to deny protected individuals access to business establishments, public accommodations, and city services or to discriminate in the rental, sale, financing, or insurance of real property. Also, no one can be required to undergo any medical test for AIDS except for blood or organ collection activities. The effectiveness of these ordinances is largely untested. Complaints are generally filed with the city human relations commissions.

A broader public accommodation ordinance without specific reference to AIDS has been successfully used to combat AIDS-based discrimination in New York. There, the Manhattan Supreme Court upheld the right of the New York City Commission of Human Rights to investigate alleged discrimination by funeral homes against persons with AIDS. The complaint, brought pursuant to a City Human Rights Law, charged discriminatory inflation of fees and insistence on costly extras for attending persons who died of AIDS-related complications. Dimiceli and Sons Funeral Home v. NYC Commission on Human Rights, Index No. 19527/86 (Sup. Ct., N.Y. Co., January 9, 1987). The court held that the legal protection against discrimination on the basis of handicap extends beyond the moment of death, that the funeral home is a public accommodation within the meaning of the city's administrative code, and that the Commission had exercised proper jurisdiction.

Furthermore, a family member, including the life partner, of a person with AIDS who encounters discrimination in making funeral arrangements is a "person aggrieved" under the Human Rights Law and is entitled to file a discrimination complaint with the Commission. See id.

Similarly, many cities have sexual orientation nondiscrimination ordinances which could be used as a "boot strap" for bringing an AIDS claim. As discussed under the state statutes above, a handicap claim appears much more effective.

IV. Conclusion

Although no specific state legislation protects persons with AIDS from nursing home discrimination, the use of federal and state handicap laws are appropriate and fitting to remedy such discrimination. Additionally, local ordinances prohibiting AIDS or handicap discrimination may provide alternative remedies. Nursing homes must accept the responsibility of patient care or face the consequence of litigation.

CHILD CUSTODY AND AIDS

Arlene Zarembka

The issue of AIDS has been raised in two contexts in connection with child custody. First, it has arisen when one parent has sought to limit the custody rights of a parent with AIDS. Second, it has arisen when one parent has sought to condition the temporary custody rights of the other parent on that parent taking the HIV antibody test and showing a negative result on the test. An attorney who faces the AIDS issue in a custody matter must not only learn in detail the scientific facts concerning modes of transmission, HIV antibody testing, and the inappropriateness of conditioning custody on having a negative HIV antibody test, but must be prepared to educate all the personnel involved in the case —judges, lawyers, social workers and juvenile authorities. Moreover, this educational process must begin before there is the first hearing on the AIDS issue.

While there have been few court cases involving AIDS and custody to date, we can expect the number of such cases to increase so long as people are ignorant of the modes of transmission of AIDS. Moreover, while most cases to date have involved fathers, we can expect this to change as more women become carriers of the virus or contract AIDS.

Past Court Decisions.

As of the date of this writing, there are no appellate court decisions concerning AIDS and custody. However, there have been several trial court cases in which the AIDS issue has been injected by a parent into the custody dispute.

a. Parents with AIDS.

In G.R.M. v. J.R.A. ,[1] a case in the Superior Court of Puerto Rico, the father had been granted temporary custody rights

---

Arlene Zaremka is an attorney practicing law in St. Louis, Missouri, and a member of the Advisory Board of the National Lawyers Guild AIDS Network.

every other weekend in the original divorce decree. The father subsequently contracted AIDS through intravenous drug use, and the mother sought to limit the father's custody rights. Two doctors testified to the fact that the virus is not transmitted casually, and the trial court judge believed this testimony. Moreover, the court found that fears of infection have been exaggerated by the media, and lack a scientific basis. Nonetheless, because the court believed that there was a possibility that there might be routes of transmission of the virus other than the routes already detected, it ordered that the father's custody be restricted to four hours visitation each weekend at the home of the father's grandparents. In addition, during the visits, the father was ordered not to kiss the children, not to share his food or eating utensils with the children, to limit physical contact with the children, to prevent the children from coming into contact with his personal hygiene items, to avoid play with the children that would expose the children to wounds, and to a have a monthly physical examination, with reports of the exam to be given to the court. Finally, the father's sister-in-law was to accompany the father to each visit to ensure that he complied with the court order. In Jordan v Jordan,[2] a case from the Superior Court of New Jersey, the court ordered the temporary custody rights of a father with AIDS limited to supervised visitation under the direction of the Probation Department.[3]

b. HIV antibody positive parent.

In Stewart v. Stewart,[4] Marion County Superior Court, Indiana, the trial judge forbade a gay man who had tested positive for the HIV antibody from seeing his daughter. The judge in the case refused to allow the father to present any expert medical testimony, while allowing the mother to present expert testimony. The judge also seemed to assume that the father had AIDS because he had tested positive for the HIV antibody. The case is now on appeal.

In Buck v. Grein,[5] a Campaign County, Illinois court held that the temporary custody rights of a mother who was a nurse who treated AIDS patients could be conditioned on the mother taking the HIV antibody test. (The mother tested negative.)

c. Gay fathers.

There are at least three known cases where a mother has sought to require the father (either acknowledged or alleged to be gay) to undergo HIV antibody testing as a condition for visitation. In all three cases, the mother was ultimately unsuccessful, although the fathers were put to significant expense in contesting the mothers' request. [6]

Strategy Suggestions

The attorney needs to be prepared to make not only legal arguments, but also to present scientific evidence regarding AIDS and the HIV antibody test, and facts concerning the father's parenting skills to defend against a request limiting the father's custody rights based on AIDS. In addition, as is the case in many custody disputes, psychological factors may be as important as legal and factual matters in accomplishing our client's goals, as the mother may agree to a settlement when the length and expense of a contested court hearing becomes apparent to her, particularly where the issue is HIV antibody testing rather than AIDS itself.

a. Legal arguments.

Although the best interest of the children is, of course, the standard used in custody cases, counsel should remind the court that the rights attaching to parenthood are among "basic civil rights." Stanley v Illinois, 405 U.S. 645, 651 (1972). "It is plain that the interest of a parent in the companionship, care, custody, and management of his or her children 'come[s] to this Court with a momentum for respect lacking when appeal is made to liberties which derive merely from shifting economic arrangements.'" Id. at 645. In addition, while courts have a fairly broad range of power in custody matters, the courts cannot abuse their discretion. To deny a parent temporary custody because of having AIDS, or to condition temporary custody on a negative HIV antibody test result, is an abuse of discretion, since there is no scientific basis for a restrictive order in either situation.

In a situation where a parent already has AIDS, the case of In re Marriage of Carney, 157 Cal. Rptr. 383, 389 (Cal. 1979), is helpful to cite for the proposition that physical disability cannot be used to deny custody unless there is shown to be a substantial and lasting adverse effect on the children.

In addition, counsel may wish to refer to two recent cases involving parents who had contracted herpes. In Bailey v. Bailey, 677 S.W.2d 874 (Ark. App. 1984), the court held that the mere fact that the mother had contracted herpes genitalis was not sufficient to change custody from the mother to the father. In A.K.P. v. J.A.P., 684 S.W.2d 762 (Tex. App. 1984), the appellate court upheld an expansion of custody rights granted the father by the trial court, although the mother opposed the increase on the grounds that the father and his new wife had herpes. While these cases may be somewhat analogous to a case involving a parent with AIDS, counsel should be careful to stress to the court that the HIV virus is even more difficult to transmit than the herpes virus.

In cases involving a request that custody rights be conditioned on a negative HIV antibody test, counsel may wish to raise fourth amendment issues of unreasonable search and seizure, since requiring a father to undergo periodic blood tests amounts to a search which is unreasonable.

Finally, a court order that a gay father be required to undergo HIV antibody testing as a precondition to custody would be a violation of Equal Protection where other parents are not also required to undergo such testing. However, counsel should be wary of using this argument if it will result merely in the court ordering antibody testing for all individuals.

b. Development of factual evidence

In all cases where AIDS is raised, counsel should be prepared to educate the court, as well as opposing counsel, as to the fact that the HIV virus is not easily transmitted, and cannot be transmitted except by exchange of bodily fluids, using the scientific articles noted in footnote 7.

Where the issue is a demand by the mother that the father undergo HIV antibody testing as a condition for custody, counsel should not only argue that it is irrelevant whether or not the father is positive, due to the fact that the virus is not transmitted easily, but must also educate the court and opposing counsel on the potential fallibility of the test. Testing is questionable because: 1) The ELISA test was licensed by the FDA to screen blood products, not people, for the HIV antibodies. 2) It tests only for whether the person has been exposed to the virus, not as to whether the person actually has the virus. 3) The test is not 100% reliable, and the lower the risk that a person has the virus, the greater the probability that a positive test result will be false. While the court should be educated as to the fact that both the ELISA and Western Blot tests at times yield false positives, the percentage of false positives is very low for persons in high-risk groups where the virus has spread widely. Therefore, this argument probably should not be made when representing a person in a high-risk population. The argument would be most relevant when representing persons in communities or risk groups where the virus is not yet widespread. 4) A negative test result does not indicate whether or not the person has the virus.[8] (It may or may not be wise to raise this fourth point in the case, because the judge may merely conclude that the father should undergo repeated HIV antibody testing.)

In addition to supplying the court, opposing counsel, the guardian ad litem, and any social workers with the scientific articles regarding transmission of the virus and the problems with the HIV antibody test, counsel should have local medical experts prepared to testify. If county public health officials will make good witnesses, they may be the best experts to present to the court, as they carry the mantel of being public health officials, beholden to neither side.

In order to ensure that the only issue before the court is the question of the relevancy of AIDS or the HIV antibody test to custody, counsel should take the deposition of the opposing party as soon as possible. This deposition is important for several reasons. First, counsel may get admissions from the opposing party that the father has good parenting skills and a good and healthy relationship with the children. (This will serve to negate any later allegation that the children could obtain the virus from sexual contacts with the father.) Second, the deposition should be used to obtain admissions from the mother that the father appears to be in good health. Third, scheduling a deposition immediately after the AIDS issue is raised will put the opposing parent on notice that the father is going to fight. This may cause the mother to start to a back off on her position, as the time and expense of litigation begins to become apparent. Fourth, the opposing counsel may lose interest in the case if he or she sees that it will be a lengthy, and very possibly losing, court battle.

Conclusion

While the AIDS hysteria is extending into the custody realm, counsel can at times defeat motions to limit a parent's custody rights, particularly where the parent does not actually have AIDS or any signs of illness, and particularly if counsel takes an aggressive stance toward educating opposing counsel and court personnel. However, the process of establishing our client's right to unrestricted custody rights may take months or more than a year.

Notes

1. Decision can be obtained from William Ramirez, Administrating Attorney, Instituto Puertorrigueno de Derechos Civiles, Calle Blanco Romano No. 7, Tercer piso, Rio Riedras, P.R. 00925.

2. Decision can be obtained from Richard W. Bennett, Executive Director, Union County Legal Services Corporation, 60 Prince Street, Elizabeth, NJ 07208.

3. See also W. v. W., a suit presently pending in California concerning the custody rights of a father with AIDS. Contact Roberta Achtenberg, Executive Director, Lesbian Rights Project, 1370 Mission St., 4th Floor, San Francisco, CA 94103, for more information.

4. For more information regarding the case, contact David Hamilton, Suite 312, Victoria Centre, 22 East Washington St., Indianapolis, IN 46204, or Rick Waples, Indiana Civil Liberties Union, 445 N. Pennsylvania St., Suite 501, Indianapolis, IN 46204-1883.

5. 1986 Lesbian/Gay Law Notes of Bar Association for Human Rights of Greater New York 54-55.

6. See In the Matter of Smalley, No. 83-112 (Muskingum County Domestic Relations Court, Ohio)(for more information, contact Elliot Fishman, Case Officer, Affirmative Action, Ohio State University, 1800 Cannon Drive, Columbus, OH 43210); Doe v. Doe, No. 77D 5040 (Circuit Court of Cook County, Ill.)(for more information, contact Paul Rocklin, ACLU of Illinois, 220 State Street, Suite 816, Chicago, IL 60604);, J.R. v. L.R.(Circuit Court of St. Louis County, Mo.)(for more information, contact Arlene Zarembka, 225 So. Meramec, #214, St. Louis, MO 63105).

7. See Chapter II of this Manual on Medical Aspects. See also Centers for Disease Control, Summary: Recommendations for preventing Transmission of Infection with Human T-Lymphotropic Virus Type III/Lymphadenopathy-Associated Virus in the Workplace, 34 MMWR 34 (1985); Sande, Transmission of AIDS: The Case Against Casual Contagion, 312 New Eng. J. of Med. 380 (Feb. 6, 1986); Fischi, et al., Evaluation of Heterosexual partners, Children, and Household Contacts of Adults with AIDS, 257 J.A.M.A. 640 (1987).

8. See Barry, et al., Screening for HIV Infection: Risks, Benefits, and the Burden of Proof 14 Law, Medicine and Health Care 259 (Dec., 1986); Meyer, et al., Screening for HIV: Can We Afford the False positive Rate? 317 New Eng. J. of Med. 238 (July 23, 1987); National Lawyers Guild AIDS Network, AIDS-Related Testing: An Overview, The Exchange, August 1987 (reprinted in the appendix to this Manual).

MILITARY POLICY ON AIDS
AND HIV ANTIBODY TESTING

Kathleen Gilberd

As public concern about AIDS increases, federal agencies have begun to develop internal policies about the disease and about HIV antibody testing. The military has been in the forefront of this effort, developing a comprehensive and discriminatory policy for servicemembers with AIDS or AIDS-related conditions and for antibody testing of all service personnel. For those concerned about the legal and social implications of the AIDS crisis, the military's policies are a frightening example of governmental bias against people with--or people suspected of being at risk for--AIDS.

Until October of 1985, the Department of Defense (DoD) as a whole had no policy about AIDS, and the various services were left on their own to develop informal policies about the treatment of servicemembers with AIDS. As a result each service developed separate guidelines. The Army and Air Force appeared to assume that soldiers had acquired the disease through heterosexual prostitution (a belief still cherished, at least publicly, by the Army). The Navy and Marine Corps routinely screened the medical records of persons with AIDS for any statements to health care workers about gay sex, attempting to process people with AIDS for administrative discharge by reason of homosexuality wherever possible.

On October 24, 1985, after many months of debate and conflicting statements, the Department of Defense issued a uniform policy for the armed services. The policy provided for HIV antibody testing of all new recruits, active duty servicemembers and reservists. It required medical retirement of those with AIDS or AIDS-related conditions and retention on active duty of those who were antibody positive but healthy (including people with some minimal immune system deficiency). The policy prohibited discharges for homosexuality or drug use on the basis of statements made to health workers in the course of HIV

Kathleen Gilberd is Chair of the Military Law Task Force of the National Lawyers Guild.

evaluations, but permitted discharge for "convenience of the government" on the basis of the same information.

In October of 1986, Congress enacted legislation, as part of a Defense Authorization bill, prohibiting any use of statements made to health care workers during HIV epidemiological assessments for "adverse personnel action," including involuntary administrative discharge, court-martial, unfavorable entries into a personnel record, or similar purposes. See "Restriction on Use of Information Obtained During Certain Epidemiological-Assessment Interviews," Section 705 of the National Defense Authorization Act of 1987, amending 10 U.S. Code Section 55. This legislation resulted from public and Congressional concern about a number of cases in which the military had attempted to discharge persons with AIDS without medical benefits or pension solely on the basis of information about gay sex or drugs provided in medical interviews. The most widely publicized of these was the case of Bryon Kinney, a San Diego sailor who sued the Navy to halt a homosexual discharge based entirely on statements made during medical examinations related to his AIDS diagnosis. In the wake of widespread public anger, the Navy agreed to medically retire Kinney, just a few weeks before his death.

On April 20, 1987, the DoD promulgated a new policy, titled "Policy on Identification, Surveillance and Administration of Personnel Infected with Human Immunodeficiency Virus (HIV)"(hereafter "Policy Memo"). This memo, current at the time of this writing, addresses the 1986 legislation and makes some revisions in the prior DoD policy. It also adds several new provisions which raise problems for seropositive personnel, including contact-tracing.

Each branch of the service is required to publish regulations in keeping with the DoD memo. The service regulations are not available at the time of this writing, and practitioners should obtain the new regulations for their branch of the service when handling current cases. This chapter is based on the requirements of the DoD policy rather than service provisions and will now address selected aspects of the policy, including HIV antibody testing, disposition of HIV symptomatic personnel, lack of confidentiality and administrative action, administrative discharge, disciplinary action, harassment and contact tracing.

HIV ANTIBODY TESTING

The DoD policy requires testing of all active-duty and reserve personnel, as well as all new recruits, for the presence of HIV antibodies. Testing is done through the FDA-approved Enzyme-Linked Immunosorbent Assay (ELISA or EIA). Those who test positive on a repeat ELISA receive a confirmatory Immunoelectrophoresis test (Western Blot). The ELISA test has shown a high percentage of false positive results and a lower incidence of false negatives, while the more expensive Western Blot is considered more reliable. See the discussion in Chapter II, Medical Aspects of AIDS-Related Litigation, and in Appendix I of this Manual.

The Policy Memo, and other statements made by DoD, advance several reasons for the testing program. Officials suggest, for example, that servicemembers must be screened for the antibody to prevent transmission of the virus in battlefield blood transfusions. Person-to-person blood transfusions in the field are not commonly used by the military, and have not been for many years; the military blood supply is already protected by HIV antibody testing of all blood donors. Other suggested reasons are equally flawed. The unspoken, but more probable, reason for the testing is that the military views it as a way to screen out homosexuals and intravenous drug users and to avoid the political and financial questions associated with AIDS.

New recruits receive HIV antibody testing at the Military Entrance Processing Stations (formerly AFEES) or, where that does not occur, at their initial point of entry onto active duty. Candidates for officer service are screened during pre-appointment or pre-contracting physical exams. The Policy Memo gives detailed guidelines for separation of officer applicants who are already in the service as enlisted personnel or are in ROTC and service academy programs. New recruits testing positive are barred from military service regardless of their health status.

Active-duty and reserve personnel are also tested and periodically re-tested as part of regular physical examinations. Those on active duty who test positive receive medical evaluations to determine whether or not they are symptomatic. Each service has designated a number of

hospitals for this follow-up testing, so that all seropositive personnel are removed from their commands at least temporarily for medical examinations. Reservists not on extended active duty are referred to their own physicians for evaluation after being "counseled" on the significance of the test.

Active-duty people who show "no evidence of clinical illness or other indication of immunologic or neurologic impairment related to HIV infection" are normally retained in the service. The policy requires that they be medically evaluated at least once a year, that they not be stationed outside the continental US, and adds that "the Secretaries of the Military Departments ... may limit assignment of such individuals with respect to the nature and location of the duties performed in accordance with operational requirements." Policy Memo, Part B.7.

Members of reserve components who are seropositive but healthy are ineligible for extended active duty (i.e., duty for more than 30 days) except during mobilizations. The Policy Memo states that seropositive reservists who are not on extended active duty or on extended full time National Guard duty "shall be transferred to the Standby Reserve only if they cannot be utilized in the Selected Reserve as determined [by the assignment limitations described above]." Policy Memo, Part C.2.

The Coast Guard, which is part of the Department of Transportation rather than the Department of Defense, has developed guidelines of its own for a mandatory testing program. While there are many similarities between Coast Guard regulations and the policy, the Coast Guard routinely separates all members who test positive, regardless of their health. Seropositive but healthy members may petition for retention on active duty, although so far no petitions have been granted. When it became clear that a number of seropositive and healthy Coast Guard members intended to challenge this provision, the Coast Guard decided to provide medical retirement and a modest pension to healthy seropositive servicemembers.

DISPOSITION OF HIV SYMPTOMATIC
PERSONNEL

Active duty and reserve personnel who show symptoms of any HIV-related condition are evaluated for medical fitness and, in the absence of information requiring administrative separation (see below) will be medically retired. Servicemembers with more than the most minimal symptoms of immunological illness, not just those with AIDS, are currently being retired under this provision. Medical retirement entitles servicemembers to military medical care and to a pension; the amount of the pension is based on the severity of the illness and the amount of pay the servicemember would receive on active duty.

As a general rule, decisions about medical retirement involve a case-by-case evaluation of medical problems and the actual ability of a servicemember to fulfill his or her military duties. This personalized evaluation is not provided in HIV related cases. Instead, the military has developed its own "staging system," different from the classification used by the Centers for Disease Control and other civilian medical authorities. The scale is generally called the Staging System, except by the Army, which refers to it as the Walter Reed Staging System. (The Navy, not to be outdone, combines the staging system with its own categories.) See Attachment 1. Retention or retirement is based entirely on a person's classification on this scale, rather than his or her overall health or ability to perform duties. As a result, practitioners will frequently encounter servicemembers facing retirement who wish to remain on active duty, and others seeking discharge despite a categorization requiring retention.

The original policy specifically stated that information provided to health care workers could not be used in "line of duty" determinations (determining eligibility for medical disability monies) and thus could not affect servicemembers' entitlement to a pension after medical retirement. While that language is not in the current DoD policy statement, other language prohibiting adverse personnel actions on the basis of admissions to medical personnel may provide the same protection.

A new provision of the 1987 policy permits seropositive and healthy servicemembers to request discharge under the "plenary authority" of the Secretary of their service. Plenary authority is provided for the Secretaries to separate servicemembers where no specific grounds for discharge exist. The discharge is technically administrative, rather than medical, and honorable or general in character, although those on active-duty for less than six months might receive uncharacterized entry level separations. There is no right to the discharge, however, and it is difficult to predict how each service will handle requests. Such discharges would in all likelihood not include any commitment of military medical care or pension, but should not affect the servicemember's right to VA care or pensions.

LACK OF CONFIDENTIALITY
AND ADMINISTRATIVE ACTION

The DoD policy prohibits the use of test results themselves for non-medical discharges, except the voluntary discharge described above, for disciplinary action or for administrative action, except for the geographic and other limitations mentioned above. However, statements made by servicemembers in the course of medical evaluations may still cause a number of administrative and disciplinary problems.

Lack of confidentiality in the military medical setting has long been of concern to military counselors and attorneys (see Rule 501(d) of the Military Rules of Evidence, and Department of Defense Directive 1332.14, Encl. 3, Part 3, Section 5.3). Medical records, including diagnostic information and statements made by patients to their physicians, are routinely available to the patient's command, and there are no general limitations on their use in courts-martial or other military proceedings. This problem received widespread public attention early in the military's dealings with AIDS issues as a result of the Navy's efforts to discharge sailors with AIDS for homosexuality where the only "evidence" was contained in medical records made during diagnosis and treatment of their condition. The DoD policy places real limitations on the use of diagnostic information, but also contains a number of problems.

Underlying these problems is the military's policy of excluding homosexuals. Military policy holds that "homosexuality is incompatible with military service" and defines as homosexual anyone who engages in or desires or intends to engage in homosexual acts. Since homosexual acts include any touching of another person of the same sex for sexual gratification (i.e., kisses and hugs as well as behavior more commonly thought of as sex acts), and since bisexuals are treated as homosexuals, the policy potentially covers a very large number of servicemembers.

Suspected lesbians and gay men are routinely discharged on the basis of homosexuality. While such discharges are normally honorable or general in character (depending on the person's service record), other than honorable discharges may be given where certain "aggravating circumstances" are found. These include acts, or attempts or solicitations of acts, in public or aboard a ship or airplane; where there is force, coercion or intimidation; with a person under age 16; with a subordinate in rank; for compensation; or, under most circumstances, on a military base. Evidence of homosexuality before the current enlistment or commission may also result in a less than honorable discharge. On occasion, a servicemember may face court-martial for homosexual acts, usually involving one of the "aggravating circumstances," though most commands prefer to avoid trial and simply discharge the servicemember.

A somewhat similar policy makes it illegal for servicemembers to use drugs, and requires the discharge of those who have used even small amounts. Discharges are usually under other than honorable conditions, and courts-martial are a very real risk in these cases.

Thus, lack of confidentiality in the military medical setting normally poses serious dangers for those who tell physicians about gay sex or drugs during medical examinations. The new DoD regulation provides some significant limitations on those dangers, but problems remain. The policy states that:

> "Information obtained from a service member during or as a result of an epidemiological assessment interview may not be used against the servicemember in a court-martial; non-judicial punishment; involuntary separation (other than for medical reasons); administrative or punitive reduction in grade; denial of promotion; an unfavorable entry in a personnel record; a bar to reenlistment; and any other action considered by the Secretary concerned to be an adverse personnel action." Policy Memo, Part F.1.

This addition to the old DoD policy is obviously a direct response to the 1986 legislation. However, the new policy attempts to limit the protections offered by that legislation, stating that these limitations do not apply to:

> "the introduction of evidence for impeachment or rebuttal purposes in any proceeding in which the evidence of drug abuse or relevant sexual activity (or lack thereof) has first been introduced by the service member or to disciplinary or other action based on independently derived evidence; or, nonadverse personnel actions such as reassignment, disqualification (temporary or permanent) from a personnel reliability program, denial, suspension, or revocation of a security clearance, suspension or termination of access to classified information, and, removal (temporary or permanent) from flight status or other duties requiring a high degree of stability

or alertness such as explosive ordnance disposal or deep-sea diving." Policy Memo, Part F.3.

DoD's creation of a new category of "non-adverse" personnel actions which may result from statements to health care workers is an obvious attempt to circumvent the 1986 Congressional action, and it is likely that some categories of "non-adverse" action will be challenged. It is also likely that the individual services will attempt to further circumvent the new law.

It is quite possible, for example, that the services will attempt to expand the category of "non-adverse" action created by the DoD memo, though they are not permitted to directly contradict the memo. It is also possible that the service Secretaries will simply refuse to label any non-enumerated actions as adverse, despite the invitation in the DoD policy and the legislation to do so.

Additionally, services may try to limit the statements covered by the policy. While a liberal reading of the legislation or the DoD policy would cover statements made during most medical interviews of seropositive personnel, the military may interpret this section more closely, and try to use statements which are made in follow-up examinations, on-going treatment or other 'non-epidemiological' interviews as a basis for discharge or other action.

It is important to note that the DoD policy and legislation provide no protection at all for statements made in non-medical settings or for medical interviews not related to HIV positivity (unless they are somehow "a result of" the HIV assessment interview). Servicemembers may not understand these distinctions, and it is quite likely that statements made during protected interviews might be repeated to doctors examining an unrelated knee problem, or to members of the person's command. Local commands, affronted that they cannot use information about sex or drugs contained in medical reports, may also attempt to "set up" servicemembers by intentionally eliciting supposedly independent statements.

These protections apply to statements, and not the test results themselves. In some cases, results of the tests may be used for personnel action, and conceivably as a bar to reenlistment. As noted above, the DoD policy does permit the Secretaries to "limit assignment of such [seropositive] individuals with respect to the nature and location of the duties performed in accordance with operational requirements." Policy Memo, Part B.7.

ADMINISTRATIVE DISCHARGE

While many of the personnel actions mentioned above can have serious and permanent consequences for service-members' careers, the danger of administrative discharge is most significant. Unlike the prior DoD policy, the current memo does not permit "convenience of the government discharge" on the basis of statements to health care workers. However, the policy does not prohibit discharges for homosexuality or drug abuse which are ostensibly based on independently derived evidence. Some practitioners and clients have noted an increased--but theoretically entirely independent--scrutiny of those who are found to be sero-positive.

Commands which learn of the sexual preference of service-members through medical records, or who assume it simply because of test results, may make a zealous effort to obtain their own statements or other evidence of homosexuality and then pretend they are proceeding solely on the basis of independent evidence. Determinations about the inde-pendence of that evidence will generally be made by non-attorneys who are more responsive to the command than to constitutional niceties. The risk of discharge for homo-sexuality or drug abuse thus remains a real one for those who test positive, particularly if they make admissions of sexual preference or drug use to their physicians.

Another danger of involuntary administrative discharge exists for seropositive persons who are found to have engaged in unprotected sexual activity. The DoD policy states that seropositive servicemembers "who are found not to have complied with lawfully ordered preventive medi-cine procedures for individual patients are subject to appro-priate administrative and disciplinary action which may include separation." Policy Memo, Part D.2. This is an addition to prior DoD policy, and there is no information available about the character or type of discharge involved.

Any administrative discharge would bar medical care and benefits from the military itself, leaving the servicemember to the questionable mercy of the Veterans Administration for treatment and pension. If the discharge is under other than honorable conditions, it is likely that VA care would also be unavailable.

When both medical retirement and administrative dis-charge are appropriate, the military must decide which to pursue. Some service regulations permit discretion here, though the services have historically preferred to separate people without medical benefits when possible. Particu-larly in the Navy, practitioners have seen an informal (and not uniform) tendency to avoid administrative discharges where it is apparent that the servicemember will be medi-cally retired because of AIDS or a related condition. The tendency seems to result from the Navy's desire to avoid further unpleasant publicity, and practitioners confronted with administrative processing of servicemembers who are ill may be able to encourage the Navy to quietly medically retire the person.

DISCIPLINARY ACTION

DoD policy prohibits court-martial or non-judicial punish-ment on the basis of the test results themselves, or on the basis of statements made to physicians. However, the policy allows disciplinary action for misconduct independ-ently determined or for failure to follow "lawfully ordered preventive medicine procedures for individual patients."

Practitioners have noted a zealousness in efforts to prose-cute seropositive personnel who are found to have engaged in unsafe homosexual acts. Under the prior DoD policy, HIV test results could not be introduced in court-martial proceedings, so that such prosecutions were difficult. Servicemembers suspected of engaging in unsafe gay sex occasionally found themselves confronted with courts-martial, charged with failure to follow "orders" to engage in safe sex only. While the unsafe sex charges might not be upheld, accompanying sodomy charges would be. Person-nel who have not tested positive were much less likely to face court-martial for the same behavior. An attempt to court-martial Adrian Morris, Jr., a soldier stationed at Ft. Huachuca, on charges of having unsafe sex after being told he had tested HIV antibody positive, led to a determination that the results of the test could not be introduced as evidence. See U.S. v. Morris, reported in BNA AIDS Policy and Law, Aug. 12, 1987, at 7. However, this case is currently under review by appelate courts, and, in any case, its value has been diminished by the new DoD policy.

The current DoD memo includes language which, while somewhat vague, is obviously intended to permit introduc-tion of HIV antibody test results in criminal prosecutions, and to allow prosecution of those who engage in unsafe sex, shared needle use or, presumably, other activities contrary to preventive medicine procedures. Abstractly, this could be expanded to include failure to follow other medical advice, although such an effort would fly in the face of a long-standing right to refuse medical treatment. In addition to the reference to disciplinary action for those who fail to follow lawfully ordered preventive medicine procedures, the Memo notes that HIV antibody test results may be used "in any other manner consistent with law or regulation." Policy Memo, Part F.2. On the other hand, the memo states that "the occurrence of HIV infection or serological evidence of HIV infection shall not be used as a basis for any disciplinary action against an individual." Policy Memo, Part B.3. The possible conflict between these provisions has not yet been explored, but may be useful in future courts-martial in which HIV positivity is a factor.

HARASSMENT

Throughout the development of the military's testing program, the Department of Defense and the various services have assured the public that the strictest confidentiality would be maintained regarding test results and HIV medical conditions, so that other servicemembers would not have access to such information. The Policy Memo does not include language on this point, but service regulations have in the past been uniform in requiring confidentiality of test results and any HIV-related diagnoses. Only those with a demonstrated need to know, such as the commanding officer (and perhaps executive officer) and medical person in any command, should know the names of seropositive personnel assigned to the command.

In reality, test results and medical diagnoses have often been made known widely throughout commands, causing considerable embarrassment for servicemembers. Practitioners have frequently found that many members of a command with absolutely no need to know about a client's HIV positivity have extensive, and not necessarily accurate, information about the person. Moreover, even where confidential medical information is not revealed, a soldier or sailor's removal to a hospital for several weeks of testing, or limitations on duty assignments, may clue in members of the command about his or her condition. Since the military has done very little to educate members about the meaning of the test, methods of transmission, and so on, the results of breaches of confidentiality are predictable: seropositive (or suspected seropositive) servicemembers are often ostracized, harassed, denied services, and occasionally threatened.

Since the service regulations are clear in prohibiting breaches of confidentiality about test results, practitioners should consider vigorous challenges to breaches and resulting harassment. Complaints under Article 138 of the Uniform Code of Military Justice, Congressional inquiries, and pursuit of criminal charges may be appropriate in such cases.

CONTACT TRACING

It has not been uncommon in the past for medical personnel to ask people receiving follow-up HIV evaluations about their sexual partners. Under the DoD policy, the services are now encouraged to engage in a vigorous contact tracing effort. The memo states specifically that "Epidemiological investigation shall attempt to determine potential contacts of the patient with serologic or other laboratory or clinical evidence of HIV infection." Policy Memo, Part B.5.a.(2). The policy also provides for counseling of those contacts who are military health care beneficiaries (military personnel, "dependents," and retirees), and notification of non-military health care beneficiaries.

The policy offers no assurance that the protections provided to a servicemember during epidemiological assessment would apply to persons named as homosexual or IV drug use partners. If Greg names Peter as a sexual contact, Greg is protected; Peter is probably protected concerning statements he later makes if he tests positive and is evaluated. But the policy does not guarantee that Peter will not be discharged or disciplined on the basis of the information obtained from Greg about their relationship.

COUNSELING SUGGESTIONS

Military counselors and attorneys are confronted with a number of important legal (and personal) issues in HIV testing and AIDS cases. They can play an important role in protecting the rights of servicemembers affected by these policies. The following are some general suggestions:

1. In order to reach military personnel who are affected by (and may know little about) the policies, counselors and attorneys need to develop better ties with local and national organizations providing medical and personal assistance to people with AIDS and with agencies that provide HIV testing. Similarly, practitioners need to develop relationships with local lesbian and gay organizations on these issues. These groups will need accurate information about the military rights of their patients and clients. They can, in turn, make sure that servicemembers know supportive legal counseling is available about their military problems.

2. The confidentiality problem must be explained to servicemembers who are concerned about AIDS or who may be tested for HIV antibodies. The decision to talk to a military physician or a command about AIDS or one's sexual or drug history must be an educated one based on an understanding of the general lack of confidentiality, the

limitations of the specific confidentiality provisions of current regulations, the particular service's policies, and the possibility of harassment. Getting the word out about this problem is essential. Leaflets and articles discussing confidentiality problems, and urging those concerned to seek legal assistance, can provide an essential warning.

3. When soldiers or sailors are processed for medical retirement or discharge on the basis of HIV infection, counselors and attorneys must make sure that their rights are respected in the medical process and that attempts are not made to limit their disability ratings. Those being processed for administrative discharges may wish assistance in challenging the discharges and, where appropriate, demanding medical retirement.

4. Those with AIDS and those suspected of having AIDS face discrimination and harassment by the military, above and beyond the official policies. For those who may be trying to cope with a disabling and fatal disease, such discrimination is an added layer of suffering. The assistance of military counselors and attorneys in challenging such harassment and minimizing mistreatment is essential.

5. Where possible, counselors and attorneys should consider participating in coordinated challenges to the military's policies on HIV testing and AIDS. The organizations listed in the resource section of the Manual can provide information on pending litigation and other challenges.

DEPARTMENT OF DEFENSE STAGING CLASSIFICATION

The chart below is an Army description of the DoD staging classification system for HIV infection. Servicemembers categorized as State 1 or 2 are normally retained on active duty; those in stages 3 through 6 are normally medically retired.

Walter Reed Staging Classification of HTLV-III Infection

Stage	HTLV-III Antibody	Chronic Lymphadenopathy	T Helper Cells/mm^3	DHS	Thrush	O.I.
WR 0	-	-	>400	NI	-	-
WR 1	+	-	>400	NI	-	-
WR 2	+	+	>400	NI	-	-
WR 3	+	+/-	<400	NI	-	-
WR 4	+	+/-	<400	P	-	-
WR 5	+	+/-	<400	C or +	-	-
WR 6	+	+/-	<400	P/C	+/-	+

- Indicates that this criterion is required for the given stage

Suffices:
K - Kaposi's Sarcoma, Indicate presence by adding "K" (e.g.,WR4K)
B - The suffix "B" should be added in the presence of constitutional symptoms (i.e., T>100.5˚ for 3 weeks, weight loss > 10% of body weight over 3 months, night sweats for 3 weeks, or chronic diarrhea for greater than 1 month).

WR 0 - designates high risk contacts (sexual contacts, newborns, and recipients of blood products from pts documented to have AIDS [antibody + or virus isolation +])
WR 5 - the occurrence of either complete anergy and/or thrush (i.e., DHS = P/"Thrush +" or C/"Thrush -" or C/"Thrush +")
HTLV-III Antibody - defined by the presence of antibody to the HTLV-III virus as determined by the Western Blot technique (gp 41 is a requirement for diagnosis: "+" = present, "-" = absent)
Chronic lymphadenopathy - defined as two or more extrainguinal sites w/ lymph nodes ≥ 1 cm in diameter persistent for > 3 months ("+" = present, "-" = absent)
T Helper Cells - Quantitative depletion (<400 cells/cu.mm.) must be present for at least 3 months for WR3 classification.

DHS - (Delayed Hypersensitivity) NI - normal DHS is defined as an intact cutaneous response to at least two of the following 4 test antigens: tetanus, trichophyton, mumps, and candida. P of the above antigens. C - "complete" cutaneous anergy (no response to any antigen).
Thrush - Clinical oral candidiasis including + KOH prep.
O.I. - (Opportunistic Infection): pneumocystis carinii pneumonia, CNS or disseminated toxoplasmosis, chronic cryptosporidiosis, candida esophagitis, disseminated histoplasmosis, CNS or disseminated cryptococcosis, disseminated atypical mycobacterial disease, extra-pulmonary tuberculosis, disseminated nocardiosis, disseminated CMV, or chronic mucocutaneous herpes simplex. Other disseminated or chronic non self-limited infections with agents in which CMI plays a pivotal role in host defence should be anticipated to cause opportunistic disease in pts with stages WR5 and WR6. Kaposi's sarcoma alone does not fulfill staging criteria for WR6.

FURTHER ISSUES

NON-U.S. CITIZENS

Bruce Fodiman

Non-U.S. citizens, including permanent residents (green card holders), non-immigrants (e.g., students, refugees and asylees) and undocumented immigrants ("illegal aliens) who have AIDS/ARC, are seropositive or are members of at-risk groups face special problems under the complex, often contradictory, immigration laws of the United States. These laws may affect their ability to remain in or return to the U.S. and their access to public benefits.

Under the so-called reentry doctrine, all non-citizens returning to the U.S. after a trip of any length outside the country, even long-term permanent residents, are treated as if they were entering the U.S. for the first time and therefore may be barred from reentry under the exclusion provisions of the immigration laws. These laws now classify HIV infection as a "dangerous contagious disease" for which a non-citizen can be excluded from entry or reentry into the country. 42 CFR 34.2(b); 8 USC 1182(a)(6).

This provision may arise in various ways. Non-citizens applying for permanent residence or amnesty under the Immigration Reform and Control Act of 1986 (IRCA)[1] are required to take a "serologic test to detect HIV infection" as part of the mandatory medical exam. A positive test result is sufficient grounds for denying the applicant resident status. Thus, any applicant for lawful resident status, including long-term illegal residents considering applying for amnesty or students wishing to adjust their status, should ascertain his/her antibody status before

applying or perhaps even before submitting the medical examination form to an INS-designated "civil surgeon" authorized to do such examinations as INS regulations provide that positive test results are to be reported to health authorities if local law requires. In addition, since the INS instructions to the civil surgeons are confusing and misleading, it can be expected that individuals testing positive may not be properly counseled as to medical or immigration consequences.

Whether the section 1182(a)(6) exclusion of HIV antibody positive applicants can be waived depends on the type of application. In immigrant and fiance(e) visa cases, the INS stressed in a cable to its field officers dated July 6, 1987 that there is no statutory authority to waive the provision. On the other hand, in refugee, amnesty and nonimmigrant cases, the statutory authority for such a waiver exists. However, it is construed narrowly, prohibiting the grant of a discretionary waiver unless the applicant can establish that "(1) the danger to the public health of the United States created by the alien's admission to the U.S. is minimal, (2) the possibility of spread of the disease created by the alien's admission to the U.S. is minimal, and (3) there will be no cost incurred by any level of government agency of the U.S. without prior consent of that agency." INS File CO 234-P.

Non-citizens who travel outside of the country may be stopped at the border and denied reentry if they are seropositive or have "a physical defect, disease or disability" that may affect their ability to earn a living (8 USC 1182(a)(7)) as well as for "sexual deviation" (8 U.S.C. 1182(a)(4)). It thus may not be advisable for noncitizens to make even brief trips outside the U.S. (such as trips to purchase medicine in Mexico).

Non-citizens can also be excluded from reentry if they have received certain forms of public assistance, most notably SSI, because they will be classified as persons "likely to become a public charge." An alien is deport-

Bruce Fodiman is an attorney in private practice in San Francisco, California, who focuses on immigration law.

able if within five years of entry s/he "has become a public charge from causes not affirmatively shown to have arisen after entry." 8 USC 1251(a)(8). Thus, an alien may apply for SSI after five years in permanent residence status, but must be very cautious about making any trips abroad.

Non-citizens who have no legal immigration status ("illegal aliens") are specifically excluded from most forms of public assistance, but are otherwise accorded the protection of U.S. law and may sue to enforce nondiscrimination laws, etc. They are, however, prima facie deportable, although it is within the discretion of the Attorney General to allow an undocumented immigrant to remain in the U.S. pending the outcome of a lawsuit or for humanitarian reasons.

In light of the complexity and drastic nature of these laws, it is recommended that an immigration specialist be consulted.

Note: Up to the minute developments immigration law are reported in Interpreter Releases a weekly publication available in most law libraries.

Note

1. Under IRCA, persons who have been residing illegally and continuously in the U.S. since on or before January 1, 1982, or have qualified as seasonal agricultural workers because they have performed at least 90 "man days" of agricultural labor between May 1985 and May 1986 may apply for temporary and, ultimately, permanent residence.

Tax Issues

Leonard Graff

A thorough income tax analysis for people with ARC or AIDS is beyond the scope of this publication. There are, however, some questions that are asked with some degree of regularity that the practitioner should be familiar with. The following is a brief summary of those questions -- and the answers:

Leonard Graff is Legal Director of National Gay Rights Advocates.

1. Are medical expenses deductible? Yes, but only to the extent they exceed 7 1/2% of adjusted gross income. "Medical expenses" include any payment for the diagnosis, cure, treatment, mitigation or preventation of disease; costs of insurance to cover medical care; and transportation expenses primarily for and essential to medical care. Also included are laboratory and x-ray fees and the costs of prescription medications.

2. My lover who lives with me has ARC and cannot work. Can I deduct my expenses for his support and medical care? You can recover a portion of the expenses you have incurred in supporting your lover by claiming him as a dependent. However, your lover must have less than $1,080 gross income, and you must have provided over half of his total support. If your lover receives any income, including pensions, social security, or state public assistance, he will be considered as having contributed to his own support.

If you claim your lover as a dependent, then you may also be able to deduct your expenses for his medical care -- but only to the extent that these expenses exceed 7.5% of your adjusted gross income.

3. Will the beneficiary of my life insurance policy have to pay income tax on the proceeds when I die? No. Life insurance proceeds paid upon the death of the insured are not taxable.

4. Will there be a tax on my estate after I die and will the beneficiaries who receive an inheritance from me have to pay tax on their gifts? There is a federal estate tax but not an inheritance tax. The law on estate and inheritance taxes collected by the states varies from state to state. Usually the value of an estate or inheritance has to be quite high before the tax will kick in.

5. Are the payments I receive from a disability insurance policy taxable? If you paid the premiums, the proceeds are excludable from your income. But, if your employer paid the premiums, e.g., as part of a group policy, the benefits are includable in your income.

6. Are the payments I receive from Supplemental Security Income (SSI) taxable? No, SSI benefits are not subject to income tax.

Material for this section taken, by permission, from Tax Strategies for Lesbians and Gay Men, National Gay Rights Advocates, c. 1987.

The tax law is complex and constantly changing. Anyone with a specific tax problem should consult a CPA or lawyer who specializes in this area.

Suicide

Leonard Graff

Sometimes when a person is diagnosed with AIDS, or tests positive to HIV antibodies, he or she will become despondent and contemplate suicide. And, such a person may try to enlist the help of a friend, lover, or family member to carry out the plan.

While there are many medical and ethical issues involved in the question of suicide, this brief paper addresses only the legal issues. Most states used to consider suicide, or "self-murder," a felony. Thus, an attempted suicide, which failed, was a punishable crime.

Now, it is generally established that neither an attempted, nor successful, suicide entails penal liability. However, the law does come to bear on those considered "accomplices" to the act.

People can discuss, and even advocate, suicide including detailed techniques to accomplish the act. But, when a discussion of generalities becomes advocacy of individual action, the conduct may be punishable. The possibility of criminal charges being brought for solicitation, conspiracy, or aiding and abetting, increase as mere speech becomes a plan of action.

Other legal problems may also arise. A pharmacist or physician who supplies lethal drugs risks losing his or her license. Most insurance companies will not pay a death benefit unless the policy is in effect for at least two years prior to a suicide. Beneficiaries of an estate may be precluded from sharing in the distribution if they helped cause the testator's death. And, there is also the possibility of being sued for negligence or wrongful death for helping another to commit suicide.

Material used to write this paper came from <u>Let Me Die Before I Wake</u> by Derek Humphry. For additional information, see the accompanying newspaper article or contact: The Hemlock Society, PO Box 66218, Los Angeles, CA 90066.

AIDS-related suicides rising

Health officials fear virus is becoming a psychiatric problem

By Rob Stein
UNITED PRESS INTERNATIONAL

BOSTON — Scattered reports of AIDS-related suicides and attempted suicides are emerging across the nation, causing health officials to fear such problems may become more common as the deadly virus infects increasing numbers of people.

"We have a second epidemic," said Peter Goldblum, a psychologist at UC-San Francisco. "AIDS is not only a medical problem. It is also a psychiatric problem. Despair and anxiety are epidemic."

Suicide and suicidal thoughts have long been a problem associated with fatal and chronic diseases such as cancer. But experts say suicide may be more of a problem with acquired immune deficiency syndrome because of its social stigma.

In San Francisco, for example, as many as a dozen people with AIDS committed suicide in 1985. The San Francisco Suicide Prevention Center says it gets up to 100 AIDS-related calls each month.

AIDS "is a metaphor for many people for all the things we don't want to face in our society," said Dr. Marshall Forstein, a psychiatrist at Harvard Medical School.

Many researchers believe AIDS-related suicide may become more frequent, especially as the virus spreads, infecting and killing more people and giving more people first-hand experience with how AIDS victims die.

"AIDS is in its infancy; when it comes to full flower and we have a million AIDS patients, we're going to have a lot more of these things to cope with," said Dr. Jerome Motto of UC-San Francisco.

The Centers for Disease Control in Atlanta say as of Feb. 9 there were 30,632 cases of AIDS in the United States, of which 17,542 resulted in death. AIDS was first diagnosed in 1981 in San Francisco, Los Angeles and New York.

Because the virus is so new, and suicides in general are difficult to document, no one knows how many AIDS-related suicides have occurred or whether the risk of suicide is actually higher among people who have AIDS or related disorders or those who have tested positive for exposure to the AIDS virus.

But state and local health officials, U.S. AIDS counselors and suicide experts report cases of suicide and attempted suicide that raise questions about whether enough is being done to deal with the psychiatric problems associated with the virus.

"It is something that creates a tremendous amount of stress and anxiety in an individual," said Philip Ramu, who counsels AIDS patients in New York City.

While stressing that the number of suicides is probably relatively small, especially compared with the loss of life associated with the virus itself, mental health workers say the deaths illustrate the intense emotional cost of the virus.

"The psychological aspects, including depression and substance abuse, is a major aspect of AIDS," Goldblum said.

Most agree that AIDS-related suicide is probably underreported because it is difficult to document. A gravely ill patient may simply take too much medication, or stop going to the doctor.

Although one study found patients with ARC — AIDS-related complex — suffer the most anxiety, experts say it is unclear which aspect of the virus creates the most stress.

"For most people AIDS symbolizes death and suffering," Goldblum said. "When a person is given a positive result at least momentarily they are confronted with their own death. They have to ask, 'Is life worth living now, and will it be worth living if I develop AIDS?'"

The most frightening misconception is that the test is a test for AIDS itself. In fact, it is only a test for antibodies to the virus that causes AIDS. A positive result only means an individual has been exposed to the virus.

"Just telling them their antibody status without any counseling or education is risking their mental health," said Rodger McFarlane, an AIDS educator in New York City. "Basically, you're giving that person a chance to jump out a window."

Even if they understand the test, the most difficult aspect about getting a positive result on an AIDS virus test is its ambiguity, experts said.

No one knows what percentage of those who test positive will actually develop the virus.

"They walk around feeling like a time bomb," McFarlane said. "I'm not saying it's easier to die than to worry about dying. But you can come to grips with a terminal virus much better than with ambiguity."

Officials at blood banks, which test all donations for AIDS, and the military, which tests all applicants and members of the military, stress that they offer counseling to people they notify of positive test results.

AIDS counselors stress that support groups, counseling and education can make a difference.

"Nobody gets a certificate from God saying you're guaranteed 90 years of life," said Monsignor Fred Tondalo, an Orthodox Catholic clergyman who counsels AIDS patients in Fort Lauderdale, Fla. "When you get them into a support group, they begin to realize there were no guarantees beforehand."

The potential problem has spurred efforts throughout the country, including studies in New York and San Francisco, to assess the extent of the current problem and the risk.

"It's important because AIDS is a public health problem of huge proportions," said Dr. Mark Rosenberg, who studies suicide for the CDC.

"If this happens to people after hearing that they are positive for the virus," he said, "we're talking about a lot of people who are, at risk."

Manual Appendices

Appendix I	Resource List of Organizations
Appendix II	AIDS Related Testing: An Overview, The Exchange (National Lawyers Guild AIDS Network, August 1987).
Appendix III	AIDS and Handicap Discrimination: A Survey of the 50 States and the District of Columbia, National Gay Rights Advocates (1986).

APPENDIX I

Resource List of Organizations

This section lists organizations involved in AIDS-related legal work. This list will be updated and we urge readers to send us names of additional organizations.

Disability Rights Education and Defense Fund
Jeoff Merideth
2212 6th St.
Berkeley, CA 94710
415 644-2555

American Civil Liberties Union
Southern California
Susan McGreivy, Esq.
633 Shatto Place
Los Angeles, CA 90005
213 487-1720

L.A. Gay/Lesbian Community Center
Tom Coleman, Esq.
1213 North Highland Ave.
Los Angeles, CA 90038
213 467-4141

Los Angeles Office of the City Attorney
David Schulman, Esq.
200 N. Main Street
Los Angeles, CA 90012
213 485-4579

Protection & Advocacy, Inc.
Trevis Wall
2131 Capitol Ave.
Sacramento, CA 95816
916 447-3324

Military Law Task Force
National Lawyers Guild
Kathleen Gilberd, Director
1168 Union Street, Suite 202
San Diego, CA 92101
619 233-1701

AIDS Network
National Lawyers Guild
Paul Albert, Director
211 Gough St., Suite 311
San Francisco, CA 94102
415 861-8884

Bay Area Lawyers for Individual Freedom (BALIF)
AIDS Legal Referral Panel
Clint Hockenberry, Administrator
1663 Mission St., Suite 400
San Francisco, CA 94103
415 864-8186

Bayview Hunter's Point Foundation
Multicultural AIDS Legal Assistance Project
6025 Third St.
San Francisco, CA 94124
415 822-7500

Department of Fair Employment and Housing
State of California
30 Van Ness Avenue, Third Floor
San Francisco, CA 94102
415 557-2005

Employment Law Center
Chris Redburn
1663 Mission St.
San Francisco, CA 94103
415 864-8848

American Civil Liberties Union of Northern California
Matt Coles
1663 Mission St., Suite 460
San Francisco, CA 94103
415 621-2488

Lesbian Rights Project
Roberta Achtenberg, Directing Attorney
1370 Mission St.
San Francisco, CA 94103
415 621-0674

Multicultural Alliance for the Prevention of AIDS
Henn Norms, Esq.
6025 3rd St.
San Francisco, CA 94102
415 822-7500

National Gay Rights Advocates
Leonard Graff, Legal Director
Benjamin Schatz, Director, AIDS Civil Rights Project
540 Castro St.
San Francisco, CA 94114
415 863-3624

San Francisco Human Rights Commission
Norm Nickens, AIDS Discrimination Representative
1095 Market St., Suite 501
San Francisco, CA 94103
415 558-4901

ACLU of the National Capitol Area
Liz Symonds, Staff Attorney
1400 20th St., NW
Washington, DC 20036
202 457-0800

DC AIDS Task Force
Whitman-Walker Clinic AIDS Program
Mauro Montoya, Legal Services Coordinator
2335 18th St., NW
Washington, DC 20001
202 332-5295

National Prison Project of the ACLU
1616 P St. NW, Suite 300
Washington, DC 20001
202 331-0500

Gay & Lesbian Advocates & Defenders (GLAD)
Kevin Cathcart, Executive Director, GLAD
Denise Williams, Director, AIDS Law Project
PO Box 218
Boston, MA 02112
617 426-1350

Cambridge Human Rights Commission
Sarah Wunsch, Esq.
57 Inman St.
Cambridge, MA 02139
617 498-9049

American Civil Liberties Union
National Office
Nan Hunter, Staff Attorney
132 West 43rd St.
New York, NY 10036
212 944-9800

Center for Constitional Rights
Joan Gibbe
666 Broadway
New York, NY 10012
212 614-6464

Gay Men's Health Crisis
Mark Senak, Legal Services Coordinator
Box 274, 132 West 24th St.,
New York, NY 10011
212 206-8640

Lambda Legal Defense & Education Fund, In.
Abby Rubenfeld, Legal Director
666 Broadway
New York, NY 110012
212 995-8585

New York City Commission on Human Rights
AIDS Discrimination Unit
Mitchell Karp, Administrator
52 Duane St., 7th Floor
New York, NY 10007
212 566-7638

Prisoners' Legal Services of New York
John Gresham, Associate Director
105 Chambers St., 5th Floor
New York, NY 10007
212 513-7373

Prisoners' Legal Services of New York
Deborah Schneer, Staff Attorney
2 Catherine St.
Poughkeepsie, NY 12601
914 473-3810

Philadelphia AIDS Task Force
Advocacy Committee
David Webber, Legal Director
1425 Walnut St.
Philadelphia, PA 19102
213 568-5188

Texas Human Rights Foundation
Dara Gray, Executive Director
1014-G North Lamar
Austin, TX 78703
512 479-8473

AIDS NETWORK

THE EXCHANGE

Issue 5 August 1987

AIDS- RELATED TESTING: AN OVERVIEW

The manner in which we as a society respond to the AIDS crisis will, in many regards, be a test of our collective moral fibre. We can, on the one hand, respond to persons infected with Human Immunodeficiency Virus[1] (HIV) with caring and compassion, viewing the epidemic as an international tragedy that requires an immediate, cooperative and whole-hearted response. We can, in the alternative, react out of fear: identifying the infirm, labeling them with epithets, attempting to segregate them from "the rest of us," and accusing them of bringing the disease upon themselves. We can, in short, let the disease become an arena for public hysteria, prejudice and fear.

The current public controversy over mandatory HIV antibody testing illustrates the dangers of allowing AIDS to be treated as a political football rather than a medical emergency. Most public health leaders, including the Surgeon General, the Centers for Disease Control, and the National Academy of Sciences oppose mandatory testing. Nonetheless, politicians on both the local and national level are ignoring the advice of public health authorities in forging ahead with testing policies that are counter to the best advice of the medical community. No doubt encouraged by the lack of public education about AIDS, public opinion polls reveal broad support for mandatory testing. As a result, bills requiring such testing have been introduced throughout the country.[2]

In this issue of The Exchange, *we discuss the reasons behind policy choices concerning HIV antibody testing and their legal and practical implications. It is our position that all mandatory testing programs are counterproductive to efforts to control the spread of AIDS, cause great trauma to thousands of individuals, and divert funds that are badly needed for research, education and counseling. We believe that all HIV testing programs should be both voluntary and anonymous, that testing must at all times be accompanied by counseling and that testing is only useful in the context of broad, explicit and responsible educational programs.*

A mixture of policies resulted, rationalized by the division of infected persons into the culpable and the innocent: prostitutes were quarantined and subjected to forced examination and treatment, while soldiers were given prophylactics, education, and treatment for their disease (efforts which ended after the war).

In much the same way, people tend to divide those with AIDS into culpable and blameless categories. For gay men and intravenous drug users, AIDS has been described as "God's punishment". Gay men have been blamed for the AIDS epidemic, indeed Congressman Dannemeyer has repeatedly stated that "The genus of AIDS is perverse sex."

A second similarity to the earlier controversies is that the recommendations of government scientists have been rejected by political leaders and the public when they conflict with moral views and fears. Thus, policy makers promote chastity in lieu of safe sex education, and school board members urge that antibody positive students be segregated because "no one really knows how the virus is passed."

AIDS generates even greater and widespread fear than earlier epidemics for several reasons. The fact that AIDS is invariably fatal, the fact that it can be contracted from nonsexual activities and that much is still unknown about the virus leads some persons to want to "err on the side of caution" by requiring an impos-

The HIV antibody testing controversy is similar in several respects to the dilemmas surrounding the venereal disease epidemic in the first half of this century.[3] The rapid spread of venereal disease (particularly during the First and Second World Wars) challenged accepted standards of morality, which held that sexual promiscuity was immoral. This led people to see venereal disease as punishment for those who transgressed moral standards, and to resist "sanctioning" immoral behavior by facilitating education about the spread of the disease and the use of prophylactics.

National Lawyers Guild AIDS Network
211 Gough Street Third Floor   San Francisco CA 94102   415 861-8884

sible 100 percent certainty of safety before placing themselves or their children in contact with a person with AIDS. In addition, the fact that over 70 percent of people with AIDS are gay men has provided persons hostile to gay rights a perfect vehicle for attempting to set back the gains of the gay and lesbian rights movement over the last twenty years.

These factors have been played upon by top officials of the Reagan administration. In 1986, Attorney General Edwin Meese issued an opinion stating that irrational fear of AIDS could justify discrimination against a person thought to have AIDS. In 1987, he publicly applauded the use of plastic gloves by law enforcement officials in arresting persons demonstrating for greater amounts of federal funding for AIDS research, even though the demonstrators posed no risk to the officers. This kind of misdirection from the top law enforcement official of the nation creates an atmosphere where public officials at all levels and the public at large are encouraged to view persons with AIDS without compassion and sympathy and to ignore uncontroverted medical evidence.

REAGAN ADMINISTRATION TESTING POLICIES

It is in this context of hostility, fear and rejection of public health authority and advice that the HIV antibody testing policies of the Reagan administration have been formulated. Mandatory testing was instituted of all recruits in the Armed Services in 1985, for Foreign Service personnel stationed overseas and applicants for the Job Corps and Peace Corps in early 1987. In a speech in late May of this year, the President went further by proposing:

- The mandatory testing of immigrants seeking permanent U.S. residence;

- The mandatory testing of federal prisoners upon arrival or parole;

- An examination of the appropriateness of testing in veterans hospitals and other federal agencies;

- That states "require routine testing" for prisoners and "offer routine testing" to those applying for marriage licenses or seeking treatment in sexually transmitted disease and drug rehabilitation clinics.

The President made no specific recommendations with respect to provisions for anti-discrimination and confidentiality measures to protect the rights of seropositive persons. The language that the President has used in discussing HIV testing proposals has been ambiguous, if not deliberately vague and confusing.[4]

Public health officials have unanimously opposed the type of mandatory testing provisions supported by the President. In June, 1987, 1,317 physicians and researchers attending the Third International AIDS Conference signed a petition calling on government officials to heed their advice. The opinions of top public health experts were set forth in two major documents: a November 1986 report by a blue ribbon committee of medical and scientific experts published by the National Academy of Sciences (NAS) and a report on testing by the Centers for Disease Control (CDC) dated April 30, 1987. Both reports opposed mandatory testing and called for the passage of stringent confidentiality and anti-discrimination laws.[5] These views have been consistently supported by the Surgeon General, C. Everett Koop.[6]

The NAS Report concludes that

AIDS differs from other diseases in several significant ways. These differences include the greater stigma attached to AIDS, the legitimate fear of discrimination faced by seropositive persons, the life-long nature of the infection, and the lack of a vaccine or satisfactory treatment available to seropositive persons. In addition, the Committee considered the fact that the test would provide thousands of false positive results in the testing of low risk populations such as marriage license applicants.[7]

As noted by the NAS Committee, consideration of mandatory HIV antibody testing must include an understanding of the stigma associated with AIDS, which to many people is identified with homosexuality or illicit drug use. Persons have been left by their spouses or lovers as a result of a positive test result. Wide-spread alarm about AIDS exacerbates homophobia and racism and has led to discrimination in employment, housing, medical treatment and insurance. Seropositive inmates are routinely segregated in many jails.

Stigma and discrimination are only a part of the drastic implications of a positive test result. Because current research indicates that 36 percent of sero-positive persons develop AIDS within eight years of infection, persons receiving a positive test must face the possibility of a shortened life-span. Severe psychological reactions often result, including anxiety, nightmares, sleep disturbance, depression, suicidal behavior, rage reactions, sexual dysfunction, hypochondria and severe social withdrawal.[8] Positive test results have had a particularly devastating effect upon women who are faced with the possibility of not being able to bear children. Because of the severe implications of the test, the period of waiting for the result is also full of anxiety.

In light of these adverse consequences, it can be expected that persons will avoid contact with agencies administering mandatory tests until they are ready to deal with the implications of a positive result and feel assured that they will not suffer discrimination due to breaches in the confidentiality of the records. As a consequence, many persons who suspect they may be antibody positive will avoid counseling centers, drug and venereal disease clinics, and hospitals where mandatory tests are administered. The result will be to drive the disease underground, making both treatment and education more difficult.

The problem is compounded where there are laws requiring the reporting of positive results to a state health agency. A number of states currently require such reporting, either by statute or by administrative regulation.[9] The NAS Committee recommended strongly against reporting requirements, noting that they do not produce accurate statistics and make counseling and testing programs less effective. This prediction was fulfilled in Colorado, where there was a sharp decline in the number of persons visiting clinics following enactment of a reporting law.[10] Agency pressure on seropositive persons to reveal the identities of their sexual or drug-sharing partners may further discourage the use of testing and counseling programs.[11]

Public health officials have recognized that gaining the trust of the communities most at risk is more effective in combating AIDS than imposition of mandatory testing or reporting programs. In this regard, it is important that these officials be "in the forefront" of supporting strong confidentiality and anti-discrimination provisions.[12]

Anonymous and Confidential Testing

The confidentiality of HIV antibody test results is of great importance because of the stigma associated with seropositivity and the risk of discrimination if records are made public. The CDC has recognized that "the ability of health departments to assure confidentiality - and the public confidence in that ability - are crucial" to efforts to slow the spread of HIV.

Experience has shown that anonymous testing provides the only true guarantee of confidentiality of test results. Those tested anonymously are identified only by code, and the counselor and testing agency never learn of their identities. Where testing is not or cannot be conducted anonymously, strict laws must be enacted and enforced to ensure the confidentiality of those tested.

Because of the nature of the medical business, however, records are subject to release from a number of sources and the achievement of confidentiality is extremely difficult.

The list of persons with routine access to hospital and clinic records is long, and includes social workers, physical therapists, and the institution's credit department. Third party payors (such as Blue Cross) are demanding ever-increasing amount of personalized medical information. Medical records may also be made available to state and federal courts and agencies through their extensive subpoena powers.

This ready access to records has made unauthorized disclosures widespread. A Congressional committee found that surreptitious trafficking in medical records is "common" and "nationwide." A Colorado grand jury investigated

a firm that for over twenty-five years had engaged in a nationwide business of obtaining medical information without the patient's consent.[13]

There are no easy answers to these problems and various approaches are needed. Some Illinois hospitals have developed special procedures for handling sensitive information and will not release charts containing highly confidential material without a court order. Some hospitals also sequester information in special files (as is currently the practice with charts relating to alcohol and drug abuse).[14]

The California legislature has enacted statutes which impose criminal and civil penalties for the unauthorized release of HIV antibody status. The statutes also protect this information from the subpoenas of state and local courts and agencies.[15]

Unfortunately, these statutes have not been taken seriously by the medical industry or state prosecutors to date. Berkeley attorney Alice Philipson represents a number of persons whose antibody status was revealed in violation of the law. She states that antibody records are often kept in the general medical record file, and that doctors often fail to supervise their staff when copies of the file are made in response to a general medical release form. Her requests to district attorneys and the state Attorney General to prosecute the doctors involved have been uniformly denied. She has several suits pending, and sees large damage awards as the only way to make the medical and insurance industries take the issue seriously. In spite of the problems with the California statute, Philipson favors passage of a similar federal law, although reliance on such statutes to protect confidentiality may be misplaced since any statute can be amended or repealed.[16]

Counseling

Testing has been advocated on the theory that persons who test seropositive are more likely to engage in safe sex and needle practices if they know their antibody status. This may not always be the case. Some studies reveal that among self-identified gay and bisexual men, knowledge of HIV seropositivity had little influence on behavior while knowledge of being seronegative had an adverse influence on behavior change for some men. While testing may prove more useful in other populations, in general its ability to spark positive changes in sex and needle practices is thoroughly dependent on the counseling that accompanies the tests.[17]

In the case of persons who test seropositive, counseling is essential both because of the potentially devastating emotional impact of the test results and because of the need to educate the testee about preventing transmission to others. Persons who test negative must be informed of the possibility of false negatives and of ways to help avoid future infection. Without such counseling, negative test results can create a false sense of security, thereby promoting the unsafe behavior that testing is supposed to discourage.

Although counseling is a critical component of any testing program, it may also be the most labor intensive and expensive.[18] Cost estimates for pre and post test counseling have ranged from $15 to $26 or more per person, depending on the region and whether a person is antibody positive. All testing proposals should be analyzed to ensure that counselling is an integral component and to guard against budgetary slighting in this area.

We turn now to a more detailed consideration of the various forms of mandatory testing which are currently being implemented or which have been proposed.

HIV Testing in the Military

In October, 1985 the Department of Defense announced a program of mandatory testing all military recruits for HIV antibodies. Those who tested positive would not be eligible for appointment or enlistment. The Department grounded the policy on four concerns, most of which are contradicted by current reliable medical research regarding the virus, and all of which attempt to mask the Department's actual goal to rid the military of gay and lesbian people. First, the Department projected that HIV antibody positive individuals might not be able to complete their tours of service if they were to become ill. Here, the military has singled out HIV seropositivity for special treatment where other medical conditions such as high blood pressure and a history of smoking are not similarly used to screen job applicants form military employment.

Second, despite significant medical evidence to the contrary, Defense was concerned that seropositive persons could have an adverse reaction to immunizations administered to all service members. Third, the Department sought to screen seropositive people from military employment on the basis of the remote chance that they would be called upon to administer a battlefield person-to-person blood transfusion. It is well known that such transfusions rarely, if ever, occur in our modern army. Finally, Defense maintained that it wished to avoid the potential medical costs presented by individuals with HIV infection.

In April, 1987, the Secretary of Defense expanded the military's HIV testing program to include mandatory testing of all active duty personnel, members of the Reserve Officers Training Corps (ROTC), and students at the various military academies, as well as Reserve members. Active duty personnel who are seropositive and asymptomatic will not be terminated solely on the basis of antibody status, however they will be prosecuted if they are found to have engaged in any high risk behavior as defined by the Department's safe sex guidelines. All seropositive active duty servicepersons will be fired once they become symptomatic. The Department's Health Affairs Office will also do contact tracing for all active duty servicepeople found to be seropositive. HIV seropositive ROTC members and students in the service academies shall be disenrolled in those programs at the end of the current semester.[19]

HIV Testing by the Department of State

In January, 1987, the Department of State began a program of compulsory testing for HIV antibodies of all Foreign Service and Peace Corps employees and applicants as well as their spouses and dependents. If an applicant or his or her spouse or dependent tests positive, the applicant will automatically be denied employment. If a current employee or his or her spouse or dependent tests positive, that person will be given a restricted medical clearance and the employee will be denied most overseas postings.

The Department of State attempted to justify this policy in several ways. As in the military context, the government was concerned about screening from federal employment those individuals who might not complete their tour of service and who are thought to be overly sensitive to immunizations with live viruses. In the Foreign Service context, the Department of State was particularly concerned about what it called a world wide perception of AIDS as an American disease and wanted to protect against damage to foreign relations where Foreign Service employees are seen as "instruments" in the spread of AIDS in other nations.

HIV Antibody Testing in the Job Corps

In February, 1987, the Department of Labor added a negative HIV antibody test to the list of conditions for entrance to the Job Corps program. Job Corps is a federally funded, primarily residential, job training program for economically deprived youths between the ages of 16 and 21. Those applicants who test positive will be denied admission to any residential program. Clearly, antibody status has absolutely no rational nexus to a person's ability to receive job training, and the testing program will in no way slow the spread of the virus. As such, the policy represents a patent form of discrimination on the basis of perceived handicap.

HIV Antibody Testing by the Immigration and Naturalization Service

On June 8, 1987, the INS published proposed regulations which would add HIV infection to the Public Health Service's list of "dangerous contagious diseases," the effect of which will be to require a negative HIV antibody test

as a condition for obtaining a permanent or immigrant visa or for determining admissability as a permanent resident of the United States. Under these regulations, aliens seeking admission to the U.S. must present at the U.S. port of entry a negative HIV test. Unlike tests for every other excludable condition, may not be administered at the port of entry when it is not available in the immigrant's country of origin. As a result, regardless of their antibody status, hundreds of thousands of applicants for admission to the U.S. will be rejected simply because the antibody test is not available in most other countries, or because the test is prohibitively expensive in those countries where it is available.

In addition, the INS also proposed requiring all applicants for legalization under the Immigration Reform and Control Act's amnesty program to demonstrate the absence of HIV infection. On its face, this requirement may seem designed to prevent further importation of HIV. However, given that all amnesty applicants have been living in the U.S. for at least five years, those applicants who do test positive have been infected in this country. In addition, given the fact that amnesty applicants will not be deported on the basis of any information obtained in connection with an amnesty application, this policy will only serve to prevent the legalization of seropositive aliens. In effect, it will simply force those amnesty applicants who do test positive to remain underground without access to health care or appropriate education regarding high risk behavior which may put other persons at risk of exposure to the virus.

HIV Testing In The Federal Prison System

As of June 15, 1987, all federal prisoners are mandatorily administered the HIV-antibody test upon initial incarceration and upon release from prison. The plan presently calls for seropositive inmates with no manifestations of disease to continue to be housed with the general prison population, while symptomatic prisoners will be sent to the Springfield, Missouri or Lexington, Kentucky prison medical facilities.

Confidentiality provisions of the plan are minimal and unclear at best. Seropositive inmates will be notified of their antibody status, and such results will be forwarded to the chief probation officer where the inmate is to be released. Medical employees of the prison system may divulge an inmate's test result only to the warden; prison staff are generally not to be informed of the test results. The wardens in turn, are authorized to release test information on a "need-to-know" basis. Precisely what this entails is unclear. Dr. Robert Brutsche, Medical Director for the Federal Bureau of Prisons, made clear the lack of any cohesive confidentiality scheme by stating that each of the forty-eight federal correctional institutions will most likely interpret differently their need to divulge test results. The inmate testing plan is slated to undergo initial evaluation after sixty (60) days.

The reasoning behind instituting the testing of federal inmates as one of the seminal government testing programs is clear. The inmate population constitutes a captive audience (literally and figuratively) with traditionally fewer rights and fewer avenues of redress than other groups in the population. Their status as prisoners, however, does not divest them of all rights.

The succinct rationale put forth by Attorney General Edwin Meese posits that law enforcement officials "run a much higher risk of exposure to acquiring the virus through contact with suspects and offenders than do most other professionals." (Mr. Meese does not elaborate whether this is because these officials engage in sex with inmates or whether they share IV-drug needles with the inmates, the two common routes of transmission applicable to the prison setting.) However, in Mr. Meese's mind, such a "risk of exposure" can only be lessened by full and indiscriminate disclosure of test results. As set forth elsewhere in this article, such disclosure poses it own substantial risks to inmates which belie any potential benefits of testing. The true rationale lies in the general lack of political power held by inmates and the lack of a solid political voice on their behalf. They present a population easily forced to serve as an initial testing ground for the administration's mandatory testing programs, and from which other testing programs are likely to stem. As discussed in previous issues of *The Exchange*, it is significant to note that 90% of antibody positive inmates are people of color.

The simple solution proffered by mandatory testing in prisons is, in fact, neither simple nor a solution. Problems exist with both the general rationale presented to justify mandatory testing in prisons, as well as with the specifically-enacted plan for testing. Chief among these failings is the lack of provision for adequate and effective counseling and education concerning AIDS. The relatively small size of the individual prison populations, coupled with the variety of cultures represented, necessitates a higher educator-to-subject ratio than in other settings, and no single style of presenting information can be successful to reach the subject population as a whole. Therefore, either more funds will need to be dedicated to such counseling and education programs, or such

programs will necessarily be inadequate.

The consequences of such inadequacies in the prison testing program are grave. Inmates testing seropositive, or believed by other inmates or guards to be seropositive, have been subjected to serious harassment and, at times, physical abuse either induced or encouraged by the prison guard staff. This is likely the by-product of several factors, including a general lack of knowledge concerning AIDS, and a lack of provisions for adequate and accessible medical equipment, including plastic-shield resuscitators and surgical-thickness rubber gloves, when necessary. These factors, among others, led to the support of mandatory prison testing proposals by the American Federation of Government Employees, the very union which has so vigorously opposed testing in other contexts, i.e., testing of foreign service employees.

Discrimination against seropositive prisoners has been proposed at all junctures in the legal system. Secretary of Education William Bennett recently suggested that seropositive prisoners who pose a threat of spreading the disease may be detained beyond their established release date. Proposals have been made to deny probation and/or parole to those testing positive. States, too, have begun to enact legislation providing for testing within their own prison systems. The contours and ramifications of such programs may be even graver than the current federal program which served as their impetus.

Antibody testing in prisons presents recurring issues in a unique setting. Due to their relative powerlessness and the ease with which compliance can be compelled, the prison population is a particularly easy and attractive segment for initial mandatory test-

ing programs. The safeguards and prerequisites of effective testing programs called for by the U.S. medical community (namely, voluntariness and confidentiality) have been summarily dismissed. Whether this testing program is an aberration or the harbinger of broader acceptability for testing will be shown with time.

Testing In Hospitals

In the past years of the AIDS epidemic, public and private health authorities have developed guidelines on testing hospital patients for HIV antibodies.[20] Those guidelines rejected routine screening of all patients as a matter of infection control. Instead, emphasis has been placed on close adherence to standard precautionary measures recommended for any patient. Those standard measures include use of protective clothing when handling blood or other body fluids, frequent hand-washing, precautions against needle sticks, decontamination procedures, and proper handling of laboratory specimens.[21]

Due to the CDC's report of the seroconversion of three health care workers (HCWs) after exposure to the blood of AIDS patients, and recent overbroad statements by the Reagan Administration, renewed concern on this topic has been aroused. Despite attempts to cast the question in political terms, testing of hospital admissions remains a medical issue. The merits of testing have been and should continue to be measured solely by the medical indications determined for each individual patient.

Testing of hospital patients can have two goals. First, a test for the HIV antibody can be an important diagnostic tool. Even when a patient has not developed AIDS, a positive antibody test may affect the physician's treatment decisions. For instance, the patient's condition may call for use of medication with immunosuppressive properties. A positive test result may dictate use of alternate medication if available. Like any medical treatment, testing should be conducted only on a voluntary, informed basis, when combined with the proper counseling and strict confidentiality. Also, in light of the increasing phenomenon of states enacting laws requiring physicians to report test results, informed consent must include full patient appreciation of the severe legal ramifications that may result from the reportability of antibody status.

A second goal of testing all hospital patients is protection of HCWs. Doctors, nurses and other medical personnel are commonly exposed to the blood and other body fluids of patients. Identification of all patients who are antibody positive would allow HCWs to use extra precautions, it is said.

Much media attention was focused on the three HCWs reported to have tested seropositive after exposure to blood or body fluids of AIDS patients. The circumstances of those three cases were described in detail in the CDC's weekly report, Morbidity and Mortality Weekly Report, on May 22, 1987. After careful analysis the conclusion was drawn that "It is unlikely that routine serologic testing for HIV infection of all patients admitted to hospitals would have prevented these exposures since two of the three exposures occurred in the outpatient clinic setting, and one occurred during a resuscitation effort in an emergency room shortly after the arrival of the patient."[22] The CDC concluded that "these three cases represent rare events, [and] reemphasize the need for health care workers to adhere rigorously to existing infection control recommendations for minimizing the risk of exposure to blood

and body fluids of all patients."

Despite the sympathy evoked by the personal situation of the three HCWs involved, mass testing of hospital patients is no answer. The cost, the lack of feasibility, and the logistical problems involved simply do not outweigh the extremely low risk posed. That the risk is low is demonstrated by three ongoing studies. In a CDC study of 1,097 HCWs with parental (needlestick) or mucous-membrane exposure to the blood of AIDS patients, only one seroconverted. In a University of California study of 63 exposed workers with open wounds or mucous membranes exposed, none was seropositive. And in a National Institutes of Health study, none of 103 workers with percutaneous exposures and none of 229 workers with mucous-membrane exposure was seropositive.[23]

With the millions of persons who are admitted annually to hospitals, the cost of administering the antibody test would be enormous. In addition, since these confirmatory tests are time-consuming and not readily available[24,] the delay attendant to completion of the tests would pose significant logistical barriers to the delivery of the needed health care procedures that occasion many hospital admissions. It is not surprising, then, that the University of California San Francisco Task Force on AIDS concluded that "screening for the purpose of assigning infection-control procedures was not indicated in most health care settings."[25] The reasons cited by the Task Force included the lack of feasibility of identifying all infected patients and the extremely low risk of transmission.

Testing Of Marriage License Applicants

Another proposal loudly promoted by the Reagan Administration is the "routine" testing of applicants who apply for marriage licenses. The premise of the program seems to be that fiances have a right to know that their partners are potentially infectious, and should be informed of their future spouse's antibody status in order to protect themselves.

The proposal belies a sadly outdated conception of sexual behavior among Americans. While it might have been the case for Ron and Nancy, the date of the wedding hardly marks the initiation of sexual intercourse between contemporary adults. Cohabitation of unmarried couples has become a common phenomenon. If sexually active people are to truly protect themselves from infection they must begin practicing safe sex long before applying for a marriage license. As such, education concerning sexual transmission of HIV must be readily available in elementary schools when most people become sexually active.

An argument advanced in favor of testing marriage license applicants has been that since this group is widely tested for sexually transmitted diseases (STDs), testing for the HIV antibody should be no different. However, the difference is significant. With STDs testing, proof of treatment is commonly required before the marriage license will issue. If the same condition is placed upon a positive HIV antibody test, the marriage license may never be issued, given the current limited efficacy of medical treatment for AIDS. The ethical objections to such a denial are obvious.

1. HIV is the virus assumed to cause AIDS. Prior to June, 1986, the virus was referred to as either HTLV-III or LAV.

2. 140 testing bills were introduced in state legislatures in the first five months of 1987. In addition to testing of such groups as marriage license applicants,

prisoners, and hospital patients, bills also singled out restaurant and bar owners and employees, persons arrested for prostitution or assault, mental patients, rape victims, women seeking prenatal care or pregnancy tests, barbers, health spa owners, doctors, students and teachers. Many of these bills require that positive test results be reported to state officials. See INTERGOVERNMENTAL HEALTH POLICY PROJECT, A SYNOPSIS OF STATE AIDS RELATED LEGISLATION (JANUARY - JUNE 1987). The Project can be contacted at 202 872-1445.

3. See BRANDT, NO MAGIC BULLET: A SOCIAL HISTORY OF VENEREAL DISEASE IN THE UNITED STATES SINCE 1880 (Oxford 1987).

4. The Reagan administration has muddied the testing issue by confusing "routine" and "mandatory" testing. "Routine" is a benign-sounding word which can be used to refer to either mandatory or voluntary tests. On the one hand, a test may be routinely administered, in which case the test is given to every person applying for a particular position or service. Alternatively, testing may be routinely offered, in which case the test is made available to each individual but is administered only with the testee's informed consent. Finally, when the test is voluntarily administered, the testee must initiate a request for testing.

5. NATIONAL ACADEMY OF SCIENCES, CONFRONTING AIDS: DIRECTIONS FOR PUBLIC HEALTH, HEALTH CARE AND RESEARCH 129, 135 (1986) (hereafter "NAS Report"); CENTERS FOR DISEASE CONTROL, RECOMMENDED ADDITIONAL GUIDELINES FOR HIV ANTIBODY COUNSELING AND TESTING IN THE PREVENTION OF HIV INFECTION AND AIDS 4, 9-14 (April 30, 1987) (hereafter "CDC Report"). The CDC Report was submitted to the Assistant Secretary for Health but not officially released by the Reagan administration. See Resource Section for further information.

6. The Surgeon General stated in a hearing before the House Energy and Commerce Subcommittee on May 1 that he opposed any program which would re-

quire testing as it would "force people underground." AIDS POLICY & LAW (BNA) May 6, 1987, at 2. For the same reason, the Surgeon General's influential report issued in 1986 explicitly opposed any form of reporting of seropositive individuals and stressed the importance of securing the "strictest confidentiality" of antibody test records. U.S. DEP'T OF HEALTH AND HUMAN SERVICES, SURGEON GENERAL'S REPORT ON ACQUIRED IMMUNE DEFICIENCY SYNDROME at 30.

7. NAS Report, at 112-13, 121. The percent of false positives varies with the population tested and is much higher for low-risk groups or when the test is performed with less sophisticated equipment.

8. See Goldblum & Seymour, Whether to Take the Test: Counseling Guidelines, FOCUS: A GUIDE TO AIDS RESEARCH, April 1987, at 2.

9. States requiring reporting of seropositivity include Arizona, Colorado, Georgia, Idaho, Illinois, Kentucky, Minnesota, Montana, and Wisconsin. The Missouri Department of Health has issued proposed regulations which would add seropositivity to the list of reportable conditions.

10. Gay Community News, May 24, 1987.

11. The San Francisco Public Health Department has begun a low-profile tracing program aimed at contacting heterosexual women who have had contact with seropositive men with whom they would have not reason to believe were at-risk. AIDS POLICY & LAW (BNA), February 11, 1987, at 5.

12. See CDC Report, App. I, p.11.

13. It is important that counseling take place both before testing and at the time that test results are given. A primary purpose of pretest counseling is to ensure that the consent to the test is informed. Information provided should include a description of the test and its diagnostic significance, a list of possible results, the reporting and recording methods of the results, a realistic evaluation of the limitations of confidentiality guarantees, and

the risks of discrimination based upon antibody status.

14. See Weldon-Linne, Weldon-Linne & Murphy, AIDS-Virus Antibody Testing: Issues of Informed Consent and Patient Confidentiality, 75 ILLINOIS BAR JOURNAL 205, 211 (December 1986).

15. Calif. Health & Safety Code Sections 199.20-.22.

16. There is, in fact, a bill pending to repeal the California confidentiality provisions.

17. It is important that counseling take place both before testing and at the time that test results are given. A primary purpose of pretest counseling is to ensure that consent to the test is informed.

18. The costs of testing and counseling have been evaluated by the CDC, and vary considerably depending on whether the population being tested is at high or low risk. The cost of a program of low risk population (of 1 seropositive person per 1,000) is estimated at $18,197 per infected person, while dealing with a high-risk group it is only $128. CDC Report, App. V.

19. See also the National Lawyers Guild Military Law Taskforce newsletter, "On Watch," May, 1987 for a comprehensive discussion of the Department of Defense's HIV antibody testing program. "On Watch" can be obtained from the Military Law Taskforce, 1168 Union Street, Suite 201, San Diego, CA 92101 at a yearly subscription of $10 for individuals and $15 for institutions.

20. 34 MMWR 681 (November 15, 1985); J.L. Gerberding and UCSF Task Force on AIDS, "Special Report, Recommended Infection-Control Policies for Patients With Human Immunodeficiency Virus Infection," 315 New England J. Med. 1562-1564 (December 11, 1986).

21. Id., at 1563.

22. Id., at 1563.

23. Id., at 1564.

24. 36 MMWR 287-288 (May 22, 1987).

25. Id., at 287.

RESOURCES

Helpful materials on the issue of HIV antibody testing are listed in the footnotes to this issue and should include:

-The Centers for Disease Control report, "Recommended Additional Guidelines for HIV Antibody Counseling and Testing in the Prevention of HIV Infection and AIDS" (April 30, 1987). This report contains helpful appendices prioritizing and estimating the costs of various antibody testing programs. The report was officially submitted by the CDC to the Undersecretary for Health, but has not been officially released by the Reagan administration. It is available from the Network for $7.00 copying and handling costs.

- National Academy of Sciences, "Confronting AIDS: Directions for Public Health, Health Care and Research" provides a thorough analysis of many aspects of the AIDS crisis and, being published by the NAS, carries a lot of credibility.

- Brandt, No Magic Bullet (Oxford 1987) is a history of the treatment of venereal disease in the United States since 1880. As many of the issues are similar, it provides a valuable perspective to the current debates.

-The ACLU has published a second set in its series "AIDS: Basic Documents." The April 1987 version contains the official CDC Recommendations for prevention of transmission in schools, the workplace, perinatally and during surgery. It also has useful scientific articles on the lack of household transmission, heterosexual transmission and ethical issues of testing as well as court decisions. In addition, the ACLU has published a 133 page

docket of AIDS and sexuality cases. These materials are available from Nan Hunter, ACLU, 132 West 43rd St., New York NY 10036 for $5.00 (Basic Documents) and $10 (Docket).

-The AIDS and Employment Project has prepared a general survey of the protections against employment discrimination on the basis of physical handicap in each state and the District of Columbia. It is available from Katherine Franke, 1663 Mission St., #400, San Francisco 94103.

-In November, 1986, National Gay Rights Advocates and the American Civil Liberties Union filed an amicus brief in support of a man whom law enforcement authorities sought to forcibly test in connection with criminal charges stemming from a biting incident. The brief examines published medical literature concerning the transmissibility of HIV. Copies of the brief are available for $2.50 from Mark Vermeulen, 1231 Market Street-Penthouse, San Francisco, CA 94103-1488.

Networking and Notes

-AIDS Network members are encouraged to respond to regulatory or legislative testing proposals in their states by submitting comments and/or testimony to the appropriate bodies. Arlene Zarembka, an attorney in private practice in St. Louis, recently wrote comments on a Missouri regulation which would have mandated the reportability of the names of seropositive persons.

-A conference will be held on the impact of AIDS on minorities in Houston on September 11 - 12. For further information, contact Eugene Harrington, Texas Southern University, Thurgood Marshall School of Law, 3100 Cleburne St., Houston, TX 77004. 713 748-3555.

-The San Francisco Chapter will hold a fund raiser for the AIDS Network on August 9 at 5:00 PM. A reception at Route 66, one of San Francisco's chicquest new restaurants, will be followed by the local premiere of Justice is a Constant Struggle, a documentary history of the Guild narrated by Studs Terkel and created by chapter president Abby Ginzberg. Thanks to the hard work of the chapter's Executive Board, over 150 members have agreed to be sponsors and patrons. Tom Steel, a member of our Executive Committee, is to be especially thanked for organizing much of the work out of his office.

-The Denver Chapter of the NLG held an extremely successful CLE program, according to AIDS Network regional contact Lynn Palma. Denver members are thinking of repeating it in the Fall. This program follows a similarly successful one in Seattle, which netted the chapter over $2,000.

-Our consultant list is constantly being updated and now contains over 115 attorneys and legal workers. Participants who wish the most recent version should send us a stamped envelope.

-Back issues of The Exchange are available for $2.25 each. The topics are Quarantine (#1), Jails and Prisons (#2), Health Insurance (#3) and Race (#4).

Editorial Board

**National Lawyers Guild
AIDS Network
211 Gough Street, 3rd Floor
San Francisco, CA 94102**

Name _____

Firm/Org. _____

Address _____

_____

Telephone _____

Send me _____ The Exchange ($10)
_____ Practice Manual

____ I am interested in participating in the
Network. Please send me details.

Enclosed is a contribution for your work: $ ____
Make checks payable to NLG AIDS Network.
Thank you.

National Lawyers Guild
AIDS Network
211 Gough Street, 3rd Floor
San Francisco, CA 94102

The Exchange is published bimonthly by the National Lawyers Guild AIDS Network. The NLG is an organization of 10,000 members of the legal community in 120 chapters nationwide. It has a fifty year history of defense of civil rights and advocacy for progressive social change. The purpose of the NLG AIDS Network is to encourage members of the legal community to represent people with AIDS and related conditions, to take part in advocacy and public education about the law and AIDS, and to assist local AIDS organizations.

The Exchange is part of our educational support program, which also includes publication of a Practice Manual (with forms) and a list of consultants. A one year subscription to The Exchange is $10 ($5 low income) and the second edition of the Practice Manual is available to individuals and community-based AIDS organizations for $20 and to other institutions for $35. Please use this form to order materials or obtain further information.

AIDS AND HANDICAP DISCRIMINATION:

A Survey Of The 50 States And The District of Columbia

NATIONAL GAY RIGHTS ADVOCATES
PUBLIC INTEREST LAW FIRM
540 CASTRO STREET
SAN FRANCISCO, CALIFORNIA 94114
(415) 863-3624

INTRODUCTION

The information compiled in the following pages is the result of a survey of the fifty states and the District of Columbia by National Gay Rights Advocates.

Results are extremely encouraging. <u>Fully two thirds of the nation's states (34) have indicated that they are willing to accept AIDS-related discrimination complaints or have declared such discrimination to be improper.</u> Only one state (Kentucky) has indicated that AIDS is not a protected handicap--and only because state law expressly excludes communicable diseases from protection. Significantly, Georgia, the only other state with a similar exception, is unwilling to assume that exclusion pertains to AIDS. In its letter to NGRA, the Georgia Department of Human Resources reports that it "advises employers to continue the employment of AIDS victims since the disease is not transmitted through casual contact."

Another positive sign is the fact that many of the states which have not yet made a determination are in the process of developing a position. Others are waiting to receive discrimination complaints before deciding the issue. Thus, further positive declarations can be expected in the upcoming months.

<u>Perhaps most encouraging is the overwhelming rejection by the states of the U.S. Justice Department's legal analysis of AIDS discrimination under federal law. Not one state agency indicated that it would join the Justice Department in permitting discrimination based upon the fear of transmission of AIDS.</u> The unwillingness of state officials to distort the clear meaning of the law by transforming antidiscrimination statutes into tools for discrimination is to be applauded.

State laws are thus an increasingly critical tool in the battle against AIDS-related discrimination. Nonetheless, the need for a reasoned and compassionate federal approach to the problem remains compelling. While all fifty states and the District of Columbia have now passed laws which prohibit discrimination against the physically handicapped, these laws vary widely. A few laws protect only public employees, while some others protect only those with "actual" as opposed to "perceived" handicaps. Many laws cover only discrimination in employment, while others also forbid discrimination in such areas as housing, public accomodation, credit and state services. In light of these differing approaches, and the rapidly changing medical, legal and political landscape of the AIDS crisis, continued monitoring and education of state and federal agenciess, as well as litigation, will remain important.

STATE	OFFICIAL DECLARATION: AIDS IS A HANDICAP; DISCRIMINATION PROHIBITED	INFORMAL RECOMMEN- DATION: AIDS-BASED DISCRIMINATION IS IMPROPER	ACCEPT AND INVESTIGATE AIDS DISCRIMINATION COMPLAINTS	NO DETERMINATION OR NO RESPONSE	OTHER	COMMENTS:
Alabama				X		
Alaska	X					
Arizona				X		
Arkansas				X		
California	X					Position of California Department of Fair Employment and Housing in *Chadbourne v. Raytheon Co.* (case pending)
Colorado	X					
Connecticut	X					
Delaware			X			
District of Columbia	X					
Florida	X					Opinion of Florida Commission on Human Relations in *Shuttleworth v. Broward County*, December 11, 1985.
Georgia		X				Georgia's handicap statute exempts persons with communicable diseases. However, "the law does not define 'communicable disease' and . . . the Depart- ment of Human Resources advises employers to con- tinue the employment of AIDS victims since the disease is not transmitted through casual contact."
Hawaii	X					Testimony of Department of Commerce and Consumer Affairs before state legislature. Spring 87
Idaho				X		
Illinois	X					
Indiana				X		
Iowa				X		
Kansas			X			
Kentucky					X	State handicap statute explicitly excludes persons with communicable diseases from protection.
Louisiana		X				"The Department of Health and Human Resources has determined that any employee with AIDS, ARC and HTLV-III antibodies would be treated the same as an employee with any other sickness or illness in the terms and conditions of employment."
Maine	X					
Maryland	X					Letter of 11/18/86
Massachusetts	X					
Michigan	X					
Minnesota	X					Department of Human Rights has issued a probable cause determination of discrimination in an AIDS dis- crimination case.
Mississippi				X		
Missouri	X					

STATE	OFFICIAL DECLARATION: AIDS IS A HANDICAP; DISCRIMINATION PROHIBITED	INFORMAL RECOMMEN-DATION: AIDS-BASED DISCRIMINATION IS IMPROPER	ACCEPT AND INVESTIGATE AIDS DISCRIMINATION COMPLAINTS	NO DETERMINATION OR NO RESPONSE	OTHER	COMMENTS:
Montana		X				"The Montana Human Rights Commission has informally taken the position that AIDS constitutes a handicap."
Nebraska			X			
Nevada				X		
New Hampshire		X				
New Jersey	X					
New Mexico	X					
New York	X					Court ruling in *People v. 49 W. 12 Tenants Corp.* as well as policy statement by New York State Division of Human Rights.
North Carolina		X				Human Relations Council has encouraged North Carolina Attorney General to rule that AIDS is a handicap and thus within the purview of state civil rights laws.
North Dakota				X		
Ohio	X					*Lambda Update 5 Nov. 1986*
Oklahoma				X		
Oregon	X					"Adverse employment decisions based on AIDS, ARC, or a seropositive finding would be a violation [of state law]. Such a decision based on a perception that an individual employee or applicant is a member of a high risk group . . . would also be a violation."
Pennsylvania	X					"The Pennsylvania Human Relations Commission treats AIDS and AIDS-related complaints as it would any other handicap or disability case . . . we have also conducted an orientation session on AIDS for all staff."
Rhode Island	X					
South Carolina				X		
South Dakota				X		
Tennessee			X			
Texas	X					
Utah					X	"Some of the conditions resulting from AIDS may be deemed a 'handicap' under appropriate factual circumstances, but the application of the diagnosis of AIDS alone is insufficient."
Vermont			X			
Virginia				X		
Washington	X					State has printed poster saying state law prohibits discrimination against "persons with AIDS, persons perceived to have AIDS, persons perceived to be particularly susceptible because they are related to or reside with someone with AIDS, [and] persons who have tested positive for HTLV-3 antibody."
West Virginia	X					
Wisconsin	X					Decision by Department of Industry, Labor and Human Relations in *Racine Educational Association v. Racine Unified School District.*
Wyoming			X			
TOTAL	24	5	7	13	2	

SUMMARY

OFFICIAL DECLARATION: AIDS IS A HANDICAP; DISCRIMINATION PROHIBITED	INFORMAL RECOMMENDATION AIDS-BASED DISCRIMINATION IS IMPROPER	ACCEPT AND INVESTIGATE AIDS-RELATED COMPLAINTS	NO DETER-MINATION OR NO RESPONSE	OTHER
California	Georgia	~~Alaska~~	Alabama	Kentucky
Colorado	Louisiana	Delaware	Arizona	Utah
Connecticut	Montana	Kansas	Arkansas	
D.C.	New Hampshire	Nebraska	~~Hawaii~~	
Florida	North Carolina	~~Ohio~~	Idaho	
Illinois		Tennessee	Indiana	
Maine		Vermont	Iowa	
Massachusetts		Wyoming	~~Maryland~~	
Michigan			Mississippi	
Minnesota			Nevada	
Missouri			North Dakota	
New Jersey			Oklahoma	
New Mexico			South Carolina	
New York			South Dakota	
Oregon			Virginia	
Pennsylvania				
Rhode Island				
Texas				
Washington				
West Virginia				
Wisconsin				

Ohio
Maryland
Alaska
Hawaii

INFORMATION REQUEST FORM

Please send me additional information about

_____ AIDS Network of the National Lawyers Guild.

_____ Enclosed is a check for $10 for a one year subscription to The Exchange.

_____ National Gay Rights Advocates.

Name _____

Firm _____

Address _____

_____ Zip _____

This form may be sent to either of the addresses below. If information about more than one organization is requested, the form will be circulated.

AIDS Network
National Lawyers Guild
211 Gough Street, Third Floor
San Francisco, CA 94102
415 861-8884

National Gay Rights Advocates
540 Castro Street
San Francisco, CA 94114
415 863-3624

GAMCO